Debrett's Handbook

Debrett's Handbook
Published by Debrett's Limited
MPA House
66 Baker Street
Weybridge KT13 8AL

Editor
Elizabeth Wyse

Contributing Editors
**Wendy Bosberry-Scott, Jo Bryant, Lucy Hume,
Celestria Noel, Laura Winter**

Consulting Editors
Charles Kidd, Davina Alexander

Index
Christine Shaw

Creative Director
Sarah Elton

Design
Karen Wilks

Additional design
Lucy Frinton

Copyright © Debrett's Limited 2014, 2015, 2018, 2021;
Revised Coronation Edition 2023
All information correct at the time of going to press

All rights reserved. No part of the publication may be reproduced, stored in a retrieval system, or transmitted in any form or by any means, without the prior permission of the publisher, nor be otherwise circulated in any form of binding or cover other than that in which it is published and without similar condition being imposed on the subsequent purchaser.

ISBN 978-1-9997670-9-9
Printed and bound by L.E.G.O. SPA, Italy

Debrett's
Handbook

About this Book

Debrett's Correct Form was first published in 1970 as an invaluable guide to forms of address after the upheavals of the 1960s, when institutions such as local government, the armed forces, the judiciary and the Church had been subjected to a great deal of change.

Regularly revised and updated, Debrett's *Correct Form* has never been out of print. In 2014, it was amalgamated into the *Debrett's Handbook*. Debrett's authoritative advice covers addressing the Royal Family, titles, Crown honours, precedence and protocol, as well as professional forms of address. Effective communication is the cornerstone of good manners and formal correspondence is an area where traditional rules still have their place. *Debrett's Handbook* contains a comprehensive guide to correspondence, from the most formal to business and social, including use of email and social media, undreamt of in 1970.

As well as encompassing *Correct Form*, the *Debrett's Handbook* is also an extensive guide to contemporary manners. It examines traditions and behaviour in a range of contexts and widely-encountered situations, from very formal events and major rites of passage, such as christenings, weddings and funerals, to home entertaining and hosting informal gatherings. It also offers a modern interpretation of the foundations that underpin all manners: introductions, small talk, conversation, compliments. It will help the reader to feel at ease, and put others at ease, in every situation.

Following the death of Queen Elizabeth II in September 2022, the *Debrett's Handbook* has been comprehensively revised and updated, reflecting many changes in nomenclature as well as increased informality in some areas of British society.

Preface

We live in a cosmopolitan and egalitarian age and customs and manners are increasingly less prescriptive. Yet this fluidity can present a challenge, as politeness and consideration, which should underpin social behaviour and etiquette, may get lost. Ironically, the more relaxed society becomes, the more useful it is to have the knowledge to navigate its nuances.

Etiquette is about understanding and mastering a set of clear and pragmatic guidelines that have evolved to make everyone feel welcome and valued. Manners make everyday life easier, removing anxiety and minimising social difficulties or awkwardness. Politeness, therefore, does not intimidate or create barriers: instead it should make communication clearer. Etiquette must adapt and shift with time, especially as we become increasingly absorbed in our own digital bubble (screens, keyboards, headphones), which may erode the ability to observe, and interact with, those around us.

In a highly competitive age, manners are still valued and noticed by many, and the confidence associated with mastering social skills is an essential tool. Good manners are attractive and empowering, showing not weakness but strength. Employers bemoan the awkwardness of job candidates; educationalists are arguing that manners have their place on the national curriculum. It is proven that the confidence manners provide can set individuals apart and give them a competitive edge.

The essence of good manners is to treat other people as you would wish to be treated yourself, to show empathy, so that no one feels confused, excluded or exposed. Debrett's believes that good manners do not advertise themselves in opaque rituals and exaggerated behaviour. When used with integrity, they are the unobtrusive gestures that make the world a more civilised and agreeable place.

Debrett's Handbook

CORRECT FORM

Formal Address — 12

The Royal Family 14
Communicating with The King — 15
Invitations to Members of the Royal Family — 17
Private Secretaries to the Royal Family — 18
Entertaining Royal Guests — 20
Invitations from the Royal Family — 21

The Peerage & Baronetage 22
The Peerage — 23
Duke — 24
Marquess — 27
Earl — 30
Viscount — 33
Baron — 36
Courtesy Titles — 39
The Scottish Title of Master — 41
Life Peers — 43
Disclaimed Peerages — 43
Baronets — 45

Other Titles 48
Knights — 49
Dames — 55
Scottish Titles — 57
Irish Hereditary Knights — 60
Privy Counsellors — 61
Untitled Persons — 61

Professions — 64

Academics 66
The University Hierarchy — 67
Principal Titles — 68
Letters Denoting Degrees — 72
Academic Forms of Address — 73

The Armed Forces 74
The Royal Navy — 77
The Army — 80
The Royal Air Force — 84

The Police 86
Forms of Address — 89

Local Government 90
Lord-Lieutenants — 92
High Sheriffs — 94
Local Order of Precedence — 94
Lord Mayors, Mayors & Civic Heads — 95
Forms of Address — 97

Politics 98
Forms of Address — 101

Law 102
The Judiciary: England & Wales — 103
Forms of Address — 107
The Judiciary: Scotland — 108

Religion 110
The Church of England — 111
Archbishops — 113
Bishops — 115
Other Members of Clergy — 117
Church of Scotland — 120
Methodist Church — 121
Chaplains — 122
Roman Catholic Church — 123
Non-Christian Faiths — 128

Medicine 130
Forms of Address — 131
Medical Qualifications — 132
Fellowships & Memberships — 134

Contents

The Diplomatic Service 136	Forms of Address	139
	Commonwealth Titles	140
	Letters After the Name	**142**
Hierarchies 144	Crown Honours	146
	Commonwealth Orders	148
	Appointments	149
	Academia & Religion	150
	Societies & Professions	151
	Formal Events	**154**
Invitations 156	Sending out Invitations	157
	Replies	158
	Place cards	159
Seating Plans & Precedence 160	Seating	161
	Precedence	163
	Official Lists	164
Traditional Rituals 166	Grace	167
	Toasts	167
	Speeches	168
Guests at Formal Events 172	Arrival	173
	Procedure	174
	Departure	175
Royal Events 176	Etiquette	178
	Entertaining Members of the Royal Family	181
	Dress Codes	**182**
Formal Dress Codes 184	White Tie	185
	Black Tie	187
	Morning Dress	190
	Highland Dress	191
Informal Dress Codes 192	Lounge Suits	193
	Smart Casual	194
	Country Clothing	195

RITES OF PASSAGE

	Growing Up	**198**
Births 200	Announcements	201
	After the Birth	202
Christenings 204	Religious Rituals	205
	Godparents	206
	Invitations	207
	Naming Rituals	209
Coming of Age 210	Confirmation	211
	Bar and Bat Mitzvahs	212
	18ths and 21sts	213
	Engagements	**214**
Proposals 216	Engagement Rings	218
	Practicalities	219
Announcements 220	Formal Announcements	221
Celebrations 224	Celebrations	225

WEDDINGS — 226

Getting Started 228	The Guest List	229
	Save-the-Date Cards	231
	Wedding Presents	232
	Second Marriages	233
Wedding Invitations 234	Traditional Invitations	235
	Useful Forms of Address	240
	Postponement or Cancellation	242
	Replies to Invitations	243
The Wedding Party 244	Roles & Responsibilities	245
	Dress: The Wedding Party	250
	Wedding Rings	253
	Dress: Wedding Guests	253
The Wedding Day 254	Before the Ceremony	255
	Transport	255
	The Ceremony	256
	Traditional Church Ceremonies	258
	Civil Ceremonies	261
	The Reception	262
	The Speeches	267
	After the Reception	269
After the Wedding 270	After the Wedding	271

DIVORCE — 272

Social Conventions 274	Divorce & Weddings	276
	Divorce & Funerals	277
	Forms of Address	279

DEATH — 280

Communicating the News 282	Death Notices	285
	Condolence Letters	286
Organising a Funeral 288	Before the Funeral	289
	The Funeral Service	290
	After the Funeral	293
Attending a Funeral 294	Who Should Attend?	295
	At the Service	296
	Flowers & Donations	298
	After the Service	299
Memorial Services 300	Planning the Service	301
	Inscriptions & Memorials	303

MODERN MANNERS

COMMUNICATION — 306

Stationery 308	Writing Paper	309
	Visiting Cards	310
Invitations 312	Private Invitations	313
	Formal Invitations	314
	At Home Invitations	315
	Contemporary & Informal Invitations	316
	General Considerations	317
	Save-the-Date Cards	319
Social Correspondence 320	Cards for Special Occasions	321
	Thank-you Letters	322
	Emails and Text Messages	323
Business Correspondence 324	Business Essentials	325
	Digital Communication	326
	Other Business Stationery	328

Social Graces — 330

Introductions 332	How Do You Do?	333
	Shaking Hands	336
	Social Kissing	337
Conversation 338	Use of First Names	339
	Small Talk	340
	Social Tact	342
Polite Actions 344	Polite Actions	345

Table Manners — 346

Table Rules 348	On the Table	349
	Practicalities	350
	At the Table	352
Challenging Foods 354	Fruit & Vegetables	355
	Fish & Shellfish	356
	Other Foods	358
Drinks 360	Wine & Spirits	361
	Coffee	364
	Traditional Tea	365

At Home — 366

Dinner Parties 368	Formal Dinners	369
	Informal Suppers	376
	Buffets	377
Drinks Parties 378	Party Planning	379
	At the Party	380
Overnight Stays 382	Hospitality	383
	Guest Etiquette	387
	Children	392

Public Manners — 396

On the Street 398	General Awareness	399
Transport 402	Driving	403
	Public Transport	405
	Aeroplanes	407
Daily Life 408	Restaurants & Pubs	409
	Hotels	411
	Shops	412
	Mobile and Laptops in Public Places	412
	Managing Children in Public	414
	In Church	415
Culture & Sport 416	Performances	417
	Sporting Events	418
In the Country 420	In the Country	421

Appendices

Sample Letters 424	Sample Letters	425
The Season 428	The Season: A Brief History	429
	The Season: Calendar of Events	429
Orders, Medals & Decorations 432	How to Wear Orders, Medals & Decorations	433
The Tables of Precedence 442	The Tables of Precedence	443
Surname Pronunciation 452	Surname Pronunciation	453

Index 470

CORRECT FORM
FORMAL ADDRESS
PROFESSIONS
LETTERS AFTER THE NAME
FORMAL EVENTS
DRESS CODES

Correct Form

12 - 63

The Royal Family

The Peerage & Baronetage

Other Titles

Formal Address

There are many occasions when it is imperative to use the correct, formal, form of address. For centuries it has been considered that this is a sign of respect that is due the monarchy and people with titles and honours conferred by the Crown, and this consideration is an important and defining feature of British society.

Formal Address

The Royal Family

Communicating with The Sovereign
Invitations to Members of the Royal Family
Private Secretaries to the Royal Family
Entertaining Royal Guests
Invitations from the Royal Family

Communicating With The King and Queen Consort

The King and all members of the Royal Family have private secretaries who deal with their correspondence.

Writing to The King and Queen Consort

See p 19 for addresses of private secretaries

Unless you are personally known to the Sovereign, any letter to The King or Queen Consort should be addressed to 'The Private Secretary to His Majesty The King'. There is no need to address the private secretary by name, but if there is subsequent correspondence this should be addressed to the actual writer of the reply.

Communications from those Known Personally

For those who wish to communicate directly with the King or Queen Consort, the following style is used:

The letter should begin 'Sir', 'Madam' or 'May it please Your Majesty'. The first line of the letter itself should begin with the phrase 'With my humble duty'; the main content of the letter then follows. It should end 'I have the honour to remain, Sir/Madam, Your Majesty's most humble and obedient servant'. The word 'remain' can be replaced with 'be' if desired.

In the body of the letter alternate between 'Your Majesty' and 'Your Majesty's' and 'you' and 'your'. The envelope should be addressed to 'His Majesty The King' or 'Her Majesty The Queen Consort'.

Verbal Address

Use 'Your Majesty' for the first time and subsequently 'Sir'. When speaking to The Queen Consort, use 'Your Majesty' for the first time and subsequently 'Ma'am'. This should always rhyme with 'lamb'. Pronunciation to rhyme with 'palm' has not been correct for some generations.

In conversation, refer to 'His/Her Majesty' or 'The King/Queen', as appropriate. 'Your Majesty' should be substituted for 'you'. References to other members of the Royal Family are made to 'His (or Her) Royal Highness' or the appropriate title, such as The Princess Royal.

On Being Presented to The King/Queen Consort

Introductions to the Royal Family are known as presentations. When presenting another person to The King/Queen Consort it is only necessary to state the name of the person to be presented: 'Your Majesty, may I present Mr John Smith?'.

On Being Presented to The King/Queen Consort and Other Members of the Royal Family

Upon being presented to members of the Royal Family, and on taking leave, men should bow and women curtsy (some women may prefer to bow). The bow is an inclination of the head, not from the waist. The curtsy should be discreet but dignified, with a slow rise, maintaining eye contact. It may be acceptable to simply shake hands, especially with younger members of the Royal Family. Check with their staff for guidance.

Communicating with Other Members of the Royal Family

Unless the writer is personally known to the member of the Royal Family, it is usual to write to the private secretary, equerry, queen's companion (for The Queen Consort), lady-in-waiting or lady of the household. Letters should be addressed to the holder of the office, not by name. Subsequent correspondence should be sent to the writer of the reply.

Sending Correspondence via Intermediaries

Alternatively, correspondents may send their formal letter to the member of the Royal Family via their intermediaries with a covering letter, saying 'please will you lay my letter before His/Her Majesty or His/Her Royal Highness...'

Communications from those Known Personally

If communicating directly with a member of the Royal Family the letter should begin 'Sir/Madam' and end 'I have the honour to remain, Sir/Madam, Your Royal Highness's most humble and obedient servant'. In the body of the letter substitute 'Your Royal Highness' for 'you' and 'Your Royal Highness's' for 'your'.

See pp 146–147 for post-nominals

The envelope should be addressed to 'His/Her Royal Highness' where appropriate, followed on the next line by the name:
The Prince of Wales, KG, KT, PC
The Princess of Wales, GCVO
The Duke of Sussex, KCVO
The Duchess of Sussex
The Duke of York, KG, GCVO, CD
Princess Beatrice of York
Princess Eugenie of York
The Duke of Edinburgh, KG, GCVO
The Duchess of Edinburgh, GCVO, CD
The Princess Royal, KG, KT, GCVO, CD, QSO
The Duke of Gloucester, KG, GCVO
The Duchess of Gloucester, GCVO, CD
The Duke of Kent, KG, GCMG, GCVO, CD
The Duchess of Kent, GCVO
Prince Michael of Kent, GCVO, CD
Princess Michael of Kent
Princess Alexandra, the Hon Lady Ogilvy, KG, GCVO

Invitations to Members of the Royal Family

An invitation to a member of the Royal Family is always extended by letter, either through the lord-lieutenant of a county or to the private secretary. The former is the rule outside London. A printed invitation is not sent, although a specimen may be forwarded to the private secretary if desired.

Preliminary Enquiries

It may be both prudent and diplomatic to make an informal enquiry, to the lord-lieutenant or private secretary, as to the possibility of a favourable response prior to extending a formal invitation by letter. The approach should outline the nature and purpose of the function.

See p 19 for addresses of private secretaries

Whether the consort of a member of the Royal Family should be included in the invitation depends on the nature of the function. The point can be raised in the informal enquiry.

Only in exceptional circumstances should two or more members of the Royal Family, other than consorts, be invited to the same function, and only then by agreement with the office of the more senior member of the Royal Family.

Sending the Letter of Invitation

The titles of the royal guest/s are shown in full, but without post-nominal letters, as follows:

Their Royal Highnesses The Prince and Princess of Wales
The Duke of York
Her Royal Highness Princess Beatrice of York and Mr Edoardo Mapelli Mozzi
Her Royal Highness Princess Eugenie of York and Mr Jack Brooksbank
Their Royal Highnesses The Duke and Duchess of Edinburgh
Her Royal Highness The Princess Royal and Admiral Sir Timothy Laurence
Their Royal Highnesses The Duke and Duchess of Gloucester
Their Royal Highnesses The Duke and Duchess of Kent
Their Royal Highnesses Prince and Princess Michael of Kent
Her Royal Highness Princess Alexandra, the Hon Lady Ogilvy

AFTER THE REPLY

If an invitation is declined, it is advisable to discuss with the invitee's office which member of the Royal Family may be invited in their stead, rather than trying the next person in line.

If an invitation is accepted, the event's organiser should liaise with the private secretary (or with another nominated member of the Royal Household) to discuss important details. These include:
- time of arrival
- name of the equerry, queen's companion, lady-in-waiting or lady of the household who will accompany the royal guest
- dress
- names and positions of persons to be presented etc

ON THE INVITATION

See pp 157–158 for formal invitations

If a member of the Royal Family has accepted an invitation, it is advisable to indicate on the invitation that a member of the Royal Family will be present. One of the following is engraved or printed at the top of the invitation card:

- In the gracious presence of His Majesty the King/Her Majesty The Queen Consort
- In the presence of His Royal Highness the Prince ......

Note: the word 'gracious' is included only for the Sovereign.

PRIVATE SECRETARIES TO THE ROYAL FAMILY

HOW TO WRITE TO A PRIVATE SECRETARY

Commence the letter 'Dear Sir' and end the letter 'Yours faithfully'.

The first reference to the member of the Royal Family must be written in full, eg 'His Majesty The King' or 'His Royal Highness The Prince of Wales', and subsequently 'The King, 'The Prince' etc.

Substitute 'His/Her Majesty' or 'His/Her Royal Highness' for 'he/she' and 'His/Her Majesty's' or 'His/Her Royal Highness's' for 'his/her'.

Alternate the above with 'The King/The Queen Consort/The Prince/The Princess/ The Duke/The Duchess', as applicable, to avoid repetition of 'His Majesty' or HRH etc.

Envelopes should be addressed as follows (*see facing page*):

The Private Secretary to
His Majesty The King
Buckingham Palace
London SW1A 1AA

The Private Secretary to
Her Majesty The Queen Consort
Buckingham Palace
London SW1A 1AA

The Private Secretary to
His Royal Highness The Prince of Wales
  KG, KT, PC
Clarence House
London SW1A 1BA

The Private Secretary to
Her Royal Highness The Princess of Wales,
  GCVO
Clarence House
London SW1A 1BA

The Private Secretary to
His Royal Highness The Duke of Edinburgh,
  KG, GCVO
Bagshot Park
Bagshot
Surrey GU19 5PL

The Private Secretary to
Her Royal Highness The Duchess of Edinburgh,
  GCVO
Bagshot Park
Bagshot
Surrey GU19 5PL

The Private Secretary to
Her Royal Highness The Princess Royal,
  KG, KT, GCVO
Buckingham Palace
London SW1A 1AA

The Private Secretary to
His Royal Highness The Duke of Gloucester,
  KG, GCVO
Kensington Palace
London W8 4PU

The Private Secretary to
Her Royal Highness The Duchess of Gloucester,
  GCVO, CD
Kensington Palace
London W8 4PU

The Private Secretary to
His Royal Highness The Duke of Kent,
  KG, GCMG, GCVO, CD
St James's Palace
London SW1A 1BQ

The Private Secretary to
Her Royal Highness The Duchess of Kent, GCVO
St James's Palace
London SW1A 1BQ

The Private Secretary to
His Royal Highness Prince Michael of Kent,
  GCVO, CD
Kensington Palace
London W8 4PU

The Private Secretary to
Her Royal Highness Princess Alexandra,
the Hon Lady Ogilvy, KG, GCVO
Buckingham Palace
London SW1A 1AA

It is advised that, for the sake of simplicity, the post-nominal letters for members of the Royal Family are limited to the most senior orders of chivalry.

Entertaining Royal Guests

Close liaison between the host's office and Buckingham Palace or the office of the member of the Royal Family is essential.

Arrival and Departure Times

See pp 177–181 for formal events

Protocol rules that everyone should arrive before the royal guest and no-one should leave an event before a member of the Royal Family, except in special circumstances, with prior permission.

However, charity balls and dinners may continue well after midnight so it is probably practical for the organiser of the event to warn the private secretary that this rule may be honoured in the breach rather than in the observance. Similarly the organiser may also seek, through the private secretary, blanket permission for guests to leave before the member of the Royal Family. If necessary, individuals should seek permission to leave early through the private secretary in advance of the event.

Seating Plans for Royal Guests

When The King or Queen Consort attends an event (official or private) the host always surrenders his/her place to His/Her Majesty, and will be seated on The King or Queen Consort's right. Other members of the Royal Family are given special precedence before all non-royal guests. The husband of a female member of the Royal Family is accorded precedence immediately after her when both attend an event. If he attends alone, he retains his own precedence, unless he is the principal guest. However, the wives of male members of the Royal Family have the same precedence as their husbands.

Retinues

Those in attendance upon a member of the Royal Family should be placed reasonably near him or her (not necessarily at the same table) and must have a clear sight line between them.

When the principal guest is The King or Queen Consort, some or all of the following, and their spouses, should be invited:
- the lord-lieutenant of the county
- the lord mayor, lord provost, mayor, provost, chairman of the city/borough/district
- the high sheriff of the county
- the chairman of the county council

Table Plan Approval

The seating plan of the top table for any event attended by a royal personage must be submitted to the private secretary for prior approval, from whom the names of the suite in attendance should also be obtained.

Invitations From The Royal Family

Invitations from The King or Queen Consort

Invitations from the Sovereign (called commands) are sent by:
- The Lord Steward of the Household to a state banquet
- The Lord Chamberlain to all major court functions, such as a garden party, wedding, funeral or memorial service
- The Master of the Household to all domestic functions given by the Sovereign at a royal residence

Commands from the Sovereign may read:

*The Master of the Household
is Commanded by His/Her Majesty to invite
Mr and Mrs John Debrett
to Luncheon at Sandringham House
on Thursday, 8th October at 12.30 o'clock*

Replies to Invitations from The King or Queen Consort

Replies should be worded to reflect this and addressed to the member of the Royal Household who has issued the invitation:

Mr and Mrs John Debrett present their compliments to the Master of the Household and have the honour to obey His/Her Majesty's command to Luncheon on 8th October at 12.30 o'clock.

The date of the letter is written in the bottom left corner. Reasons for non-acceptance should always be stated. A prior engagement is not considered to be a sufficient reason:

Mr and Mrs John Debrett present their compliments to the Master of the Household, and much regret that they are unable to obey His/Her Majesty's command to Luncheon on 8th October owing to the illness of Mrs Debrett.

Replies to Invitations from the Royal Family

Invitations from other members of the Royal Family are not commands; in other respects replies follow the same formula.

Garden Parties

See pp 179–180 for garden parties

Invitations to a garden party do not require an acknowledgement unless a guest is unable to attend, in which case the admission card must be returned.

Thank Yous

When appropriate, such as after a state banquet, but not after a garden party, a letter of thanks is addressed to the relevant member of the Royal Household, asking that thanks are conveyed to the Sovereign or other member of the Royal Family.

Formal Address

The Peerage
& Baronetage

The Peerage
Duke
Marquess
Earl
Viscount
Baron
Courtesy Titles
The Scottish Title of Master
Life Peers
Disclaimed Peerages
Baronets

The Peerage

The peerage is a system of mainly hereditary titles in the United Kingdom, comprising the ranks of the British nobility, augmented by the creation of life peers under the British honours system. The holder of a peerage is termed a peer.

The Sovereign is considered the fount of honour and, as such, cannot hold a peerage. Only the holder of the title is a peer; the members of a peer's family are commoners. In this way the British system of nobility differs fundamentally from continental European ones, where entire families, rather than individuals, are considered to be members of the nobility.

Nobility in Britain is based not on bloodline, but on title. A good example is Peter Phillips, son of HRH The Princess Royal, who is a commoner even though his mother is a princess, his grandmother was the Sovereign and his uncle is now The King.

In modern times, only members of the Royal Family are granted new hereditary peerages. Only life peerages, which carry the personal right to sit and vote in the House of Lords, are generally granted to honour individuals; the last non-royal hereditary peerages were created under the Thatcher government.

Peerages are officially created when letters patent are affixed with the Great Seal of the Realm. The Sovereign will take advice from his or her government on a new peerage, under a process that scrutinises appointments to political honours.

In 1999 the Labour Government abolished the automatic rights of hereditary peers to sit in the House of Lords, with two exceptions, the Earl Marshal and the Lord Great Chamberlain. The House of Lords Act provided that 92 hereditary peers would remain in the House of Lords, together with 17 other hereditary peers who were returned to the Lords as life peers.

The majority of peers hold more than one title, but it is customary for them to use the senior one; lesser titles are therefore available for their heirs to use as courtesy titles.

DUKE

See p 16 for royal dukes

A duke is the highest of the five grades of the peerage. For guidance on how to address the five royal dukes (Sussex, York, Edinburgh, Gloucester and Kent) see Invitations to Royalty, p 17.

A duke is always so described, unlike the lower ranks of the peerage. If reference is made to only one duke he may be called 'the Duke', but if distinction is necessary, or on introduction, he should be referred to as, for example, 'the Duke of Mayfair'.

Ecclesiastical, ambassadorial and armed forces ranks precede the ducal rank, for example 'Major-General the Duke of ......'. When a duke is also a privy counsellor or has received a knighthood he may use the appropriate post-nominal letters. In official and legal documents the style 'The Most Noble ......' should still be used for both a duke and duchess.

The signature of a duke is by title only: *Mayfair*

WIFE OF A DUKE

The wife of a duke is always described as 'the Duchess', or 'the Duchess of ......' if distinction is required, or on introduction.

WIDOW OF A DUKE

Officially the widow of a duke is known as 'The Dowager Duchess of ......' (unless there is already a dowager duchess in that family still living, in which case the widow of the junior duke is known by her forename, eg Anne, Duchess of Mayfair).

In practice, many widows prefer to use their forename in place of 'Dowager'; if in doubt, this is recommended. If the present holder of the dukedom is unmarried, the widow of the previous duke continues to be known as The Duchess of Mayfair. If a marriage between a duke and duchess has been dissolved, the former wife (although no longer a peeress) may continue to use her title as a duke's wife, preceded by her forename (unless she remarries).

ELDEST SON OF A DUKE

The eldest (or only) son of a duke may use one of his father's lesser peerage titles. For example, the son and heir apparent of the Duke of Mayfair could be known as, for example, 'Marquess of Clarges' and the appropriate forms of address for a marquess by courtesy therefore apply to him and his family.

YOUNGER SONS OF A DUKE

The younger sons of a duke have the courtesy title of 'Lord' before their forename and surname.

Prefixes such as 'His Excellency', 'Major General', 'The Rt Rev', 'The Rt Hon' etc precede his courtesy title.

DAUGHTERS OF A DUKE

A daughter of a duke has the style of 'Lady' before her forename and surname, eg the elder daughter of the Duke of Mayfair could be Lady Rachel Bond.

On marriage she continues to use the same style, but with her husband's surname, ie when Lady Rachel Bond married Mr Guy Green, she became Lady Rachel Green.

Should she marry a peer she adopts his title.

EXCEPTIONS ON MARRIAGES OF DUKE'S DAUGHTERS

If she marries a courtesy peer, and the precedence she derives from this is lower than that she derives from her father (ie his title belongs to a lower rank of the peerage than duke), she has the option of:

(a) adopting the usual style of the wife of a courtesy peer, eg 'Viscountess South', or

(b) continuing her own style followed by the courtesy title, eg 'Lady Mary South'

In practice very few ladies now adopt course (b) unless the marriage has been dissolved.

If the daughter of a duke marries the younger son of a duke or marquess, again she has the option of:

(a) adopting the usual style of the wife of a younger son of a duke or marquess, eg 'Lady Charles Bond', or

(b) continuing her own style followed by her surname, eg 'Lady Mary Bond'

See table on next page

How to Address a Duke and his Family

	Salutation	Envelope	Verbal Address	Conversation
Duke (formal)	My Lord Duke	His Grace the Duke of Mayfair	Your Grace (very formal) or Duke	The Duke or The Duke of Mayfair
Duke (social)	Dear Duke	The Duke of Mayfair	Duke	The Duke of Mayfair
Duchess (formal)	Madam or Dear Madam	Her Grace the Duchess of Mayfair	Your Grace (very formal) or Duchess	The Duchess or The Duchess of Mayfair
Duchess (social)	Dear Duchess	The Duchess of Mayfair	Duchess	The Duchess or The Duchess of Mayfair
Widowed Duchess	Dear Duchess	The Dowager Duchess of Mayfair, or Anne, Duchess of Mayfair	Duchess	The Duchess or The Dowager Duchess of Mayfair or Anne, Duchess of Mayfair
Former Wife of a Duke	Dear Duchess	Rosita, Duchess of Mayfair	Duchess	The Duchess of Mayfair or Rosita, Duchess of Mayfair
Eldest Son of a Duke	By courtesy title, eg Dear Lord Clarges	Marquess of Clarges	Lord Clarges	Lord Clarges
Younger Son of a Duke	Dear Lord Edward	Lord Edward Bond	Lord Edward	Lord Edward
Wife of a Younger Son of a Duke	Dear Lady Edward	Lady Edward Bond	Lady Edward	Lady Edward
Daughter of a Duke	Dear Lady Rachel	Lady Rachel Bond (if married Lady Rachel Green)	Lady Rachel	Lady Rachel

Marquess

The second most senior grade in the peerage, the official spelling of this title, marquess, is now standardised and this is adopted on the Roll of the House of Lords. Some Scottish marquesses, in memory of the 'Auld Alliance' with France, prefer the French spelling, marquis, as does the Marquis of Headfort, who holds an Irish marquessate.

There are three marquessates which do not include the word 'of' in the title: Camden, Conyngham and Townshend.

In conversation, a marquess is referred to as, for example, 'Lord Audley' rather than 'the Marquess of Audley'.

Ecclesiastical, ambassadorial and armed forces ranks precede a marquess's rank in correspondence. For example, 'Major-General the Marquess of ......'.

When a marquess is also a privy counsellor or has received a knighthood he may use the appropriate post-nominal letters.

In official and legal documents and announcements the style of 'The Most Hon ......' should still be used for both a marquess and marchioness.

The signature of a marquess is by title only: *Audley*

Wife of a Marquess

The wife of a marquess is a marchioness and is known as 'Lady ......' (use of the title marchioness in speech is socially incorrect unless it needs to be specifically mentioned, for example in a formal introduction).

Widow of a Marquess

The widow of a marquess is officially known as 'The Dowager Marchioness of ......' (unless there is already a dowager marchioness in that family still living, in which case the widow of the junior marquess is known by her forename, eg Elizabeth, Marchioness of Audley).

In practice, many widows prefer to use their forename in place of 'Dowager'; if in doubt, this is recommended.

Former Wife of a Marquess	If a marriage between a marquess and marchioness has been dissolved, the former wife (although no longer a peeress) may continue to use her title as a marquess's wife, preceded by her forename (unless she remarries).
Marquess by Courtesy	Although the bearer of the title marquess by courtesy enjoys none of the privileges of a peer, he is addressed as such with the following exceptions: - a marquess by courtesy is never accorded the formal style of 'The Most Hon' - a marquess by courtesy is not addressed as 'The' in correspondence; this is restricted to actual peers Normally a peer by courtesy is called 'Lord ......', but if there is a special reason for a marquess by courtesy to be referred to by his precise courtesy title, he is called verbally 'the Marquess of ......'. The wife of a marquess by courtesy takes the title of marchioness but, like her husband, there are some distinctions in how she should be addressed: - she is never accorded the formal style of 'The Most Hon' - she is not given the prefix 'The' in correspondence
Eldest Son of a Marquess	The eldest (or only) son of a marquess may use either a peerage title by courtesy or a courtesy style (of a rank junior to his father) and should be addressed accordingly. For example, the son and heir apparent of the Marquess of Audley may be known as the Earl of Maddox, and the appropriate forms of address for a peer by courtesy therefore apply to him and his family.
Younger Sons of a Marquess	The younger sons of a marquess have the courtesy title of 'Lord' before their forename and surname. For example, the younger son of the Marquess of Audley could be Lord Alexander Hart. Prefixes such as 'His Excellency', 'Major General', 'The Rt Rev', 'The Rt Hon' etc precede his courtesy title.
Wife of a Younger Son of a Marquess	The wife of the younger son of a marquess has the courtesy title of 'Lady' followed by her husband's forename and surname (unless herself the daughter of a duke, marquess, or earl). For example, the wife of the younger son of the Marquess of Audley could be Lady Alexander Hart.
Widow of the Younger Son of a Marquess	Her style in widowhood does not change, except on remarriage, when she adopts the style from her husband.

DAUGHTERS OF A MARQUESS A daughter of a marquess has the style of 'Lady' before her forename and surname, eg the elder daughter of the Marquess of Audley could be Lady Clare Hart.

On marriage she continues to use the same style, with her husband's surname, ie if Lady Clare Hart married Mr Mark North, she would become Lady Clare North.

See p 25 for exceptions

How to Address a Marquess and his Family

	Salutation	Envelope	Verbal Address	Conversation
Marquess (formal)	My Lord	The Most Hon the Marquess of Audley	Lord Audley	Lord Audley
Marquess (social)	Dear Lord Audley	The Marquess of Audley	Lord Audley	Lord Audley
Marchioness (formal)	Madam or Dear Madam	The Most Hon the Marchioness of Audley	Lady Audley	Lady Audley
Marchioness (social)	Dear Lady Audley	The Marchioness of Audley	Lady Audley	Lady Audley
Widowed Marchioness	Dear Lady Audley	The Dowager Marchioness of Audley, or Kathleen, Marchioness of Audley	Lady Audley	Lady Audley or The Dowager Lady Audley
Former Wife of a Marquess	Dear Lady Audley	Elizabeth, Marchioness of Audley	Lady Audley	Lady Audley or Elizabeth, Lady Audley
Eldest son of a Marquess	By courtesy title, eg Dear Lord Maddox	Earl of Maddox	Lord Maddox	Lord Maddox
Younger Son of a Marquess	Dear Lord Alexander	Lord Alexander Hart	Lord Alexander	Lord Alexander
Wife of a Younger Son of a Marquess	Dear Lady Alexander	Lady Alexander Hart	Lady Alexander	Lady Alexander
Daughter of a Marquess	Dear Lady Clare	Lady Clare Hart (if married Lady Clare North)	Lady Clare	Lady Clare

Earl

This is the third grade in the peerage.

In conversation, an earl is referred to as 'Lord (Aldford)' rather than 'the Earl of (Aldford)'. Ecclesiastical, ambassadorial and armed forces ranks precede an earl's rank in correspondence. For example, 'Major-General the Earl of (Aldford)'.

When an earl is also a privy counsellor or has received a knighthood he has the appropriate post-nominal letters.

In official documents the style of The Rt Hon should still be used for both an earl and countess.

The signature of an earl is by title only: *Aldford*

Territorial Designations
It should be noted that although most peers of this rank are earls 'of' somewhere, there is a significant number that are not. The following titles are prefixed by 'Earl' not 'Earl of': Alexander of Tunis, Annesley, Attlee, Baldwin of Bewdley, Bathurst, Beatty, Belmore, Cadogan, Cairns, Castle Stewart, Cathcart, Cawdor, Cowley, De La Warr, Ferrers, Fortescue, Granville, Grey, Haig, Howe, Jellicoe, Lloyd-George of Dwyfor, Mountbatten of Burma, Nelson, Peel, Russell, St Aldwyn, Spencer, Temple of Stowe, Waldegrave and Winterton.

Countess in Her Own Right
A number of earldoms can be inherited in the female line and a countess in her own right would be addressed as for the wife of an earl. Her husband derives no title or style from his wife.

Wife of an Earl
The wife of an earl is a countess and is known as 'Lady (Aldford)'. Use of the title 'countess' in speech is socially incorrect unless it needs to be specifically mentioned, for example in a formal introduction.

Widow of an Earl
The widow of an earl is officially known as 'The Dowager Countess of ......' (unless there is already a dowager countess in that family still living, in which case the widow of the junior earl is known by her forename, eg 'Elizabeth, Countess of ......'). In practice, many widows prefer to use their forename in place of 'Dowager'; if in doubt, this is recommended.

If the present holder of the earldom is unmarried, the widow of the previous earl continues to be known as, for example, 'The Countess of Aldford'.

FORMER WIFE OF AN EARL If a marriage between an earl and countess has been dissolved, the former wife may continue to use her title as an earl's wife, preceded by her forename (unless she remarries).

EARL BY COURTESY Although the bearer of the title earl by courtesy enjoys none of the privileges of a peer, he is addressed as such with the following exceptions:
- an earl by courtesy is never accorded the formal style of 'The Rt Hon' unless he also happens to be a privy counsellor
- an earl by courtesy is not addressed as 'The' in correspondence

ELDEST SON OF AN EARL
See p 41 for Scottish title of master if the earl is of the peerage of Scotland

Normally a peer by courtesy is called 'Lord ......', but if there is a special reason for an earl by courtesy to be referred to by his precise courtesy title, he is called verbally, eg 'the Viscount......'.

The wife of an earl by courtesy takes the title of countess but is never accorded the formal style of 'The Rt Hon' or given the prefix 'The' in correspondence. The same rules apply to the widow of a peer by courtesy.

The eldest (or only) son of an earl may use a peerage title by courtesy (of a rank junior to his father) and should be addressed accordingly, for example Viscount St James.

YOUNGER SONS OF AN EARL The younger sons of an earl have the courtesy title of 'The Honourable' (usually abbreviated to 'The Hon') before their forename and surname. The style of 'The Hon' is used on envelopes or in formal documents, but never in conversation, or on invitations or visiting cards, when the correct style is 'Mr'.

Prefixes such as 'His Excellency', 'Major General', 'The Rt Rev', 'The Rt Hon' etc precede his courtesy title.

WIVES AND WIDOWS OF YOUNGER SONS OF AN EARL The wife of a gentleman with the courtesy style of 'The Hon' is known by her husband's forename and surname, with the addition of 'Mrs' as a prefix. Thus, the wife of 'The Hon John Browne' is 'The Hon Mrs John Browne'. The same is true of a widow of a younger son (unless she remarries). If she prefers to use her own forename, she does not use 'the hon', so is simply addressed as Mrs Jane Browne.

DAUGHTERS OF AN EARL — A daughter of an earl has the style of 'Lady' before her forename and surname, eg the daughter of the Earl of Aldford could be Lady Daisy Browne. A daughter of someone who enjoys the courtesy peerage of an earl has the identical style of 'Lady'.

See p 25 for exceptions — On marriage she continues to use the same style, with her husband's surname. For example, if the Earl of Aldford's daughter Lady Daisy Browne married Nathaniel Watkins, she would become Lady Daisy Watkins.

How to Address an Earl and his Family

	Salutation	Envelope	Verbal Address	Conversation
Earl (formal)	My Lord	The Rt Hon the Earl of Aldford	Lord Aldford	Lord Aldford
Earl (social)	Dear Lord Aldford	The Earl of Aldford	Lord Aldford	Lord Aldford
Countess (formal)	Madam or Dear Madam	The Rt Hon the Countess of Aldford	Lady Aldford	Lady Aldford
Countess (social)	Dear Lady Aldford	The Countess of Aldford	Lady Aldford	Lady Aldford
Widowed Countess	Dear Lady Aldford	The Dowager Countess of Aldford, or Emma, Countess of Aldford	Lady Aldford	Lady Aldford or The Dowager Lady Aldford
Former Wife of an Earl	Dear Lady Aldford	Emily, Countess of Aldford	Lady Aldford	Lady Aldford
Eldest Son of an Earl	By courtesy title, eg Dear Lord St James	Viscount St James	Lord St James	Lord St James
Younger Son of an Earl	Dear Mr Browne	The Hon John Browne	Mr Browne	Mr Browne
Wife of a Younger Son of an Earl	Dear Mrs Browne	The Hon Mrs John Browne	Mrs Browne	Mrs Browne
Daughter of an Earl	Dear Lady Daisy	Lady Daisy Browne (if married, Lady Daisy Watkins)	Lady Daisy	Lady Daisy

Viscount

This is the fourth grade in the peerage. A viscount is, in conversation, referred to as 'Lord Tilney' rather than 'Viscount Tilney'.

There are two viscountcies where an 'of' is used in the title: the Viscount of Arbuthnott and the Viscount of Oxfuird.

Ecclesiastical, ambassadorial and armed forces ranks precede a viscount's rank in correspondence. For example, 'Major-General the Viscount ......'.

When a viscount is also a privy counsellor or has received a knighthood he may use the appropriate post-nominal letters.

The signature of a viscount is by title only: *Tilney*

Wife of a Viscount

The wife of a viscount is a viscountess and is known as 'Lady (Tilney)'. Use of the title 'viscountess' in speech is socially incorrect unless it needs to be specifically mentioned, for example in a list of patrons.

Widow of a Viscount

The widow of a viscount is officially known as 'The Dowager Viscountess ......' (unless there is already a dowager viscountess in that family still living, in which case the widow of the junior viscount is known by her forename eg 'Elizabeth, Viscountess ......'.

In practice, many widows prefer to use their forename in place of 'Dowager'; if in doubt this is recommended. If the present holder of the viscountcy is unmarried, the widow of the previous viscount does not use the term of either 'The Dowager Viscountess ......', or 'Clare, Viscountess ......', but continues to be known as 'The Viscountess ......'.

Former Wife of a Viscount

If a marriage between a viscount and viscountess has been dissolved, the former wife (although no longer a peeress) may continue to use her title as a viscount's wife, preceded by her forename (unless she remarries – for example, if Tessa, Viscountess Tilney, marries Mr George Robinson she becomes Mrs George Robinson or Mrs Tessa Robinson).

Viscount by Courtesy

Although the bearer of the title viscount by courtesy enjoys none of the privileges of a peer, he is addressed as such with the following exceptions:
- a viscount by courtesy is never accorded the formal style of 'The Rt Hon' unless he also happens to be a privy counsellor
- a viscount by courtesy is not addressed as 'The' in correspondence; this is restricted to actual peers

The wife of a viscount by courtesy takes the title of a viscountess but she is never accorded the formal style of 'The Rt Hon'. The same rules apply to the widow as to the wife of a viscount by courtesy.

Sons of Viscounts, and their Wives and Widows

All sons of a viscount have the courtesy title of 'The Hon' before their forename and surname. This style is only used on the envelope in correspondence, in written descriptions (usually only on the first mention) or in formal documents. It is never used in conversation, or on invitations or visiting cards, when the correct style is 'Mr' or 'Mrs'. The wives and widows of the sons of viscounts may use the prefix 'The Hon' until they remarry, but it is never used in conversation. Wives and Widows should either be referred to as the Hon Mrs John Whyte or Mrs Jane Whyte.

Daughters of a Viscount

A daughter of a viscount bears the courtesy style of 'The Hon'. When she is unmarried this style is precedes her forename (eg The Hon Jane Whyte). After marriage she drops the use of her forename and her surname only, eg 'The Hon Mrs Wharton'. The style of 'The Hon' is not used before 'Miss'.

The style of 'The Hon' is only used on the envelope in correspondence, in written descriptions (usually only on the first mention) and in formal documents. It is never used in conversation or on invitations or visiting cards, when the correct style is 'Mrs', 'Miss' or 'Ms'.

Exceptions

Should the daughter of a viscount marry the younger son of an earl, or the son of a viscount or baron (ie when both partners are 'The Hon'), she should be addressed as 'The Hon Mrs Wharton', not 'The Hon Mrs John Wharton'.

How to Address a Viscount and his Family

	Salutation	Envelope	Verbal Address	Conversation
Viscount (formal)	My Lord	The Rt Hon the Viscount Tilney	Lord Tilney	Lord Tilney
Viscount (social)	Dear Lord Tilney	The Viscount Tilney	Lord Tilney	Lord Tilney
Viscountess (formal)	Madam or Dear Madam	The Rt Hon the Viscountess Tilney	Lady Tilney	Lady Tilney
Viscountess (social)	Dear Lady Tilney	The Viscountess Tilney	Lady Tilney	Lady Tilney
Widowed Viscountess	Dear Lady Tilney	The Dowager Viscountess Tilney or Lisa, Viscountess Tilney	Lady Tilney	Lady Tilney or The Dowager Lady Tilney
Former Wife of a Viscount	Dear Lady Tilney	Tessa, Viscountess Tilney	Lady Tilney	Lady Tilney
Son of a Viscount	Dear Mr Whyte	The Hon James Whyte	Mr Whyte	Mr Whyte
Wife of a Son of a Viscount	Dear Mrs Whyte	The Hon Mrs James Whyte	Mrs Whyte	Mrs Whyte
Daughter of a Viscount	Dear Miss Whyte	The Hon Jane Whyte (if married, The Hon Mrs Wharton)	Miss Whyte or Mrs Wharton	Miss Whyte or Mrs Wharton

Baron

The following guidelines apply to hereditary and life barons and Lords of Parliament in the peerage of Scotland and their wives.

The fifth degree of the peerage, a baron is always referred to, both verbally and in correspondence, as 'Lord (Hays)' rather than 'Baron (Hays)'. The title baron is never used, except in formal or legal documents.

In the peerage of Scotland, the fifth grade of the peerage is a 'Lord' (lord of parliament) in any case.

Ecclesiastical, ambassadorial and armed forces ranks precede a baron's rank in correspondence. For example, 'Major-General the Lord ......'.

The signature of a baron is by title only: *Hays*

Wife of a Hereditary Baron

The wife of a baron is known as 'Lady (Hays)'. The use of her exact rank in speech is socially incorrect, unless it needs to be specifically mentioned, for example in formal introductions.

Widow of a Hereditary Baron

The widow of a baron (or lord of parliament in the peerage of Scotland) is officially known as 'The Dowager Lady ......' (unless there is already a dowager baroness in that family still living, in which case the widow of the junior baron is known by her forename, eg 'Elizabeth, Lady ......'). In practice, many widows prefer to use their forename in place of 'Dowager'; if in doubt this is recommended.

If the present holder of the barony is unmarried, the widow of the previous baron does not use the term of either The Dowager Lady Hays or Barbara, Lady Hays, but continues to be known as The Lady Hays.

Former Wife of a Hereditary Baron

If a marriage between a baron and baroness has been dissolved, the former wife (although no longer a peeress) may continue to use her title as a baroness's wife, preceded by her forename (unless she remarries). This also applies to the former wife of a lord of parliament in the peerage of Scotland.

Baroness in Her Own Right and Life Baroness

A number of baronies can be inherited in the female line and there are many female life baronesses.

At present, all peeresses in their own right are either countesses or baronesses. In the peerage of Scotland, the term 'Lady' (ie lady of parliament) is the legal term for the fifth grade of peerage because the term 'Baroness' is used in Scotland in a feudal sense relating to land tenure.

A countess in her own right is addressed in the same way as an earl's wife, but a baroness in her own right, whether hereditary or life, has two alternatives, 'Baroness' or 'Lady'.

Since the Peerage Act 1963, and the growing numbers of female life peers, the use of the continental style of 'Baroness', both verbally and in writing, has become widespread. Most baronesses in their own right, however, prefer to be styled 'Lady', and the same is true of a minority of life baronesses. Children of a baroness in her own right or a life baroness will be styled in the same way as children of barons.

Sons of a Baron

All sons of a baron, a baroness in her own right and a life baroness have the courtesy title of 'The Honourable' (usually abbreviated to 'The Hon') before their forename and surname. The style of 'The Hon' is used on the envelope in correspondence, in written descriptions (usually on the first mention) or in formal documents. It is never used in conversation or on invitations or visiting cards, when the correct style is 'Mr'.

Wife of the Son of a Hereditary or Life Baron

The wife of a man with the courtesy style of 'The Hon' is known by her husband's forename and surname, with the addition of 'Mrs' as a prefix. Thus, the wife of 'The Hon John Mount' is 'The Hon Mrs John Mount'. 'The Hon' is never used in conversation or on invitations or visiting cards. If she prefers to use her own name, she is styled Mrs Jane Mount.

If she is the daughter of a duke, marquess or earl (ie with the style of 'Lady' followed by her forename), she continues to use her own style and name with her husband's surname, eg 'Lady Mary Mount'.

If she is the daughter of a viscount or baron, with the style of 'The Hon', she does not use her husband's forename. For example, if The Hon Jane Whyte marries The Hon John Mount, she is known as 'The Hon Mrs Mount.'

| | | Widow or Former Wife of the Son of a Baron | There is no difference in the form of address in widowhood, or on the dissolution of her marriage. Should she remarry, however, she adopts her style from her new husband. |

WIDOW OR FORMER WIFE OF THE SON OF A BARON — There is no difference in the form of address in widowhood, or on the dissolution of her marriage. Should she remarry, however, she adopts her style from her new husband.

DAUGHTERS OF BARONS — Daughters of barons are styled 'the Honourable' (usually shortened to 'The Hon'). When she is unmarried this style precedes her forename, eg 'The Hon Rose Hays'. After marriage she uses her surname only (eg The Hon Mrs Smythe). Her husband is not entitled to use her style.

Should the daughter of a baron marry the younger son of an earl, or the son of a viscount or baron, she would also be addressed as 'The Hon Mrs Hays'. In this case, the joint form of address would be 'The Hon Dominic and the Hon Mrs Hays'.

HOW TO ADDRESS A BARON, A BARONESS AND THEIR FAMILY

	SALUTATION	ENVELOPE	VERBAL ADDRESS	CONVERSATION
Baron (formal)	My Lord	The Rt Hon the Lord Hays	My Lord	Lord Hays
Baron (social)	Dear Lord Hays	The Lord Hays	Lord Hays	Lord Hays
Baroness (formal)	Madam or Dear Madam	The Rt Hon the Baroness Hays	Madam	Lady Hays
Baroness (social)	Dear Baroness Hays or Lady Hays	The Baroness (or Lady) Hays	Baroness Hays or Lady Hays	Lady Hays
Widowed Baroness	Dear Lady Hays	The Dowager Lady Hays or Therese, Lady Hays	Lady Hays	Lady Hays or The Dowager Lady Hays
Former Wife of a Baron	Dear Lady Hays	Barbara, Lady Hays	Lady Hays	Lady Hays
Son of a Baron	Dear Mr Hays	The Hon Dominic Hays	Mr Hays	Mr Hays
Wife of a Son of a Baron	Dear Mrs Hays	The Hon Mrs Dominic Hays	Mrs Hays	Mrs Hays
Daughter of a Baron	Dear Miss Hays	The Hon Rose Hays (if married, The Hon Mrs Smythe)	Miss Hays or Mrs Smythe	Miss Hays or Mrs Smythe

Courtesy Titles

A courtesy title is a title such as 'Lord', 'Lady' or 'The Hon', which is usually borne by the sons, daughters, daughters-in-law, brothers, sisters and sisters-in-law of a peer.

- The son and heir apparent of a duke, marquess or earl may use one of his father's peerage titles 'by courtesy', providing it is of a lesser grade than that used by his father.
- The younger sons of a duke or marquess have the courtesy style of 'Lord' before their forename and surname.
- The younger sons of an earl, and all sons of a viscount or baron, have the courtesy style of 'The Hon' before their forename and surname.
- The daughters of a duke, marquess or earl have the courtesy title of 'Lady' before their forename and surname.

A peer's sons and daughters who are legitimated under the Legitimacy Act 1926 (amended 1959) are now, under Earl Marshal's Warrant 1970, accorded the same courtesy styles as the legitimate *younger* children of peers. However, they have no right of succession to the peerage (except under certain circumstances in Scotland), or precedence from it.

Courtesy styles may continue to be borne by the children of peers who have disclaimed their peerage.

Eldest Sons of Peers

There is no hard and fast rule about which title borne by a peer is selected for use by his eldest son as a peer by courtesy, though in most families custom is followed.

The eldest son of the Marquess of Lansdowne is usually known as Earl of Kerry or Earl of Shelburne in alternate generations.

The late Earl of Wemyss and March, after the untimely deaths of successive Lords Elcho, decided his only surviving son should use the courtesy peerage title of Lord Neidpath instead of Elcho. The present Earl of Wemyss's son has reverted to Elcho.

When the 11th Duke of Devonshire died in 2004, he was succeeded by his only son, previously known by courtesy as the Marquess of Hartington. The new Duke of Devonshire's son, however, is not known as the Marquess of Hartington, preferring to retain his courtesy title of Earl of Burlington (traditionally the title of the grandson of the Duke of Devonshire).

ADOPTED CHILDREN Children adopted into a family do not acquire rights of succession to a title, and children adopted out of a family do not lose their rights.

An Earl Marshal's Warrant dated 30 April 2004 decreed that the adopted children of peers should be accorded the styles and courtesy titles as are proper to the *younger* children of peers, but without right of succession to the peerage.

FORMS OF ADDRESS Although the bearer of a peerage title by courtesy enjoys none of the privileges of a peer, he is addressed as such with the following exceptions:
(i) a marquess by courtesy is never accorded the formal style of 'The Most Hon'
(ii) an earl, viscount or baron by courtesy is never accorded the formal style of 'The Rt Hon', unless he also happens to be a privy counsellor
(iii) a peer by courtesy is not addressed as 'The' in correspondence; this is restricted to actual peers

Normally a peer by courtesy is called 'Lord ......', but if there is a special reason for a marquess or earl by courtesy to be referred to by his precise courtesy title, he is called verbally 'the Marquess of ......' or 'the Earl of ......', the usual colloquial form of reference. The definite article is not given to courtesy viscounts or barons.

WIVES AND WIDOWS OF PEERS BY COURTESY Wives of peers by courtesy take the titles of marchioness, countess or lady, as appropriate, but never have the formal style of 'The Most Hon' or 'The Rt Hon'. The wife of a peer by courtesy is not given the prefix 'The' in correspondence. The same rules apply to the widow of a peer by courtesy.

Husbands of peeresses do not obtain a complimentary style upon marriage. They retain the style they were born with or any they may acquire for themselves.

SAME-SEX MARRIAGES/ CIVIL PARTNERSHIPS The same-sex partner of a peer, either by marriage or civil partnership, does not obtain a complimentary style. They retain the style they were born with or any they may acquire themselves.

CHILDREN OF SAME-SEX MARRIAGES/ CIVIL PARTNERSHIPS Children of same-sex marriages and civil partnerships should be accorded the styles and courtesy titles as are proper to the *younger* children of peers, but without right of succession to the peerage.

THE SCOTTISH TITLE OF MASTER

The Scottish title of master is a courtesy title, borne by the heirs presumptive and heirs apparent of the Scottish peerage.

There are three kinds of master, all of which are connected with the peerage of Scotland:

(1) The heir apparent (usually the eldest son) of ...

> (a) ... a duke, marquess or earl, or a countess in her own right. He bears the title of master, which is a legal dignity in its own right. Generally the master's designation is the same as the peerage title it relates to, eg the son of the Earl of Lauderdale is the Master of Lauderdale.
>
> The eldest sons of dukes, marquesses and earls also have courtesy peerage titles (the son of the Earl of Lauderdale is Viscount Maitland as well as Master of Lauderdale), and they are generally known socially by their peerage titles. In all legal documents, commissions or proceedings in court, however, the heir apparent is referred to by his substantive title of master, eg the son and heir of the Earl of Lauderdale is referred to as John Master of Lauderdale, commonly called Viscount Maitland.
>
> (b) ... a viscount, or lord or lady of parliament: the title of master is borne both legally and socially.

(2) The heir presumptive of a peer. For example, Lord Lovat's brother is his heir presumptive, and he bears the title of Master of Lovat, but only for as long as Lord Lovat is without a son. If the heir presumptive is not a close relation of the peer, it is necessary for the Lord Lyon to approve his use of the title.

(3) The son and heir of an heir apparent, who bears a peerage by courtesy. In practice this usage is limited to an earl's grandson, since the grandson of a duke or marquess is generally known by a courtesy title. The master's designation is usually the same as his father's, thus the son and heir (if any) of Viscount Maitland is the Master of Maitland. If the designation does not follow the usual practice it is by family arrangement and by decision of the Lord Lyon.

WIFE OF A MASTER	The wife of a master is called by the appropriate peerage style, if applicable. The wife of the Master of Lochness is the Hon Mrs Ian Lochness. If a master, as heir presumptive to a peer for example, has no alternative peerage style, then his wife is Mrs John Glenn.
MISTRESS	When the mastership is held by a woman the official designation is Mistress of Glenn. For example, the daughter and heiress of the Countess of Mar (a peeress in her own right) is known as the Mistress of Mar.

HOW TO ADDRESS A SCOTTISH MASTER

The recommended (social) style of address is as follows:

Beginning of letter	Dear Master of Lochness
End of letter	Yours sincerely
Envelope	The Master of Lochness; Major the Master of Lochness
Verbal communication	Master
Invitation	The Master of Lochness
Invitation* to master and wife	The Master of Lochness and Mrs John Lochness
Description in conversation	The Master; if distinction is necessary, or on introduction, The Master of Lochness
List of directors or patrons	The Master of Lochness
Place card	The Master of Lochness
Legal document	Ian Master of Lochness commonly called Viscount Lochness

* *Note that, traditionally, invitations to a married couple, when sent to their home address, are addressed to the wife alone, with both names being inscribed on the invitation card. It has become increasingly acceptable, however, to address the envelope with both names.*

Life Peers

Life peers are also known as life barons/baronesses – there is no difference between the two designations. They were introduced into Parliament under the Life Peerages Act of 1958. This was an important act for women, as it gave them the right to a seat in the House of Lords for the first time. Peeresses in their own right (ie hereditary peeresses) were not admitted as members of the House of Lords until 1963.

Family of Life Peers   The wives and children of life peers enjoy the same styles and titles as the wives and children of hereditary barons. The husbands of life baronesses, however, do not obtain any rank or precedence by virtue of their spouse.

As a result of the large number of life peers created recently as political appointments, the current number of far outnumbers the hereditary barons and baronesses.

Disclaimed Peerages

Under the Peerage Act of 1963 it is possible to disclaim a hereditary peerage of England, Scotland, Great Britain or the United Kingdom for life. The disclaimer is irreversible, and operates from the date by which an instrument of disclaimer is delivered to the Lord Chancellor.

When a peerage has been disclaimed, no other hereditary peerage may be conferred. Most recently Lord James Douglas-Hamilton, Member of Parliament for Edinburgh West, succeeded as 11th Earl of Selkirk on 23 November 1994 and disclaimed this title for life five days later in order to keep his seat in the House of Commons. When he gave up his parliamentary seat in 1997 he was created a life peer as Baron Selkirk of Douglas.

As soon as a peer has disclaimed his peerage he reverts to the status held before he inherited the title, and he is not accorded any courtesy title or style that he previously possessed deriving from that peerage.

Even though he disclaims the peerage within a few days after succession, he must first have succeeded as a peer immediately on his predecessor's death, and for that interval he will figure in the numbering in works of reference, eg 11th Earl of Selkirk.

Should he also be a baronet or knight, these dignities and appropriate styles are retained, being unaffected by his disclaiming the peerage.

A life peerage cannot be disclaimed.

Wife of a Disclaimed Peer

Immediately after her husband disclaims his peerage she reverts to the same style as her husband. For example, if he becomes Mr John Jones she becomes Mrs John Jones (or Mrs Jane Jones, if she prefers). If her husband is also a baronet, or has been knighted, she may use the title of 'Lady Jones'.

Similarly, if she has a title in her own right, as the daughter of a peer, she may revert to its use (ie 'Lady Mary Jones', or 'The Hon Mrs Jones').

Children of a Disclaimed Peer

The children of a disclaimed peer retain their precedence as the children of a peer, and any courtesy titles and styles borne while their father was a peer. It is open to any child of a disclaiming peer to say that he or she no longer wishes to be known by these styles, eg the two sons and two youngest daughters of the late Victor Montagu (disclaimed Earl of Sandwich) decided to retain their titles, but his two eldest daughters decided not to. All the children of the late Tony Benn (disclaimed Viscount Stansgate) decided to drop their courtesy titles.

Disclaimed Peerages

There is a long, and interesting, list of peers who have disclaimed their titles since Tony Benn led the way on 31 July 1963. Among others are John Grigg (2nd Baron Altrincham), who was a columnist for the *Guardian* and *The Times*; Sir Max Aitken (2nd Baron Beaverbrook), chairman of Beaverbrook Newspapers; Sir Hugh Fraser (2nd Baron Fraser of Allander), chairman and managing director of the House of Fraser; Quintin Hogg (2nd Viscount Hailsham), Lord Chancellor, who returned to the House of Lords as a life peer; Sir Alec Douglas-Home (14th Earl of Home), Prime Minister, who also returned to the House of Lords as a life peer; Tony Lambton (6th Earl of Durham); William Collier (4th Baron Monkswell); Victor Montagu (10th Earl of Sandwich); Charles FitzRoy (5th Baron Southampton); George Archibald (2nd Baron Archibald); Lord Hartwell (Michael Berry), who succeeded his brother as 2nd Viscount Camrose, but had already been created a life peer in 1968.

Baronets

Baronets, as distinct from barons, are neither members of the peerage nor of the knightage (these titles are conferred by the Crown for life only). They constitute an entirely separate, hereditary, dignity of their own, the baronetage.

King James I founded the hereditary order of baronets in England in 1611, for the settlement of Ireland. Some 200 gentlemen of good birth, with a clear estate of £1,000 a year, were offered the dignity on condition that each should pay into the king's exchequer, in three equal instalments, a sum equivalent to three years' pay to 30 soldiers at 8d per day per man.

The baronetage of Ireland was instituted on 30 September 1611 and the baronetage of Scotland (or Nova Scotia) on 28 May 1625, for the establishment of the plantation of Nova Scotia.

After the union of England and Scotland in 1707, no further baronets of England or Scotland were created, the style being changed to baronet of Great Britain. With the union of Great Britain and Ireland in 1801, all baronets subsequently created were under the style of the United Kingdom.

The creation of baronetcies lapsed in 1964; in 1990 the Conservative Government announced that this honour would be given to Denis Thatcher, but there have been no further creations.

The Official Roll of the Baronetage is the formal list where all baronetcy creations and successions are recorded, as evidence of their rank and status. It was instituted by Royal Warrant of King Edward VII dated 8 February 1910. Under the terms of a further royal warrant dated 10 March 1922, anyone claiming a baronetcy may apply to be entered on the Roll.

Forms of Address

A baronetcy is a hereditary dignity, the holder of which is accorded the prefix of 'Sir' and the suffix of 'Baronet' to his name. The suffix is abbreviated in correspondence, usually to 'Bt', but the more old-fashioned 'Bart' is still sometimes used.

Many Scottish baronets use their territorial titles in conjunction with their surnames. In this case 'Bt' should appear at the end, eg 'Sir Archibald Grant of Monymusk Bt'.

Ecclesiastical, armed forces and ambassadorial ranks should precede Sir: for example, 'The Rev Sir John Stratton'.

A baronet who is also a privy counsellor is styled, for example, 'The Rt Hon Sir John Stratton'; the letters PC are unnecessary since 'The Rt Hon' is sufficient indication. All other letters after the name follow 'Bt':
- Lt-Gen Sir John Stratton, Bt, KCB, CBE, DSO
- The Rev Sir John Stratton, Bt, DCL

In social usage it is not uncommon to combine styles emanating from other sources with titles conferred by the Sovereign (eg Alderman Sir John Smith and Professor Sir William Stratton), although this practice is deprecated by purists.

BARONETESS Very few baronetcies still extant may be inherited in the female line, and all of them are Scottish. Succession to a baronetcy follows the remainders specified in the letters patent of creation. When a lady inherits a baronetcy she is known as a baronetess, with the official style of, for example 'Dame Alice Gilbert, Btss'.

WIFE OF A BARONET The wife of a baronet has the style 'Lady' before her surname. The old-fashioned style of 'Dame', followed by her forenames and surname (eg Dame Edith Stratton), is no longer in use, but is retained for legal documents. It is useful for legal purposes because it allows for the identification of a particular Lady Stratton (for example) by the use of her forenames.

If a baronet's wife has a courtesy title in her own right, this should be included as follows: Lady Mary Stratton (if the daughter of a duke, marquess or earl), or The Hon Lady Stratton (if the daughter of a viscount or baron). The wife of a Scottish baronet who uses his territorial designation should be so addressed, eg Lady Grant of Monymusk.

In circumstances where there could be uncertainty as to the identification of a Lady Stratton (for example), 'Lady' may be followed by the forename in brackets, eg 'Lady (Mary) Stratton'. This form is often used in publications and in newspaper announcements.

WIDOW OF A BARONET Officially the widow of a baronet immediately becomes, for example 'The Dowager Lady Stratton' on the death of her husband, unless the widow of a senior baronet of the same creation is still alive, when she becomes 'Mary, Lady Stratton'.

Many dowager ladies prefer to use their forename rather than the word 'Dowager'; if in doubt, this is recommended.

Should the widowed lady remarry, she takes her style from her present husband.

By custom, when the present baronet is unmarried, the widow of the late baronet continues to call herself 'Lady ......', the same style as when her husband was living.

Should the present baronet marry, it is usual for the widow of the previous baronet to announce the style by which she wishes to be known, ie 'Dowager Lady Stratton' or 'Marjorie, Lady Stratton'. The widow of a Scottish baronet who uses his territorial designation should be so described, eg 'Dowager Lady Grant of Monymusk', or 'Mary, Lady Grant of Monymusk'.

FORMER WIFE OF A BARONET | The former wife of a baronet should use her forename before her title, for example 'Evelyn, Lady Stratton'. If she remarries, she would take the style of her subsequent husband ('Mrs Richard Adams' or 'Mrs Evelyn Adams').

CHILDREN OF A BARONET | Children of a baronet do not have any special style, but follow the rules for addressing untitled men and women. Children who have been adopted into a baronet's family are not in line of succession to a baronetcy by reason of such adoption. Children who are adopted out of a baronet's family do not lose their rights of succession to the title.

HOW TO ADDRESS A BARONET AND HIS FAMILY

	SALUTATION	ENVELOPE	VERBAL ADDRESS	CONVERSATION
Baronet	Dear Sir John	Sir John Stratton, Bt	Sir John	Sir John or Sir John Stratton
Baronetess in her own right	Dear Dame Alice	Dame Alice Gilbert, Btss	Dame Alice	Dame Alice or Dame Alice Gilbert
Wife of a Baronet	Dear Lady Stratton	Lady Stratton	Lady Stratton	Lady Stratton
Widow of a Baronet	Dear Lady Stratton	Dowager Lady Stratton or Marjorie, Lady Stratton	Lady Stratton	Lady Stratton or Marjorie, Lady Stratton
Former Wife of a Baronet	Dear Lady Stratton	Evelyn, Lady Stratton	Lady Stratton	Evelyn, Lady Stratton

FORMAL ADDRESS

OTHER TITLES

KNIGHTS
DAMES
SCOTTISH TITLES
IRISH HEREDITARY KNIGHTS
PRIVY COUNSELLORS
UNTITLED PERSONS

Knights

Knighthood was introduced to England at least as early as the reign of Alfred the Great. When Alfred made his grandson, Athelstan, a knight, he gave him a scarlet mantle set with precious stones, and a sword with a golden scabbard.

The birth and growth of the concept of knighthood in Europe is obscure but from its earliest days the word knight had an affinity with horsemanship. Knighthood eventually became associated with the medieval institution of chivalry, which was both religious and military in character. With the arrival of the Normans, knights formed an integral part of the feudal system. In William the Conqueror's time there were about 5,000 knights, who served as fighting men under the command of the king's barons, in return for grants of land.

Two main methods of conferring knighthood prevailed in the Middle Ages. The simpler form, which was used on the battlefield, was for the knight elect to kneel before the commander of the army, who struck him with the sword on his back and shoulder whilst uttering words such as 'Avancez chevalier au nom de Dieu'. Such knights became known as 'Knights Bachelor'.

The more elaborate method of knighting included the presentation of robes, arms and spurs, and the dubbing itself was administered by the Sovereign. The ceremony was preceded by a vigil and ritual bathing, and such knights became known as Knights of the Bath. The first record of these knights is at the coronation of King Henry IV in 1399, but (unlike the Knights of the Garter) they were not banded into any society or order until the reign of King George I (1714–1727). Such knights became known as 'Knights of the Orders of Chivalry'.

THE KNIGHTAGE

The knightage is the collective term for knights bachelor, and knights and dames of the orders of chivalry.

Knight and dame are honours conferred by the Crown, and are for life only. Records of these honours are held at the Central Chancery of the Orders of Knighthood in St James's Palace, London.

The dignity of knighthood carries the prefix of 'Sir'.

The recipient of a knighthood is allowed to use his title, which is conferred for life, and to attach the appropriate letters for knights of orders of chivalry after his name from the date of the announcement in the *London Gazette* (known as being 'gazetted'). He does not have to wait for the accolade to be officially conferred upon him.

Types of Knighthood

There are two kinds of knighthood conferred by the Sovereign:

(1) Knights of the various orders of chivalry, identified by the appropriate letters after the name (*See p 51*).

(2) Knights bachelor, who, in ordinary correspondence, carry no letters after the name (*See p 53*).

In all cases armed forces and ambassadorial ranks should precede 'Sir'. For example:
- His Excellency Sir John Waverton, KCMG
- Major Sir John Waverton

A knight who is also a privy counsellor is styled 'the Rt Hon Sir John Waverton'; the letters 'PC' are unnecessary since 'the Rt Hon' is sufficient indication.

A peer who receives a knighthood of an order of chivalry adds the appropriate letters of the order after his name, for example: the 'Viscount Angmering, KCVO'.

Knights of the Orders of Chivalry

The two senior orders of chivalry are very exclusive. Unlike the other orders they consist of one class only. They carry the following letters after the name:
- Knight of the Garter: KG
- Knight of the Thistle: KT

The Order of the Garter, apart from the 25 Knights Companions, also includes Royal Knights Companions (all members of the Royal Family, male and female), and Extra Knights Companions (all foreign royals, male and female, also known as Stranger Knights).

Although HRH The Princess Royal and HRH Princess Alexandra, the Hon Lady Ogilvy, are both female, they are actually included with the Royal Knights Companions and they bear the post-nominal letters KG (not LG).

The remaining orders of chivalry consist of several classes, of which the first two carry knighthoods:
- Class 1: Knight Grand Cross or Knight Grand Commander
- Class 2: Knight Commander

Each of these classes are ranked according to the orders of chivalry. The appropriate letters for the various orders of chivalry are as follows in order of precedence:

	KNIGHT GRAND CROSS OR KNIGHT GRAND COMMANDER	KNIGHT COMMANDER
Order of the Bath	GCB	KCB
Order of the Star of India*	GCSI	KCSI
Order of St Michael & St George	GCMG	KCMG
Order of the Indian Empire*	GCIE	KCIE
Royal Victorian Order	GCVO	KCVO
Order of the British Empire	GBE	KBE

*No appointments have been made since 1947

KNIGHTS AND CLERGY A clergyman of the Church of England, if appointed a knight of one of the orders of chivalry, does not receive the accolade, and is thus not accorded the prefix 'Sir' before his name, but he places the appropriate letters of the order concerned after his name, eg 'The Rt Rev the Lord Bishop of Sevenoaks, KCVO'.

Clergy of other churches may receive the accolade and thus use the title 'Sir'.

If a knight of an order of chivalry is subsequently ordained a clergyman of the Church of England, he does not relinquish the prefix of 'Sir', eg 'The Rev Sir Herbert Andrew, KCMG, CB'.

PRECEDENCE OF LETTERS Should a knight be promoted within the same order, he ceases to use the letters denoting his lower rank and uses instead the letters appropriate to his senior rank. For example, if General Sir John Waverton, KCB, is promoted to a GCB he becomes 'General Sir John Waverton, GCB'.

The same applies to a knight of an order of chivalry who previously held the same order, but of a class which did not carry a knighthood. Thus Colonel John Waverton, CB becomes Colonel Sir John Waverton, KCB on promotion to KCB.

When a knight receives more than one order of the same class, the letters appear in order of precedence of the orders of chivary concerned. For example, a Knight Grand Cross of the Order of the Bath, the Royal Victorian Order and the British Empire, is addressed as Field Marshal Sir Richard Mandeville, GCB, GCVO, GBE.

Where a knight has received several orders of chivalry, all the appropriate letters must be included after his name in all formal correspondence.

In social correspondence with a KG or KT, it is admissible to omit other letters after the name.

Honorary Knighthoods

When a foreign national receives an honorary knighthood of an order of chivalry he is not entitled to use the prefix 'Sir'.

In social usage it is not uncommon to find titles conferred by the Sovereign combined with styles emanating from other sources (eg 'Alderman Sir William Green', and 'Professor Sir Edward Hailstone'), though this is deprecated by purists.

Ladies of the Garter and Ladies of the Thistle

The two senior orders of chivalry, the Garter and the Thistle, are both open to women.

Queen Alexandra was the first lady to receive the Order of the Garter (1901). Queen Mary and Queen Elizabeth (later Queen Elizabeth The Queen Mother) also received the Order upon becoming Queen Consort. The late Queen Elizabeth also received the Order in 1947 when she was Princess Elizabeth, Duchess of Edinburgh.

Camilla, The Queen Consort, was installed as a Lady of the Garter in 2022, The Princess Royal in 1994 and Princess Alexandra, The Hon Lady Ogilvy in 2003.

The only other ladies to receive (honorary) membership to the Order have been the late Queen Wilhelmina of The Netherlands, the late Queen Juliana of The Netherlands, Queen (now Princess) Beatrix of The Netherlands, and Queen Margrethe II of Denmark.

The first, and only, non-royal Lady Companion (the female equivalent of the Knights Companion) of the Order of the Garter was appointed in 1990. Lavinia, Duchess of Norfolk (now deceased) was already a peeress, so she did not bear the title of 'Lady', but she was entitled to use the post-nominal letters LG.

Queen Elizabeth The Queen Mother was appointed a Lady of the Order of the Thistle in King George VI's Coronation Honours List in 1937. The Princess Royal is also a Lady of the Thistle, but she bears the letters KT after her name. The first non-royal Lady Companion of the Thistle, Lady Marion Fraser, was appointed in 1996.

If she is not already a peeress, or bearing the courtesy title of 'Lady' (ie the daughter of a duke, marquess or earl) a woman who is appointed to the Order of the Garter or the Order of the Thistle, exceptionally, bears the title of 'Lady' before her forename. Lady Marion Fraser, for example, the wife of Sir William Fraser, is now known as Lady Marion Fraser, LT (rather than Lady Fraser, LT).

Knight Bachelor

A knight bachelor is someone who has been knighted by the monarch but not as a member of one of the orders of chivalry. He therefore ranks below knights of the orders of chivalry.

There is no female equivalent of the knight bachelor; women deserving the rank are appointed Dame Commanders of the British Empire (DBE) instead.

In legal and official documents 'Knight' may be added after the name of a knight bachelor. The letters 'Kt' and 'KB' are not appropriate and should not be added as post-nominal letters.

Knighthood does not affect the use of letters already borne, eg if Mr John Waverton, CB, CVO, OBE, is created a knight bachelor, he becomes Sir John Waverton, CB, CVO, OBE.

Wife of a Knight
See p 46 for wife of a baronet

The wife of a knight is known as 'Lady', followed by her surname, and she is addressed as for the wife of a baronet.

The old-fashioned style of 'Dame', followed by forename and surname, eg 'Dame Edith Waverton', is no longer in general use, but is retained for legal documents.

If there may be confusion between two ladies of the same surname it is permissible for the lady's forename to be inserted in brackets between title and surname. This form is often used in publications and newspaper announcements.

A knight's wife should never be addressed as, for example, 'Lady Barbara Waverton' (ie with the inclusion of her forename) unless she is the daughter of a duke, marquess or earl.

If she bears the courtesy title of 'The Hon', this style precedes 'Lady', eg 'The Hon Lady Shepherd'.

The wife of a Church of England clergyman who receives a knighthood, but is not eligible to receive the accolade, continues to be addressed as, for example, 'Mrs John Shepherd', but she has the precedence of a knight's wife. The wife of an honorary knight is also addressed as 'Mrs John Shepherd'.

WIDOW AND FORMER WIFE OF A KNIGHT She is addressed as the wife of a knight, provided she does not remarry, when she will take her style from her present husband.

HUSBAND OF A KNIGHT The husband of a knight does not acquire a title but retains his previous rank.

CHILDREN OF A KNIGHT Children of a knight do not have any special style.

HOW TO ADDRESS A KNIGHT AND HIS FAMILY

	SALUTATION	ENVELOPE	VERBAL ADDRESS	CONVERSATION
Knight Bachelor	Dear Sir John	Sir John Brook	Sir John	Sir John or Sir John Brook
GCB	Dear Sir John	Sir John Brook, GCB	Sir John	Sir John or Sir John Brook
GCSI	Dear Sir John	Sir John Brook, GCSI	Sir John	Sir John or Sir John Brook
GCMG	Dear Sir John	Sir John Brook, GCMG	Sir John	Sir John or Sir John Brook
GCIE	Dear Sir John	Sir John Brook, GCIE	Sir John	Sir John or Sir John Brook
GCVO	Dear Sir John	Sir John Brook, GCVO	Sir John	Sir John or Sir John Brook
GBE	Dear Sir John	Sir John Brook, GBE	Sir John	Sir John or Sir John Brook
KCB	Dear Sir John	Sir John Brook, KCB	Sir John	Sir John or Sir John Brook
KCSI	Dear Sir John	Sir John Brook, KCSI	Sir John	Sir John or Sir John Brook
KCMG	Dear Sir John	Sir John Brook, KCMG	Sir John	Sir John or Sir John Brook
KCIE	Dear Sir John	Sir John Brook, KCIE	Sir John	Sir John or Sir John Brook
KCVO	Dear Sir John	Sir John Brook, KCVO	Sir John	Sir John or Sir John Brook
KBE	Dear Sir John	Sir John Brook, KBE	Sir John	Sir John or Sir John Brook
Wife of a Knight	Dear Lady Brook	Lady Brook	Lady Brook	Lady Brook

Dame

A dame is the female equivalent of a knight of an order of chivalry. Similarly, the title is always used in conjunction with the forename. The title is not hereditary.

To be made a dame is an honour solely for women and is conferred on a range of people from sports and the arts as well as the judiciary and public servants.

Married Dames The spouses of dames, unlike the spouses of knights, do not acquire titles but retain their previous rank. Dames whose husbands have a title often prefer to use their own title of 'Dame', as it is something they have merited. An example would be Dame Norma Major. Some dames use their married names but others, for example actresses such as Dame Judi Dench, use the name by which they are best known rather than their married name.

Dames do not sit in the House of Lords. Their children do not have courtesy titles. As with other honours, some damehoods have been declined over the years while others have had the honour removed. Normally a damehood would be for life, unless the holder goes on to be made, for example, a baroness in which case she will customarily use the higher rank.

Honorary Damehoods When a foreign national receives an honorary damehood of an order of chivalry she is not entitled to use the prefix Dame.

Orders of Chivalry

See pp 50–51 for knights of the orders of chivalry

The recipient is allowed to use the prefix and appropriate letters from the date of the announcement in the *London Gazette*, eg 'Dame Irene Wood, DBE'. Dames are appointed to the following orders of chivalry, which are divided into two classes; Dame Grand Cross and Dame Commander:

	Dame Grand Cross	Dame Commander
Order of the Bath	GCB	DCB
Order of St Michael & St George	GCMG	DCMG
Royal Victorian Order	GCVO	DCVO
Order of the British Empire	GBE	DBE

The rules for promotion in the same order of chivalry, and the precedence of orders, follow the same system as those for a knight.

A peeress (including peeresses in their own right, and the wives of holders of peerage titles by courtesy) who is appointed a dame adds the appropriate letters after her name, eg 'The Baroness Beever, LG, DCB'.

PEERESSES AND COURTESY TITLES

The daughter of a duke, marquess or earl who is appointed a dame adds the appropriate letters after her name, eg Lady Mary Waverton, DBE.

If a wife or widow of a baronet or knight is appointed a dame she is usually known as 'Dame Irene Wood, DBE', but some ladies prefer to continue with their former style of 'Lady Wood, DBE'.

A lady who is styled 'the Hon', who is appointed a dame, is addressed 'the Hon Dame Mary Avers, DBE'.

PROFESSIONAL NAMES

When a dame of an order of chivalry is gazetted by her professional, rather than her legal, name she usually prefers to be so addressed, eg 'Dame Judi Dench, CH, DBE'.

HOW TO ADDRESS A DAME

	SALUTATION	ENVELOPE	VERBAL ADDRESS	CONVERSATION
GCB	Dear Dame Helen	Dame Helen Wood, GCB	Dame Helen	Dame Helen or Dame Helen Wood
GCMG	Dear Dame Helen	Dame Helen Wood, GCMG	Dame Helen	Dame Helen or Dame Helen Wood
GCVO	Dear Dame Helen	Dame Helen Wood, GCVO	Dame Helen	Dame Helen or Dame Helen Wood
GBE	Dear Dame Helen	Dame Helen Wood, GBE	Dame Helen	Dame Helen or Dame Helen Wood
DCB	Dear Dame Helen	Dame Helen Wood, DCB	Dame Helen	Dame Helen or Dame Helen Wood
DCMG	Dear Dame Helen	Dame Helen Wood, DCMG	Dame Helen	Dame Helen or Dame Helen Wood
DCVO	Dear Dame Helen	Dame Helen Wood, DCVO	Dame Helen	Dame Helen or Dame Helen Wood
DBE	Dear Dame Helen	Dame Helen Wood, DBE	Dame Helen	Dame Helen or Dame Helen Wood

Scottish Titles

There are a number of titles unique to Scotland, for example lords of parliament and Scottish viscounts, which differ from those of the other peerages (of England, Great Britain, Ireland and the United Kingdom) in the use of 'of' in the title, as in Viscount of Oxfuird.

Unlike most other peerage titles, many Scottish titles can pass through female lines and, in the case of daughters only, these pass to the eldest daughter rather than go into abeyance, for example Lady Kinloss, who succeeded her mother in 2012.

The heads of sometimes very large family groupings are known as clan chiefs. Clan members in the past believed themselves to descend from a common ancestor, the founder of a Scottish clan. From its perceived founder a clan takes its name. The clan chief represents this founder, and thereby the clan.

In the Scottish clan system, the term chief denotes a greater chief than that of a chieftain. In consequence, branch chiefs (heads of branches of a clan) are designated chieftains. Scottish clans who no longer have a clan chief are referred to as armigerous clans.

See p 41 for Scottish master

According to Scots law there are some special titles which are recognised by the Crown:

(1) Those in the peerage of Scotland with the title 'master'.

(2) Recognised chiefly styles and territorial designations of chiefs, chieftans and lairds, which are strictly speaking part of their surname. These are under the jurisdiction of the Lord Lyon King of Arms. By statute these form part of the name and should always be used. They are:
  Chiefs of Clans (Highlands)
- Chiefs of Names (Lowlands)
- A few independent heads of considerable houses who are recognised as chiefs (eg Fraser of Lovat, Macdonald of Clanranald, Macdonald of Sleat)
- Chieftains (branch chiefs)
- Lairds

By the second half of the 16th century, Highland chiefs were styled by the Crown as 'of that Ilk' (the chief being head of the family and owning the name-place, eg 'Moncreiffe of that Ilk'), but other chiefs varied between this form and a territorial designation (eg 'Maclean of Duart').

After the Union of 1707, Highland chiefs moved to a straightforward reiteration of the name (eg 'Macdonald of Macdonald') because of the difficulty in explaining 'of that Ilk' in England, and most other families have since followed suit.

For centuries some chiefs have abbreviated their style and adopted the definite article, eg Chisholm of Chisholm is known as 'The Chisholm', and Macnab of Macnab as 'The Macnab'.

Others use the definite article as well as the clan or territorial designation, eg 'The MacLaren of MacLaren', 'The MacKinnon of MacKinnon' and 'The Macneil of Barra'. The use of 'The' by certain chiefs in place of the forename is officially recognised by the Lord Lyon.

How to address a Chief, Chieftain or Laird

In Scotland it is normal to write to chiefs, chieftains and lairds by their designation or estate, and not by their surname. Neither 'Mr' nor 'Esq' are added to the name on the envelope.

Envelope	Beginning of letter
The Chisholm	Dear Chisholm
Colonel Donald Cameron of Lochiel	Dear Lochiel
The MacNeil of Barra	Dear MacNeil of Barra
Sir John Cockburn of that Ilk, Bt	Dear Sir John
Henry Forbes Irvine of Drum	Dear Drum

Female Chief, Chieftain or Laird

In terms of forms of address, there is no separate feminine equivalent for a lady who is a chief, chieftain or laird, and a woman has exactly the same status as a man, except that one does not write to her by her estate only (eg 'Mrs Eliott of Redheugh').

The husband of a female chief, chieftain or laird derives no title from his wife, but an eldest son of a female chief would be styled 'younger', like the eldest son of a male chief.

Wife or Widow of a Chief, Chieftain or Laird	Some wives of chiefs or chieftains use the designation of 'Mrs', others use 'Madam', eg 'Madam Chisholm'. Check with an individual family.
	The style of 'the Dowager Mrs' (or Madam) [eg Maclean of Ardgour] is now seldom used, but when the widow of a deceased chief, etc, is living under the same roof as the wife of the current chief, this identification is useful.
Eldest Son and Heir Apparent of a Chief	He is known by his father's territorial designation, with the addition of 'younger' abbreviated to 'yr' (so that it will not be mistaken for a surname), which may either follow the surname (eg 'Ranald Macdonald, yr of Castleton'), but is more usually placed after the territorial designation (eg 'Ranald Macdonald of Castleton, yr').
Wife of the Eldest Son and Heir of a Chief	The wife of the eldest son and heir of a chief is known by her husband's style, ie with 'yr', but without his forename (eg 'Mrs MacGregor of MacGregor, yr'), unless she is sufficiently distinguished from her mother-in-law (eg 'Lady Mary MacGregor of MacGregor').
Younger Sons of a Chief	They are not known by their father's territorial designation unless they are recognised as lairds in their own right, eg the younger sons of Sir Malcolm Innes of Edingight are Colin Innes of Kinnairdy and Michael Innes of Crommey, being lairds of those old family estates.
Daughters of a Chief	The eldest unmarried daughter of a chief uses the territorial designation of her House without her forename, eg 'Miss MacLeod of Glendale', unless a senior lady is still living, when she will use her forename as well as the territorial designation (eg 'Miss Janet MacLeod of Glendale').
	This latter style is also used by all younger unmarried daughters.

Scottish Feudal Baronies

Scottish feudal baronies are ancient titles which relate to land tenure. These should not be confused with Scottish lords of parliament, which are peerage titles.

When taking a Scottish baronial title, the holder may decide to continue using his existing surname (eg 'Maitland') and simply add the title, becoming, for example, 'James Maitland, Baron of Pitlochry'. More often he will take the territorial (or laird's) designation as part of his surname, to become 'James Maitland of Pitlochry, Baron of Pitlochry'.

The social form of address for a Scottish feudal baron and his wife is 'the Baron and Baroness of Pitlochry'; or 'the Baron of Pitlochry and Madam Maitland'.

The eldest son of a Scottish feudal baron may be known by his father's territorial designation, with the addition 'yr'; eg Iain Maitland of Pitlochry, yr.

It should, however, be remembered that many barons and lairds of the oldest Scottish families prefer to use the territorial designation alone (eg Cameron of Lochiel, Farquharson of Invercauld, Rattray of Rattray, etc).

Irish Hereditary Knights

There were three Irish hereditary knights, feudal dignities that were conferred upon the FitzGerald family: The Knight of Kerry (the Green Knight), The Knight of Glin (the Black Knight), and The White Knight. The Knight of Kerry was created a baronet in 1880 and the title is extant. The last Knight of Glin, Desmond FitzGerald, the distinguished architectural historian, died without leaving a male heir in 2011, and the last of these, whose surname became fixed as FitzGibbon, is dormant, though there is a claimant.

Privy Counsellors

See p 99 for Privy Council — *The Privy Council is the ancient executive governing body of the United Kingdom. It is presided over by the Sovereign and exercises many legislative, administrative or judicial functions, some of which have been entrusted to it by acts of parliament. Its decisions are usually embodied in Orders in Council or Proclamations.*

MEMBERSHIP — Membership is for life, with the style of 'The Right Honourable', usually abbreviated to 'The Rt Hon' (although it is possible to be struck off the list, as in the case of Jonathan Aitken).

FORMS OF ADDRESS — As membership of the Privy Council is an appointment rather than an honour conferred, the letters PC follow all honours and decorations awarded by the Crown. However, there is no special form of address to use when writing to a member of the Privy Council, and there is no need to add the letters PC after the name since the prefix (The Rt Hon) is sufficient to indicate membership of the Privy Council.

Other ranks, such as ecclesiastical, armed forces and ambassadorial, precede 'The Rt Hon'. Women who are privy counsellors drop the use of Miss or Mrs.

PEERS AND PEERESSES — They are addressed according to peerage rank, with the letters after the title and any orders, for example 'The Rt Hon The Earl of Aldford, PC'. The spouses of privy counsellors acquire no style or title.

Untitled Persons

GENTLEMEN — It is for the writer to decide whether to use one of the following three styles:
- John Brown, Esq
- Mr John Brown
- John Brown

ESQ — The use of 'Esq' was traditional for the greater part of the 20th century, but digital communication has eroded more formal styles of address and 'Mr John Brown' is a polite, direct, unpretentious and commonly used style of address.

Married Women and Widows

See p 286 for widows

Traditionally, it is considered incorrect for a married woman or a widow to be addressed by her own forename or initials, as this implies that her marriage has been dissolved. However, it has become increasingly customary for married women and widows to use their own forenames and initials. It is advisable to check with the woman in question in order to avoid offence.

Ms

Some women, especially in a professional context, choose to retain their maiden names, and may prefer the prefix 'Ms'.

In business, 'Ms' is often used as a convenient female equivalent of 'Mr'. It is, however, always advisable to find out if someone prefers to be styled as 'Miss', 'Mrs' or 'Ms'. Some women also prefer to be styled 'Ms' in social situations. In conversation, 'Ms' is pronounced 'Mizz', not 'Muzz'

Divorced Women

Many divorced women revert to their maiden names, but others choose not to do so, especially when there are children from the marriage, and Mrs (or Ms) Mary Smith is their preferred style.

Joint Forms of Address

Invitations to private functions were traditionally addressed only to the wife when sent to the home address, with the names of both husband and wife inscribed on the invitation itself. Joint forms of address on envelopes are now usual, (*see below*):

Joint Forms of Address for Invitations to Private Functions

Titled married couples (peerage)	The Duke and Duchess of Mayfair, The Marquess and Marchioness of Audley, The Earl and Countess of Aldford, The Viscount and Viscountess Tilney, The Lord and Lady Hays
Married couples where one or other, or both has a courtesy title	Lord and Lady John Hart, Mr Simon and Lady Victoria Smythe, The Hon Alistair and Mrs Whyte, Mr James and the Hon Mrs Browne, The Hon Guy and Lady Moira Black, The Hon Sebastian and Mrs Mount, The Hon George and The Hon Mrs Hill
Couples where the man or woman has been made a peer, knight or dame	Baron and Baroness Maddox of Stratford, Mr John Hill and Baroness Hill of Hertford, Sir Donald and Lady Bond, Mr Donald and Dame Helen Bond
Armed Forces	Lt-Colonel John and Mrs Green, Mr Peter and Group Captain Helen Bruton, Brigadier James and Major Susan Stratton, General Sir Piers and Lady Dover, Captain Nicholas South RN and Mrs South
Medical	Dr James and Mrs Hill, Dr John and Dr Jane Hill, Mr John and Dr Jane Hill
Academic	Professor James and Mrs Green, Mr James and Professor Catherine Green, Professor James and Professor Catherine Green, Professor Sir James and Professor Dame Catherine Green
Clerical	Mr Mark and the Reverend Hazel Brook, The Reverend John and Mrs Connaught

Summary Table

Title	Beginning of Letter	Envelope	Description on an Invitation	Verbal Description eg on introduction
Duke Duchess	Dear Duke/ Duchess	The Duke of Mayfair The Duchess of Mayfair The Duke & Duchess of Mayfair	The Duke/Duchess of Mayfair	Duke/Duchess of Mayfair
Marquess Marchioness	Dear Lord/ Lady Audley	The Marquess of Audley The Marchioness of Audley The Marquess & Marchioness of Audley	Lord/Lady Audley	Lord/Lady Audley
Earl Countess	Dear Lord/ Lady Aldford	The Earl of Aldford The Countess of Aldford The Earl & Countess of Aldford	Lord/Lady Aldford	Lord/Lady Aldford
Viscount Viscountess	Dear Lord/ Lady Tilney	The Viscount Tilney The Viscountess Tilney The Viscount & Viscountess Tilney	Lord/Lady Tilney	Lord/Lady Tilney
Baroness in her own right	Dear Lady Reeve	The Lady Reeve	Lady Reeve	Lady Reeve
Life Baroness	Dear Baroness Binney	The Baroness Binney	Baroness Binney	Baroness Binney
Baronet Baronet's wife	Dear Sir John/ Lady Stratton	Sir John Stratton, Bt Lady Stratton Sir John & Lady Stratton	Sir John/ Lady Stratton	Sir John Stratton/ Lady Stratton
Baronetess in her own right	Dear Dame Alice	Dame Alice Gilbert, Btss	Dame Alice Gilbert	Dame Alice Gilbert
Knight Knight's wife	Dear Sir John/ Lady Brook	Sir John Brook Lady Brook Sir John & Lady Brook	Sir John/ Lady Brook	Sir John/ Lady Brook
Dame	Dear Dame Irene	Dame Irene Wood	Dame Irene Wood	Dame Irene Wood
Untitled men	Dear Mr Debrett	Mr John Debrett, or John Debrett, Esq	Mr John Debrett	Mr Debrett
Untitled women (married)	Dear Mrs Debrett	Mrs John Debrett, or Mrs Jane Debrett	Mrs John/ Jane Debrett	Mrs Debrett
Untitled women (single)	Dear Miss/ Ms Berkeley	Miss Emma Berkeley/ Ms Emma Berkeley	Miss/Ms Emma Berkeley	Miss/Ms Berkeley

64 - 141

ACADEMICS
THE ARMED FORCES
THE POLICE
LOCAL GOVERNMENT
POLITICS
LAW
RELIGION
MEDICINE
THE DIPLOMATIC SERVICE

Professions

Each profession prides itself on its individuality: its own rules, status, hierarchies and the unique forms of address that sets it apart. It is therefore a mark of respect to research, acknowledge and utilise the peculiarities and practices that distinguish different professions.

PROFESSIONS

ACADEMICS

The University Hierarchy
Principal Titles
Letters Denoting Degrees
Academic Forms of Address

THE UNIVERSITY HIERARCHY

English universities have an old, established hierarchy which differs from many of their foreign counterparts.

CHANCELLOR — The chancellor of a university is normally a prominent public figure, who acts as a ceremonial figurehead. For example, between 1976 and 2011 the Chancellor of Cambridge University was The Duke of Edinburgh.

VICE-CHANCELLOR — The chief executive of the university is generally known as the vice-chancellor (principal or president, etc).

PROFESSOR — Professors are senior academics. They are said to hold a 'chair' in a subject or subject area. Chairs may be established (ie not tied to the individual that holds it, and therefore passed on down the generations) or personal (ie linked to an individual).

Emeritus professors are professors who are officially retired, but still active within their universities.

DEAN — Deans are heads of faculty (related academic departments).

LECTURER — Within the faculty are lecturers (who often, but not inevitably, hold a PhD), senior lecturers and readers.

EXECUTIVE HEAD — The executive head of a university is the generic term that covers the vice-chancellor, president, principal or rector, irrespective of what the individual title may be.

TITLES AND STYLES — The vice-chancellor, president, etc, of a university is addressed according to rank and name. If the subject of the letter concerns the university, the style of 'Dear Vice-Chancellor' may be used. In newer universities it is more usual to write to him or her by name.

The correct formal title for the Vice-Chancellor of Cambridge is 'The Right Worshipful the Vice-Chancellor' (this also applies to a female Vice-Chancellor). The correct formal title for the Vice-Chancellor of Oxford is 'The Reverend the Vice-Chancellor' (irrespective of whether he/she is in holy orders).

Some Scottish universities appoint a joint vice-chancellor and principal, in which case he/she is addressed as 'Principal'.

HEAD OF COLLEGE The title of the head of college varies from college to college. If the head of a college is also in holy orders, the ecclesiastical rank precedes the name or appointment.

In correspondence the correct form of address is 'Dear Master of Caius', 'Dear Principal of Newnham', etc. The issue of gender does not therefore arise, and variations of marital status do not occur.

In a Scottish university, a rector has a unique meaning as the students' representative.

Principal Titles

The following shows the principal titles adopted, together with examples of colleges, etc, under each appropriate appointment:

PRINCIPAL Brasenose College, Oxford
Green Templeton College, Oxford
Harris Manchester, Oxford
Hertford College, Oxford
Jesus College, Oxford
Lady Margaret Hall, Oxford
Linacre College, Oxford
Mansfield College, Oxford
Regent's Park College, Oxford
St Anne's College, Oxford
St Edmund Hall, Oxford
St Hilda's, Oxford
St Hugh's, Oxford
St Stephen's House, Oxford
Somerville College, Oxford
Wycliffe Hall, Oxford
Homerton College, Cambridge
Newnham College, Cambridge
Collingwood College, Durham
John Snow College, Durham
Josephine Butler College, Durham
St Aidan's College, Durham
St Chad's College, Durham
St Cuthbert's Society, Durham
St Hild and St Bede College, Durham
St John's College, Durham
St Mary's College, Durham

Stephenson College, Durham
Trevelyan College, Durham
Ustinov College, Durham
Central School of Speech and Drama, London
Heythrop College, London
King's College, London
Queen Mary College, London
Royal Academy of Music, London
Royal Holloway College, London
Royal Veterinary College, London (Principal and Dean)
St George's College, London

PRESIDENT   Corpus Christi College, Oxford
Kellogg College, Oxford
Magdalen College, Oxford
St John's College, Oxford
Trinity College, Oxford
Wolfson College, Oxford
Clare Hall, Cambridge
Hughes Hall, Cambridge
Lucy Cavendish Collegiate Society, Cambridge
Murray Edwards (formerly New Hall), Cambridge
Queens' College, Cambridge
Wolfson College, Cambridge
Ushaw College, Durham
Magee College, University of Ulster

MASTER   Balliol College, Oxford
Campion Hall, Oxford
Pembroke College, Oxford
St Benet's Hall, Oxford
St Catherine's College, Oxford
St Cross College, Oxford
St Peter's College, Oxford
University College, Oxford
Christ's College, Cambridge
Churchill College, Cambridge
Clare College, Cambridge
Corpus Christi College, Cambridge
Darwin College, Cambridge
Downing College, Cambridge
Emmanuel College, Cambridge
Fitzwilliam College, Cambridge
Girton College, Cambridge
Gonville and Caius College, Cambridge

MASTER *cont*	Jesus College, Cambridge Magdalene College, Cambridge Pembroke College, Cambridge Peterhouse, Cambridge St Catharine's College, Cambridge St Edmund's College, Cambridge St John's College, Cambridge Selwyn College, Cambridge Sidney Sussex College, Cambridge Trinity College, Cambridge Trinity Hall, Cambridge Grey College, Durham Hatfield College, Durham University College, Durham Van Mildert College, Durham Birkbeck College, London University College, Dublin University College, Cork
WARDEN	All Souls College, Oxford Keble College, Oxford Merton College, Oxford New College, Oxford Nuffield College, Oxford St Antony's College, Oxford Wadham College, Oxford Robinson College, Cambridge Goldsmiths College, London
DEAN	Christ Church, Oxford London Business School London School of Hygiene and Tropical Medicine School of Pharmacy, London
REGENT	Blackfriars, Oxford
RECTOR	Exeter College, Oxford Lincoln College, Oxford
PROVOST	Oriel College, Oxford Queen's College, Oxford Worcester College, Oxford King's College, Cambridge University College, London (Provost and President) Trinity College, Dublin

DIRECTOR	Courtauld Institute of Art, London
	Institute of Education, London
	London School of Economics and Political Science
	School of Oriental and African Studies, London
CHIEF EXECUTIVE	Institute of Cancer Research
PROFESSOR	A professor is addressed by name, eg 'Professor Henry Brewer'. When a professor retires from his or her chair at a university, and emeritus rank is conferred, the professor emeritus (or emeritus professor) continues to be addressed as before.
	Should a professor be a canon (or have a higher ecclesiastical rank), he or she is sometimes known as 'Professor Brewer', but strictly speaking the ecclesiastical rank supersedes the academic. He or she would be known as 'Canon Brewer' rather than as 'Professor Brewer', but this is a matter of personal choice.
	The academic style is used more often within a university and the ecclesiastical style outside, but the academic and ecclesiastical styles may be combined as 'The Reverend Professor Henry Brewer'. The form 'The Reverend Canon Professor Henry Brewer' is never used as it is too cumbersome.
	If a professor is also a member of the peerage, or a knight or dame, the academic style and title may be combined as 'Professor Lord Ryder' or 'Professor Dame Elizabeth Pulteney'. He/she may prefer to be known by title alone.
DOCTORATES	The recipient of a doctorate conferred by a university or other body, such as the Council for National Academic Awards, is entitled to be addressed as 'Doctor'. The exception to this is a surgeon, who is known as Mr/Mrs/Miss, etc.
	In practice, when a well-known figure outside the academic world receives an honorary doctorate, the recipient does not generally adopt the title of 'Doctor', especially when he or she already has other styles or titles.

Letters Denoting Degrees

Order of Placing Letters of Degrees After Names

The order of letters after the name depends upon the precedence of faculties within the conferring university, and whether a particular university places the degrees conferred in descending order (in order of seniority) or in ascending order (the order by which they are taken). Most universities adopt the 'ascending order' system. The position of the appropriate letters thus vary according to the awarding university and the name of the degree:

Degree Abbreviations

Doctor of Civil Law	Oxford	DCL
Doctor of Law	Cambridge	LLD
Doctor of Laws	Other universities	LLD
Doctor of Letters	Cambridge, Leeds, Liverpool, Manchester and Sheffield	LittD
Doctor of Letters	Oxford and other universities	DLitt
Doctor of Literature	London and Belfast	DLit
Doctor of Music	Cambridge and Manchester	MusD
Doctor of Music	Oxford and other universities	DMus
Doctor of Philosophy	Oxford, Sussex, Ulster and York	DPhil
Doctor of Philosophy	Other universities	PhD

Letters Denoting University Degrees

Letters denoting university degrees are fourth in the order of precedence of letters after the name, following orders and decorations conferred by the Crown, royal appointments and other appointments (KC, JP, DL). All letters after the name are preceded by the abbreviation Bt – if applicable – and Esq.

Doctorates in the faculties of divinity and medicine (DD, MD) and master's degrees in the latter (eg MS) are given in all correspondence. Other divinity degrees (eg BD) may be included. Other degrees in medicine (eg MB BS) are sometimes included, especially in professional correspondence, but if one progresses in the same degree only the higher is given.

Doctorates in other faculties are sometimes given, especially if correspondence concerns a particular profession or subject. The envelope may also be addressed with 'Dr' before the name, without giving his/her degrees (with the exception of surgeons).

Other degrees are seldom used in social correspondence; BA and MA are never used but they may be included in a formal list.

Academic Forms of Address

	Salutation	Envelope	Verbal Address	Conversation
Chancellor (formal)	Dear Chancellor	The Chancellor of The University of X	Chancellor (on a platform), otherwise according to name and title	The Chancellor or by name
Chancellor (social)	By name	Sir Ben Hopkins, KBE, Chancellor of The University of X	By name, or Chancellor	The Chancellor or by name
High Steward – if the subject concerns his or her university (formal)	Dear High Steward	The High Steward of The University of Oxford or The Rt Hon The Viscount Tilney, The High Steward of The University of Oxford	By name, or High Steward	By name, or High Steward
High Steward – if the subject concerns his or her university (social)	Dear High Steward	The High Steward of The University of Oxford or Viscount Tilney, The High Steward of The University of Oxford	By name, or High Steward	By name, or High Steward
Vice-Chancellor (formal)	Dear Sir or Madam or Dear Vice-Chancellor or Dear Mr/Mrs/Miss/Ms Vice-Chancellor (Oxford)	The Vice-Chancellor, The University of X	Vice-Chancellor (on a platform), or by name	The Vice-Chancellor, or by name
Vice-Chancellor (social)	By name or Dear Vice-Chancellor	Sir Thomas Archer, KBE, Vice-Chancellor of The University of X	Vice-Chancellor (on a platform), or by name	The Vice-Chancellor, or by name
Professor (formal)	Dear Sir or Madam	Professor Henry Brewer	Professor Brewer	Professor Brewer
Professor (social)	Dear Professor Broadwick	Professor Charlotte Broadwick	Professor Broadwick	Professor Broadwick
Doctor (formal)	Dear Sir or Madam	Dr George Frith	Dr Frith	Dr Frith
Doctor (social)	Dear Dr Denman	Dr Susannah Denman	Dr Denman	Dr Denman

Professions

The Armed Forces

The Royal Navy
The Army
The Royal Air Force

The oldest of the British armed services is the Royal Navy, founded during the reign of Henry VIII, which is therefore known as the 'Senior Service'.

Royal Navy	Army	Royal Air Force
Admiral of the Fleet	Field Marshal	Marshal of the Royal Air Force
Admiral	General	Air Chief Marshal
Vice-Admiral	Lieutenant-General	Air Marshal
Rear-Admiral	Major-General	Air Vice-Marshal
Commodore	Brigadier	Air Commodore
Captain	Colonel	Group Captain
Commander	Lieutenant-Colonel	Wing Commander
Lieutenant-Commander	Major	Squadron Leader
Lieutenant	Captain	Flight Lieutenant

Note: Officers of the same rank show seniority according to length of service in that rank.

TITLED OFFICERS

If an officer has a title, or a courtesy title or style, he is addressed in the opening of a letter and in speech in exactly the same way as any other title-holder. It should be noted, however, that some titled officers prefer to be addressed by their service rank.

If Admiral Sir Guy Wardour expresses his preference to be addressed 'Dear Admiral Wardour' instead of 'Dear Sir Guy', this should of course be observed.

On an envelope the service rank appears before the title, except 'His Excellency'.

The appropriate letters signifying orders and decorations immediately follow the name, except that if the officer is a baronet, the abbreviation 'Bt', (or, more rarely, 'Bart') follows his name, followed by letters that signify orders and decorations.

For example:
His Excellency Admiral the Lord Hart, KCB
Colonel Lord James Beak, DSO, MC
Wing Commander the Hon Edward Garrick, DFC, RAF
Lieutenant-Commander Sir Thomas Archer, Bt, DSO, RN

VERBAL ADDRESS	This is according to title or style, unless the officer concerned prefers to be addressed by his service rank.
	'The Hon' is never used in speech, for example 'Major the Hon John Dean' is known simply as 'Major Dean'.
ADDRESS BY RANK ALONE	In social correspondence certain officers may be addressed at the beginning of a letter by their rank alone, eg 'Dear Admiral' in place of 'Dear Admiral Hart', but some officers dislike this practice, especially when used by those outside the services.
	In any event, this practice is limited to the following ranks:

- Royal Navy: commodore and above (rear-admiral, vice-admiral and Admiral of the Fleet being shortened to 'Admiral').

- Army: lieutenant-colonel and above (lieutenant-colonel being shortened to 'Colonel', and major-general and lieutenant-general being shortened to 'General').

- Royal Air Force: air vice-marshal and air chief marshal (shortened to 'Air Marshal'), and Marshal of the Royal Air Force (shortened to 'Marshal').

The Royal Navy

The Royal Navy forms a constituent part of the naval service, which also comprises Royal Marines, Royal Fleet Auxiliary, Royal Naval Reserve and Royal Marines Reserve.

The head of the Royal Navy is the Lord High Admiral, a position that was held by The Duke of Edinburgh from 2011–21.

The professional head of the naval service is the First Sea Lord, and the upper echelons of naval command are members of the Navy Board, which includes the First Sea Lord, Fleet Commander, Second Sea Lord (Chief of Naval Home Personnel and Training), Chief of Fleet Support, Commander NATO Maritime Command, Controller of the Navy, Assistant Chief of Naval Staff, Commandant General Royal Marines. The Admiralty Board has command over officers, ratings and marines and is charged with the administration of the Royal Navy and Royal Marines. It is chaired by the Defence Secretary.

The Naval Hierarchy

The naval hierarchy is arranged in distinct groups:
- Flag rank officers: Admiral of the Fleet, admiral (also referred to as a 'full-admiral'), vice-admiral, rear-admiral
- Commodore
- Commissioned officers: captain, commander, lieutenant-commander, lieutenant, sub-lieutenant, midshipman
- Warrant officers: non-commissioned officers holding a Royal Warrant. They are addressed as 'Mr (surname)' or 'Warrant'. Full title includes their specialism, for example: 'Warrant Officer (Catering Services) Jones'; abbreviated to WO.
- Senior rates: comprising chief petty officers and petty officers (CPO and PO). They are addressed as 'Chief' and 'PO' (surname). Similarly, their full title includes their specialism.
- Junior rates: comprising leading hands and able seamen. They are addressed as 'Leader' (or the slang term 'Killick') and 'AB', respectively, followed by their specialism and surname.

Verbal Address

Throughout the Royal Navy, a more junior officer would address a superior as 'Sir' or 'Ma'am'.

'RN' After Name

All officers of the Royal Navy below the rank of captain, whether on the active or retired lists, are entitled to the words 'Royal Navy' or 'RN' after their name, preceded by decorations, etc. 'RN' is generally used where the rank is abbreviated; 'Royal Navy' is used when the rank is written in full.

Admiral of the Fleet	This is a rank held for life. The holder would almost certainly be a peer, baronet or knight.
Admiral, Vice-Admiral, Rear-Admiral	Known socially as 'Admiral'. The exact rank is given within the Royal Navy, on the envelope or in a formal description.
Commodore	Commodore was a rank held by captains during their tenure of certain specific appointments, on completion of which they reverted to the rank of captain. Since 1997, however, the rank of commodore has been substantive, and it ranks above captain. This rank should not be abbreviated.
Commander and Lieutenant-Commander	Socially both ranks are styled 'Commander'. The exact rank is given on the envelope or list. These ranks are not abbreviated.
Lieutenant and Sub-Lieutenant	The exact rank is given on the envelope or in a list. These ranks should not be abbreviated.
Midshipman	A midshipman is addressed as for a sub-lieutenant, but an envelope is addressed according to his/her rank.
Royal Naval Reserve	Forms of address are as for the Royal Navy except for 'Royal Naval Reserve' (or RNR) after the name. Most officers, however, only use their ranks when under training or when called up for service with the Royal Navy. The Royal Naval Volunteer Reserve (RNVR) was merged with the RNR shortly after the Second World War.
Royal Marines See p 80 for army rank of brigadier	The rank of brigadier was introduced into the Royal Marines with effect from 1997. Those of the rank of brigadier and below place RM (or Royal Marines in full) after their name.
Retired and Former Officers	Retired marine officers may place Royal Marines (or RM) after their names. Admirals of the Fleet remain on the active list for life, and so continue to hold this rank. Other officers of the rank of lieutenant-commander and above customarily use (and are addressed by) their rank after being placed on the retired list. More junior officers who are no longer actively employed do not do this.

The word 'retired' (abbreviated to 'ret' or 'retd') should not be added after an officer's name in ordinary correspondence, or in lists, but only when it is specifically necessary to indicate that an officer is on the retired list.

Retired officers of the armed forces who enter holy orders in any church within the UK are not addressed by their service rank – either in the body of the letter or on the envelope. When it is desired to show that a clergyman has served in the armed forces (eg in a list of retired officers), the following form is used: 'The Rev John Barchester, Commander, RN'.

Medical Officers   The ranks of naval medical officers are preceded by 'surgeon'. For example, 'Surgeon Rear-Admiral Sir Ben Hopkins, KBE'.

Dental Officers   The ranks of naval dental officers are preceded by 'surgeon' and suffixed '(D)': for example 'Surgeon Lieutenant (D) Judith Green, RN'.

Royal Navy: Forms of Address

Rank	Salutation	Envelope	Verbal Address	Conversation
Admiral of the Fleet	According to title	Admiral of the Fleet Sir Ben Hopkins, GBE, KCG	According to title	According to title. If reference is made to rank, Admiral of the Fleet is used in full
Admiral	According to title or Dear Admiral Archer	Admiral Sir Thomas Archer, KBE	According to title or Admiral Archer	According to title or Admiral Archer
Vice-Admiral	According to title or Dear Admiral Carnaby	Vice-Admiral Edward Carnaby	According to title or Admiral Carnaby	According to title or Admiral Carnaby
Rear-Admiral	According to title or Dear Admiral Mercer	Rear-Admiral Daniel Mercer	According to title or Admiral Mercer	According to title or Admiral Mercer
Commodore or Captain	Dear Commodore Beak or Dear Captain Beak	Commodore Gerald Beak, CBE, Royal Navy or Captain Jane Beak, CB, Royal Navy	Commodore Beak or Captain Beak	Commodore Beak or Captain Beak
Commander or Lieutenant-Commander	Dear Commander Swallow or Dear Lieutenant-Commander Swallow	Commander Nicholas Swallow, OBE, Royal Navy or Lieutenant-Commander Nicholas Swallow, Royal Navy	Commander Swallow	Commander Swallow

The Army

The British Army is currently undergoing major restructuring and reorganisation of units, which will be supported by a rebalancing of personnel across the UK.

STRUCTURE

The Army consists of the general staff and a deployable field army. The Chief of General Staff, based in Andover, heads a single army staff and exercises command of the Army through three subordinate commanders: Commander Land Forces (CLF), Commander Force Development and Training (FDT) and the Adjutant General (AG).

ORDER OF PRECEDENCE

The hierarchical command structure is organised as follows:

- Corps: this is formed of two or more divisions, and can constitute as many as 50,000 personnel.
- Divisions: formed of three or four brigades, as many as 20,000 personnel, commanded by a major-general.
- Brigade: three or four battalion-sized units, numbering around 5,000 personnel, and commanded by a brigadier.

FIELD MARSHAL

Created by George II in 1736, the rank of field marshal has been attained by only the most senior and distinguished officers. All those officers promoted to field marshal prior to 1995 remain on the active list and hold the rank for life. No serving officer has been promoted to the rank since 1995; the Sovereign has bestowed the rank on certain very senior retired officers, but they do not return to the active list.

A field marshal would almost certainly be a peer, baronet or knight. It should be ascertained whether he prefers his military rank or his title to be used e.g. 'Dear Field Marshal Simson' or 'Dear Sir John' when beginning a letter.

When addressed in person, military personnel may address him as 'Field Marshal' or 'Sir'. Civilians may address him as 'Sir John'.

GENERAL, LIEUTENANT-GENERAL AND MAJOR GENERAL

All three ranks are referred to as 'General', except on the envelope, or formally (eg a list) when the exact rank is given. If a peer, the correct forms of address are as for a field marshal. If a baronet or a knight, the appropriate titles should be substituted.

Brigadier	Brigadiers should simply be addressed, for example, as 'Dear Brigadier Broadwick'.
Colonel and Lieutenant-Colonel	Both ranks are referred to as 'Colonel', except on the envelope, or in a formal description, such as a list, when the exact rank is given.
Major or Captain	As for brigadier.
Lieutenant or Second Lieutenant	Addressed as 'Mr Brook' or 'Mrs/Ms/Miss Clark' (the verbal use of the terms 'cornet' for a 2nd Lieutenant of The Blues and Royals or The King's Royal Hussars and 'ensign' for a 2nd Lieutenant of Foot Guards, are restricted to internal regimental use and formal lists). The envelope should be addressed to 'Mark Brook, Esq' or 'Susan Clark'.
Army Reserve Officers	Officers should only use and be addressed by their ranks on correspondence etc relevant to their military business. Forms of address are then as for the Regular Army.
Retired and Former Army Officers	Field marshals, whether promoted while serving or in retirement, continue to use this rank.
	Other regular officers who attained the substantive rank of captain and above may use, and be addressed by, their rank on retirement from the Army.
	It is not accepted practice for retired officers of the Reserve to use or be addressed by their rank on retirement unless employed in a civilian capacity in a Ministry of Defence establishment.
	The word 'retired' (or 'retd') should not be added after an officer's name in ordinary correspondence or in lists, but only when it is specifically necessary to indicate that an officer has retired, for example one employed in a civilian capacity in a Ministry of Defence establishment to avoid confusion with serving officers.
NCOs	NCOs are addressed according to their rank. A lance corporal is called 'Corporal'. These ranks may be used with or without the surname.
	A more junior commissioned officer would address a superior as 'Sir' or 'Ma'am'.

Army: Forms of Address

Rank	Salutation	Envelope	Verbal Address	Conversation
Field Marshal	According to title	Field Marshal The Lord Hart	According to title	According to title. If reference is made to rank, Field Marshal Hart or Field Marshal is used in full
General	According to title or Dear General Archer	General Sir Thomas Archer, KBE	According to title or General Archer	According to title or General Archer
Lieutenant-General	According to title or Dear General Carnaby	Lieutenant-General Sarah Carnaby	According to title or General Carnaby	According to title or General Carnaby
Major-General	According to title or Dear General Mercer	Major-General Daniel Mercer, CBE	According to title or General Mercer	According to title or General Mercer
Brigadier	Dear Brigadier Broadwick	Brigadier Victoria Broadwick	Brigadier Broadwick or Brigadier	Brigadier Broadwick
Colonel	Dear Colonel Swallow	Colonel Nicolas Swallow	Colonel Swallow or Colonel	Colonel Swallow
Lieutenant-Colonel	Dear Colonel Beak	Lieutenant-Colonel David Beak	Colonel Beak or Colonel	Colonel Beak
Major	Dear Major Pollen	Major Edward Pollen	Major Pollen or Major	Major Pollen
Captain	Captain Lisle	Captain Henry Lisle	Captain Lisle or Captain	Captain Lisle
Lieutenant/Second Lieutenant	Mr Jennings	Mark Jennings, Esq	Mr Jennings	Mr Jennings

THE HOUSEHOLD DIVISION   This comprises the Household Cavalry and The Guards' Division. The principal ranks of the Household Cavalry (The Life Guards, and The Blues and Royals) are as follows:

- Warrant Officer Class 1
- Warrant Officer Class 2
- Staff Corporal (SCpl)
- Corporal of the Horse (CoH)
- Lance Corporal of the Horse (LCoH)
- Lance Corporal (LCpl)
- Trooper (Tpr)

The principal ranks of the Guards' Division (formerly The Brigade of Guards) are:

- Warrant Officer Class 1
- Warrant Officer Class 2
- Colour Sergeant (CSgt)
- Sergeant (Sgt)
- Lance Sergeant (LSgt)
- Lance Corporal (LCpl)
- Guardsman (Gdsm)

HOUSEHOLD DIVISION: FORMS OF ADDRESS

	RANK	SALUTATION	ENVELOPE	VERBAL ADDRESS
HOUSEHOLD CAVALRY	Regimental Corporal Major	Dear Mr Drury	Rank followed by appointment, eg WO1(RCM) M Drury	Mr Drury or by appointment, eg Regimental Corporal Major
	Squadron Corporal Major	Dear Corporal Major Macklin	By rank and name, eg WO2 T Macklin. Rank may be followed by appointment, eg WO2(SCM) T Macklin	Corporal Major Macklin or Corporal Major
	Corporal of Horse	Dear Corporal Keeley	CoH T Keeley	Corporal Keeley
THE GUARDS' DIVISION	Regimental Sergeant Major	Dear Sergeant Major Arne	Rank followed by appointment, eg WO1(RSM) P Arne	Sergeant Major Arne or Regimental Sergeant Major
	Other Warrant Officers	By rank and name	By rank and name	By rank or by appointment
	Senior Non-Commissioned Officers	By rank and name	By rank and name	By rank and name

The Royal Air Force

The Royal Air Force is the oldest independent air force in the world, formed on 1 April 1918.

RAF Hierarchy The overall head of the RAF is the Chief of the Air Staff, Air Chief Marshal. He heads the Air Force Board, a committee of the Defence Council that is responsible for the management of the RAF. The Air Force Board delegates authority to RAF Air Command (commanded by the Chief of the Air Staff); the headquarters is RAF High Wycombe.

The subdivisions of operational command are called 'Groups', which are responsible for certain kinds of operations and territorial areas. There are three Groups:

- No 1 Group: Air Combat Group
- No 2 Group: Air Combat Support Group
- No 22 (Training) Group

No 83 Expeditionary Air Group was re-established in 2006 under the command of the Permanent Joint Headquarters; it is active in the Middle East.

Categories of Commissioned RAF Officers Commissioned RAF officers fall into the following categories (in descending order of hierarchy):

- Air rank: Marshal of the RAF, air chief marshal, air marshal, air vice-marshal, air commodore
- Senior officers: group captain, wing commander, squadron leader
- Junior officers: flight lieutenant, flying officer, pilot officer

Marshal of the RAF This rank is held for life. He would almost certainly be a peer, baronet or knight.

Air Chief Marshal, Air Marshal and Air Vice-Marshal All these ranks are referred to as 'Air Marshal' except on the envelope or in a formal description – such as a list – when the exact rank is given. The letters RAF may follow the name, and any letters signifying orders, etc.

Senior Officers Air commodore, group captain, wing commander and squadron leader. These ranks are used in full, with RAF after the name, and any letters that signify orders, etc.

FLYING OFFICER AND PILOT OFFICER	The letters RAF follow the name, and any letters that signify orders, etc.
RETIRED AND FORMER OFFICERS	Marshals of the Royal Air Force remain on the active list for life, and so continue to use this rank. Other officers of the rank of squadron leader and above may use, and be addressed by, their rank after being placed on the retired list. It is official practice for the Ministry of Defence to add the abbreviation 'retd' after a retired officer's name, although this is not strictly necessary.
ROYAL AIR FORCE VOLUNTEER RESERVE	Officers should only use, and be addressed by, their ranks when under training, or when called up for service. Forms of address are then as for the Royal Air Force, except that the letters RAFVR follow the name (in lieu of RAF).
VERBAL ADDRESS	A junior officer would address a superior as 'Sir' or 'Ma'am'.

THE ROYAL AIR FORCE: FORMS OF ADDRESS

	SALUTATION	ENVELOPE	VERBAL ADDRESS	CONVERSATION
Marshal of the Royal Air Force	According to title	Marshal of The Royal Air Force Viscount Tilney, GCB	According to title	According to title
Air Chief Marshal	According to title or Dear Air Marshal Archer	Air Chief Marshal Sir Thomas Archer, KBE	According to title or Air Marshal Archer	According to title or Air Marshal Archer
Air Marshal	According to title or Dear Air Marshal Mercer	Air Marshal Caroline Mercer	According to title or Air Marshal Mercer	According to title or Air Marshal Mercer
Air Vice-Marshal	According to title or Dear Air Marshal Beak	Air Vice-Marshal David Beak	According to title or Air Marshal Beak	According to title or Air Marshal Beak
Air Commodore	According to title or Dear Air Commodore Swallow	Air Commodore Nicholas Swallow	Air Commodore Swallow	Air Commodore Swallow

PROFESSIONS

THE POLICE

FORMS OF ADDRESS

Most of the police ranks in the UK are standardised across the service, with slight variations in the most senior ranks of the Metropolitan Police Service and the City of London Police. Policing in Scotland and Northern Ireland has been devolved to the Scottish Parliament and Northern Ireland Assembly respectively.

COMMISSIONER The police forces within Greater London – the Metropolitan Police Service and the City of London Police – are both headed by an appointed commissioner. The Commissioner of the City of London Police has the status of a justice of the peace.

The term 'chief police officer' refers to a commissioner or chief constable ('senior police officer' refers to their deputy).

CHIEF OFFICER RANKS The Metropolitan Police Service has five ranks above the level of chief superintendent (commander, deputy assistant commissioner, assistant commissioner, deputy commissioner and commissioner) and The City of London Police has three (commander, assistant commissioner and commissioner).

Each territorial police force is headed by a chief constable.

POLICE RANKS OF THE UNITED KINGDOM

Metropolitan Police Service	City of London Police	Police
Commissioner	Commissioner	–
Deputy Commissioner	–	–
Assistant Commissioner	–	Chief Constable
Deputy Assistant Commissioner	Assistant Commissioner	Deputy Chief Constable
Commander	Commander	Assistant Chief Constable
Chief Superintendent	Chief Superintendent	Chief Superintendent
Superintendent	Superintendent	Superintendent
Chief Inspector	Chief Inspector	Chief Inspector
Inspector	Inspector	Inspector
Sergeant	Sergeant	Sergeant
Constable	Constable	Constable

Ranks	Below the rank of chief superintendent, police forces in England, Scotland and Northern Ireland share the same titles, and officers should be addressed in the same way.

There is no longer any differentiation between male and female officers.

For the Criminal Investigation Department (CID) the prefix 'Detective' is added to the ranks from constable to chief superintendent, eg 'Detective Inspector Sheraton'.

At the beginning of a letter to a chief inspector, inspector, police sergeant or police constable, the appropriate rank is placed before the name, eg 'Dear Chief Inspector Lisle'. The rank is also placed on the envelope before the name.

Abbreviations Police sergeant is often abbreviated to PS, police constable to PC, detective sergeant to DS and detective constable to DC. The table on page 89 does not differ in Scotland or Northern Ireland.

Verbal Address 'Ma'am' is commonly used to verbally address female officers of the rank of inspector and above in British police forces.

Although the correct pronunciation is to rhyme the word with 'lamb', female officers are still generally addressed as 'Ma'am' rhyming with 'harm'.

Police and Crime Commissioners Police and Crime Commissioners (PCCs) are elected to a four-year term in a police area of England and Wales. They were first elected in 2012, replacing the police authorities. Their role is to cut crime and deliver an effective and efficient police service within their force area, as well as being the voice of the people. They are not warranted police officers.

CORRECT FORM | PROFESSIONS [89]

THE POLICE: FORMS OF ADDRESS

	SALUTATION	ENVELOPE	VERBAL ADDRESS	CONVERSATION
Commissioner (Metropolitan Police)	According to title or Dear Commissioner	Sir Ben Hopkins, KBE, Commissioner of The Metropolitan Police	According to title or Commissioner	According to title or The Commissioner
Commissioner (City of London Police)	According to title or Dear Commissioner	Dame Cornelia Archer, DBE, Commissioner of Police for The City of London	According to title or Commissioner	According to title or The Commissioner
Chief Constable (other police forces)	According to title or Dear Chief Constable	Sir Edward Carnaby, KBE, Chief Constable of Gloucestershire Constabulary	According to title or Chief Constable	According to title or The Chief Constable
Deputy Commissioner (Metropolitan Police)	According to title or Dear Deputy Commissioner	Alison Mercer, Deputy Commissioner of The Metropolitan Police	According to title or Deputy Commissioner	According to title or The Deputy Commissioner
Assistant Commissioner (Metropolitan Police/City of London Police)	According to title or Dear Assistant Commissioner	David Beak, Esq, Assistant Commissioner, for The City of London/ Metropolitan Police	According to title or Assistant Commissioner	According to title or Assistant Commissioner
Deputy Assistant Commissioner (Metropolitan Police)	According to title or Dear Deputy Assistant Commissioner	Barbara Swallow, Deputy Assistant Commissioner, Metropolitan Police	According to title or Deputy Assistant Commissioner	According to title or Deputy Assistant Commissioner
Commander (Metropolitan Police/City of London Police)	According to title or Dear Commander Pollen	Commander Edgar Pollen, Metropolitan Police/City of London Police	According to title or Commander	According to title or The Commander
Ranks below Chief Superintendent are all addressed in the same way	Chief Superintendent Brewer (or appropriate rank)	Chief Superintendent Brewer (or appropriate rank), or Henry Brewer, Esq	Chief Superintendent (or appropriate rank) or by name	Chief Superintendent (or appropriate rank) or by name

PROFESSIONS

LOCAL GOVERNMENT

LORD-LIEUTENANTS
HIGH SHERIFFS
LOCAL ORDER OF PRECEDENCE
LORD MAYORS, MAYORS & CIVIC HEADS
FORMS OF ADDRESS

The English system of local government is highly complex. England is subdivided into nine regional authorities, and only one of these – London – has an elected assembly and mayor.

Below this regional level there are two main types of local government: county councils and district councils. Unitary authorities combine these two strata into a single authority.

Since the Local Government Act 2000 most councils have moved to an executive-based system, either with a council leader and a cabinet acting as an executive authority, or with a directly elected mayor. A number of district councils (those with populations of less than 85,000) are governed by a committee system.

Metro Mayors

Metro mayors, introduced piecemeal since 2017, are the directly elected leaders of a combined authority (CA), with significant executive powers to make decisions across whole city-regions. By 2021 a total of nine city-regions already had metro mayors: Cambridgeshire and Peterborough; Greater Manchester; Liverpool City Region; North of Tyne; South Yorkshire; Tees Valley; West of England; West Midland City Region; and West Yorkshire.

In 2022 there were 16 directly elected mayors, each responsible for the administration of a single local authority area.

A civic mayor, or chairman of council, carries out ceremonial duties or chairs meetings, but cannot make decisions about council business.

Local councillors are elected for four-year terms by the local community to represent its views.

Lord-Lieutenants

The British Sovereign's personal representatives in the UK are known as lord-lieutenants. They are appointed by The King, on the advice of the Prime Minister, for each county in England and Wales, and each area in Scotland (other than the cities of Aberdeen, Dundee, Edinburgh and Glasgow where the Lord Provost is, by virtue of his office, lord-lieutenant for that city).

These non-political appointees are normally retired people with a substantial local reputation.

Within each county, high sheriffs are appointed for a year as the Sovereign's judicial representative.

Lord-Lieutenants

As a personal representative of The King, the prime duty of a lord-lieutenant is to maintain the dignity of The King and fulfill key functions such as arranging visits by members of the Royal Family, presenting medals and honours, taking part in civic activities, liaising with local units of the armed forces and leading the local magistracy. It is a non-political, unpaid post, held until retirement at the age of 75. Although assigned no place in the table of precedence for England and Wales, by Royal Warrant in 1904 a lord-lieutenant (or lieutenant) has precedence within their own county immediately after the Sovereign (except sometimes on civic premises).

See p 94 for local table of precedence

How to Address a Lord-Lieutenant

The title applies to both male and female appointees. Letters to a lord-lieutenant open with 'Dear Lord-Lieutenant'. Invitations are addressed to 'The Lord-Lieutenant of (County)'. A joint invitation would read, for example, 'The Lord-Lieutenant of (County) and Lady Hart/Mr James Cavendish'.

On an envelope the full title is 'His Majesty's Lord-Lieutenant' and this may be abbreviated to 'HM Lord-Lieutenant' or 'Lord-Lieutenant of (County)'. The hyphen is always included. If a lord-lieutenant is also a peer he or she would be addressed:
The Earl of Cirencester or *The Countess of Aldford*
HM Lord-Lieutenant of (County).

Vice and Deputy Lord-Lieutenant

A vice lord-lieutenant and a number of deputy lieutenants support the lord-lieutenant. A deputy lieutenant must live in the county or within seven miles of the county border. All deputy lieutenants are entitled to use the initials DL after their name, but there is no formal way of addressing them.

How to Address a Vice Lord-Lieutenant

The vice lord-lieutenant is appointed by the lord-lieutenant from among the deputies. Should a vice lord-lieutenant be acting for the lord-lieutenant he or she would take his or her superior's precedence.

If writing to a vice lord-lieutenant in his or her official capacity, the style of address on an envelope is:
Mark Brook, Esq, DL*
Vice Lord-Lieutenant of (County)

*The letters DL may be placed after his/her name (following JP), although in social correspondence these are often omitted.

Lord-Lieutenancies of England, Scotland, Wales and Northern Ireland

England	Scotland	Wales
Bedfordshire Berkshire The City and Council of Bristol Buckinghamshire Cambridgeshire Cheshire Cornwall Cumbria Derbyshire Devon Dorset County Durham Essex Gloucestershire Hampshire Hertfordshire Isle of Wight Kent Lancashire Leicestershire Lincolnshire London (Greater) Manchester (Greater) Merseyside Norfolk Northamptonshire Northumberland Nottinghamshire Oxfordshire Rutland Shropshire Somerset Staffordshire Suffolk Surrey Sussex: East; West Tyne and Wear Warwickshire West Midlands Wiltshire Worcestershire Yorkshire: South; East Riding; North Riding; West Riding	Aberdeenshire Aberdeen City Angus Argyll and Bute Ayr and Arran Banffshire Berwickshire Caithness Clackmannan Dumfries Dunbartonshire The City of Dundee East Lothian The City of Edinburgh Fife The City of Glasgow Inverness Kincardineshire Lanarkshire Midlothian Moray Nairn Orkney Perth and Kinross Renfrewshire Ross and Cromarty Roxburgh, Ettrick and Lauderdale Shetland Stewartry of Kirkcudbright (Dumfries and Galloway) Stirling and Falkirk Sutherland Tweeddale Western Isles West Lothian Wigtown	Clwyd Dyfed Mid Glamorgan South Glamorgan West Glamorgan Gwent Gwynedd Powys
		Northern Ireland
		County Antrim County Armagh County Down County Fermanagh County Londonderry County Tyrone The City of Londonderry The County Borough of Belfast

High Sheriffs

The office of high sheriff dates back over 1,000 years. The role is largely ceremonial but key duties include acting as the returning officer in parliamentary elections and attending high court judges sitting in local courts. The post is unpaid.

How to Address a High Sheriff

There is no special form of address for either high sheriff or under sheriff although the appointment may follow the name in official correspondence:
John Hill, Esq
High Sheriff of (County)

In speeches and introductions, the individual would be referred to by name followed by:
The High Sheriff of (County)

The title applies to both male and female holders of the office.

Note: The office does not exist in Scotland where the title Sheriff refers to a different position. For a list of current High Sheriffs in England and Wales see www.highsheriffs.com

Precedence

The high sheriff takes precedence in the county immediately after the lord-lieutenant, except when precedence is deferred to a lord mayor, mayor or chairman of the local authority when they are undertaking municipal business in their own district.

Local Order of Precedence

The Lord-Lieutenant of the County *
The High Sheriff of the County
The Lord Mayor **
The elected Mayor **
The Chairman of the County Council **
The Deputy Mayor
Aldermen
Councillors
Justices of the Peace
The Clerk of the County Council
The Town Clerk
The Chief Constable
The County Engineer or Borough Engineer

* *Unless there are specific representatives of The King present such as an equerry.*
** *Lord mayors, mayors and chairmen of the council would take precedence when hosting their own civic functions.*

Lord Mayors, Mayors & Civic Heads

A lord mayor is the chief citizen of a UK city – the title being an honour bestowed on a limited number of cities by the Sovereign.

In the Scottish cities of Aberdeen, Dundee, Edinburgh and Glasgow the equivalent position is lord provost and the holders are *ex officio* lord-lieutenants for their respective cities.

Cities Granted Lord Mayor Status by the Sovereign		
Aberdeen*	Dundee*	Norwich
Armagh	Edinburgh*	Nottingham
Belfast	Exeter	Oxford
Birmingham	Glasgow*	Plymouth
Bradford	Kingston-upon-	Portsmouth
Bristol	Hull	Sheffield
Canterbury	Leicester	Southampton
Cardiff	Leeds	Stoke-on-Trent
Chester	Liverpool	Swansea
City of London	Manchester	Westminster
Coventry	Newcastle	York

* *'Lord Provost' in Scottish cities*

'The Rt Hon' — The Lord Mayors of London, York and Belfast (and the Lord Provost of Edinburgh) have been styled 'The Rt Hon' since time immemorial. This privilege has also been granted by the Sovereign to the Lord Mayor of the city of Cardiff and the Lord Provost of Glasgow.

The style 'The Rt Hon' refers to the office rather than the person. Thus 'The Rt Hon the Lord Mayor of York' is correct, but 'The Rt Hon Neil Green' is not.

The lord mayor customarily takes precedence when hosting civic events (see local order of precedence, *left*).

'The Rt Worshipful' — All other lord mayors are styled 'The Rt Worshipful'. A Lord Mayor is addressed as such, irrespective of gender. The name (preceded by 'Councillor' – where applicable) may follow the office (not applicable to the Lord Mayor of London). For example: 'The Rt Worshipful the Lord Mayor of Westminster, Councillor Edward Pollen'.

Lady Mayoress	A lady mayoress (ie the wife or other chosen female consort of a lord mayor) is addressed as 'Lady Mayoress', not styled 'The Rt Hon' or 'The Rt Worshipful'.
Mayors	Other mayors, with the exception of directly elected mayors (see below) are addressed as 'The Right Worshipful or 'The Worshipful'. The policy of individual local councils should be checked on appropriate websites. In all cases the courtesy title 'The Right Worshipful or 'The Worshipful' should precede the individual's position in the council: eg 'The Right Worshipful the Mayor of Bath, Councillor Edward Pollen' or 'The Worshipful the Mayor of Brighton, Councillor Emma Brewer'.
Deputy Mayor/Mayoress	A deputy mayor/mayoress is addressed as such, but without the courtesy title 'The Right Worshipful' or 'The Worshipful'.

Directly Elected Mayors

Cities, Towns and Boroughs that Directly Elect a Mayor in England		
Bedford	Leicester	Newham
Bristol	Lewisham	North Tyneside
Copeland	Liverpool (City)	Salford
Croydon	Mansfield	Tower Hamlets
Doncaster	Middlesbrough	Watford
Hackney		

Addressing directly elected Mayors and Metro Mayors	Mayors that have been directly elected by local voters (*see above*) do not use the titles 'The Right Worshipful' or 'The Worshipful'. They will instead be known as either, for example, 'Mayor Daniel Mercer' or 'Daniel Mercer, Mayor of ......'. This would also apply to directly elected metro mayors. Individual councils' websites should be checked for the preferred form of address.
The Mayor of London	London's first directly elected mayor took office in 2000, alongside a separately elected assembly (the London Assembly). The mayor and assembly are elected for four-year terms.
Addresing the Mayor of London	The Mayor of London is formally referred to as 'Mr Mayor' or 'The Mayor of London'.
Chairman of Council	Mayors are not appointed to district councils that have not adopted the title of borough. Their role is undertaken by the chairman of council, who undertakes exactly the same functions and is the civic head of the district concerned.

Local Government: Forms of Address

Name	Placecard	Salutation	Envelope	Verbal Address
Chairman of a County Council	Chairman	Dear Chairman (even if a woman)	The Chairman of X County Council	Chairman (even if a woman)
Lord Mayor (also applies to female office-holders)	Lord Mayor	Dear Lord Mayor	The Right Honourable The Lord Mayor of X or The Right Worshipful The Lord Mayor of X	My Lord Mayor or Lord Mayor
Lord Provost (also applies to female office-holders)	Lord Provost	Dear Lord Provost	The Rt Hon The Lord Provost of Edinburgh/Glasgow; The Lord Provost of Aberdeen/Dundee	My Lord Provost
Lady Mayoress (usually the wife or daughter of a mayor)	Lady Mayoress	Dear Lady Mayoress	The Lady Mayoress of X	Lady Mayoress
Consort of a female Lord Mayor	Mr John Hill	Dear Mr Hill	John Hill, Esq	Mr Hill
Lady Provost (usually the wife or daughter of a Lord Provost)	Lady Provost	Dear Lady Provost	The Rt Hon The Lady Provost (but not if married to the Lord Provost of Edinburgh or Glasgow)	My Lady Provost
Mayor	Mayor of X	Dear Mr or Madam Mayor	The Right Worshipful The Mayor of X or The Worshipful the Mayor of X	Mr or Madam Mayor
Provost	Provost of X	Dear Mr Provost	The Provost of X	Mr Provost
Alderman	Alderman Beak	Dear Alderman or by name	**Men:** Mr Alderman Beak/Alderman Sir David Beak/Alderman The Rt Hon the Lord Beak/Major and Alderman Beak (also correct for **women,** who may also be styled Mrs, Miss or Ms Alderman, followed by her name)	**Men:** Alderman, which may be followed by the name, and where applicable, title. **Women:** Alderman, which may be followed by her name, preceded by Mrs/Miss/Ms or, where applicable, her title
City, Borough or District Councillor	Councillor Ryder	Dear Councillor (followed by name, preceded, where applicable, by rank and title)	Councillor (followed by name, preceded where applicable by rank and title)	Councillor (followed by name, where applicable by rank and title)

Professions

Politics

Forms of Address

The Cabinet is composed of senior government ministers chosen by the Prime Minister. Most cabinet members are heads of government departments, and therefore have the title 'Secretary of State'.

GOVERNMENT DEPARTMENTS

Government departments are led politically by a government minister, assisted by a team of junior ministers. The administration of the department is the responsibility of a civil servant known as a permanent secretary.

Non-ministerial departments are headed by senior civil servants, and generally have responsibility for areas where political control is inappropriate – for example regulation or inspection.

PRIVY COUNCIL

The Privy Council is the ancient executive governing body of the United Kingdom. It is presided over by the Sovereign and exercises many functions, some of which have been entrusted to it by Acts of Parliament, which may be legislative, administrative or judicial. Its decisions are usually embodied in Orders in Council or Proclamations.

See p 61 for privy counsellors

Privy counsellors are appointed by the Crown and include the Lord Chancellor, all members of the cabinet, some senior members of the Royal Family, senior judges, the Archbishops of Canterbury and York, the Bishop of London, the Speaker of the House of Commons, leaders of opposition parties and leading Commonwealth spokesmen and judges.

The Lord President of the Council is usually a senior member of the cabinet.

Membership of the Privy Council is an appointment that is held for life, although it is possible to be struck off the list (for example Jonathan Aitken).

The Privy Council meets, on average, once a month, but most of its business is transacted in discussion and correspondence between its ministerial members and the government departments that advise them. A secretariat is provided by the Privy Council Office for these discussions.

Councils – held by The King and attended by some ministers (usually four) and the Clerk of the Council – take place to allow The King to give his formal approval to a number of Orders previously discussed and approved by ministers.

The Rt Hon — Privy counsellors have the prefix 'The Rt Hon' before their names. 'Mr' is dispensed with, but if a privy counsellor is also a knight, his correct style of address would be 'The Rt Hon Sir Thomas Archer'.

If the privy counsellor is female 'The Rt Hon' replaces Mrs/Miss/Ms in her style of address; if she is also a dame, her style of address would be 'The Rt Hon Dame Elizabeth Kean'.

As membership of the Privy Council is an appointment rather than an honour conferred, the letters PC follow all honours and decorations awarded by the Crown.

Members of Parliament — The UK has members of two different parliaments.

- Members of parliament (MPs) refers to the House of Commons, the lower house of the Parliament of the United Kingdom. All members of the House of Commons of the United Kingdom have the letters MP after their names.

- MSPs are elected members of the Scottish Parliament.

Senedd (Welsh Parliament) — Members of the Senedd (Welsh Parliament) use the letters MS after their names. They were formerly known as Assembly Members (AMs), until 2020 when the Welsh Assembly changed its name.

Nothern Ireland Assembly — Elected members of the Northern Ireland Assembly are known as Members of the Legislative Assembly (MLA).

Speaker — The Speaker of the House of Commons is an MP who is elected by other MPs. Politically impartial, the Speaker chairs debates in the Commons Chamber, keeping order and calling MPs to speak. The Speaker also chairs the House of Commons Commission.

'Mr Speaker' or 'Madam Speaker' is the usual designation on parliamentary matters, otherwise according to his or her rank.

Lord Speaker — The Lord Speaker presides over proceedings in the House of Lords from the Woolsack. They are politically impartial, and act as an ambassador for the work of the Lords. They are elected by members of the House of Lords for a period of five years and a maximum of two terms.

The post of Lord Speaker was created under the Constitutional Reform Act 2005; previously the Lord Chancellor presided over debates in the House of Lords.

The Lord Speaker is addressed as 'Lord Speaker' (even if female) on parliamentary matters, otherwise according to his/her rank.

LIFE PEERS   Life peers, who sit in the House of Lords, are also known as life barons. *See forms of address p 43.*

POLITICS: FORMS OF ADDRESS

	SALUTATION	ENVELOPE	VERBAL ADDRESS	CONVERSATION
Prime Minister	Dear Prime Minister	The Rt Hon Charles Berkeley, MP, The Prime Minister	Prime Minister	The Prime Minister
Deputy Prime Minister	Dear Deputy Prime Minister	The Rt Hon Marian Maddox, MP, The Deputy Prime Minister	Deputy Prime Minister	The Deputy Prime Minister
Chancellor of the Exchequer	Dear Chancellor	The Rt Hon Emily Sutcliffe, MP, The Chancellor of the Exchequer	Chancellor of the Exchequer	The Chancellor of the Exchequer
Lord Privy Seal	Dear Lord Privy Seal	The Rt Hon The Lord Chesterfield, PC, The Lord Privy Seal	Lord Privy Seal	The Lord Privy Seal
Minister	Dear Minister or by name	The Rt Hon Henry Bruton, MP, Secretary of State for the Environment	Minister	The Secretary of State for the Environment or by name
Backbencher	Dear Mrs Hill	Mrs C Hill, MP	Mrs Hill	Mrs Hill

Professions

Law

The Judiciary: England & Wales
Forms of Address
The Judiciary: Scotland

The Judiciary: England & Wales

Supreme Court of the United Kingdom

Under the provisions of the Constitutional Reform Act 2005, a Supreme Court of the United Kingdom (UKSC) was established with effect from 1 October 2009. It assumed the responsibilities of the House of Lords (the Law Lords), including a final appellate jurisdiction over civil cases throughout the UK, and criminal cases in England, Wales and Northern Ireland. The Supreme Court is the highest court in the United Kingdom.

The existing Law Lords became the first justices of the UKSC; they continue to be members of the House of Lords but are unable to sit and vote.

New justices appointed after October 2009 are not members of the House of Lords; they are known as 'Justices of the Supreme Court'. Justices of the Supreme Court, though not necessarily life peers, are styled 'Lord' and 'Lady' for life.

The Lord Chancellor

Appointed by The King on the advice of the Prime Minister, the Lord Chancellor is a senior member of the Cabinet. He or she heads the Ministry of Justice as the Secretary of State for Justice.

Prior to the Constitutional Reform Act 2005, the Lord Chancellor was also Speaker of the House of Lords (replaced by the post of Lord Speaker), head of the judiciary (now the responsibility of the Lord Chief Justice) and the senior judge of the House of Lords in its judicial capacity (the Lord Chancellor may no longer sit as a judge).

The Lord or Lady Chief Justice

The Lord or Lady Chief Justice presides over the King's Bench Division of the High Court, is the Head of the Judiciary of England and Wales, President of the Courts of England and Wales, and Head of Criminal Justice. He or she represents the views of the judiciary to parliament and the government.

The Lord/Lady Chief Justice is supported by and chairs the Judicial Executive Board (JEB) that meets monthly during term time. Members of the JEB are: Lord/Lady Chief Justice; Master of the Rolls; President of the King's Bench; President of the Family Division; Chancellor of the High Court; Vice President of the King's Bench Division and Deputy Head of Criminal Justice; Chairman of the Judicial College; Senior President of Tribunals; Senior Presiding Judge; Chief Executive of the Judicial Office.

THE MASTER OF THE ROLLS	The Master of the Rolls is the Head of Civil Justice, and the second most senior judicial position in England and Wales after the Lord Chief Justice. By virtue of the office, he/she is a judge of the Court of Appeal and the president of its Civil Division. As a head of division and member of the Privy Council, he/she has the prefix of 'Right Honourable'.
ATTORNEY GENERAL AND SOLICITOR GENERAL	His Majesty's Attorney General and Solicitor General are known as the Law Officers of the Crown for England and Wales, or simply 'the Law Officers'. The Attorney General for England and Wales is chief legal adviser to the government and oversees the Law Officers' departments including the Crown Prosecution Service, the Serious Fraud Office, His Majesty's Crown Prosecution Service Inspectorate and the Treasury Solicitor's Department. Usually a member of parliament, the Attorney General also holds the office of Advocate General for Northern Ireland, is head of the Bar in England and Wales (taking precedence over all barristers) and has a number of independent public interest functions. The Solicitor General – a King's Counsel – is the Attorney General's deputy (and junior in precedence), offering support across the range of responsibilities. A Solicitor General is also appointed for Scotland.
LORD/LADY JUSTICE OF APPEAL	Known officially as 'Lords Justices', a judge who sits in the Court of Appeal is known as a Lord Justice of Appeal. They are privy counsellors and are styled, professionally, as 'The Right Honourable Lord/Lady Justice ......', or sometimes shortened to 'Lord/Lady Justice ......' or '[Surname] LJ'. The judicial title is not used in social correspondence. The Heads of Division – the Lord Chief Justice of England and Wales, the Master of the Rolls, the President of the King's Bench Division, the President of the Family Division and the Chancellor of the High Court – are also judges of the Court of Appeal.
THE HIGH COURT	The High Court has three divisions: the King's Bench Division, the Family Division and the Chancery Division. Heads of Division are generally appointed from among the Lords of Appeal in Ordinary (the Law Lords) or Lords Justices of Appeal. The King's Bench Division, the biggest of the three divisions, is headed by the President of the King's Bench Division.

The President of the Family Division is also the Head of Family Justice; he/she will be a knight or a dame but is addressed according to their judicial title (not to be used socially).

The Chancellor of the High Court presides over the Chancery Division and is vice-president of the Court of Protection. He/she is an *ex officio* judge of the Court of Appeal and, as a member of the Privy Council, has the prefix 'The Right Honourable'.

HIGH COURT JUDGE Justices of the High Court are almost always referred to as High Court judges and are assigned to one of the three divisions of the High Court – the King's Bench Division, the Family Division and the Chancery Division.

A male High Court judge is, by convention, knighted on appointment, but he is styled, for example, as 'The Hon Mr Justice Cane'. The letters KC do not appear after his name. His style may be shortened to '[Surname] J'.

A female High Court judge is, by convention, made a dame on appointment but is traditionally styled, for example, as 'The Hon Mrs Justice Macklin', whether married or single. Since 2014, she may also be styled as, for example, 'The Hon Ms Justice Macklin'. The letters KC do not appear after her name. Her style may be shortened to '[Surname] J'.

The prefix 'The Hon Mr/Mrs/Miss/Ms Justice' is dropped on retirement and retired judges are then styled, for example, as 'The Hon Sir Jonathan Dean' or 'The Hon Lady Macklin'.

A person appointed to sit (part-time) as a deputy High Court judge is addressed in court as for a High Court judge. Outside court, he/she reverts to his/her usual style.

CIRCUIT JUDGE Circuit judges are appointed to one of six regions of England and Wales: Midlands; North (also known as the North Western Circuit); North East; South East (also known as the London and South Eastern Circuit); Western (also known as the South Western Circuit) and Wales. They sit in the Crown and County Courts within their region. In professional correspondence, they are addressed as 'His/Her Honour Judge ......'; if they were a King's Counsel when at the Bar, the letters KC follow the name. The forename is used if there is more than one judge with the same surname. On retirement, the style 'Judge' is dropped, becoming, for example, 'His Hon John ......'.

Recorder	Historically, recorders presided at the Courts of Quarter Sessions. Today a recorder is a part-time circuit judge, usually a practising barrister or solicitor, who may sit in both Crown and County Courts.
District Judge	On appointment, district judges are assigned to a particular circuit and may sit at any of the county courts or district registries of the High Court on that circuit; they usually hear cases. By virtue of their office they are justices of the peace.

In correspondence, they are addressed as 'District Judge ……'. On retirement, district judges are not referred to by any title; they are simply referred to as 'Mr', 'Miss', 'Mrs' or 'Ms'.

The senior district judge is also known as the chief magistrate. |
| King's Counsel and Barrister | Barristers are divided into King's Counsel and Junior Counsel. When a barrister becomes a KC, he/she is said to 'take silk', after their silk gowns. On the direction of the Bar Council they are no longer termed 'Barrister-at-law', simply 'Barrister'.

The letters KC are placed after the name of King's Counsel while they are at the Bar, or after appointment to the Circuit Bench. They are not used after the names of High Court judges or persons holding other higher legal appointments.

King's Counsel may also be appointed from the ranks of solicitor advocates or (*honoris causa*) distinguished academic lawyers. |
| Magistrate (Justice of the Peace) | Magistrates (also known as Justices of the Peace or JPs) are volunteers who hear cases in courts in their community. The Secretary of State and Lord Chancellor appoint magistrates in England and Wales on behalf of, and in the name of, The King. Local advisory committees recommend candidates.

Magistrates' courts are the first tier within the justice system and are where all criminal cases begin. They pass serious crimes to the Crown Court; they also hear some civil and family cases.

In court, a magistrate is addressed as 'Your Worship', or 'Sir' or 'Madam'. In correspondence, the letters 'JP' may be used after the name on the envelope, but this is not obligatory. Note that 'JP' precedes 'DL' as the former is a Crown appointment and the latter a lord-lieutenant's appointment. |

The Judiciary, England & Wales: Forms of Address

	Salutation	Envelope	Verbal Address	Conversation
Lord Chancellor	My Lord (formal) or Dear Lord Chancellor (social)	The Rt Hon The Lord Chancellor	According to title or Lord Chancellor	According to title or The Lord Chancellor
Lord Chief Justice	My Lord (formal) or Dear Lord Chief Justice (social)	The Rt Hon The Lord Chief Justice of England	According to title or Lord Chief Justice	According to title or The Lord Chief Justice
Master of the Rolls	Dear Master of the Rolls or according to title	The Rt Hon The Master of the Rolls	According to title or Master of the Rolls	According to title or The Master of the Rolls
President of the Family Division	Dear President or Dear Sir John	The Rt Hon The President of the Family Division	According to title or President	According to title or The President of the Family Division
President of the King's Bench Division	Dear President or Dear Dame Margaret	The Rt Hon The President of the King's Bench Division	According to title or President	According to title or President of the King's Bench Division
Chancellor of the High Court	Dear Chancellor	The Rt Hon The Chancellor of the High Court	According to title or Chancellor	According to title or The Chancellor of the High Court
Justice of the Supreme Court	Dear Lord/Lady Black	The Rt Hon Lord/Lady Black	According to title	According to title
Lord Justice of the Court of Appeal (male)	Dear Lord Justice	The Rt Hon Lord Justice Beak	Lord Justice	The Lord Justice or His Lordship (judicial matters)
Lord Justice of the Court of Appeal (female)	Dear Lady Justice	The Rt Hon Lady Justice Hill, DBE	Lady Justice	The Lady Justice or Her Ladyship (judicial matters)
Judge of the High Court (male)	Dear Sir Ben or Dear Judge or My Lord	The Hon Mr Justice Noel or Sir Ben Noel	My Lord or Mr Justice Noel or Sir Ben (out of court)	According to title
Judge of the High Court (female)	Dear Madam or Dear Dame Amy or Dear Judge	The Hon Mrs/Ms Justice Lisle or Dame Amy Lisle, DBE	My Lady or Mrs/Ms Justice Lisle or Dame Amy (out of court)	According to title
Circuit Judge	Dear Judge	His Hon Judge Pollen	Judge or according to title	According to title
District Judge	Dear Judge or Dear Sir/Madam	District Judge Sheraton	Judge or according to title	According to title

By convention it is never considered wrong to address a judge of any seniority (from district judge up to Justice of the Supreme Court) when not in court as 'Judge'.

The Judiciary: Scotland

Lord President and Lord Justice General

The Lord President is the most senior judge in Scotland and the head of the judiciary, acting as both Lord President of the Court of Session (Scotland's highest civil court) and the Lord Justice General of the High Court of Justiciary (Scotland's supreme criminal court). The Lord President is a privy counsellor and may be a peer, but is always described by office.

Lord Advocate

The Lord Advocate is the most senior of the two Law Officers (the other being the Solicitor General) and the office corresponds with that of the Attorney General in England and Wales.

As a minister of the Scottish Government, the Lord Advocate acts as principal legal advisor and is the ministerial head of Scotland's Crown Office and Procurator Fiscal Service (COPFS).

The Lord Advocate is appointed by The King on the recommendation of the First Minister, with the agreement of the Scottish Parliament.

Lord Justice Clerk

As the second most senior judge in Scotland, the Lord Justice Clerk plays a prominent role in the criminal appeals system and holds the office of President of the Second Division of the Inner House of the Court of Session.

The Lord Justice Clerk receives a judicial title on appointment as a judge, but like the Lord President, is always described by office. The Lord Justice Clerk is a privy counsellor and may be a peer.

Senators of the College of Justice

Judges of the Court of Session (the supreme civil court), who are also the judges of the High Court of Justiciary (the supreme criminal court), are appointed by The King as senators of the College of Justice.

On appointment, the courtesy style of 'Lord' or 'Lady' is used, unless already a peer. Judges of the Outer House of the Court of Session have the prefix 'honourable'; judges of the Inner House are privy counsellors with the prefix 'The Right Honourable'.

Chairman of the Land Court

The Chairman of the Scottish Land Court is addressed in the same way as a judge of the Court of Session.

SHERIFF PRINCIPAL — There are six sheriffdoms in Scotland and each sheriffdom is headed by a Sheriff Principal who is usually a King's Counsel. They are supported by permanent or resident sheriffs. Within his/her own sheriffdom, the Sheriff Principal takes precedence immediately after the lord-lieutenant.

SHERIFF — The main role of sheriffs is to sit as a trial judge (but they have some appellate functions). Sheriffs are either advocates or solicitors; many are also King's Counsel.

THE JUDICIARY, SCOTLAND: FORMS OF ADDRESS

	SALUTATION	ENVELOPE	VERBAL ADDRESS	CONVERSATION
The Lord President and Lord Justice General	My Lord/Lady (formal) or Dear Lord President or Dear Lord Justice General	The Rt Hon The Lord/Lady Macklin Lord President of The Court of Session (Civil, if a peer)/Lord Justice General of Scotland (Criminal, if a peer) or The Rt Hon Lord/Lady Macklin Lord President of The Court of Session/Lord Justice General of Scotland (if not a peer)	My Lord/Lady or Lord President or Lord Justice General	Lord President or Lord Justice General
Lord Justice Clerk	My Lord/Lady (formal) or Dear Lord Justice Clerk	The Rt Hon Lord/Lady Macklin Lord Justice Clerk (if not a peer) or The Rt Hon The Lord/Lady Macklin Lord Justice Clerk (if a peer)	My Lord/Lady or Lord/Lady Macklin	Lord/Lady Macklin
Senators of the College of Justice	My Lord/Lady (formal) or Dear Lord/Lady Macklin	The Hon Lord/Lady Macklin (if not a privy counsellor) or The Rt Hon Lord/Lady Macklin (if a privy counsellor) or The Rt Hon The Lord/Lady Macklin (if a peer)	My Lord or Lord/Lady Macklin	Lord/Lady Macklin
Sheriffs Principal	Sheriff Principal Macklin	Sheriff Principal Macklin (KC, if applicable)	My Lord/Lady	Sheriff Principal Macklin
Sheriff	Sheriff Macklin	Sheriff Macklin (KC, if applicable)	My Lord/Lady	Sheriff Macklin

Professions

Religion

The Church of England
Archbishops
Bishops
Other Members of Clergy
Church of Scotland
Methodist Church
Chaplains
Roman Catholic Church
Non-Christian Faiths

The Church of England

The Church of England is the officially established Christian Church in England and the Mother Church of the worldwide Anglican Communion. The British monarch still has the constitutional title of 'Supreme Governor of the Church of England'. The Church of England is episcopally led and synodically governed.

Provinces   The Church of England comprises two provinces: the Southern Province, led by the Archbishop of Canterbury, and the Northern Province, led by the Archbishop of York.

Dioceses   Each province is broken down into dioceses. Each English diocese is a territorial unit of administration – with boards and councils who have responsibility for different aspects of the Church's work – under the pastoral care of one or more bishops, typically a diocesan bishop assisted by one or more suffragan bishops.

Sub-Divisions   Dioceses are divided into archdeaconries, deaneries (a group of parishes forming a district within an archdeaconry) and parishes (overseen by a parish priest, also called a vicar or rector).

General Synod   The General Synod is the legislative body of the Church of England. Elected from the laity and clergy of each diocese, it meets in London or York at least twice annually. The Archbishops of Canterbury and York are the joint presidents.

The General Synod consists of the House of Bishops and the House of Clergy (these two houses join together the Convocations of Canterbury and York), and the House of Laity.

The House of Bishops consists of all diocesan bishops of the Church of England, the Bishop of Dover and seven suffragan bishops (four from the Province of Canterbury, three from York). The House of Bishops also meets separately from the Synod. The Archbishops of Canterbury and York are the presidents.

The House of Clergy comprises clergy (other than bishops) who have been elected, appointed or chosen, together with *ex officio* members and up to five co-opted members. The House of Laity consists of elected members from each diocese of the two Provinces, or those chosen by and from the lay members of religious communities, and *ex officio* members.

GENERAL SYNOD (CONT)	The General Synod considers and approves Church legislation, formulates new forms of worship, debates matters of religious or public interest and approves the annual Church budget. Legislation can be passed in two ways: by 'measures', which require approval by both Houses of Parliament and the receipt of Royal Assent, and by 'Canon', which are subject to Royal Licence and Assent.
ARCHBISHOPS' COUNCIL	This central executive body co-ordinates and leads the work of the Church. It comprises 19 members and seven directors; the Archbishops of Canterbury and York are the presidents.
CHURCH COMMISSIONERS	The Church Commissioners manage the Church's investments. They are accountable to the General Synod, Parliament and the Charity Commission. They are: the Archbishops of Canterbury and York; three Church Estates Commissioners (appointed by the Crown or the Archbishop of Canterbury); 11 elected from the General Synod (four bishops, three clergy, four lay people); two cathedral deans; nine appointed by the Crown and the archbishops; six holders of state office (the Prime Minister, Lord Chancellor, Lord President of the Council, Secretary of State for Digital, Culture, Media and Sport, Speaker of the House of Commons and the Lord Speaker).
THE CHURCH OF ENGLAND'S PENSION BOARD	This provides retirement services for those who have served or worked for the Church. There are 12 members of the Board, led by a chairman who is appointed by the Archbishops of Canterbury and York with the approval of the Synod.
THE CHURCH IN WALES	The Church in Wales is a member of the Anglican Communion and, therefore, recognises the primacy of the Archbishop of Canterbury as the spiritual leader of the Anglican Communion. Unlike the Archbishops of Canterbury and York, who are appointed by The King upon the advice of the Prime Minister, the Archbishop of Wales is one of the six diocesan bishops of Wales, elected to hold this office in addition to his own diocese.
THE CHURCH OF IRELAND	The Church of Ireland is also a member of the Anglican Communion; it is one church embracing Northern Ireland and the Republic of Ireland. There are two Archbishops of the Church of Ireland: Armagh and Dublin.
WOMEN	Women have been ordained into the Church of England since 1994. On 14 July 2014 the General Synod gave final approval for women to become bishops in the Church of England.

TITLED MEMBERS OF THE CLERGY	Ordained clergymen of the Church of England, and other churches within the Anglican Communion, do not receive the accolade of knighthood, though the letters signifying an order of knighthood are placed after a name (for example, 'The Right Reverend the Lord Bishop of Brompton, KCVO'). If a clergyman succeeds to a title or has a courtesy title or style, the ecclesiastical style precedes the temporal, eg 'The Venerable Sir John Garrick, Bt'; 'The Reverend the Hon John Brewer'.
ARMED FORCES AND THE CLERGY	When it is desired to show that a clergyman has served in the armed forces – in a list of retired officers, for example – the following form is used: 'The Reverend Nicholas Swallow, Commander, Royal Navy'.
DEGREES	Doctorate degrees are added on the envelope where appropriate.
SPOUSES	Spouses of the clergy do not have any special form of address.
USE OF THE FORENAME	In reference to a member of the Anglican clergy or in starting a social letter or in speech, use the forename in place of initials.
'THE REVEREND'	'The Reverend' is often abbreviated to 'The Rev', although some clergymen prefer it to be written in full; others prefer the abbreviation 'The Revd'. Where a personal preference is known, it is courteous and advisable to follow it.
	When referring to an Anglican clergyman in letters or in speech, never use the form 'The Reverend Hays' or 'Reverend Hays' – this is an American style. If the forename or initials are unknown, use 'The Reverend Mr/Mrs/Miss Swallow' instead.
MARRIED CLERGY	There is no universally accepted form of addressing an envelope to a married couple who are both in holy orders; 'The Reverend Mark Brook and The Reverend Hazel Brook' is acceptable.

ARCHBISHOPS

THE ARCHBISHOPS OF CANTERBURY AND YORK	The two provinces, Canterbury and York, each have an archbishop who, as the 'metropolitan', has authority and jurisdiction. The Archbishop of Canterbury is 'Primate of all England and Metropolitan'. He (or potentially she) is also the Bishop of the Diocese of Canterbury. The Archbishop of York is 'Primate of England and Metropolitan'. He is also the Bishop of the Diocese of York.

The Archbishops of Canterbury and York confirm the election of new diocesan bishops and ordain all new bishops within their province. Alternately they chair sessions of the Crown Nominations Commission (who identify and approve candidates for appointment as diocesan bishops). The Archbishop of Canterbury has the right to preside at the Eucharist, during which he anoints and crowns a new British monarch.

STYLES The Archbishops of Canterbury and York are privy counsellors and are accordingly addressed as 'The Most Rev(erend) and Right Hon(ourable)' and have seats in the House of Lords.

PRECEDENCE The Archbishop of Canterbury ranks next in precedence to the Royal Family and above the Lord Chancellor. The Archbishop of York ranks immediately below the Lord Chancellor.

SIGNATURES When signing their name on official documents, archbishops preface their signature, written in capital letters, with a cross.

The Archbishop of Canterbury usually signs his first name and 'Cantuar' (from the Latin for Canterbury), eg + *Justin Cantuar:*

The Archbishop of York signs with his surname and 'Eboracensis' (from Eboracum, the Roman name for York), eg + *Cottrell Eboracensis:* (or just + *Cottrell Ebor* may be used) Note: when the abbreviated Latin name of the See is used it is usual to put a colon instead of a full stop.

The archbishop of the Church in Wales signs, after a cross, the forename followed by *'Cambrensis'*.

RETIRED ARCHBISHOPS On resigning, an archbishop reverts to the status of a bishop, and should in principal be addressed as 'The Rt Rev', rather than 'The Most Rev'. By courtesy, however, he may still be addressed as 'Archbishop', unless he is actually appointed as a bishop in this country, when he will be addressed as 'Bishop'.

LORDS SPIRITUAL The lords spiritual are Church of England bishops who serve in the House of Lords along with the lords temporal (life or hereditary peers). They comprise the Archbishops of Canterbury and of York, the Bishops of London, Durham and Winchester, as well as the 21 longest-serving English diocesan bishops.

The former Archbishops of Canterbury and York are created lords temporal (ie receive life peerages).

BISHOPS

BISHOP OF LONDON The Bishop of London is always a privy counsellor and accordingly is addressed as 'The Right Reverend and Right Honourable'. When the Bishop of London retires he/she is addressed as any other retired diocesan bishop, except that as a privy counsellor he/she retains the aforesaid designation 'The Rt Hon' (so his/her description does not change).

DIOCESAN BISHOPS The Bishops of London, Durham and Winchester have permanent seats in the House of Lords. When a vacancy arises, it is filled by the senior diocesan bishop without a seat and the vacated See is placed at the foot of the list of those awaiting seats. Translation of a bishop from one See to another does not affect his/her right to sit in the House of Lords. The Bishop of Sodor and Man is an *ex officio* member of the Legislative Council of the Isle of Man.

BISHOPS' SIGNATURES Bishops sign, after a cross, their Christian name, followed by the first diocese in their title.

SUFFRAGAN BISHOPS In each diocese, suffragan bishops are appointed to assist the bishop, styled by the name of an ancient town or place within the See. There may be a number of suffragans each responsible for a geographical area in the diocese, or one suffragan operating on behalf of the bishop throughout the diocese. While enjoying full episcopal rights, they do not qualify for membership of the House of Lords. It is open to question whether they may use the style of 'Lord/Lady' Bishop (ie whether the title is ecclesiastical or temporal); the prefix is usually given by custom or courtesy, but they are not so styled in an official document.

RETIRED BISHOPS Retired bishops are addressed by their names, but otherwise as for English bishops, ie 'The Rt Rev Nicholas Swallow'. The recommended style of address in a letter would be: 'Dear Bishop', and it should be finished with 'Yours sincerely'; the envelope is addressed to 'The Rt Rev Nicholas Swallow'.

In conversation, a retired bishop is addressed as 'Bishop' and is referred to as 'The Bishop of Blankshire'. Any invitation or place card should be addressed to 'The Rt Rev Nicholas Swallow', or in the case of married retired bishops, to 'The Rt Rev Nicholas and Mrs Swallow'.

Retired bishops sign their name after a cross, followed by Bishop.

Bishops: Scottish Episcopal Church

Since the Scottish Episcopal Church is not the State Church of Scotland, a bishop has no official precedence and recognition and is, therefore, addressed as 'The Right Rev John Macklin, Bishop of ......', and not as 'The Right Rev the Bishop of ......'.

Socially, the style is as for a diocesan bishop of the Church of England, except for the Primus of Scotland who acts as the Presiding Bishop. He is elected by the other bishops and has no metropolitan power. The style is 'The Most Reverend the Primus'.

Welsh Bishops

The styles of address for the bishops of the Church in Wales are as for diocesan bishops of the Church of England.

A bishop of the Church in Wales also signs, after a cross, his Christian name and diocese. The Bishop of Llandaff (if he is currently the Archbishop of Wales) would sign as '*Landav*'; the other bishops sign by the usual spelling of the diocese.

Irish Bishops

Bishops are styled as for diocesan bishops in the Church of England, except for the Bishop of Meath (Premier Bishop of the Church of Ireland) who is styled 'The Most Rev' instead of 'The Rt Rev'.

A retired Irish bishop would be addressed on an envelope as 'The Rt Rev John Carnaby', and a letter would begin 'Dear Bishop'.

Bishops of Overseas Churches

They are styled as for bishops in the Church of England.

The Presiding Bishop of the Protestant Episcopal Church in the United States has the style 'The Most Rev the Presiding Bishop'.

In the Anglican Church overseas, bishops coadjutor may be appointed to assist an archbishop. They have no separate territorial style, and are addressed by name, with the addition of their office. For example:
The Rt Rev David Beak
Bishop Coadjutor of ......

Retired overseas bishops are addressed in the same way as other retired bishops.

Other Members of Clergy

General Address Unless otherwise stated, deans, provosts, archdeacons, canons and prebendaries should be addressed formally in writing as 'Very Reverend Sir or Madam', and the letter concluded 'I have the honour to remain, Very Reverend Sir or Madam, your obedient servant' or 'Yours sincerely'.

Deans A dean is the incumbent of a cathedral or collegiate church. Some cathedrals were appointed a provost rather than a dean as their incumbent.

In the case where a dean is a female, substitute 'Madam Dean' for 'Dean' and 'Mr Dean'. An invitation sent to a married dean who is a woman would be inscribed 'Mr Henry Brewer and the Dean of Lincoln'.

After retirement, a dean is addressed as for other clergy, ie 'The Reverend' instead of 'The Very Reverend', unless he/she remains an archdeacon, canon or prebendary, or is appointed to emeritus rank, when he/she is addressed accordingly. The word 'emeritus' is only used in official documents.

Archdeacons An archdeacon is a senior member of the clergy, appointed by the bishop, whose duty it is to supervise his/her fellow clergy and to administer part of a diocese, hence his/her territorial designation. As well as pastoral duties, archdeacons are in charge of the fabric of parish churches and their contents.

In the case where an archdeacon is a female, substitute 'Madam Archdeacon' for 'Archdeacon' and 'Mr Archdeacon'. An invitation sent to a married archdeacon who is a woman would be inscribed 'Mr Lisle and the Archdeacon of Exeter'.

After retirement, an archdeacon is addressed as for other clergy, ie 'The Rev' instead of 'The Venerable', unless he/she remains a canon or prebendary, or is appointed to emeritus rank, when he/she is addressed accordingly. The word 'emeritus' is only used in official documents.

Canon A canon is either residentiary, with duties in his/her cathedral, or honorary. The latter role is usually given to incumbents with a record of honourable service in the diocese. A minor canon is a cleric attached to a cathedral or collegiate church to assist the daily services.

The address is as for other clergy. Canons are referred to in traditional form as 'The Reverend Canon John May' and in less formal circumstances and speech as 'Canon May'.

Prebendaries

Prebendaries have a Prebend Stall in certain cathedrals or collegiate churches. The appointment is similar to a non-residentiary canon. After retirement he/she is addressed as other clergy, unless he/she is appointed to emeritus rank. In this case he/she continues to be addressed as prebendary. Again, the word emeritus is only used in official documents.

Formally prebendaries should be addressed as 'The Reverend Prebendary John Ryder', and in speech, an informal letter or in reference he/she can be referred to as 'Prebendary Ryder'.

Rectors and Vicars

The difference between a rector and a vicar is now purely nominal. A rector was in receipt of greater and lesser tithes, and a vicar of the lesser tithes only. Tithes were virtually abolished in 1936. Vicars are now appointed to most new livings.

Religious Communities

When members of religious orders are ordained, the correct formal style is 'The Reverend John/Jane Drury'. Verbally and informally they are known as 'Father [John]', 'Mother [Jane]' or Sister [Joanna].

Lay members of religious orders are addressed as 'Brother [John]' and 'Sister [Jane]', except in the case of Franciscans or the Society of St Francis, where all the members (including those who have been ordained) are called 'Brother'.

The male head of a religious community may be:

- The Right Reverend the Abbot
- The Reverend the Prior
- The Reverend Superior-General
- The Reverend Pro-Superior
- The Reverend Superior

Female heads of religious communities may be addressed as: Mother Superior (including an abbess), Prioress, Reverend Mother or Sister Superior.

The preferred style of individual religious communities should be checked.

The Church of England: Forms of Address

	Salutation	Envelope	Verbal Address	Conversation
Archbishops of Canterbury and York	My Lord/Lady Archbishop or Your Grace (formal) Dear Lord/Lady Archbishop or Dear Archbishop (social)	The Most Reverend and Right Hon The Lord/Lady Archbishop of Canterbury/York	Your Grace (formal) Archbishop (social)	The Archbishop (of Canterbury/York)
Archbishops of the Church of Ireland and Other Provinces	My Lord/Lady Archbishop or Your Grace (formal) Dear Lord/Lady Archbishop or Dear Archbishop (social)	The Most Reverend The Lord/Lady Archbishop of Blank	Your Grace (formal) or Archbishop (social)	The Archbishop of Blank
Bishop of London	Dear Bishop	The Right Reverend and Right Hon The Lord/Lady Bishop of London	Bishop	The Bishop (of Blank)
Bishop, Diocesan and Suffragan, Church of England and the Church in Wales	Dear Bishop	The Right Reverend The Lord/Lady Bishop of Blank or The Right Reverend The Bishop of Blank	Bishop	The Bishop (of Blank)
Assistant and Retired Bishops and Retired Archbishops	Dear Bishop	The Right Rev Amy Hill (if a privy counsellor, The Right Rev and Right Hon Amy Hill)	Bishop	The Bishop (or by name, ie Bishop Hill)
Bishops, Scottish Episcopal Church	Dear Primus	The Most Reverend the Primus	Primus	The Primus
Dean	Dear Dean	The Very Reverend the Dean of Norwich	Dean or Mr or Miss/Mrs/Ms Dean	The Dean (of Norwich)
Provost	Dear Provost	The Very Reverend the Provost of Ely	Provost	The Provost (of Ely)
Archdeacon	Dear Archdeacon	The Venerable The Archdeacon of Exeter	Archdeacon	The Archdeacon (of Exeter)
Canon	Dear Canon (Frith)	The Reverend Canon John/Jane Frith	Canon (Frith)	The Canon or Canon Frith
Prebendary	Dear Prebendary (Kean)	The Reverend Prebendary Tim/Anne Kean	Prebendary/ Prebendary Kean	Prebendary or Prebendary Kean
Other Clergy	Dear Mr/Mrs/Ms/Miss Dent, (for beneficed clergy Dear Rector or Dear Vicar)	The Reverend John/Jane Dent (not Reverend Dent or The Reverend Dent)	Mr/Mrs/Ms/ Miss Dent	Mr/Mrs/Ms/Miss Dent or Rector or The Vicar

Church of Scotland

This is the Established Church in Scotland, and is Presbyterian by constitution. The Supreme Court of the Church is the General Assembly, which meets annually in May and is presided over by a moderator, who is appointed each year by the Assembly.

The General Assembly comprises around 850 commissioners – ministers, elders and members of the diaconate (deacons). The General Assembly has the authority to make laws determining how the Church of Scotland operates. It is also the highest court of the Church, the other courts being the kirk session and the presbytery, where cases can be heard in matters of litigation.

The Sovereign either attends the Assembly in person, or is represented by the Lord High Commissioner to the General Assembly who is appointed by the Crown.

Moderator of the General Assembly of the Church of Scotland

The Moderator of the General Assembly is nominated by a committee of the Assembly every year. His or her duties are to preside at meetings of the Assembly, to lead daily worship, to keep order, to rule on points of law, and to sign documents on behalf of the Assembly. It is an honorary role.

If the moderator is a minister, he or she is addressed as 'The Rt Rev the Moderator of the General Assembly of the Church of Scotland' or 'The Right Rev John Macklin'. If he/she is an elder or a deacon, a formal letter should begin 'Dear Sir/Madam' or 'Dear Moderator' or socially as 'Dear Mr Macklin' or 'Dear Moderator'. The verbal address is 'Moderator' or, in conversation, 'The Moderator'.

Lord High Commissioner

The Lord High Commissioner to the General Assembly of the Church of Scotland is appointed by the Crown. The Lord High Commissioner takes up residence for the week of the Assembly in the Palace of Holyroodhouse.

The same style is used for men and women when addressing the holder of this post. A letter should begin 'Your Grace' and end 'I have the honour to remain, Your Grace's most devoted and obedient servant'. The envelope is addressed to 'His/Her Grace the Lord High Commissioner'. Verbal address is 'Your Grace', while the description in conversation is 'The Lord High Commissioner'.

When The Princess Royal was appointed, she was styled as 'Her Grace' for the duration rather than her normal dynastic style 'Her Royal Highness' because the Lord High Commissioner is ranked higher in the order of precedence.

If a woman is appointed to the office, the alternative title 'His Majesty's High Commissioner' may be used.

Former Moderators On retirement he/she is styled 'The Very Reverend John Macklin'; otherwise as 'Mr Smith' or 'Mr Minister'.

Dean of the Chapel Royal and Dean of the Thistle They are styled The Very Reverend. One person can hold both appointments.

Other Clergy Other clergy are addressed at the beginning of a formal letter as 'Dear Sir' or 'Dear Minister' or, socially, as 'Dear Mr or Miss/Mrs/Ms Macklin' or 'Dear Minister'. Verbally, they are addressed as 'Mr Macklin' or 'Minister'. In conversation, they are described as 'Mr Macklin' or 'The Minister'.

The envelope would be addressed to 'The Reverend John Macklin' (followed by 'The Minister of Blanktown' if a minister of a parish). If a woman was ordained, she would be styled 'The Reverend Mary Macklin'. Miss/Mrs/Ms should not be used.

Methodist Church

Methodists belong to local churches, or ecumenical partnerships, but are also part of a larger connected community, or 'connexion'.

The annual Methodist Conference meets in different places every year and is the supreme decision-making body of the Church. A new president and vice-president are appointed to preside over that conference and represent the Methodist Church.

Ministers The beginning of a letter is 'Dear Sir/Madam' (traditional), or 'Dear Mr/Miss/Mrs/Ms Green' (contemporary) and the envelope is addressed 'The Reverend John/Mary Green'. The verbal address is 'Mr/Miss/Mrs/Ms Green' and in conversation ministers are referred to as 'The Minister', 'The Pastor', 'The President' or 'Dr/Mr/Miss/Mrs/Ms Green'.

Deaconess of the Methodist Church She is referred to as 'Sister Jane Adam', is known as 'Sister Jane' and, in writing, may be referred to as 'Deaconess Jane Adam'.

Chaplains

A chaplain serving with HM Forces is addressed in speech by his/her ecclesiastical rank and never in speech by his/her relative service rank. It is not necessary to write the service rank, but when used formally it must appear in brackets after the ecclesiastical title and before the chaplain's forename or initials.

It is no longer the case, in any of the services, that the role is always taken by an Anglican – Heads of Chaplaincy can be chaplains from any of the contributing churches, so there is no title common to them.

Principal Chaplain

The principal Anglican chaplain in each of the services (who may or may not be the service's Head of Chaplaincy) will continue to be made an archdeacon with the title 'The Venerable'. The principal Roman Catholic chaplain in each of the services (who may or may not be the service's Head of Chaplaincy) will continue to be made Vicar General of the Bishopric of the Forces with the title 'Monsignor'.

Other Chaplains

Other chaplains are addressed by name/appointment: for example, 'Dear Canon Ryder' or 'Dear Mr Ryder'. If the name is used, the appointment is placed after it: 'The Reverend John Ryder, OBE, CF, Assistant Chaplain General, HQ, Blankshire Command'.

See pp 75–85 for armed forces

Army chaplains have the letters 'CF' (Chaplain to the Forces) after the name, following any decorations etc. The letters 'RN' or 'RAF' are placed after the names of chaplains to these services, following any decorations etc.

Verbally a chaplain is addressed by name or ecclesiastical title, or, informally, as 'Padre'.

When the chaplain's name is not known, correspondence should be addressed to, for example, 'The Church of England Chaplain, RAF Station, Blanktown'.

Correspondence to a Jewish chaplain is addressed to, for example, 'The Reverend David Golden, CF, Senior Jewish Chaplain, Blanktown Garrison', etc; the verbal address is 'Rabbi', 'Minister' or 'Padre', as may be appropriate.

Roman Catholic Church

The Catholic Church is the world's largest Christian church, representing over half the Christians in the world. It comprises 23 autonomous ritual churches (Roman/Latin Rite, Coptic Rite, Chaldean Rite, etc) in communion with the Bishop of Rome.

The Bishop of Rome, or Pope, is the spiritual leader of the Catholic Church and head of its college of bishops. He is also the head of Vatican City State, a sovereign state within the city of Rome. Each Pope is elected for life by the College of Cardinals – however, as illustrated by Pope Benedict XVI in 2013, resigning the office of Bishop of Rome is possible.

In England and Wales, the senior Catholic prelate is the President of the Catholic Bishops' Conference, a post usually held by the Archbishop of Westminster.

The Catholic Church in England and Wales consists of 22 dioceses, the Bishopric of the Forces (Military Ordinariate), the Apostolic Eparchy of the Ukrainian Church in Great Britain, the Ordinariate of Our Lady of Walsingham, and the Apostolic Prefecture of the Falkland Islands.

Provinces and Archdioceses

England and Wales is also divided into five provinces or metropolitan archdioceses: Birmingham, Cardiff, Liverpool, Southwark and Westminster. The five metropolitan archdioceses of the Catholic Church of England and Wales have a total of 17 suffragan dioceses, each overseen by a bishop. These are:

- Westminster: Brentwood, East Anglia, Northampton, Nottingham
- Southwark: Arundel and Brighton, Plymouth, Portsmouth
- Birmingham: Clifton, Shrewsbury
- Liverpool: Hallam, Hexham and Newcastle, Lancaster, Leeds, Middlesbrough, Salford
- Cardiff: Menevia, Wrexham

In Scotland there are two metropolitan archdioceses with a total of six suffragan dioceses:

- St Andrews and Edinburgh: Aberdeen, Argyll and The Isles, Dunkeld, Galloway
- Glasgow: Motherwell, Paisley

ORDINATION Men are ordained into the Catholic Church through the sacrament of holy orders. Ordained clergy form a three-part hierarchy of bishops, priests and deacons. Only priests and bishops may celebrate the eucharist and administer the sacraments of penance and anointing the sick.

In the Roman/Latin rite, only celibate men are ordinarily ordained as priests, whereas in the Eastern rites of the Catholic Church, married men may be ordained as priests. Married men may become deacons. Marriage is not allowed, however, after ordination as a deacon or priest has taken place. Only celibate men may be ordained as bishops.

Married Anglican vicars, however, may be reordained as Roman Catholic priests.

THE POPE An invitation to the Pope is not sent directly; it should be addressed through His Holiness's Apostolic Nuncio to Great Britain.

CARDINALS A cardinal is a senior cleric – usually a bishop – in the Roman Catholic Church. Cardinals are collectively known as 'the College of Cardinals', and their duties are to act as counsellors to the Pope, elect a new Pope, and attend regular meetings of the College. Cardinals also have their own ecclesiastical duties, often related to the dioceses over which they preside. The territorial designation is not officially used when letters are addressed to the person and not to the province or diocese.

ARCHBISHOPS In Britain, Roman Catholic archbishops have no statutory claim to territorial titles or to the use of the salutations 'Your Grace' or 'My Lord', and such modes of address are not permitted in official and legal documents. However, unofficially and within the Roman Catholic community, these styles are used.

On retirement, a Roman Catholic archbishop is normally referred to as the 'Archbishop Emeritus of Blank'.

BISHOPS Roman Catholic bishops are addressed in speech within their community as 'My Lord' or 'Your Excellency', and are styled Right Reverend, except in Ireland where they are styled Most Reverend. In Ireland, the abbreviation 'Dr' is included on the envelope before the name, as in 'The Most Reverend Dr John Frith, Bishop of Kildare'.

In lists compiled by non-Roman Catholic organisations, a Roman Catholic bishop should be mentioned by name, for example: 'The Right Reverend John Denman'. If the territorial designation is given, and there is a Church of England bishop whose See has the same name, it should be stated, as in 'Roman Catholic Bishop of Liverpool'.

On retirement from his See or office, a bishop is appointed to a titular See, and addressed by name. Though it is not the usual practice, the titular See may be appended on the envelope after the name if desired.

As with archbishops, Roman Catholic bishops in Britain have no statutory claim to territorial titles or to the use of the salutations 'Your Grace' or 'My Lord', and such modes of address are not permitted in official documents. However, unofficially and within the Roman Catholic community, these styles are in common usage.

ABBOTS — Abbots are addressed in speech as 'Father Abbot' and addressed on a letter as 'The Rt Rev David Lisle'.

MONSIGNORS — Monsignor is an honorific title conferred on priests by the Pope. There are three categories: Protonotary Apostolic, Prelate of Honour or Chaplain to his Holiness.

Monsignori are addressed in speech as 'Monsignor' and addressed on letters as 'The Reverend Monsignor David Lisle' instead of 'The Right Reverend' or 'The Very Reverend'.

CANONS — Priests who have been appointed by their bishop as a member of a Cathedral Chapter of Canons are addressed in speech as 'Canon' and addressed on a letter as 'The Very Reverend Canon'.

PROVINCIAL — A provincial is the superior of the province of a religious order or congregation, such as the Dominicans, the Franciscans or the Jesuits. A provincial is addressed in speech as 'Father Provincial' and addressed on a letter as 'The Reverend Father Provincial David Lisle'.

The Roman Catholic Church: Forms of Address

	Salutation	Sign Off	Envelope	Verbal Address & Communication
The Pope	Your Holiness or Most Holy Father	For Roman Catholics: I have the honour to be, Your Holiness's most devoted and obedient child (or most humble child) or, for non-Roman Catholics, obedient servant	His Holiness The Pope	Verbal: Your Holiness Conversation: His Holiness or The Pope
Cardinal	Your Eminence or My Lord Cardinal (formal) or Dear Cardinal Rose (social)	I have the honour to be, My Lord Cardinal, Your Eminence's devoted or obedient child (very formal) or I remain, Your Eminence, Yours faithfully (formal) or I have the honour to be Your eminence's obedient servant (officially recognised) or Yours sincerely (social)	His Eminence The Cardinal Archbishop of Westminster (if an archbishop) or His Eminence Cardinal Rose (if not an archbishop)	Verbal: Your Eminence (formal) or Cardinal (Smith) (social) Conversation: His Eminence (formal) or Cardinal Rose (social)
Archbishop	My Lord Archbishop (formal) or Most Reverend Sir or Dear Archbishop (social)	I have the honour to be, Your Grace's devoted and obedient child (very formal) or I remain, Your Grace, Yours faithfully (formal), or I have the honour to be, Most Reverend Sir, Your obedient servant (officially recognised) or Yours sincerely (social)	His Grace The Archbishop of Blank or The Most Reverend Archbishop Rose	Verbal: Your Grace (formal) or Archbishop (social) Conversation: His Grace (formal) or Archbishop (of Blank) (social)
Bishop	My Lord or My Lord Bishop (formal), Right Reverend Sir (officially recognised) or Dear Bishop (Rose) (social)	I have the honour to be, Your Lordship's obedient child (very formal), I remain, my Lord, Yours faithfully (formal) or I have the honour to be, Right Reverend Sir, Your obedient servant (or Most Reverend Sir for an Irish bishop) (officially recognised) or Yours sincerely (social)	His Lordship The Bishop of Blank or The Right Reverend John Rose, Bishop of Blank, or The Right Reverend John Rose, Auxiliary Bishop of Blank (formal and social) or The Right Reverend Bishop Rose (officially recognised)	Verbal: My Lord or My Lord Bishop Conversation: His Lordship or The Bishop

	Salutation	Sign Off	Envelope	Verbal Address & Communication
Abbot	My Lord Abbot or Right Reverend and Dear Father Abbot (formal), Right Reverend Sir (officially recognised) or Dear Father Abbot (social)	I beg to remain, My Lord Abbot, Your devoted and obedient servant (very formal for Roman Catholics) or Yours faithfully (formal) or Yours sincerely (social)	The Right Reverend The Abbot of Blank (followed by initials of his order) (Formal and social) or The Right Reverend John Rose (initials of order) (officially recognised)	Verbal: The Abbot (of Blank) Conversation: Father Abbot (formal) or Abbot (social)
Monsignor	Reverend Sir (formal) or Dear Monsignor Rose or Dear Monsignor (social)	Yours sincerely	The Reverend Monsignor John Rose or The Reverend Monsignor or The Very Reverend Monsignor (Canon) John Rose	Verbal: Monsignor or Monsignor Rose Conversation: Monsignor Rose
Provincial	Very Reverend Father Provincial or Very Reverend Father (formal) or Dear Father Provincial or Dear Father Rose (social)	Yours sincerely	Very Reverend Father Provincial (initials of order) or Very Reverend Father or The Very Reverend Father Rose (initials of order)	Father Provincial
Prior	Very Reverend (very formal) or Dear Father Prior (formal and social)	Yours sincerely	The Very Reverend the Prior of Blank or The Very Reverend John Rose (initials of order)	Verbal: Father Prior Conversation: The Prior (of Blank)
Canon	Very Reverend Sir (formal) or Dear Canon (Rose) (social)	Yours sincerely	The Very Reverend Canon John Rose	Canon Rose
Priest	Dear Reverend Father (formal) or Dear Father Rose (social)	Yours sincerely	The Reverend John Smith or The Reverend Fr Rose	Verbal: Father Conversation: Father Rose

Non-Christian Faiths

Many faiths are now practised for which no indisputable body of conventions exists in the UK.

The Baha'i, Buddhist, Hindu, Humanist, Islamic, Jainist, Sikh and Zoroastrian faiths all have their cultural centres and places of worship, and it is recommended that an approach should be made therein to ascertain the correct forms of address for the various hierarchies of priests, ministers and officials of each faith.

ISLAM — While there are close to four million Muslims in the UK, there is no central organisation or authority for Islam. For further information, contact The Muslim Council of Britain, one of the UK's largest Muslim organisations.

JUDAISM — There are over 350 synagogues in the United Kingdom, and it is estimated that 70 per cent of the country's Jews are affiliated to a synagogue.

The Board of Deputies of British Jews, which was founded in 1760, is the main representative body of British Jewry. It receives deputies elected by individual synagogues, confederations of synagogues and other organisations within the Jewish community.

THE CHIEF RABBI — The Chief Rabbi is the spiritual head of the United Synagogue, the largest synagogue body in the UK, and therefore the Chief Rabbi of the mainstream British orthodox synagogues, receiving widespread recognition from the majority of UK Jews. He is styled as Chief Rabbi of the United Hebrew Congregations of the Commonwealth. The Chief Rabbi Emeritus is styled as for the Chief Rabbi, with the addition of 'Emeritus'.

RABBIS — Rabbis are teachers and spiritual guides. Rabbis can be teachers in schools or Talmudic academies or can act as spiritual leaders of Synagogue communities.

They can run outreach movements and charities, act as hospital/army/prison/university chaplains or in some cases, hold down everyday jobs without using their Rabbinic qualification.

RABBI DOCTORS — A Rabbi Doctor is simply a person who has both a Rabbinic ordination and a university doctorate (PhD).

	Rabbi Doctors are addressed and referred to in speech as, for example, 'Dr Golden'.
READERS	Readers are professional officiants in a synagogue (sometimes called 'minister', although this archaic term is rarely used nowadays). They lead the services.

Readers are addressed and referred to in speech as 'Mr/Mrs/Miss Golden', or 'Dr Golden', as appropriate. An envelope should be addressed to 'The Rev Joseph Golden', for example, or 'The Rev Dr Joseph Golden', as appropriate.

There are two styles of address for members of the Jewish Synagogue: formal and contemporary. In most circumstances the social form is used.

JUDAISM: FORMS OF ADDRESS

	SALUTATION	ENVELOPE	VERBAL ADDRESS	CONVERSATION
Chief Rabbi	Dear Sir (formal) or Dear Chief Rabbi (social)	The Chief Rabbi Dr Joseph Golden	Chief Rabbi	The Chief Rabbi
Rabbi	Dear Sir or Madam (formal) or Dear Rabbi Golden	Rabbi J Golden	Rabbi Golden	Rabbi Golden
Readers (Ministers)	Dear Sir or Reverend Sir (formal) or Dear Mr Golden (social)	The Reverend Joseph Golden	Mr Golden	Mr Golden

Professions

Medicine

Forms of Address
Medical Qualifications
Fellowships & Memberships

Formal qualifications in all divisions of the British medical profession are extremely complex and, despite adhering to many customs and traditions, are often subject to revision.

BRITISH MEDICAL EDUCATION

There are several stages to British medical education and it takes many years to qualify. Undergraduate education at a medical school is followed by a two-year Foundation Programme, replacing what was formerly known as the Pre-registration House Officer (PRHO) year and the first year of Senior House Officer (SHO) training. After this, postgraduate doctors undertake either run-through, specialty or GP training.

Run-through programmes, providing recruitment for the duration of the training period, are offered by some specialties. Other specialties – eg surgery or paediatrics – require 'uncoupled' training, consisting of two to three years of core training followed by four to five years of higher specialty training. Training to specialise in general practice lasts for approximately three years. The final stage of qualification is membership exams after which a Certificate of Completion of Training (CCT) is awarded. The newly qualified medics are put on the specialist register of the appropriate Royal College and can apply for consultant or GP posts.

DOCTORS, PHYSICIANS AND SURGEONS

Doctors and physicians are always referred to both in written and verbal communication by the title of 'Doctor', which is abbreviated to 'Dr'. Surgeons are referred to both in written and verbal communication as 'Mr'.

DENTISTS

Dentists are correctly addressed as surgeons (unless additional qualifications allow their title to be that of doctor). Dentists with additional qualifications (eg DChD, FDS RCS) are usually addressed as a doctor.

MEDICINE: FORMS OF ADDRESS

	SALUTATION	ENVELOPE	VERBAL ADDRESS	CONVERSATION
Doctor	Dear Dr Adam	Dr Jane Adam, MD, FRCP	Dr Adam	Dr Adam
Physician	Dear Dr Brewer	Dr Mary Brewer, MB BS	Dr Brewer	Dr Brewer
Surgeon	Dear Mr Frith	John Frith, Esq, MS, FRCS	Mr Frith	Mr Frith
Dentist	Dear Mr Garrick	Edward Garrick, Esq, FDS RCS	Mr Garrick	Mr Garrick

Medical Royal Colleges and Faculties	
	Royal College of Surgeons of Edinburgh (RCSEd)
	Royal College of Physicians of London (RCP)
	Royal College of Physicians and Surgeons of Glasgow (RCPSG)
	Royal College of Physicians of Edinburgh (RCPE)
	Royal College of Surgeons of England (RCS)
	Royal College of Psychiatrists (RCPsych)
	Royal College of Nursing (RCN)
	Royal College of Obstetricians and Gynaecologists (RCOG)
	Royal College of General Practitioners (RCGP)
	Royal College of Radiologists (RCR)
	Royal College of Pathologists (RCPath)
	Royal College of Ophthalmologists (RCO)
	Royal College of Anaesthetists (RCoA)
	Royal College of Paediatrics and Child Health (RCPCH)
	Royal College of Surgeons of Ireland (RCSI)
	Royal College of Physicians of Ireland (RCPI)
	College of Emergency Medicine (CEM)
	Faculty of Occupational Medicine (FOM)
	Faculty of Public Health (FPH)
	Faculty of Pharmaceutical Medicine (FPM)
	Faculty of Dental Surgery (Royal College of Surgeons of England) (FDS)

Medical Qualifications

Post-nominal Letters   By custom, those letters denoting medical qualifications follow those of orders, decorations and medals bestowed by the Crown.

They are usually placed in the following order:
- Doctorates
- Masterships
- Baccalaureates (degrees of bachelor)
- Postgraduate diplomas
- Qualifying diplomas

CORRESPONDENCE   It is the custom for letters indicating doctorates, masterships and fellowships to be given in correspondence.

Baccalaureates, memberships and qualifying diplomas may be shown if no higher qualifications are held.

It is sufficient for a maximum of three series of letters to be shown: for example, MD, FRCS, FRCOG.

The following is the list of some letters commonly used in medicine in the UK:

Doctorates	Style: 'Doctor of...'
DM; MD	Doctor of Medicine
DCh; DS	Doctor of Surgery
DDS	Doctor of Dental Surgery
Masterships	Style: 'Master of...'
MCh; MChir; MS; ChM	Master of Surgery
MDS; MChD	Master of Dental Surgery
MAO	Master of the Art of Obstetrics
MChOrth	Master of Orthopaedic Surgery
MClinPsychol	Master of Clinical Psychology
MClSc	Master of Clinical Science
MCommH	Master of Community Health
MMed	Master of Medicine
MMedSci; MMS	Master of Medical Science
Baccalaureates	Style: 'Bachelor of...'
BM or MB	Bachelor of Medicine
BDS; BChD; BDentS	Bachelor of Dental Surgery
BAO	Bachelor of the Art of Obstetrics
BAc	Bachelor of Acupuncture
BASc	Bachelor of Applied Science
BMedSci	Bachelor of Medical Science
BPharm	Bachelor of Pharmacy
MB BChir; MB ChB; MB BCh; MB BS; BM BCh; BM BS; BM	Bachelor of Medicine, Bachelor of Surgery

Medicine: Fellowships and Memberships

Fellowships	Style: *'Fellow of the Royal College of...'*
FDSRCS	Fellow in Dental Surgery, Royal College of Surgeons of England
FRCA	Fellow of the Royal College of Anaesthetists
FRCN	Fellow of the Royal College of Nursing
FRCOphth	Fellow of the Royal College of Ophthalmologists
FRCP	Fellow of the Royal College of Physicians
FRCPCH	Fellow of the Royal College of Paediatrics and Child Health
FRCPEd	Fellow of the Royal College of Physicians of Edinburgh
FRCP(Glas)	Fellow of the Royal College of Physicians and Surgeons of Glasgow
FRCS	Fellow of the Royal College of Surgeons of England
FRCSEd	Fellow of the Royal College of Surgeons of Edinburgh
FRCS(Glasg)	Fellow of the Royal College of Physicians and Surgeons of Glasgow
FRCSI	Fellow of the Royal College of Surgeons of Ireland
FRCOG	Fellow of the Royal College of Obstetricians and Gynaecologists
FRCGP	Fellow of the Royal College of General Practitioners
FRCPath	Fellow of the Royal College of Pathologists
FRCPI	Fellow of the Royal College of Physicians of Ireland
FRCPsych	Fellow of the Royal College of Psychiatrists
FRCR	Fellow of the Royal College of Radiologists
FDS RCS	Fellow in Dental Surgery, Royal College of Surgeons
FDS FRCSEd	Fellow in Dental Surgery, Royal College of Surgeons of Edinburgh
FDS RCPS(Glas)	Fellow in Dental Surgery, Royal College of Physicians and Surgeons of Glasgow
Other Fellowships	Style: *'Fellow of the College/Faculty of...'*
FCEM	Fellow of the College of Emergency Medicine
FFICM	Fellow of the Faculty of Intensive Care Medicine
FFOM	Fellow of the Faculty of Occupational Medicine
FFPH	Fellow of the Faculty of Public Health
FFPM	Fellow of the Faculty of Pharmaceutical Medicine
FFSRH	Fellow of the Faculty of Sexual and Reproductive Healthcare

Memberships	Style: 'Member of the College/Faculty/Royal College of...'
MCEM	Member of the College of Emergency Medicine
MFDS (RCS Eng)	Member of the Faculty of Dental Surgery, Royal College of Surgeons of England
MFDS RCPS(Glasg)	Member of the Faculty of Dental Surgery, Royal College of Physicians and Surgeons of Glasgow
MFICM	Member of the Faculty of Intensive Care Medicine
MFOM	Member of the Faculty of Occupational Medicine
MFPH	Member of the Faculty of Public Health
MFPM	Member of the Faculty of Pharmaceutical Medicine
MFSRH	Member of the Faculty of Sexual and Reproductive Healthcare
MJDF (RCS Eng)	Member of the Joint Dental Faculties, Royal College of Surgeons of England
MRCA	Member of the Royal College of Anaesthetists
MRCN	Member of the Royal College of Nursing
MRCOphth	Member of the Royal College of Ophthalmologists
MRCP	Member of the Royal College of Physicians
MRCPCH	Member of the Royal College of Paediatrics and Child Health
MRCPEd	Member of the Royal College of Physicians of Edinburgh
MRCP(Glas)	Member of the Royal College of Physicians and Surgeons of Glasgow
MRCP(UK)	Member of the Royal Colleges of Physicians of the United Kingdom
MRCOG	Member of the Royal College of Obstetricians and Gynaecologists
MRCS(Glasg)	Member of the Royal College of Physicians and Surgeons of Glasgow
MRCSI	Member of the Royal College of Surgeons of Ireland
MRCGP	Member of the Royal College of General Practitioners
MRCPath	Member of the Royal College of Pathologists
MRCPI	Member of the Royal College of Physicians of Ireland
MRCPsych	Member of the Royal College of Psychiatrists
MRCR	Member of the Royal College of Radiologists
MRCS	Member of the Royal College of Surgeons of England
MRCSEd	Member of the Royal College of Surgeons of Edinburgh

PROFESSIONS

THE DIPLOMATIC SERVICE

FORMS OF ADDRESS
COMMONWEALTH TITLES

The very rigid form of diplomatic address that was followed in the last century has been replaced by a polite, yet slightly less deferential, style of approach.

ORIGINS Internationally recognised diplomatic ranks were agreed at the Congress of Vienna in 1815.

Ambassador is the most senior diplomatic rank, and ambassadors are formal representatives of the Head of State.

In Commonwealth countries, the equivalent of the ambassador is normally the high commissioner.

The collective term for a group of diplomats residing in another county is a diplomatic mission. Any diplomat who heads a diplomatic mission is known as chief of mission or head of mission. They are normally ambassadors.

A diplomatic mission headed by an ambassador is known as an embassy; a diplomatic mission headed by a high commissioner is known as a high commission.

HIERARCHIES Most ambassadors represent their government in a single country; 'ambassadors-at-large' work in several (normally neighbouring) countries, or represent their nation at intergovernmental organisations.

Below the ambassador in the diplomatic hierarchy come the following: minister; minister-counsellor; counsellor; first secretary; second secretary; third secretary; attaché; assistant attaché.

In the absence of an ambassador or a senior diplomat, a *chargé d'affaires* will temporarily head the diplomatic mission. At formal events, the *chargé d'affaires* has a lower precedence than the ambassador.

Attachés are generally staff, acting in an advisory or administrative capacity, who are not members of their country's diplomatic service, and are therefore temporarily 'attached' to the mission.

CONSULS

A consul is appointed to represent the government of one state in the territory of another, and is responsible for looking after the welfare of the citizens of his/her own country in a foreign land. A consul differs from an ambassador, who represents his/her head of state in a foreign country, and is concerned with diplomatic relations between the two nations.

Consuls are based in consulates (which may be within the embassy itself).

FOREIGN AMBASSADOR ACCREDITED TO THE UNITED KINGDOM

An ambassador accredited to the Court of St James is accorded the style of 'His/Her Excellency' within the United Kingdom and Colonies.

It is always correct to describe an ambassador by name, adding the country after the name.

For example, 'His Excellency M Maurice Dansey, the French Ambassador'.

It is correct, and often preferable, to use the adjectival form, if it is of long established use, for example 'His Excellency the Spanish Ambassador'. There is, however, a growing use of the name of the country in place of its adjectival equivalent, as for example 'The Jordan Ambassador' rather than 'The Jordanian Ambassador'.

'Netherlands' is used in diplomatic circles in preference to 'Dutch'.

For precedence within the diplomatic corps see The London Diplomatic List, published by The Stationery Office, or online the Foreign and Commonwealth Office website

If in doubt, check with the secretary of the ambassador in question.

In a letter to an ambassador, it is usual to mention 'Your Excellency' in the opening and closing paragraphs. In a long letter, further references may be made to 'you' or 'your'.

BRITISH AMBASSADOR ACCREDITED TO A FOREIGN COUNTRY

A British ambassador accredited to a foreign country is known as 'His/Her Excellency' within the country to which he/she has been accredited (and often by courtesy when travelling outside it on duty), but not in the United Kingdom.

An ambassador who is head of a United Kingdom mission abroad (eg to the United Nations) is styled 'His/Her Excellency'.

CORRECT FORM | PROFESSIONS [139]

A female ambassador is called ambassador, and not ambassadress. Her husband is not accorded any style as such.

COMMONWEALTH HIGH COMMISSIONER

A commonwealth high commissioner in the United Kingdom is accorded the same style and precedence as an ambassador.

It is always correct to describe the high commissioner by name, adding the country after the name, for example, 'His Excellency Mr Pat Ayres, High Commissioner for* Australia'. If in doubt, check with the secretary of the high commissioner in question.

*Note: it is correct to use the word 'for' in respect of Commonwealth countries.

In a letter to a high commissioner, it is usual to mention 'Your Excellency' in the opening and closing paragraphs. In a long letter, further references may be made to 'you' or 'your'.

DIPLOMATIC SERVICE: FORMS OF ADDRESS

	SALUTATION	SIGN OFF	ENVELOPE	VERBAL ADDRESS	CONVERSATION
Ambassador (formal)	Your Excellency	I have the honour to be, with the highest consideration, Your Excellency's obedient servant	His Excellency The Ambassador of Norway or His Excellency Mr Mathias Bergen	Your Excellency should be mentioned at least once in conversation, and thereafter Sir or Ma'am or by name	His Excellency
Ambassador (social)	Dear Ambassador	Yours sincerely	His Excellency The Ambassador of Norway or His Excellency Mr Mathias Bergen	Ambassador or by name	The Norwegian Ambassador or The Ambassador of Norway or by name
High Commissioner (formal)	Your Excellency	I have the honour to be Your Excellency's obedient servant	Her Excellency The High Commissioner of South Africa or Her Excellency Miss Elizabeth Port	Your Excellency should be mentioned at least once in conversation, and thereafter Sir or Ma'am or by name	Her Excellency
High Commissioner (social)	Dear High Commissioner	Yours sincerely	Her Excellency The High Commissioner of South Africa or Her Excellency Miss Elizabeth Port	High Commissioner or by name	The South African High Commissioner or The High Commissioner of South Africa or by name

Commonwealth Titles

Governor-General, Governor or Lieutenant-General

A governor-general or governor is styled 'His/Her Excellency', which precedes all other titles and ranks, while administering a government and within the territory administered.

The lieutenant-governors of Jersey, Guernsey and the Isle of Man are accorded the same style. Their spouses have no formal style.

It is interesting to note that British Overseas Territories are administered by a governor, not a governor-general, and usually, although not invariably, a senior retired member of the armed forces.

Governor-General of Canada

The Governor-General of Canada also has the rank of 'Rt Hon' for life, and his/her spouse is accorded the style of 'His/Her Excellency' within the country administered by the Governor-General, but this does not apply to the spouse of a governor.

Governor-General of Australia

The Governor-General of Australia is accorded the style of 'His/Her Excellency' and the spouse/partner is also accorded the style of 'His/Her Excellency' within the country administered by the Governor-General.

Lieutenant-Governor of a Canadian Province

A lieutenant-governor of a Canadian province is accorded the style of 'The Honourable' for life. At the present time there are lieutenant-governors for the provinces of Alberta, British Columbia, Manitoba, New Brunswick, Newfoundland and Labrador, Nova Scotia, Ontario, Prince Edward Island, Quebec and Saskatchewan.

Northwest Territories, Nunavut (previously part of Northwest Territories) and Yukon each have a commissioner, who is also accorded the style of 'The Honourable' for life.

British Consul-General

A consul-general, consul or vice-consul who holds His Majesty's Commission is entitled to the letters 'HM' before the appointment.

Other consuls, vice-consuls and consular agents, appointed other than by the Crown, are known as the British consul, vice-consul, etc, and do not have the prefix 'HM'.

An officer in charge of a consular appointment, during the absence of the incumbent, takes for the time being the rank of the incumbent, but is addressed as 'The Acting British Consul-General, Consul', etc.

Consuls of the other Commonwealth countries are addressed as 'The Australian Consul', etc.

AGENT-GENERAL Most states in Australia are represented in London by an agent-general.

An agent-general is not accorded any special form of address, but his/her appointment should be placed after his/her name. For example:

Daniel Mercer, Esq
Agent-General for ......

Agents-general for the states of Australia should be placed as follows:
- Victoria
- Queensland
- South Australia
- Western Australia

New South Wales and Tasmania are no longer represented.

No Canadian provinces are represented by agents-general at the present time, although Quebec has a government office in London.

142 - 153

Hierarchies

Letters After The Name

Post-nominal letters may be a recognition of status or an acknowledgement of achievement, or may denote an educational or professional qualification. They advertise certain key facts about the person who has been granted them, and in many cases are a matter of great pride. It is therefore vitally important that they are correctly deployed in all formal communications.

Letters After The Name

HIERARCHIES

Crown Honours
Commonwealth Orders
Appointments
Academia & Religion
Societies & Professions

The use of letters after an individual's name (post-nominal letters) follows a prescribed order. The abbreviation 'Bt' (for a baronet) and 'Esq', if applicable, precede all other letters.

The series of other letters are grouped, and ordered, either by regulations or by custom as follows:

ORDER OF LETTERS

1. Orders and decorations conferred by the Crown (Crown honours).

2. Crown appointments in the following order: Privy Counsellor, Aide de Camp to HM, Honorary Physician to HM, Honorary Surgeon to HM, Honorary Dental Surgeon to HM, Honorary Nursing Sister to HM, and Honorary Chaplain to HM (PC, ADC, KHP, KHS, KHDS, KHNS and KHC).

3. King's Counsel, Justice of the Peace and Deputy Lieutenant: thus KC, JP and DL.

4. University degrees.

5. (a) Religious orders (b) medical qualifications.

6. (a) Fellowships of learned societies, (b) Royal Academicians and associates, (c) fellowships, memberships etc, of professional institutions, associations etc, and (d) Writers to the Signet, *see p 153.*

7. Member of Parliament.

8. Membership of one of the armed forces, such as RN or RAF.

The nature of the correspondence determines which series of letters normally should be included under groups 4, 5 and 6. For instance, when writing a professional letter to a doctor of medicine, one would normally add more medical qualifications than in a social letter.

On a formal list, those who have letters signifying Crown honours and awards are usually given only the principal letters in groups 4, 5 and 6 (for example MD, FRCS, FRS).

A peer who is a junior officer in the armed forces is not usually addressed by his/her service rank in social correspondence, unless he/she so wishes.

Crown Honours and Decorations

See pp 433–441 for a guide to wearing orders, medals and decorations

The Honours and Decorations listed below entitle the holder to use the appropriate letters after the name. All letters should be shown in the same order as listed, with the exception of 'Bart' or 'Bt' (Baronet) and 'Esq' (if applicable) which is shown immediately after the surname and before all other letters after the name. If an individual has more than one set of letters after their name, the letters should appear in this order:

VC	Victoria Cross
GC	George Cross
KG/LG	Knight of the Garter; Lady of the Garter
KT/LT	Knight of the Thistle; Lady of the Thistle
GCB	Knight Grand Cross of the Order of the Bath
OM	Order of Merit
GCMG	Knight Grand Cross of the Order of St Michael and St George
GCVO	Knight Grand Cross of the Royal Victorian Order
GBE	Knight Grand Cross of the Order of the British Empire
CH	Companion of Honour
KCB/DCB	Knight/Dame Commander of the Bath
KCMG/DCMG	Knight/Dame Commander of St Michael and St George
KCVO/DCVO	Knight/Dame Commander of the Royal Victorian Order
KBE/DBE	Knight/Dame Commander of the British Empire
CB	Companion of the Order of the Bath
CMG	Companion of the Order of St Michael and St George
CVO	Commander of the Royal Victorian Order
CBE	Commander of the Order of the British Empire
DSO	Distinguished Service Order
LVO	Lieutenant of the Royal Victorian Order
OBE	Officer of the Order of the British Empire
ISM	Imperial Service Medal
MVO	Member of the Royal Victorian Order
MBE	Member of the Order of the British Empire
BEM	British Empire Medal

These honours are followed, in order of precedence, by:

Decorations for Gallantry & Distinguished Service

GM	George Medal
RRC	Royal Red Cross Class I
DSC	Distinguished Service Cross
MC	Military Cross
CGC	Conspicuous Gallantry Cross

DFC	Distinguished Flying Cross
AFC	Air Force Cross
ARRC	Royal Red Cross Class II
StJ	Service Medal of the Order of St John
KGM	King's Gallantry Medal
RVM	Royal Victorian Medal (Gold, Silver and Bronze)
KPM	King's Police Medal for Distinguished Service
KFSM	King's Fire Service Medal for Distinguished Service
KAM	King's Ambulance Service Medal
KVRM	King's Volunteer Reserves Medal
OTPM	Overseas Territories Police Medal

The above list shows the currently awarded Orders and Decorations following the reorganisation of the Honours system in 2003 and updates following the death of Queen Elizabeth II in 2022, and incorporates the Honours and Decorations instituted from that date. Obsolete medals have been excluded.

OBSOLETE MEDALS   The Order of the Star of India, the Crown of India, the Indian Order of Merit, the Order of Victoria and Albert and the Colonial Police Medal for Gallantry are no longer conferred.

Medals conferred during the reign of Elizabeth II, which incorporated the Sovereign's title, such as the Queen's Police Medal (QPM) retain the name and abbreviation that was used at the time of the award.

ELIZABETH CROSS   The Elizabeth Cross was created in 2009 to provide national recognition for the families of forces personnel who have died on operations or as a result of terrorism. It has no place in the order of precedence.

Commonwealth Orders

Some Commonwealth countries have their own orders, which are indicated in the same way as the British system.

The Order of Australia

The Order of Australia was established in 1975. The Order, of which The King is Sovereign, consists of a General Division and a Military Division, and is divided into the following classes:

AK	Knight of the Order of Australia; precedence after OM
AD	Dame of the Order of Australia; precedence after OM
AC	Companion of the Order of Australia; precedence after GBE
AO	Officer of the Order of Australia; precedence after Knight Bachelor
AM	Member of the Order of Australia; precedence after DSO
OAM	Medal of the Order of Australia; precedence after RRC (2nd class)

The Order of New Zealand

The Order of New Zealand (ONZ) was established in 1987. The Order, of which the King is Sovereign, confers no title and ordinary membership is limited to 20.

New Zealand Order of Merit

Next in precedence is the New Zealand Order of Merit, which was instituted by Royal Warrant dated 30 May 1996.

GNZM, KNZM, DNZM

On 8 March 2009 it was announced that the late Queen Elizabeth II had given approval for the reinstatement of the titles of Knight and Dame Grand Companion (GNZM) and Knight and Dame Companion (KNZM and DNZM).

KSO	The King's Service Order (KSO) and The King's Service Medal (KSM) were instituted by Royal Warrant in 1975 and were then known as the Queen's Service Order (QSO) and Queen's Service Medal (QSM): Companion of The King's Service Order; precedence after OBE
KSM	The King's Service Medal; precedence after KGM

The Order of Canada

The Order of Canada, of which The King is Sovereign, was established in 1967. It is divided into the following grades:

CC	Companion of the Order of Canada; precedence after VC and GC before all other letters
OC	Officer of the Order of Canada; precedence after CC
CM	Member of the Order of Canada, precedence after OC

Appointments

Royal Appointments

Letters after the name denoting privy counsellors and Crown appointments follow immediately after orders and decorations conferred by the Crown.

They are arranged in the following order:

Privy Counsellor (PC)
Aide de Camp to HM (ADC)
Honorary Physician to HM (KHP)
Honorary Surgeon to HM (KHS)
Honorary Dental Surgeon to HM (KHDS)
Honorary Nursing Sister to HM (KHNS)
Honorary Chaplain to HM (KHC)

See p 99 for privy counsellors

In a social style of address for a peer who is a privy counsellor it is advisable that the letters PC should follow the name. For all other members of the Privy Council the prefix 'Rt Hon' before the name is sufficient identification.

As the other appointments to the Crown (KHP, KHS etc) are held for a limited period only, they are not always used by recipients.

Other Appointments

In the order of precedence of letters after the name, these letters follow the abbreviation 'Bt' (Baronet) and 'Esq' (Esquire), orders and decorations conferred by the Crown and Royal appointments. They appear in the following order:

King's Counsel (KC)
Justice of the Peace (JP)
Deputy Lieutenant (DL)

The letters KC are always shown for a King's Counsel, including a County Court judge, but not a High Court judge.

The letters JP for justice of the peace, and DL for a deputy lieutenant may be included in that order. They may be omitted for a peer, or for someone with several honours and decorations.

Note: there is no official abbreviation for a lord-lieutenant or a vice lord-lieutenant.

Academia & Religion

University Degrees

Letters denoting university degrees are fourth in the order of precedence of letters after the name.

Doctorates in the faculties of Divinity and Medicine (DD, MD) and masters degrees in the latter (eg MS) are given in all correspondence. Other divinity degrees (eg BD) are sometimes included.

Other degrees in medicine (eg MB BS) are sometimes included, especially in professional correspondence, but if one progresses in the same degree only the higher is given.

See p 72 for university degrees

Doctorates in other faculties are sometimes given, especially if the correspondence concerns the particular profession or subject (eg LLD, DSC). Alternatively, except for surgeons, the envelope may simply be addressed as 'Dr' before the name.

Fifth in the order of precedence are letters denoting membership of religious orders and medical qualifications.

Religious Orders

Letters for members of religious communities, when used, should be included, for example 'SJ' (Society of Jesus). Members of the Order of St Benedict may choose not to use the letters 'OSB', preferring the prefix 'Dom' or for a nun, 'Dame'.

See p 118 for religious orders

Medical Qualifications

Medical fellowships are given in all correspondence, for example FRCP and FRCS. Other qualifications are sometimes given, especially those that are the highest held. They are usually given when writing professionally.

See pp 131–135 for medical qualifications

When all letters signifying qualifications are included they should appear in the following order:

Medicine
Surgery (except MRCS)
Obstetrics
Gynaecology and other specialities
Qualifying diplomas (for example MRCS, LRCP)
Other diplomas (for example DPH, DObst, RCOG)
In practice a maximum of three series of letters, including MD, is usually sufficient in ordinary correspondence (for example MD, MS, FRCS).

Societies & Professions

Sixth in the order of precedence of letters after the name come the following (in order):

(a) Fellowships of learned societies
(b) Royal Academicians and associates
(c) Fellowships, memberships etc, of professional institutions, associations etc.
(d) Writers to the Signet

Fellowships
Fellowships fall into two categories:
(a) Honorific, ie nomination by election
(b) Nomination by subscription
Normally only honorific fellowships are used in social correspondence, such as FRS or FBA.

Fellowships by subscription are generally restricted to correspondence concerning the same field of interest, for example a writer to a Fellow of the Zoological Society on the subject of zoology will include FZS after the name.

There is no recognised order for placing these letters. In practice, where one society is indisputably of greater importance than another the letters are usually placed in that order. Alternatively, the fellowship of the junior society may be omitted, letters may be placed in order of conferment, or even in alphabetical order.

Where a fellow is pre-eminent in a particular subject, the fellowship of a society connected with this interest may either be placed first, or his other fellowships omitted.

Principal Learned Societies and Dates of Incorporation

Fellow of the Royal Society	FRS	1662
Fellow of the Society of Antiquaries	FSA	1707
Fellow of the Royal Society of Edinburgh	FRSE	1783
Fellow of the Royal Society of Literature	FRSL	1823
Fellow of the British Academy	FBA	1901

Some presidents use letters signifying their appointment, eg the President of the Royal Society has 'PRS' after his/her name, but these letters are used only within the particular society.

The Royal Society of Literature bestows an award limited to ten recipients, the Companion of Literature. The letters 'CLit' are placed before the fellowship (CLit, FRSL).

ROYAL ACADEMICIANS Although Royal Academicians come second in this list, it is not suggested that they yield in precedence to fellows of learned societies. In practice the two lists do not coincide.

The president and past presidents are indicated as follows:

President of the Royal Academy	PRA
Past President of the Royal Academy	PPRA
President of the Royal Scottish Academy	PRSA
Past President of the Royal Scottish Academy	PPRSA

Royal Academicians and Associates are indicated as follows:

Royal Academician	RA
Royal Scottish Academician	RSA
Associate of the Royal Academy	ARA
Associate of the Royal Scottish Academy	ARSA

Similarly with other academies, for example President of the Royal Hibernian Academy (PRHA) and academicians (RHA).

PROFESSIONAL INSTITUTIONS AND ASSOCIATIONS Letters denoting fellowships and memberships of professional institutions are usually restricted to correspondence concerning the particular profession.

As there is no recognised order for placing qualifications awarded by different bodies, a recipient usually places these letters on headed paper, business cards, etc, in order of importance to his particular profession.

Those whose fellowships are by subscription generally only use letters after the name in the particular field of interest. For example, if John Smith is a chartered engineer and a Fellow of the Royal Historical Society, he would normally be described professionally as 'John Smith, Esq, CEng'.

When corresponding on historical subjects, however, he would normally be described as 'John Smith, Esq, FRHistS'. If both series of letters are placed after his name, it is usual to place first those appropriate to the particular function or subject that is being addressed.

Writers to the Signet

The Writers to the Signet is an ancient society of solicitors in Scotland that dates back to 1594. Its members originally held special privileges in relation to the drawing up of legal documents. The society is now an independent association of solicitors, using the post-nominal letters 'WS'.

It is customary for the letters 'WS' to follow the name after university degrees and those that signify fellowship or membership of a society or institution, despite the fact that the WS Society is considerably older than many institutions. This is simply a way of indicating the profession. It is not customary for the letters 'WS' to be used socially.

Members of Parliament

In formal address, the letters 'MP' are always shown for a member of parliament. They are shown seventh in the order of precedence of letters after the name.

Armed Forces

Letters denoting membership of one of the armed forces come last in the order of precedence of letters after the name.

Royal Navy
See pp 77–79 for Royal Navy

The letters RN (or Royal Navy, which this service prefers) are placed after the names of serving officers of the rank of captain and below. They are also placed after the names of retired captains, commanders and lieutenant-commanders. The letters RNR are likewise used by officers of the Royal Naval Reserve.

Army
See pp 80–83 for Army

The appropriate letters that signify a regiment or corps may be placed after the name for officers on the active list of and below the rank of lieutenant-colonel, but are often omitted in social correspondence. These letters are not used for retired officers. Corps have letter abbreviations (for example RE for Royal Engineers, RAMC for Royal Army Medical Corps, RAOC for Royal Army Ordnance Corps, REME for Royal Electrical and Mechanical Engineers). Most regiments are written in full.

RAF
See pp 84–85 for RAF

The letters RAF are placed after serving and retired officers, except for marshals of the Royal Air Force. Officers above the rank of group captain do not often use these letters. The same rules apply to the Royal Air Force Volunteer Reserve (RAFVR).

The letters RM (or Royal Marines, which some officers prefer) are placed after the names of serving and retired officers of the rank of lieutenant-colonel and below. The same rules apply to the Royal Marines Reserve (RMR).

154 – 181

Invitations
Seating Plans & Precedence
Traditional Rituals
Guests at Formal Events
Royal Events

Formal Events

Very formal or official events, often hosted by an organisation such as a livery company, charity, corporation or business, are different from social events hosted by individuals. There are set conventions that have become established, including elements of protocol and precedence not usually required at purely social events. A knowledge and understanding of such conventions will help the smooth running of these events for both organisers and guests.

Formal Events

Invitations

Sending Out Invitations
Replies
Place Cards

Sending Out Invitations

See pp 17–18 for invitations to members of the Royal Family

Invitations to official events are usually issued on a card, which may be engraved or flat-printed in script or Roman type. The invitation should make clear the nature of the event, the date and location, the dress (if applicable), the time of the event and, if desired, the time it will end.

Style of Names and Titles on Invitations to Official Events

Invitations to official events name the host by his/her office and/or name. This means his or her full title, rank etc, followed by his/her decorations etc.

Prefixes such as 'His Grace', 'His Excellency' and 'The Right Worshipful' are, however, omitted, with the exception of 'The Rt Hon', which is included for a privy counsellor. The courtesy title 'The Hon', and the suffix 'Esq' are never used.

The younger sons of a duke or a marquess are shown as 'Lord Edward Bond', for example, and the daughters of dukes, marquesses and earls are shown as 'Lady Alice Hart'.

Invitations to non-married pairs of guests take these forms:
- brother and sister: *Mr John Debrett and Miss Emma Debrett*
- mother and son: *Mrs George Chesterfield and Mr William Chesterfield* (note that invitations to adult offspring are usually sent separately from those to their parents)
- unmarried couple: *Mr Richard Maddox and Miss Ilsa Curzon*

Examples of forms of address for official events
The Rt Hon the Prime Minister and Mrs Downing or Mr Whitehall
The Duke and Duchess of Mayfair
The Lord Mayor and Lady Mayoress of London
The President of the Royal Academy, Sir John Burlington, KBE, and Lady Burlington
The Master of the Worshipful Company of Haberdashers, and Mrs Green
The Archbishop of Canterbury and Mrs Lampton
The Cardinal Archbishop of Westminster
The Earl of Aldford, OBE, MC, and the Countess of Aldford
Mr Thomas and Dame Helen Wood, DBE
Brigadier and Mrs Donald Hertford
Dr and Mrs John Debrett or Mr James and Dr Emma Hill
The Reverend John and Mrs Bolton

A NOTE ON DRESS — For an event during the day, including early evening drinks, the dress need only be specified if it is other than lounge suits: for example, morning dress or academic robes. For an evening event, dress can be specified: for example, black tie or uniform. Decorations may also be specified when appropriate.

See pp 185–195 for dress codes
See pp 433–441 for decorations

ENVELOPES — An invitation to an official event should be addressed only to the guest invited in their own right if sent to their official address, even if their partner is invited. They are given their full prefix, title, rank and decorations, as for a formal letter.

Note that, traditionally, invitations to a married couple, when sent to their home address, are addressed to the wife alone, with both names being inscribed on the invitation. It is increasingly acceptable, however, to address the envelope with both names.

REPLIES

Replies to invitations are sent on good quality writing paper. It is customary to use paper with a letterhead (*see p 309*) showing the sender's address and to reply in the third person.

Sample replies are as follows:
Mr and Mrs John Debrett thank the President and Council of the National Society of ...... for their kind invitation for Saturday, 12th February, which they have much pleasure in accepting (or: which they have the honour to accept).

Lord and Lady Hays thank the Master of the Worshipful Company of Clockmakers for his kind invitation for Saturday, 12th February, which they much regret being unable to accept. (If the host is known personally, a reason may be given, eg a previous engagement etc.)

REPLY CARDS — Printed reply cards may be sent out with the invitations and should be of small postcard size. Guests should always use the printed card for their reply. Should they wish to add anything, such as an explanation for their inability to accept, this should be done in a separate letter.

To assist the toastmaster and increasingly as a security measure, the words 'please bring this invitation with you' may be added at the bottom of the invitation card. Traditionally these words signalled the presence of a royal personage.

ADMISSION CARDS Alternatively, and especially for an evening event for which a large invitation card cannot easily be carried in a pocket or handbag, the following wording may be added: 'An admission card will be sent on receipt of your acceptance'. Admission cards should be printed in Roman type and should not exceed W5½ x H3½ inches (14 x 9 cm) in size.

An admission card to a ceremony may be used to allocate a specific seat. Separate admission cards should be sent for couples who have both been included on the same invitation card.

NAMES ON ADMISSION CARDS The guest is shown on an admission card by office or by name, in the form in which he or she is to be announced to the hosts.

If by name, this is limited to title, rank and name, except that the following prefixes should be used:
- 'His [or Her} Grace' for the Archbishops of Canterbury/York
- 'His Eminence' for a cardinal
- 'His [or Her] Excellency' for ambassadors and high commissioners (this may be abbreviated to 'HE' on the card, but not by the announcer)
- The Right Honourable, The Right Worshipful, The Worshipful etc for civic heads who are so styled

ENCLOSURES Additional information or instructions, for example relating to car parking, are best given on a separate sheet sent with the invitation or with the admission card.

PLACE CARDS

Table place cards should always be handwritten, and the names kept brief, with honours, decorations, degrees, etc, omitted.
- full titles may be used as opposed to social forms, for example 'Lord' or 'Lady'
- peers are shown as The Duke of Mayfair, The Marquess of Audley, The Earl of Aldford or Lord Hays, etc
- the use of 'baron' or 'baroness' is incorrect, and 'Lord' or 'Lady' should be used
- privy counsellors are accorded the prefix 'The Rt Hon'
- baronets are accorded the suffix 'Bt'
- the suffixes 'RN', 'KC' and 'MP' are given where appropriate
- styles by office are used when people are known by their office not their name (eg The Swiss Ambassador, The Lord Mayor)
- untitled men are invariably styled 'Mr' in place of 'Esq'

Formal Events

Seating Plans & Precedence

Seating
Precedence
Official Lists

Seating

Seating is different at official formal events from the conventions at a social or purely private party. The host is seated at the centre of the table and as a general principle, guests radiate out from the centre of the table in order of precedence. (At a private dinner the host would more usually be at the head of the table.)

The principal guest is placed on the host's right. Traditionally the principal guest's wife would be placed on the host's left, the host's wife being placed on the right of the principal guest. If wives are not present, the second most important guest would be placed on the host's left. It is now as likely for the host, or the principal guest, to be a woman, in which case the same basic principles may be applied, with any necessary adaptations employed to achieve the desired balance.

Guests' partners should be placed according to the precedence of the guest invited in their own right. It is up to the host to decide whether husbands and wives are to be seated together or apart. The former is easier to arrange, but the latter (which is always followed at private dinners) gives both husband and wife a chance to meet new people. It is usual to adhere to alternating the sexes. At single-sex dinners the same basic rules apply and seating is arranged in order of precedence.

At an official event when there is a governing body or organising committee, important members or other subordinate hosts – the 'home team' – should be interspersed among the principal guests. For instance, at Buckingham Palace banquets, members of the extended Royal Family would qualify under this heading.

Guests of Honour

Whereas in some situations social rank may still be deemed to be of utmost importance, at the majority of events considerations such as professional status and age are now treated as equally determining factors. In other words a hereditary peer or their spouse should not be seated in a place of honour above, say, the main supporter of a charity.

The nature of the occasion should offer indications as to the relative significance of guests. A guest of honour must be seated to reflect his or her status, and, by way of example, the chairman of a host company, the MP of the constituency in which an event is held, a foreign dignitary whose country is being honoured or a benefactor should all be recognised and seated appropriately.

Guest Lists at Official Events

For a party of not more than 30, a seating plan may be displayed. For a party of up to 100, a numbered drawing of the table may be displayed with a list of guests alongside it in alphabetical order, each with a seat number.

For parties of more than 100, each guest may be provided with a printed table plan, with the names listed in alphabetical order, and a table diagram with their seat marked or a card with their table numbers. Alternatively a number of boards may be on display.

Naming Styles

A guest list at an official event requires names and titles to be listed in full, formal style, as on an envelope, rather than in the more informal social style.

Prefixes such as 'The Rt Hon' and suffixes such as 'OBE' should be used.

Male guests without a title or rank should be styled 'Mr' rather than 'Esq'. An untitled married couple would be listed separately as 'Debrett, Mr John' and 'Debrett, Mrs Jane' (the traditional wording is 'Debrett, Mrs John').

Any guest invited by virtue of office should be so indicated: for example, 'Hertford, Sir William, KBE, President of the Society of Stationers'.

Peers are shown by their exact rank in the peerage. For example, 'Aldford, The Earl of, JP'; 'Aldford, The Countess of'. The definite article is optional for the ranks of viscount and barons and their wives and widows. Consistency in these listings is important.

Peers by courtesy are not prefixed by the definite article (ie simply 'Audley, Marquess of', 'Burlington, Earl of', etc).

Privy counsellors are accorded the prefix 'The Rt Hon'.

Baronets are accorded the suffix 'Bt'.

See pp 145–153 for letters after the name

Crown honours and decorations should be included, and degrees etc, where appropriate.

Precedence

Lord Mayors and Mayors

The Lord Mayor of London has precedence throughout the City immediately after the Sovereign, and elsewhere immediately after earls. Other lord mayors and mayors (lord provosts and provosts in Scotland), as well as council chairmen, have precedence immediately after the Royal Family on their own civic premises, and after the lord-lieutenant elsewhere in their city or borough.

See pp 443–451 for tables of precedence

On occasion these guests may, as a courtesy, yield their precedence to a guest of honour, or, for example, to an archbishop at a church event, to the Speaker of the House of Commons or the Lord Speaker at a parliamentary event, to the Lord Chief Justice or the Master of the Rolls at a legal function, etc.

Outside their areas of jurisdiction all (except the Lord Mayor of London) have no precedence, other than that which courtesy, or the occasion, may demand.

Diplomats

Ambassadors, high commissioners and *chargés d'affaires* should be placed at the top table, their relative precedence being strictly observed. It is recommended to seek advice from the Marshal of the Diplomatic Corps concerning the order of precedence at the time of an event.

As a general rule, diplomatic representatives from countries that do not enjoy diplomatic relations with each other should not be invited to the same event. When, as sometimes happens, it is necessary to invite them, care should be taken to avoid placing them near each other.

Top Table

Ministers of the Crown and privy counsellors should be placed at the top table.

Important dignitaries of the established Church, that is the Church of England, are placed high among the guests. High dignitaries of other churches and faiths should, as a courtesy, be accorded status immediately after those of the same rank from the established Church.

Representation

When an event takes place within premises belonging to an organisation or institution, a senior representative of that organisation should be invited and placed high among the guests.

When the principal guest is the Sovereign or other head of state, a member of the Royal Family, a prime minister, a member of the Cabinet or someone of comparable importance, inviting some or all of the following and their partners should be considered:
- the lord-lieutenant of the county
- the lord mayor, lord provost, mayor or provost of their specific city, borough etc
- the high sheriff of the county
- the chairman of the county council

Those who accept would be placed in this order of precedence after such principal guests.

Official Lists

Lists of Patrons etc

As a general rule, the form used on an official or similar list should be as for addressing an envelope.

Names on programmes, brochures etc are traditionally listed in order of precedence. Alternatively, an acceptable solution is to list names in alphabetical order, the sole exception being that the Sovereign and other members of the Royal Family must always come first. Members of the Royal Family are always shown with the royal style, usually in full: that is, 'Her Royal Highness ......'.

Others should be treated consistently, either in the formal or social style, whichever is to be adopted.

Formal Style	Social Style
His Grace the Duke of Mayfair	The Duke of Mayfair
Her Grace the Duchess of Mayfair	The Duchess of Mayfair
Her Grace Mary, Duchess of Mayfair	Mary, Duchess of Mayfair
The Rt Hon the Earl of Aldford	Lord Aldford
The Rt Hon the Baron Hill	Lord Hill
His Grace the Archbishop of York Or The Most Reverend the Lord Archbishop of York	The Lord Archbishop of York
The Rt Rev the Lord Bishop of Ely	The Lord Bishop of Ely
The Very Rev the Dean of Lincoln	The Dean of Lincoln
The Rev Mark Brook	The Rev Mark Brook
The Rt Hon Neil Green	The Rt Hon Neil Green

PEERS   There is no rule for the position of 'the' in lists of peers: for example, 'Rt Hon the Earl of Aldford', 'The Rt Hon Viscount Tilney' or 'Rt Hon Lord Hill' are not incorrect.
For recommended usage, see Formal Address pp 24–47.

Similarly, it is not laid down whether one should use upper or lower case for the first letter of 'the' within a sentence, except that the former must always be accorded to The King and senior members of the Royal Famil, such as The Princess Royal, The Duke of York, The Prince of Wales, The Duke of Sussex, in formal address.

Peers and peeresses are given the territorial designation only if it forms an integral part of the title: for example 'Earl Alexander of Tunis' but not 'Lord Prescott of Kingston upon Hull'.

Peers and peeresses by courtesy and former wives of peers are not accorded 'the' or any formal prefix.

UNTITLED MEN   Untitled men are either consistently shown as 'John Debrett, Esq' or as 'Mr John Debrett' and doctors (holders of academic degrees) as 'John Debrett, Esq, DSc' or 'Dr John Debrett' (not 'Dr John Debrett, DSc').

Formal Events

Traditional Rituals

Grace
Toasts
Speeches

Running Order

There is a traditional order of proceedings at formal functions but, inevitably, this may vary slightly from event to event. The established order of events would run as follows:
- grace is said, everybody sits down and food is served
- after dinner, before the toasts, a second grace may be said
- toasts are given after dinner
- speeches take place after the toasts (but occasionally speeches may be given before dinner or divided between before and after dinner).

Grace

Grace is usually said before a meal and guests should remain standing or stand if they have already sat down. There is no preamble to grace. The toastmaster announces only, 'Pray silence for grace by your president', or 'by Canon Mark Brook', etc. The member of clergy's living should not be mentioned: that is, not 'The Rt Rev John Jones, Bishop of Barchester'.

No one should sit down again until after grace; otherwise it is usual to sit down after the guest of honour, hosts and top table guests have taken their seats. Sometimes a second grace is said after the meal, in which case it precedes the loyal toast.

Toasts

Loyal Toasts

The most usual toast, given after dinner (and the second grace, if said), is the loyal toast to the Sovereign. To obtain the necessary silence the toastmaster may say, without preamble, 'Pray silence for your president/host/chairman' etc. The principal host will then stand and give the toast. The variations are as follows:

- The first and principal loyal toast, as approved by The King, is 'The King'. It is incorrect to use such forms as 'I give you the loyal toast of His Majesty The King'.

- The second loyal toast, which, if given, immediately follows the first, is 'The Queen Consort, The Prince of Wales, and the other members of the Royal Family'.

- The loyal toast in Lancashire, Greater Manchester and Merseyside, and at Lancastrian organisations elsewhere in the country, is 'The King, Duke of Lancaster'.

- In Jersey the toast of 'The King, our Duke' (ie Duke of Normandy) is local and unofficial, and used only when islanders are present. This toast is not used in the other Channel Islands.

THE NATIONAL ANTHEM

Everybody else then stands up and the entire National Anthem may then be played (just the first six bars are played after a second loyal toast). When the music ends, glasses are raised and the toast is said – 'The King' – and drunk before everybody sits down again. Glasses should never be raised during the National Anthem.

PREAMBLE TO OTHER TOASTS

A speaker proposing a toast (other than the loyal toast) should make this clear at the end of the speech in some such form as 'I give you the toast of ......', or 'I ask you to rise and drink to the toast of ......'. This obviates any need for the toastmaster to say 'The toast is ......'. The toastmaster should be given the form in which he/she is to make all announcements in writing.

SPEECHES

Speeches are usual at formal dinners or banquets. Guests should sit quietly, be still and refrain from chatting during the speeches. It is customary to clap at the beginning and the end.

ANNOUNCEMENT OF THE SPEAKER

A speaker is announced by name, followed by office where applicable. For example, 'The Right Honourable Neil Green, His Majesty's Secretary of State for ......'. For the first speaker the announcement should have a preamble, as for the toast, followed by, 'Pray silence for ......'. For subsequent speakers the preamble should be omitted.

PREAMBLE TO SPEECHES

Speeches at formal functions always open with a preamble. It is impossible to give a comprehensive list of those who should be mentioned in the preamble to a speech, since this depends so much on those present at a particular event.

In general, however, the list should be kept as short as possible, avoiding any omission that would cause justifiable offence. The speaker does not, of course, include himself/herself in this preamble.

THE KING

Should The King be present, a preamble begins: 'May it please Your Majesty'.

THE HOST	With the above exception, a preamble begins with the host, who is referred to by office, for example, 'Madam Chairman', 'Mr Chairman', 'Provost', etc. A non-royal duke or duchess is addressed as 'Your Grace and President'.
	A peer other than a duke, who is hosting an event in an official capacity, is addressed as 'My Lord and President'. It is incorrect to use the form 'My Lord President', except for the Lord President of the Council.
	A woman, either titled or untitled, with the exception of a member of the Royal Family or a duchess, is referred to as 'Madam President', not 'Lady'. An untitled man is referred to as 'Mr President'.
VICE-PRESIDENT	When a vice-president takes the chair, he or she may be referred to as 'Mr Vice-President' or 'Madam Vice-President' as appropriate, with the relevant prefix mentioned above, but he or she is more usually referred to as 'Mr Chairman' or 'Madam Chairman'.
CHAIRMAN	A chairman is called 'Mr Chairman', or 'Madam Chairman', irrespective of his or her rank, with the exception of a member of the Royal Family, who is referred to as 'Your Royal Highness'. A peer should not be called 'My Lord Chairman', simply 'Mr Chairman'.
	If a vice-chairman, managing director or other officer of the organisation takes the chair, he or she is still referred to as 'Mr Chairman' or 'Madam Chairman'. The use of these styles is not restricted to the actual chairman of the organisation.
PATRON	If a member of the Royal Family is also the president or patron of the society that is holding the event, he or she is styled 'Your Royal Highness and President'.
ORDER OF PRECEDENCE IN PREAMBLES	Most people will be familiar with such expressions as: 'Lords, Ladies and Gentlemen' in the preamble to a speech. However, at an event where a number of illustrious guests are present, it is not inevitable that the usual sequence of precedence is followed.
See p 170 for guidance	Adjustment may need to be made in order to give due respect to a patron, president or guest of honour. Courtesy and common sense will overrule conventional correct form.

If in doubt, there is no reason why the host or planner of any given event should not contact the dignitaries concerned before coming to any hard-and-fast decisions regarding matters of precedence and protocol. If there is a member of the Royal Family involved then it is best to contact their office. Homework and research are always advisable.

The following list gives the form in which important guests should be included in a preamble in order of precedence, with the exception of those already mentioned above:

Preamble to Speeches: Order of Precedence

Your Majesty and/or Your Royal Highness
My Lord Mayor, My Lord Provost etc: applies only to the civic head of the city, borough etc, in which the event takes place. A civic head from elsewhere is mentioned after 'My Lord(s)'. More than one lord mayor or lord provost may be covered by 'My Lord Mayors', 'My Lord Provosts' or by naming each. There is no plural for 'Mr Mayor' so 'Your Worships' is used.
Mr Recorder (the Recorder of London only has this precedence within the City of London, for example at Guildhall)
Mr Chairman of the Kent County Council
My Lord Chancellor
Prime Minister (or, more formally, Mr Prime Minister or Madam Prime Minister). Also at this level: My Lord President (that is, of the Privy Council), My Lord Privy Seal, Mr/Madam Chancellor (of the Exchequer or of the Duchy of Lancaster), Minister(s). This covers a secretary of state; other ministers are not mentioned in a preamble when the Prime Minister attends an event).
Your Excellency(ies) (this refers to ambassadors and high commissioners)
Your Grace(s). This covers dukes and duchesses. If the Archbishop of Canterbury is present, 'Your Grace' (or 'Your Graces' if a duke or duchess is also attending) should be mentioned before 'My Lord Chancellor'. Similarly, the Archbishop of York is covered by including 'Your Grace' immediately after 'My Lord Chancellor'. Archbishops rank before ambassadors and high commissioners.
My Lord(s). For peers other than dukes, peers by courtesy, for diocesan bishops by right and for other bishops by courtesy. In the absence of any peers, the form 'My Lord Bishops' may be used.
Ladies and Gentlemen. When only one woman is present the form should be 'Lady (or 'My Lady' if titled) and Gentlemen', or 'Mrs/Lady Blank, Gentlemen'; never 'Madam and Gentlemen'. The phrase 'Distinguished Guests' is also an acceptable alternative in this circumstance.

ROMAN CATHOLIC DIGNITARIES	A cardinal archbishop may be included in the form 'Your Eminence', placed by courtesy after 'Your Grace(s)'. Other archbishops and bishops are by courtesy mentioned in the same way as those of the Anglican Communion.
OTHER CLERGY	Clergy, other than archbishops and bishops, should not be included. In particular, the forms 'Reverend Sir' and 'Reverend Father' are archaic.
	Exceptionally 'Mr Dean', 'Madam Dean', 'Mr Provost', 'Archdeacon' or 'Madam Archdeacon' may be included.
GUEST OF HONOUR	When the guest of honour is not covered by one of the above terms, he or she is included in the preamble by office immediately before 'Ladies and Gentlemen'. This specific mention also applies when an individual who is present has provided the building in which the event is taking place, such as the director of the National Portrait Gallery.
ALDERMEN AND SHERIFFS	Within the City of London it is customary to refer to 'Mr Alderman' or 'Aldermen' and 'Mr Sheriff' or 'Sheriffs' immediately before 'Ladies and Gentlemen'. Elsewhere 'Councillors' may be included at civic events immediately before 'Ladies and Gentlemen'.

> **LOOKING BACK…**
>
> Officers in the Royal Navy are allowed to stay seated during the loyal toast. The origins of this are unofficial, but there are many stories. Various kings are said to have bumped their heads when standing up for a toast on board ship; inexperienced naval officers may have found it hard to stand before they had found their sea-legs; the position of the tables and structures of the overhead beams on board would have made it impossible to stand. However, officers were required to stand if the National Anthem was being played and when aboard the Royal Yacht.

FORMAL EVENTS

GUESTS AT FORMAL EVENTS

ARRIVAL
PROCEDURE
DEPARTURE

Arrival

It is expected that guests will be particularly punctilious in matters of punctuality, dress and behaviour. However, despite the formality of the occasion, guests should be sufficiently relaxed to make the atmosphere light and convivial. In fact it shows good manners to be appearing to have fun.

If the invitation specifies 'and partner' then the name of the person must be given to the host. Guests should not bring an unauthorised plus one. Additional guests should also be briefed, in advance, by the primary guest about the nature and purpose of the event.

Time of Arrival

Times of arrival as stated on formal invitations are strictly adhered to. If a formal invitation says reception 7.30, dinner 8.15 then it is best to arrive at or very shortly after the time given. In the case of a genuine delay then get a message to the organiser, especially when it is a seated dinner. In the case of a stand-up reception then guests running late need not notify the organiser but should try to slip in quietly.

Dress Codes

See pp 185–195 for dress codes

Dress codes for formal events are normally clearly stated but it is best if there is any doubt to contact the organiser. Guests should always dress more formally and modestly than when among friends. This is particularly important where cultural sensitivities may come into play.

Receiving Lines

When there is a formal receiving line a guest may be asked to give their name to an announcer. In this case always give the full name, with title. (In some cases guests may have filled in a presentation card.)
- peers should give their exact rank, eg 'the Duke of Mayfair' or 'the Earl and Countess of Aldford'
- professional titles should be in the form of 'Professor James Hill and Mrs Hill', or 'Mr John Adam and Dr Jane Adam'
- married couples would be 'Mr and Mrs John Debrett'
- titles such as 'The Hon' are not used nor are prefixes or suffixes such as 'Bt' or 'MP'

See p 159 for place cards

Speak clearly, move forward promptly when announced and greet the hosts briefly, even if you know them well. If it is a long line a person may want to repeat their name as they progress, or vary their greeting, for example: 'Good evening, it is so kind of you to have asked me/us'. Subsequently 'How do you do?'

FOOD AND DRINK   If a guest has an allergy or is a vegetarian or vegan then they must say so on replying to the invitation. It is unacceptable to make a fuss on the night and best not to take something from a dish or to leave food on the plate. Asking for special drinks or cross-examining waiting staff about ingredients is bad manners.

SMALL TALK   Avoid established contentious areas, such as religion and politics; personal remarks, including compliments, and jokes may be misinterpreted. Guests must make an effort to be sociable and include those who don't know anyone (particularly in a business context) during the drinks and at the table. Keep the conversation flowing and be attentive to other guests.

PROCEDURE

The usual procedure is to have a drinks reception and then to be shown through to the table. Pause before taking a seat as there may be grace, during which the guests stand with heads slightly bowed. Sometimes there are speeches before dinner; if this is the case then guests take their seats (after grace) and then the speakers are introduced. Serving food is usually delayed until after the speeches.

Once the guests have been seated they should pause before starting to eat, although it is not necessary to wait for everyone to be served before starting. Fast eaters may need to slow down to allow time for others to be served at a large gathering. Slow eaters should also be aware of others and not delay the staff.

At the end of dinner there may be a toast, for which the guests will stand. There may be grace, followed by speeches. If there is clearing going on during the speeches, or coffee being served, then guests must try to remain as still and silent as possible.

HIGH TABLES   Certain institutions, such as Oxbridge colleges, have a high table, usually literally raised on some kind of dais, a reminder of ancient customs and the banqueting halls of the Middle Ages. It is usual for those seated on the ordinary tables to be shown to their seats first and then for those at the high table to come into the room. Those at the ordinary tables will stand to greet them. Certain institutions have particular traditions, such as greeting guests of honour with a slow handclap. Guests will almost certainly have had this explained to them, but if not then take a cue from others rather than being the first to make a move.

Rose Bowls and Loving Cups

Institutions that have rose bowls, bowls passed round in which people will dip their fingers as a ceremonial form of ablution, or loving cups, which is a complex form of toast with arcane rules, should have prepared guests in advance. Guests need not be afraid of getting it wrong but should aim to copy others more familiar with the specific ritual.

Dinner Dances

It is customary and good manners for the male guests to ask each of the women from their table to dance.

Departures

Many formal invitations will include the wording 'Carriages at xx o'clock' or state the time the event finishes. As with arrivals, these guidelines are usually closely adhered to. If a guest knows they will have to leave early, they should notify the organiser. Otherwise it is best to slip away with no fuss.

At the end of an event the organiser or host may place themselves in a suitable position near the door for leave-taking, in which case guests should say goodbye and thank you. However, if the host, or organiser, has been caught up, for example by seeing off the guest of honour, then it is quite acceptable just to make a discreet exit.

Thanks

See pp 322–323 for thank-you letters

Guests must send a prompt formal thank-you letter (ie handwritten in ink), to the main host or organiser whose name was on the invitation. The letter may make reference to the provider of the building, say the Master of the College, and to the person being honoured, if applicable, but they do not need to be thanked. If the invitation came to the guest through another individual, who was not the main host, for example a member of an organisation, then that person should be thanked. A thank-you letter may contain a phrase apologising for not having been able to say good night and thank you properly on the night.

Charity Events

If the event in question was a charity fundraiser, for which a guest has bought a table, or brought guests, then they need not thank the host by letter, other than in exceptional circumstances, to congratulate them on the event, for example. The chairman of the charity (or one of the committee) should, however, in their turn, thank those who have taken tables, with a report about the sum raised and a brief explanation, such as: 'It will go towards the MRI scanner,' and possible future dates or plans.

FORMAL EVENTS

ROYAL EVENTS

ETIQUETTE
ENTERTAINING MEMBERS OF THE ROYAL FAMILY

The Royal Family does a great deal of entertaining, including state, official and private events.

KEY ROYAL EVENTS The events most familiar to the general public are state banquets, which are almost always on the first night of a state visit by an overseas head of state, and garden parties, which are held during the summer, both at Buckingham Palace and at Holyrood in Scotland, and occasionally at other locations. A huge range of people, often those involved in charitable or public service roles, the armed forces, showbusiness and the arts, are asked to garden parties. Then there are lunches, both formal and informal, often themed, for example to honour those who have worked or served in certain sectors, such as industry or the arts. Lastly there are drinks receptions.

On occasion there have been huge concerts or extravaganzas to celebrate landmarks such as the Platinum Jubilee. In addition to these there are investitures, which may also include a reception. Events such as investitures are hosted by The King, or The Queen Consort, The Prince of Wales or The Princess Royal, will deputise for the Sovereign. Other events may be hosted by other members of the Royal Family.

OTHER EVENTS There are also a number of smaller events throughout the year, hosted by various more junior members of the Royal Family, for example as patrons of their charities, which may be held at Buckingham Palace or elsewhere. For example, The Princess Royal might host an event to thank supporters of Riding for the Disabled at the Royal Mews, next to Buckingham Palace, or St James's Palace may be used for a reception for those involved in the Duke of Edinburgh's Award.

PRIVATE EVENTS Personal friends of the Royal Family may be asked to lunch, dinner or to stay at Balmoral in the summer or Sandringham for the shooting in the winter. Ascot is traditionally a Royal event where there is usually a large house party with a wide range of guests. Some people just come to lunch and others dine and sleep at Windsor Castle. Some guests may take part in the famous procession of carriages down the course and are able to watch the racing from the Royal Box.

Other Royal events may include the gardening groups The King previously invited to Highgrove or Sandringham and sporting events, such as the polo or the Royal Windsor Horse Show. Young Guards' officers may be invited to dinner or drinks at

Windsor Castle. While there will almost always be plenty of notice given, anyone encountering a member of the Royal Family unexpectedly in a social situation should just try to behave naturally but with courtesy.

ETIQUETTE

GUEST ETIQUETTE The key point for anyone receiving an invitation (technically a command when it comes from the Sovereign *see p 21*) is that it will include comprehensive guidance as to what form the event will take. The aim of the Royal Household is to make people comfortable and ensure they have a good experience. Guests are told exactly when to arrive and given advice about what to wear. Any special request can be accommodated, such as wheelchair access or food allergies.

Once at the event, members of the Royal Household are on hand to guide guests throughout. The net result is that people are far less likely to encounter any awkward moments at a royal event than at some other formal events where the hosts may be less experienced. The key recommendation is to relax, follow instructions and not to drink too much alcohol because of over-excitement or nervousness.

DRESS The modern tone of the monarchy is to be accepting and open. However, those invited to royal events usually want to do their best to be correct. Specific dress codes, such as black tie (*see pp 187–189*), should be adhered to.

It is generally best to err on the more conservative side when interpreting dress codes. For example, if black tie is specified, then women may want to respect the Royal Family's preference for modesty and wear a long dress, rather than a short cocktail dress. It is not always necessary to wear hats with day dress at more informal lunches. By the same token, although more women opt for dresses or skirts, trouser suits are acceptable. The key thing is to ask for extra guidance, which is given readily by the relevant office (noted on the invitation).

DECORATIONS
See pp 433–441 for a guide to wearing orders, medals and decorations

Decorations should be worn at formal events, such as state banquets, especially if the decoration was one awarded by the Sovereign. Instructions are written on the invitation. Rules for the wearing of, for example, papal decorations or memberships of other orders should be checked and may not be correct.

State banquets are also the moment to wear tiaras, if you have them, or other jewellery, but it is not essential to struggle to acquire finery. Looking as smart and well-groomed as possible is the main priority.

PROCEDURE

Royal events vary in their format, but guests should arrive punctually. They are then shown into a large reception room. Once guests have assembled, the Royal Family arrives, often with no fanfare. If it is an event attended by a large number of royal persons they enter in reverse order, most junior to most senior, with The King last of all.

Those who are to be presented are discreetly marshalled into position by members of the Royal Household, who will have been circulating. The usual form is a series of semi-circles rather than straight rows like a formal receiving line. Guests should try to be empty-handed, having put down any drinks or bags. Women should curtsy and men bow from the neck. The royal personage will offer their hand, in which case shake it with a light contact. Answer any question posed but do not launch into a subject or talk at any length as this holds up the proceedings.

DEPARTURES

It is made very clear when the event is over. This will have been indicated on the invitation and guests may notice that the royal personages have quietly made their exit before members of the Household start to steer people away. By tradition guests should not leave before any of the Royal Family. If it is essential to leave before members of the Royal Family, then a guest should let the relevant private office know in advance.

In practice, at a large reception, held, for example, in the long enfilade of rooms at St James's Palace, guests may simply be able to slip away.

GARDEN PARTIES

See p 21 for invitations from the Royal Family

Buckingham Palace garden parties are held in the afternoon and there are a set number that are organised every year. There are also Scottish garden parties, and sometimes others in particular years, for example at Sandringham.

At Buckingham Palace guests arrive from 3.15pm and are shown into its huge gardens. The royal party arrives punctually at 4pm and a band plays the National Anthem. The royal party usually splits up and circulates among the throng, with lanes of people formed by the Bodyguard for The King.

PRESENTATIONS Guests may be picked out and brought forward to be presented by members of the Household (males always have rolled umbrellas) or other attendants. If this happens it is correct to explain briefly who you are to the member of the Royal Household who will present you: 'Your Majesty, Lady Victoria Smythe, Chair of the Friends of the Elderly in Buckinghamshire.' It is also best practice to mention it if you have encountered the member of the Royal Family before. For example, 'I had the honour of being presented to Your Majesty at the opening of our drop-in centre five years ago, sir' (*See meeting royalty, pp 15–16*).

Anyone who feels strongly that a colleague or associate should be presented, maybe because their work has been outstanding, may approach a member of the Household and ask if that person may be presented.

TEA Tea is served in various marquees. Ordinary guests just queue up to be served and are then free to wander at will. The gardens at Buckingham Palace are well worth taking advantage of, with their lakes, borders and wooded areas, as they are not otherwise open to the public. Some preselected individuals, for example ambassadors, are invited to have tea with the royal party at five o'clock in a designated tent or location. Shortly before six the royal party returns to the palace and the National Anthem is played again, signalling that the party is ending. Guests are shepherded towards the exits.

THANK YOUS It is not considered necessary to write a thank-you letter after a royal garden party. For other events guests may write to the person who asked them, that is whose name was on the invitation, such as the Lord Steward of the Household or, in the case of formal or state events, the Lord Chamberlain. In the letter a guest may ask him to 'kindly convey my/our thanks to His Majesty The King.'

PHOTOGRAPHY Photography is not permitted officially in royal palaces. For most events there is an official photographer from whom photographs may be ordered, and many occasions will be videoed, with the film for sale as a souvenir. Cameras may be removed in palaces. With the advent of smartphones people inevitably do take photographs but these should have no place at more formal events and are frowned upon at garden parties. Any photographs to mark the occasion should be taken outside the gates before the event begins.

Entertaining Members of the Royal Family

Naturally, individual members of the Royal Family may be entertained privately by their friends. In addition, those involved with charities, institutions or organisations may wish to entertain a member of the Royal Family at some point. The extended Royal Family is numerous and each person has a number of charitable patronages and other special interests or causes, with many of them carrying out hundreds of engagements each year, often several in one day.

See pp 17–18 for formal address

If an organisation wishes to secure a royal guest of honour, a request would normally be sent to the private office of that member of the Royal Family for consideration or to the lord-lieutenant of their county (*see pp 92–93*). Since they are usually very booked up, it is sensible to allow plenty of time. Priority is usually given to a cause with which the member of the Royal Family is associated, but occasionally they may agree to attend something which catches their attention or seems worthwhile.

Once a request has been accepted in outline, the private office guides the potential host through all the formalities such as wording invitations, timings and what form the event is to take. The private office should approve the wording before an invitation is printed. No one should ever indicate that the royal personage is the host as opposed to the guest of honour. Usually the wording would be, for example, 'in the gracious presence of His Majesty The King'.

Procedure

It is essential to allow as much time as possible for this part of the process and to adhere to the advice proffered by the private office. Organisers may need to be somewhat flexible and may not get all they ask for. Hosts should brief their own guests and staff on behaviour and be well organised, so that as many people as possible will get a clear view of the royal visitor, that the right people are presented and that no one takes more than their fair share of attention.

Thanks

If a royal personage has been a guest of honour then the organiser should write to thank the private secretary afterwards, asking them to pass on thanks on behalf of himself and the organisation or institution. Guests would normally thank the organiser and not feel called upon to thank the royal personage.

182 - 195

FORMAL DRESS CODES

INFORMAL DRESS CODES

Dress Codes

Dressing appropriately is not just about understanding, and respecting, specific dress codes, such as those that may be printed on an invitation, or required at a club. It is also helpful to have an idea of the up-to-date unwritten rules and to accommodate a number of other factors: weather, terrain, comfort and the nature of the event.

DRESS CODES

FORMAL DRESS CODES

WHITE TIE
BLACK TIE
MORNING DRESS
HIGHLAND DRESS

White Tie

White tie is also known as 'full evening dress', 'full dress', 'evening dress' or, informally, as 'tails'. White tie is the most formal of dress codes and is not common today. Before the Second World War it was standard evening dress for gentlemen, as may be seen in period dramas on television.

Today white tie is worn in the evening at certain royal ceremonies and balls, and state and livery dinners. White tie may also be specified for formal evening weddings and for some charity balls. It is also the dress code for some Highland balls, for those men not entitled to wear the kilt. It is no longer seen at the theatre or opera, and opera cloaks and silk top hats, along with canes and white gloves, are now only seen on stage.

'White tie' will always be stated on the invitation itself. Many organisations hosting events will say 'white or black tie', as they are aware that the former may be difficult for some invitees.

White Tie: Men

- A black single-breasted tailcoat in black wool (barathea) or ultrafine herringbone with silk peaked lapels, often grosgrain (worn unbuttoned). The coat is shorter at the front than a morning coat.
- Black trousers with a natural taper and two lines of braid down the outside leg.
- A white marcella (cotton piqué) shirt with a starched detachable wing collar and double cuffs.
- Cufflinks and studs. The shirt will usually be closed with studs rather than buttons. These may be plain white or decorative.
- A low-cut, white marcella evening waistcoat (double or single-breasted).
- A thin, white hand-tied marcella bow tie.
- Highly polished or patent black lace-up shoes, worn with black laces (traditionally ribbon) and black socks.
- In winter, a black overcoat and white silk scarf may be worn.

White Tie: Women

- Full-length, formal evening dresses. It is traditional, but not essential, to show *décolletage*. Shorter dresses or trousers, no matter how smart, are not acceptable.
- Jewellery can be striking; this is the time for the finest jewels and gems, including tiaras. Traditionally these are worn for the first time by brides, and subsequently by married women only. It is incorrect for young girls to wear tiaras on any occasion.
- Evening bags should be small and elegant.

GLOVES
: Long evening gloves are traditionally worn at balls and dinners when the dress code is 'white tie' but are no longer compulsory at many events. They work best with sleeveless dresses but older women may wear them with cap or short sleeves. With long sleeves it is better to dispense with gloves, rather than wear short ones. Gloves should be worn *en route* to an event, in a receiving line, when shaking hands and dancing. They are removed when eating (even a canapé) and at the dinner table – they should be taken off finger by finger and rested on the lap under the napkin.

WOMEN'S EVENING COATS
: For formal evening events, daytime coats look out of place. A smart evening coat, cloak, pashmina or wrap in a suitable material is preferable.

VARIATIONS ON WHITE TIE
: An alternative to white tie on certain occasions may be national costume, for example Indian, Chinese or Arabian. This will usually be stated on an invitation.

Certain societies or clubs may give balls at which their own evening dress coats are worn (usually coloured tail coats, red, blue or green, with special facings). These are worn with a white tie and waistcoat, but often with ordinary dinner jacket trousers. Non-member male guests, not entitled to the club coat, usually wear black tie.

The dress code 'full-dress ceremonial' is occasionally seen for very formal or state occasions. For evening this may usually be interpreted as white tie for civilians but it is important to ask and check with the host or organiser. For daytime events such as state funerals it can mean dress uniform for those in the services, robes for peers or judges, or particular vestments for clerics, and usually morning dress or simple business attire for others.

LOOKING BACK...

Long white evening gloves, worn with sleeveless evening dresses, were very fashionable during the early part of the 20th century. They were very much part of the outfit, effectively sleeves, rather than a mere accessory. They were often very tight, sometimes made from leather and fastened with a row of small pearl buttons inside the wrist, and so were not easy to take on and off. The hands could be taken out of the gloves and the empty gloves rolled back for practical purposes, instead of taking off the whole glove, which was both difficult and also considered immodest. The effect was not very elegant and modern gloves are normally shorter and made of more forgiving materials.

DECORATIONS

See pp 433–441 for a guide to wearing orders, medals and decorations

If the dress code is white tie and the event is a royal or state occasion, or a very formal event in, say, the City, then the dress code may state 'Evening Dress—Decorations'. It is correct to wear decorations in the presence of The King but very unusual to wear them at a private event or charity ball, however grand. It would generally be more of a mistake to wear them than not to do so.

If decorations are asked for, then knights and dames should wear the most senior chivalric orders to which they belong rather than all their decorations. Stars such as the Garter or Thistle are displayed on the left side of the evening coat or dress. Knights Grand Cross of an order may also wear a sash and badge. There are also medals that may be worn on a ribbon round the neck, just below the tie. Others may be worn as miniatures on a bar, and this is also usual when the dress code is black tie and decorations.

In practice, ex-service people are usually familiar with the wearing of medals, as are members of orders. If in doubt when attending a royal event then the best thing is to ask the Palace or relevant private secretary. It goes without saying that no one should wear decorations to which they are not entitled. Even as fancy dress these may give offence, for example to genuine veterans, so treat with care.

BLACK TIE

Black tie, which is less formal than white tie, is the most frequently encountered formal evening wear, worn for dinners (both public and private), parties and balls, as well as some Season events such as Glyndebourne. It may also be described as 'dinner jackets', 'DJs', 'dress for dinner' or, in America, as 'tuxedos'. A host may also say 'we are going to change for dinner', which will traditionally indicate black tie. It should be described as a dinner jacket, not a dinner suit.

BLACK TIE: MEN

- A black wool (barathea) or ultrafine herringbone dinner jacket, single-breasted or double-breasted with no vents, silk peaked lapels (or a shawl collar) and covered buttons. White dinner jackets were traditionally worn in hot climates but not usually in Britain, even in the summer.
- Trousers are black with a natural taper, and a single row of braid down each outside leg.

- A white evening shirt, with a marcella collar, bib and double cuffs, with a turn-down collar (not a wing-collar), worn with cufflinks and studs. A plain silk shirt with buttons may be worn but any kind of ruffles or frills should be avoided. Alternatively, a fly-fronted shirt, where the buttons are concealed, is acceptable. Adults should avoid novelty shirts and ties.
- Studs may be black or decorative.
- A black hand-tied bow tie (avoid ones which are pre-tied). The size of the bow tie should be proportionate to the size of the wearer.
- Black highly polished or patent lace-up shoes and black silk socks.
- Cummerbunds are not considered essential but may be worn. A matching tie and cummerbund in a non-conventional shade (pastels rather than burgundy and black) should be treated with caution.
- Waistcoats may be worn although they are not seen very often. They would always be considered a smart option. A waistcoat and cummerbund are never worn together.
- A white handkerchief in the left breast pocket is a classic detail.

Variations on Black Tie

In the country for dinner parties with neighbours, and especially in his own home, a man may wear a velvet smoking jacket, usually navy blue, burgundy or dark green, with a black bow tie, dinner jacket trousers and evening slippers. While this dress is acceptable for the host, it would not be right for a guest to wear this for an event with the dress code black tie actually stated on an invitation, which effectively means a dinner jacket.

Evening slippers, sometimes monogrammed or crested, may be worn and are more often found in the country.

Unless national costume is specified the usual form would be 'when in Rome' but in practice smart equivalent dress from a person's home country – for example an Indian Nehru jacket or Arabian robes – may be acceptable.

A fashionable interpretation of black tie, when a black tie instead of a bow tie is worn with a dinner jacket, is often referred to as 'Hollywood black tie'. For most formal private black tie events in Britain this would look unsuitable.

BLACK TIE: WOMEN
- Women should wear an evening dress or skirt; long, or at least not very short, is usually best. There is a difference between a formal dinner and a dinner dance; avoid wearing voluminous dresses for a dinner because they're not practical. However very tight 'red-carpet' dresses or those with a dramatic split, while stunning when making an entrance, can be uncomfortable or inappropriate at a formal event that involves both a reception and a sit-down dinner.
- If not wearing a long dress, then a cocktail dress – a fitted dress to very slightly below the knee and with a little *décolletage* – is an option. The fabric should be suited to evening such as silk, crepe or chiffon.
- Tailored or palazzo-style evening trousers and a formal top are also an option. If in doubt, consult the hostess.
- Although the dress code is 'black tie', dresses need not be black. Equally, wearing black does not ensure the right level of formality.
- Tights should be worn, black or sheer, with knee-length dresses.
- Fine or costume jewellery is appropriate, but not tiaras.
- An elegant evening bag should be used.
- Ideally, an evening coat should be worn, as for white tie.

PARTIES
Parties often do not fit into the more traditional formats of white tie, black tie or smart casual. They may even be fancy dress. The key thing is to change for the event and not to wear work clothes. When an event is themed it may be hard to judge the formality, so take on board the style of event, as indicated by the invitation and the venue, and ask the host. It is now also acceptable for men at relaxed, yet formal, evening events to wear a velvet jacket, Nehru-collared jacket or moleskin suit with an open-necked party shirt. Shirts may feature non-formal prints – for example small flowers – and brighter colours. These jackets and shirts may be coupled with smart dark-coloured jeans or trousers. Such combinations indicate an effort has been made, whereas a dark suit may indicate that a man may not have tried to put together an evening look.

Women should make it clear that an effort has been made. Theme parties can be a minefield. While it is good manners to make an effort and disrespectful to ignore hosts' requests, that doesn't necessarily mean, for example, hiring a full theatrical outfit or feeling miserable all evening. At the very least, well chosen accessories or jewellery can indicate the style or period required.

Morning Dress

Morning dress is also known as 'formal day dress'. The jacket is always referred to as a 'morning coat'. Morning dress is traditional for men at weddings, formal memorial services, some official functions and formal daytime events in the presence of The King and some Season locations, such as the Royal Enclosure at Ascot. Morning dress should not be specified to be worn at an event starting after 6pm.

Morning Dress: Men

- A black or grey matt morning coat, single-breasted with peaked lapels, curved front edges sloping back into tails.
- Trousers are grey or grey and black-striped.
- A white or light-coloured shirt with a white turned-down collar, double-cuffs and cufflinks.
- Waistcoats are usually buff, grey or duck-egg blue and double or single-breasted. Double-breasted waistcoats may have a lapel, either shawl or peak, and are worn fully buttoned. Single-breasted waistcoats either have a step collar or no collar, and the lowest button is always left undone. Fancy waistcoats, such as those worn by members of the Eton Society, are sometimes worn, especially at weddings. Avoid anything backless.
- Ties are preferred to cravats. A smart woven silk tie is acceptable. A tie pin will add an extra flourish of dandyism.
- Highly polished (not patent) black lace-up/smart slip-on shoes.
- A grey or black top hat is worn with morning dress for racing but at most other events it is carried rather than worn and may be dispensed with.
- A handkerchief may be worn in the left breast pocket with an understated buttonhole.

Morning Dress: Women

- Smart daywear, such as a dress or skirt worn with a jacket.
- Dresses should not be too short or too revealing. They may be worn with no jacket in summer but if so, should be modest with sleeves or at least not narrow straps.
- Shoulders may be covered by a bolero, shrug or pashmina but a tailored jacket or coat is better for the races or smart weddings.
- Avoid very high heels or evening-style shoes – wedges are sensible if it may be soft underfoot (eg around churchyards, marquees or racecourses). Tights should be worn.
- Daytime jewellery; pearls are a good choice.
- Hats are usual, especially at weddings, but not always required. They are essential for certain Season settings, such as the Royal Enclosure at Ascot. It is best to choose a hat that may be kept on throughout the day and which is securely fitted.

Highland Dress

Scottish or Highland dress is an alternative to formal British dress. It can be worn in Scotland or south of the border for certain occasions, eg a Scottish bridegroom may wear the kilt at his wedding, even if not held in Scotland. Highland dress is worn at the Royal Caledonian Ball held in London each spring. It may also be worn when 'national dress' is stipulated.

Highland Dress: Men
- The kilt, fairly long, fastened with a pin, with a dress sporran.
- A plain white shirt, with either a black bow tie or a lace jabot.
- A Highland jacket (also called a doublet) with ornamental silver buttons. There are several styles but they are normally made from black or dark coloured baratheа, broadcloth or dark velvet. They may be worn with a waistcoat.
- Knee-length socks or stockings ('hose'), patterned, or green or red (never plain cream), secured with a silk garter (sometimes called a flash). A dagger or *sgian dubh* (pronounced 'ski-an doo') may be placed on the right-hand side.
- Black patent leather dancing pumps or buckled brogues are traditional. A black evening shoe is also acceptable.

Trews
Some men prefer tartan trousers, 'trews', which may be worn with a velvet smoking jacket and black tie in place of dinner jacket trousers. Trews are always cut without a side seam.

Highland Dress: Women
- A long dress, with a skirt full enough for dancing reels, is worn at Highland balls (eg the Skye Balls).
- White dresses are often worn with sashes, particularly at formal balls, but some wear colours or patterns.
- A tartan sash is worn diagonally. Clanswomen wear it over the right shoulder, across the breast and secured by a pin or small brooch on the right shoulder.
- The wife of a clan chief or the wife of a colonel of a Scottish regiment would wear a slightly wider sash over the left shoulder, secured with a brooch on the left shoulder.
- Non-clanswomen attending the balls should wear similar long dresses but without a sash.

Tartans
It is best not to wear a specific tartan unless connected to a specific clan. Many Scottish clans have one or more tartans – typically dress tartan and hunting tartan – which may be worn by members of that clan and their wives. Daughters may continue to wear it after marriage. For Highland balls men not entitled to wear the kilt may wear black or occasionally white tie.

DRESS CODES

INFORMAL DRESS CODES

Lounge Suits
Smart Casual
Country Clothing

Lounge Suits

'Lounge suit' is an expression only seen on invitations as a dress code. In conversation the terms dark suit or business suit or possibly business dress or business attire are used.

'Lounge suits' for Men

This dress code is used for occasions with various degrees of formality and means a suit worn with a shirt and tie. Lounge suits are worn for most business events, both daytime and evening, and for many social events, such as lunches, receptions, dinner, weddings, christenings and funerals. Dark suits are also correct for flat racing, other than events such as Ascot. They may be worn at dinner parties, especially when people come directly from the office, but are less acceptable at country dinner parties.

A three-piece suit consists of a single-breasted jacket, a single- or double-breasted waistcoat and trousers. When wearing a single-breasted waistcoat, the bottom button is always left undone. A two-piece suit consists of single-breasted or double-breasted jacket with trousers (no waistcoat). Belts should not be worn with a waistcoat or double-breasted suit.

A shirt with a turndown (not button-down) collar should be worn with a tie and the top button of the shirt must be done up. The most versatile tie knots are the four-in-hand and the half-Windsor; large Windsor knots should generally be avoided.

Dark suits are still seen on the older rural generation at formal or official events, such as agricultural shows, when there is a luncheon tent for members or notables, and for a day in London.

'Lounge suits' for Women

For evening events, a smart, or cocktail, dress (with sleeves or a jacket) is a suitable choice. For daytime events women should wear a day dress, trouser suit, or skirt and jacket or coat. The overall impression is not quite so formal as when the dress code is morning dress. A neat, tailored look is best for business, with length on or just below the knee. Printed fabric and a looser and longer silhouette works best in the country.

Day to Night: Women

If the dress code is 'lounge suits', women can alter their usual office wear, for example by opting for a smart dress underneath a fitted jacket. In the evening, the jacket can be removed. Modest-heeled shoes can be changed for something higher and a few bold accessories worn. Swap a daytime bag for something smaller and more elegant for the evening.

Smart Casual

'Smart casual' can be the hardest dress code to interpret and a great deal depends on the invitation and the type of event. A printed invitation suggests a smarter event than a text or email.

'Formal' Smart Casual for Men

It is worth remembering that town/city events will generally be more fashionable and formal than those held in the country. Similarly, if the host or hostess is very traditional or of an older generation, then the style may be more formal.

For men, smart casual requires a jacket or blazer, flannels, needlecord trousers, or chinos (not jeans), a shirt with a collar, not a t-shirt, and smart shoes, not necessarily lace-ups, but not trainers or sandals. A sweater may be worn if it is cold. Ties are not necessary but carrying one is often a good tip, just in case. Smart casual is usually a summer dress code, but if it is winter then opt for an overcoat rather than an anorak or parka. A tweed sports jacket may take the place of a blazer and may be worn with cords or old-fashioned cavalry twill.

'Formal' Smart Casual for Women

For 'formal' smart casual events, a smart day dress, worn with a jacket, is a safe choice for women. At more casual events, dress down a little – for example, smart trousers or a skirt, with a cardigan. Avoid wearing denim, unless it is immaculate and balanced with a tailored jacket and smart accessories. Also avoid high heels and wearing suits, as they look like business clothes. Sports clothes and sports shoes such as trainers are incorrect.

'Informal' Smart Casual for Men

It may be worth considering the details of the invitation before asking the host or hostess for advice. It can usually be interpreted as jeans for men but smart, clean, dark-coloured jeans. Remember you are going out so change from what you have been wearing at home. Other than in high summer or on the beach, trousers are better than shorts and polo shirts better than collarless t-shirts. Just because an event is informal it is not synonymous with making no effort.

'Informal' Smart Casual for Women

Study the invitation and dress for the occasion, the time of day and the season. Denim should be immaculate and sports or beach clothes avoided unless the occasion demands. However, too much tailoring and heels can also look wrong. If you are unsure, find out as much as possible about what other people are intending to wear and if that isn't possible ask the host or hostess. It is always more polite to the host to dress up. 'Come as you are' rarely means what it says. Be prepared to adjust your outfit at the last minute. For women, this may mean dressing down an outfit, for example swapping heels for flats, taking off dressy jewellery or removing a jacket and putting on a cardigan.

Country Clothing

Practicalities Dress codes in rural areas may be more traditional than in cities. Some guidelines on what to wear are based on practicality; clothes should be appropriate for the weather and outdoor activities, and warm enough for drafty houses. For example a woman would not wear very high heels and a short tight skirt to a Sunday lunch, which may include a walk. Instead jeans or cords, with a shirt or jumper, is correct.

Country Style and Colours Traditionally black is still seen as a city colour, other than for funerals. Men wear brown rather than black shoes, and tweeds. Women might wear black for formal dinners or dances but not for daytime. Women would not usually wear a tailored jacket indoors in a social rather than business setting, but might choose either a gilet, or a jumper or cardigan.

Outdoors weatherproof jackets are worn in preference to woollen overcoats. Colours are muted; greens and browns are more rural than black or navy blue or anything hi-vis. Country sports, even if not practised, are the inspiration for the 'correct style'; it is worth noting, however, that the wearing of jodhpurs or hacking jackets by fashionistas may cause amusement in country circles. Dressing for an activity in which a person is not taking part is unwise; for example a man who is not actually shooting should avoid plus fours.

Accessories Scarves and woollen or fake fur hats are frequently worn by women, while flat caps for men may be worn. Walking shoes or boots are left at the door and slip-on shoes such as loafers usually worn indoors. The wearing of trainers indoors and outdoors is generally frowned upon.

Formality Full-time country people tend to dress up for social and sporting events more than weekenders, who may take the opportunity to dress down, and this can cause clashes of dress codes. As for other dress codes, err on the side of effort and do not be afraid to ask in advance what others are going to be wearing.

Rites of Passage
Growing Up
Engagements
Weddings
Divorce
Death

Rites of Passage

198 - 209

BIRTHS

CHRISTENINGS

COMING OF AGE

Growing Up

Births are a time when congratulations are formally offered to new parents, and the baby is welcomed to the world and named. As new parents are coming to terms with a major change in their lives, it is important for friends and relations to be tactful, discreet and alert to their feelings and respectful of their wishes. As children grow up, their families, relations and friends celebrate the rites of passage, both religious and secular, that mark their transition into adulthood.

GROWING UP

BIRTHS

ANNOUNCEMENTS
AFTER THE BIRTH

Etiquette may not be at the forefront of the parents' minds when a baby is on its way but births and christenings are rites of passage, which have accrued traditions in British culture. There are established guidelines and contemporary considerations relating to announcing births, presents and ceremonies, about which it is helpful to be informed, although personal style will always play a major role when it comes to the choices of any given family.

Announcements

Traditionally, it is the father's responsibility to spread the good news, but a grandparent or other relation often shares the duty. Immediate family and close friends should be informed as soon as possible by telephone; it is sensible to prepare a list in advance of those nearest and dearest that require a phone call.

Other family and friends can then be contacted and it is customary to use other media – for example, text message, email – to spread the word. It is essential that the most important people have learnt of the news in person before it is announced on social media sites.

Cards

Cards, sometimes complete with a coloured ribbon (or a photograph), may be sent out at a slightly later stage, with details such as the baby's weight, if desired. Often, this may double up as a thank-you card if a present has been received.

If there are complications, the announcement may be delayed until the health or wellbeing of the mother and baby are known.

Newspaper Announcements

Birth announcements in the paper are traditionally very simple and succinct. Announcements are usually confined to the broadsheets – effectively *The Times* and *Daily Telegraph*, though fewer people now do both – or, if appropriate, a local newspaper

A traditional announcement would read: *Debrett – On 20th August to John and Charlotte (née Berkeley), a daughter, Caroline Jane.*

Unmarried couples will use both parents' first name(s) and surname. For example: *Maddox – On 20th August to Richard Maddox and Ilsa Curzon, a daughter, Alice Louise.*

Single parents may use only one parent's name. For example: *Curzon – On 20th August to Ilsa, a daughter, Lucy Claire.*

If it is not a first child the sibling may be named (for example, 'a sister for Joanna') and occasionally the hospital (certain fashionable private London hospitals include the announcements in their package and always name themselves). Additions such as 'much loved' or thanks to the medical team are less traditional but may be included and may reflect particular circumstances.

ADOPTION CARDS The traditional wording for an adoption card is:

> Mr and Mrs Debrett wish to announce the arrival of Thomas Edward into their lives.

A less formal and more contemporary version might be:

> John and Charlotte Debrett are thrilled to announce the homecoming of their son Thomas Edward.

ANNOUNCEMENTS ON SOCIAL MEDIA There are no conventions that govern announcing a birth on Facebook, Instagram, Twitter and so on, and the style and wording of the announcement will be very much dictated by the people involved. However, if they are inveterate users of social media, both parents need to agree a coordinated approach. They should decide which platform/s they will use, work out the wording and decide what they want to do about photos.

Friends of new parents must not steal their thunder by precipitately announcing the birth to the world on social media. They must wait until family and close friends have been informed.

AFTER THE BIRTH

VISITING IN HOSPITAL Visiting mothers and babies in hospital has become confined to close family and friends, as time spent there is so much shorter than it used to be. Check before going to see someone and before sending flowers, as these may not arrive in time or be permitted.

If visiting, it is usual to take a small baby present, such as clothing or a soft toy. Be aware that the mother may be exhausted and that the baby may need to be fed or changed and that its needs are paramount. Visits must be kept short.

KEEPING TRACK AND THANKING New mothers may want to have some cards ready and even stamped addressed envelopes to hand so as to send thanks for flowers and presents before going home or as soon as they get home. This can be a good idea as life can become very hectic so it is sensible to be well prepared. Alternatively, they may want to keep track of presents by making lists, as it is easy to forget in the overwhelming first few weeks at home.

It is not necessary to respond to every card immediately. It is polite, however, to acknowledge them in due course either by sending announcement cards (as discussed above), or a text message or email.

Congratulations Cards to new parents may be addressed to the mother or both parents.

Visiting at Home Meeting new babies is a great pleasure for many friends and relations but may be exhausting for the new mother, so tact and consideration are needed. Keep visits brief and uncomplicated and do not take offence if asked to postpone. Never just drop in; always arrange a time and be punctual. The baby may need to be fed during the visit or the mother may not wish to wake the baby, so visitors should not be too demanding. This is an occasion when offers of help – for example making tea or bringing some food – will really be appreciated.

A small present will be welcome but there is no need to overdo it. If you wish to be very generous then the baby's first Christmas or first birthday may be a better time, when the baby is no longer being overwhelmed with soft toys. It can also be a good idea to take along a small present for a toddler or older sibling.

Baby Showers Baby showers, which usually take place before the baby is born, are an American rather than a British tradition. If invited to one then the idea is to provide something practical; gender-neutral colours are best. The presents may be opened there and then and elaborate gift-wrapping is part of the shower culture.

It is sensible when giving clothing to size up (so choose for around six months) and consider the season in which the baby will be wearing it. It is considerate to enclose a gift receipt so that the present may be exchanged if it does not fit. Never take offence if you do not see the baby wearing the cardigan you knitted or the designer outfit on which you spent a fortune.

Some choose to give a present to the mother at the baby shower, rather than the unborn baby, and wait until the baby has safely arrived before giving a present.

Growing Up

Christenings

Religious Rituals
Naming Rituals

The ancient tradition of christening is still popular and even couples who are not regular church-goers may opt to have children christened. Other families choose a secular naming ceremony, which may take place at the same time, usually when the baby is between three months and a year old. Obviously others may belong to different religions or churches with their own traditions.

Religious Rituals

Baptism
The Church of England and the Roman Catholic Church refer officially to baptism or infant baptism. Both churches prefer the baby to be baptised during a regular Sunday service, often at the same time as other families. If the baptism is during morning service or mass, it will usually be followed by a lunch.

It is still possible to have a private christening in a church of your choice, although it may take some tact and perseverance. If you have a special relationship with a priest or vicar from a different parish, who is for instance a family friend, then you will need to clear the arrangements with the local parish priest or vicar. Private christenings are often in the afternoon and followed by a tea, but this will be dictated by the local church's timetable.

Church of England
During the baptism service, the parents and godparents gather together with the baby (traditionally wearing a white gown) and the vicar, usually around the church's font, to make a series of religious declarations. They are required to declare, in unison, their belief in God, and that the child will be brought up following Jesus. The vicar marks the sign of the cross on the baby's forehead, then pours some water on the child's head, symbolising the washing away of all sin. If the ceremony is taking place during a normal service, the congregation may join in at this point, and a candle is lit symbolising Jesus as the light of the world. During the ceremony the mother usually holds the baby, but the godmother may hold the baby at some point. The register is signed after the ceremony, usually by the father.

Roman Catholic
Baptism is one of the seven sacraments of the Catholic Church. Traditionally infants were baptised as soon as possible after they were born; today the ceremony often takes place a little later but the baby may well be younger than is usual within the Anglican Church. The child should wear a white garment and in addition to being baptised with water is anointed with oil (chrism).

Godparents

Traditionally there were three godparents, two of the same sex and one of the opposite sex. Today there may be six, sometimes more. Godparents are usually a mixture of friends and relations.

In the Church of England, godparents must have been baptised themselves, preferably confirmed too; in the case of Catholics at least one godparent, usually of the same sex as the baby, must be a full member of the Church in good standing – in other words a practising Catholic.

Being a Godparent

The aim of a good godparent should be to have a direct relationship with the child, separate from the parents.

It is an honour and a responsibility to be asked to be a godparent. If asked, it is almost impossible to say no without giving offence, but if a person really has good reason to refuse they must do so, and the parents should not take umbrage.

Choosing Godparents

Parents may choose friends or relations or both, and a mixture may be a good plan. Friendships do not always last and parents must accept that some godparents will not have much of a relationship with the child.

Parents should therefore choose people they love and trust, and not base their choice on hopes for financial gain or because they want trophy godparents for social reasons. Many people are reciprocal godparents to each other's children, which can work well. Others go down the generations within the extended family or close family friends, choosing the child of their own godparent for their baby, which can prove an enduring bond. Just occasionally someone will propose themselves as a godparent. It is polite to agree, but the parents may want to have this person in addition to others they have already chosen.

Godparents' Presents

A godparent is expected to give a christening present, which is usually something that will last rather than, for instance, a toy. Silver was traditional; laying down some good wine may be an option, or giving a pearl necklace. Premium bonds or other savings accounts may be set up, or a life membership of an organisation, for example the National Trust, may be suitable. Godparents have been known to pay school fees, buy a round-the-world ticket, host an 18th birthday party or even make a godchild their heir, if they have no other children. Generally a godparent will be expected to give a Christmas and a birthday present up to the age of 18 or 21 and then a wedding present.

Godchildren Godchildren must always be made to write thank-you letters from as soon as it is feasible, and if they do not do so they should not be surprised if the presents stop. They may invite their godparents to their 18th or 21st.

Relations with godparents may not remain as close as godchildren get older, but nevertheless godchildren should continue to write thank-you letters, and let their godparents know when they get engaged and invite them to their wedding, unless they have completely lost touch. Invitations may even be extended to christenings of their own children.

Invitations

Notification to godparents, friends and family may be by post, telephone call or email and will include mention of any party afterwards. Traditionally, formal invitations were not sent out for christenings or baptisms, but some parents do choose to send them. These are either pre-printed or bespoke cards; the style of the invitation should reflect the level of formality of the service and party.

Traditional Formal Invitations Traditionally-styled, formal invitations are usually printed on high-quality white card (600 gsm), measuring W7 x H5½ inches (14 x 18 cm). The wording should read:

> David and Lucy
>
> *John and Charlotte Debrett*
> *invite you to celebrate the christening of*
> *Thomas Edward*
> *at St Botolph's Church, Hanbury*
> *on Sunday 8th November*
> *and afterwards at the Old Hall*
>
> R.S.V.P.   11.00am Service
> lottie@gmail.co.uk   12.30pm Lunch

Pre-printed cards are available with spaces left blank for the guests' names, the baby's name, and the date, location and time of the christening, to be handwritten. The pre-printed wording usually reflects the sex of the child, for example '*...request the pleasure of your company at the christening of their son...*'.

Replies
: Guests should reply to invitations promptly. The level of formality of the reply should reflect the style and tone of the invitation. If a very formal invitation is received, it is advisable to reply in the third person, as for a wedding invitation.

Receptions
: Parties after the service may include a lunch (possibly a buffet), or tea in the case of an afternoon ceremony. The party is usually fairly informal and not all that long, as the baby's routine needs to be considered. It is best to have any party fairly near the church, whether it is in a hotel or similar venue, or a private house.

  Drinks are served, most usually champagne and wine, as well as tea or coffee and soft drinks. Traditionally the top layer of the wedding cake was saved and re-iced to use as a christening cake. A godparent may toast the baby, but long speeches are unusual.

  Parents will expect some people to bring presents, so it is sensible to have somewhere to put these, but not necessary to open them there and then. Thank-you letters should be sent promptly.

  Guests may bring small children of their own or the baby may have siblings and cousins, so it is a good idea to have some help and to have organised suitable food and possibly a play area for them. It would be very unusual not to invite children; however parents bringing children must look after them properly.

Guest Lists
: Large parties for christenings are unusual. The essential guests are the godparents, grandparents, the parents' siblings, and perhaps the godparents of the baby's siblings and the closest family friends. Cousins will not always be included, nor will neighbours or friends, even very close friends. Godparents are usually accompanied by a spouse or partner.

  Parents may need to work the date round the most important guests. If only the actual godparent can come and the spouse is away then the godparent should come alone. If a godparent is unable to come, then another close friend or family member may stand in for them – for practical reasons – during the service.

It is essential to invite the clergyman and spouse to any party or reception. Busy parish priests may not be able to come and parents must allow for this.

Photographs Photographs in church should always be non-invasive and cleared beforehand with the vicar or priest. Photographs at the party should be organised efficiently for the sake of the baby. Godparents may want to be photographed holding the baby but it is unwise to force this.

Dress It is correct to dress smartly, with men in suits, or a country jacket and tie, and women in dresses and jackets but not necessarily hats (although it is not wrong to wear one). It is no longer necessary for women to cover their heads in Catholic churches though some may choose to do so. Men should remove hats. Children should be dressed smartly.

The baby may wear a traditional christening robe, which may be a family heirloom, but these may not always fit larger babies. White is traditional and a dress and shawl look best – there are specialist companies that make modern versions.

Naming Rituals

Naming Ceremonies Naming ceremonies are a non-religious option for parents who wish to celebrate, in some official capacity, the arrival of their child with family and friends. They have no legal standing, but may be organised in association with a local authority, or through a private company. These ceremonies are often led by a trained 'celebrant' and, instead of godparents, individuals are asked to be 'supporting adults'. A certificate is usually presented as a keepsake. It is usual for the parents to host a reception for guests after the ceremony with some food, drinks and a naming cake (similar to a christening cake).

Naming Parties or Naming Days Many parents now choose to host a naming day or naming party themselves, as a non-religious alternative to a christening. The format of the day will vary from family to family, but a lunch for family and close friends is a popular option.

A few friends and/or relations are usually asked take on the role and responsibilities of godparents, and there may be a short speech followed by a toast to the new baby. It is usual for guests to take a present for the baby, as they would to a christening.

Growing Up

Coming of Age

Confirmation
Bar and Bat Mitzvahs
18ths and 21sts

Confirmation

Confirmation is the formal recognition of a baptised individual's commitment to the Christian faith. In both the Church of England and the Roman Catholic Church only bishops can conduct confirmations.

General Considerations

There is no set age, but it is usual to be confirmed during the early teens. Individuals must have been baptised before they can be candidates for confirmation. All candidates will undergo preparation for confirmation. While the detail of this varies from parish to parish, the general purpose is to ensure that they have an understanding about life as a Christian within the family of the Church.

Confirmation may take place in the church that the candidate usually attends; it is also usual to be confirmed at a school church. Roman Catholic children will have made their First Holy Communion at a younger age before confirmation, whereas in the Church of England communion follows confirmation.

The Ceremony

Only very close friends or relations will be invited to witness the ceremony. In general confirmation is seen as a private affirmation of faith and an assertion of familial religious affiliations. It is not usually celebrated by a wider circle of friends and relations. In the Church of England, godparents would be expected to attend.

In the Catholic Church, the child, who is normally confirmed in his/her early teens, will also have a confirmation sponsor, who may be nearer the child's age. This person must be a practising Catholic whose role is to keep an eye on the child's religious life. The confirmation candidate will also choose an additional saint's name, spoken by the bishop during the ceremony, but this will not become part of their official or legal names and in practice will rarely be used.

Conduct

If you are invited to a confirmation, remember that it is primarily a religious ceremony. Dress conservatively and behave respectfully in church – do not whisper, switch off your mobile and do not take photographs.

Confirmation Presents

These are often of a religious nature and may be Bibles, or gold or silver crosses and chains. However, non-religious presents such as other books or cufflinks may be preferred.

Bar and Bat Mitzvahs

Bar mitzvahs and bat mitzvahs are Jewish coming-of-age ceremonies. They are the most important rites of passage in the Jewish faith. The ceremonies are held when a boy turns 13 (a bar mitzvah) and when a girl turns 12 (a bat mitzvah), however many ceremonies are now held at the age of 13. Ceremonies are held on the first Saturday (Shabbat) after the relevant birthday.

It is quite usual for the celebrations to spread out over the whole weekend, with a family gathering on a Friday evening, the ceremony on a Saturday and the party on a Sunday.

Invitations

Formal invitations are sent out by the parents, inviting guests to the ceremony at the synagogue, and to attend the reception afterwards at their home or another venue. This may range from a celebratory meal to a lavish party. For example:

Joseph and Rachel Golden are delighted to invite you
to celebrate the Bar Mitzvah of their son
Simon
who will read Maftir and Haftorah
at 11 o'clock, on Saturday, 14 October 2023
The Central Synagogue, 36–40 Hallam Street, London W1
and afterwards for lunch at the Park Lane Hotel, London W1

The RSVP address is included in the bottom left corner and the dress code in the bottom right. Guests should respond with a handwritten reply. For less formal celebrations, invitations are often sent by email, note or postcard, or by word of mouth.

Dress Code

Men should wear a formal suit and skullcap (they will be distributed), women smart day dress (ensuring their arms are covered above the elbow and their legs above the knee) and a hat.

Conduct

Guests should arrive at the synagogue on foot (many Jews do not drive during the day on Saturdays). Men and women will often be seated separately.

While there is often singing during the ceremony, some of the service involves standing in silence. Appropriate times to leave the room may be observed from the actions of the congregation. Guests give presents and they are sent in advance or taken to the post-ceremony celebrations, never the synagogue.

18THS AND 21STS

Both 18ths and 21sts are seen as landmark birthdays for both sexes. It is advisable, therefore, to 'choose' between the two for large celebrations and more generous birthday presents.

Formal Birthday Parties

If a large formal event is planned, such as a marquee party or event in a hired venue, parents should check with their son or daughter that this is what they genuinely want, rather than using it as an excuse to indulge in celebrations they would like. They should pay careful attention to the wishes of their son or daughter to ensure the party is a success for everyone.

Themed or fancy-dress parties are a popular alternative to formal dress codes. A theme may be loosely and often wittily interpreted, while fancy-dress is a little more prescriptive and may even involve the hiring of a costume. Hosts should ensure guests are not too inconvenienced by the theme, and should always make an effort to dress up themselves.

Invitations
See pp 313–319 for invitations

The invitation should make it absolutely clear that this is a party to celebrate an 18th or 21st birthday – no guest should be taken by surprise. If there is a specific dress code, such as black tie, or a theme, this should be stated clearly on the invitation.

Party Planning

It is very common for a formal 18th or 21st party to be a mixed generation event, where contemporaries of the son or daughter are mixed with older relations, godparents and friends of their parents who have played a significant role in their lives.

The numbers should be carefully managed to ensure a balanced mix of older and younger guests. Make a decision with everyone involved as to whether to have mixed-generation tables. Food and music should have universal appeal; alternatively, communicate to the older generation that the party may be more orientated towards a younger audience as the night goes on.

It is usual to toast the boy or girl who is turning 18 or 21, and to have a speech by a parent (usually the father), godparent or elder sibling. Sometimes a close friend will also make a short speech.

Presents

Mark the occasion with a generous present, particularly if you are a godparent or close relation. Many adults treat the coming-of-age birthday as the last occasion on which they are expected to give a regular birthday present.

214 - 225

PROPOSALS

ANNOUNCEMENTS

CELEBRATIONS

ENGAGEMENTS

Traditionally, an engagement is celebrated by the families on both sides, and a public announcement of the engagement is made. It is important for the couple to understand that relationships with each other's families that are formed now are not just about the wedding, but will last well into the years to come.

ENGAGEMENTS

PROPOSALS

ENGAGEMENT RINGS
PRACTICALITIES

Asking for her Hand in Marriage

It was traditional for the man to ask his future father-in-law's permission for his daughter's hand in marriage. This convention is no longer observed, although some men still follow the formality of making their intentions known to the bride's father or parents before proposing. Some couples may choose to seek permission, as a mere formality, after they become engaged.

Proposals

A proposal of marriage is an occasion that will be recalled time and time again, so thought and planning are required to make it memorable. The manner in which a proposal is made is dependent upon the couple; the most important thing is that it is suited to the personality and style of the bride-to-be. If the prospective bride has already indicated a preferred style of proposal (eg private, not in front of family) then her suitor must not be swayed by pressure from others to ignore her wishes. It is worth remembering that there is no 'right' or 'wrong' way to ask for someone's hand in marriage.

Most suitors choose to ask the question quietly – getting down on one knee may well be appreciated. Some may choose a public proposal. It is important that the proposal is not made on an occasion when it upstages another important event such as the prospective bride's graduation or a family wedding.

Proposing is no longer solely the role of the man; it is perfectly acceptable for women to propose marriage (and not just on a leap year). Same-sex couples may choose to draw on traditional practices to create their own ritual.

It is traditional for a man to propose with an engagement ring, but many do so without one so that the couple can choose the ring together. If there is no ring for the proposal, the bride-to-be can be given a token to mark the occasion, for example a bracelet or necklace. A ring should be on her finger within a reasonable time – weeks, not months – of her accepting the proposal.

Looking Back...

There is a tradition in Britain that in leap years women may propose. It is said that in about 1288 Queen Margaret of Scotland passed a law that a man who refused a proposal could be fined; compensation ranged from a kiss to a silk gown. In 1839, Queen Victoria proposed to Prince Albert at Windsor Castle because she was The Queen and he was only a prince. As The Queen, she was able to ignore the leap year tradition, but the couple were married in 1840 – a leap year.

Engagement Rings

Choosing Some men want to propose with the engagement ring and decide to choose one on their own, or with the help of a trusted, usually female, friend. They should be confident of the bride's taste and remember that she will be wearing it every day, for many years to come.

If the couple choose the ring together, a budget should be established to assist the bride in making a realistic choice. Alternatively the bridegroom may choose a jeweller and pick out a few within an affordable price range from which the bride can make her choice. The engagement ring should be the very best that the bridegroom can afford.

If there is a family heirloom or antique ring that belonged to a grandmother or older relation, the bride should be given the option of having the ring adapted or re-set.

Use trusted and recommended jewellers where possible. A large diamond is not necessarily more valuable than a smaller, well cut, flawless stone, and a discreet ring may be more suited to everyday wear.

Styles The bride should try on and experiment with different styles and shapes of stones and settings. It is best to try them alongside a wedding band to get a true feel for how the ring will eventually sit on the finger.

Diamonds are the traditional choice, but other stones, such as sapphires and rubies, may also be chosen or used as side-settings. While solitaires are popular, other styles are also traditional.

Popular metals for engagement rings are white gold, gold and platinum, which is the most hardwearing. The metal of the wedding band should be the same as the engagement ring both to ensure that they match and to avoid a harder metal rubbing away at a softer metal.

Bridegroom's Present Many brides-to-be like to give a substantial present to their fiancé as a way of marking the significance of the occasion and giving something in return for the engagement ring. Traditional choices include a watch, cufflinks or a fountain pen.

Practicalities

Length of an Engagement

The length of an engagement varies greatly but, on average, will usually last between six and twelve months. An engagement is the time between accepting a proposal and the marriage, rather than just a separate stage or status of the relationship. Less than six months would not allow enough time to organise a wedding comfortably, but anything over twelve months may feel too long. The length of time generally depends on the work commitments of the couple, the scale and size of the wedding, the availability of the wedding venue and the season in which the couple wish to be married.

See p 229 for setting the date

The Couple

A couple that is engaged should be regarded, socially, as good as married. They should be invited jointly to parties, weddings and gatherings, even if both are not known to the host. Unlike married couples, engaged couples were conventionally seated next to one another at dinner; this tradition is now quite relaxed.

Calling off an Engagement

Traditionally, if there was an engagement announcement published in the newspaper, then it was usual to place a small cancellation notice if the engagement was called off. This procedure is now extremely unusual but, if deemed necessary – for example if the couple are of particular note or standing – then it would read: 'The marriage between Mr John Debrett and Miss Charlotte Berkeley will not now take place.'

If the invitations have already been posted, then a printed card is sent out to guests (*See p 242*). Any presents received should be returned.

Traditionally it is correct for the woman to offer to give back the engagement ring; this may vary depending on personal circumstances.

Looking Back...

Regard rings were popular in Victorian and Edwardian times; the first letters of the different stones spelt 'REGARD' with a sequence of ruby, emerald, garnet, amethyst, ruby and diamond. This fashion was sometimes adapted for other words or names; Queen Alexandra's engagement ring was set with beryl, emerald, ruby, turquoise, jacinth and a second emerald, spelling 'BERTIE' – the nickname of her fiancé the Prince of Wales, the future Edward VII.

ENGAGEMENTS

ANNOUNCEMENTS

FORMAL ANNOUNCEMENTS

SPREADING THE NEWS The parents of both the bride and bridegroom should always be the first to hear of an engagement. News should be conveyed in person wherever possible or, at the very least, by telephone. The bridegroom may already have told his own parents of the bride's parent about his intentions, so the announcement may not come as a huge surprise.

Telephone calls to the rest of the family, godparents and close friends will follow; a round-robin email or text announcing the news is fine for everyone else. Following that, social media and the grapevine can be relied upon to spread the word, or you may choose more targeted methods.

If opting to spread the news by social media, it is eye-catching and effective to post an engagement photo. If you're going to have a wedding hashtag (useful for updates, instructions and uploading photographs), don't use it in the announcement or you may find yourself spammed by planners, caterers and suppliers.

Formal Announcements

It is traditional to place a formal announcement in the newspaper, most usually *The Times, Daily Telegraph* and, if appropriate, a local paper.

The wording should include the names of the betrothed, with a heading styled either 'Mr J Debrett and Miss C Berkeley' or 'John Debrett and Charlotte Berkeley' depending upon the newspaper.

The couple's parentage is detailed, along with a geographical location. Residential addresses are usually no longer included.

A traditional announcement would read:
Mr J Debrett and Miss C Berkeley
The engagement is announced between John,
son of Mr and Mrs George Debrett of Lewes,
East Sussex, and Charlotte, daughter of Mr and
Mrs Hugh Berkeley, of Stroud, Gloucestershire.

The Hon P Maddox and Miss A Hill
The engagement is announced between Peter, only
son of Viscount and Viscountess Tilney, and Anthea,
younger daughter of Mr and Mrs Gregory Hill.

The Marquess of Audley and Lady Hermione Hays
The engagement is announced between Peregrine, eldest son of the Duke and Duchess of Mayfair, and Hermione, youngest daughter of the Earl and Countess of Aldford.

If one set of parents is divorced:
Mr J Debrett and Miss C Berkeley
The engagement is announced between John, first son of Mr George Debrett of Lewes, East Sussex and Mrs Jane Debrett of Chelsea, London, and Charlotte, third daughter of Mr and Mrs Hugh Berkeley, of Stroud, Gloucestershire.

If one set of parents is divorced and remarried:
Mr J Debrett and Miss C Berkeley
The engagement is announced between John, eldest son of Mr George Debrett of Lewes, East Sussex, and Mrs Jane Mount-Jones of Cobham, Surrey, and Charlotte, third daughter of Mr and Mrs Hugh Berkeley, of Stroud, Gloucestershire.

If the bride's mother is widowed:
Mr J Debrett and Miss C Berkeley
The engagement is announced between John, first son of Mr and Mrs George Debrett of Lewes, East Sussex, and Charlotte, third daughter of Mrs Hugh Berkeley, of Stroud, Gloucestershire.

If the bride's father is widowed:
Mr J Debrett and Miss C Berkeley
The engagement is announced between John, first son of Mr and Mrs George Debrett of Lewes, East Sussex, and Charlotte, third daughter of Mr Hugh Berkeley, of Stroud, Gloucestershire, and the late Mrs Berkeley.

A more contemporary style may be used:
Mr John Debrett of Lewes, East Sussex and Miss Charlotte Berkeley of Stroud, Gloucestershire, are delighted to announce their engagement. A summer wedding is planned.

For a same-sex engagement:
Mr R Maddox and Mr T Curzon
The engagement is announced between Richard, son of Mr and Mrs John Maddox of Tenterden, Kent, and Timothy, son of Mr and Mrs Edward Curzon of Padstow, Cornwall.

Second marriage (for a widow or divorcée):
Mr T Hill and Mrs Ilsa Maddox*
The engagement is announced between Thomas, son of Mr and Mrs James Hill of Highgate, London, and Isla, youngest daughter of Mr and Mrs Andrew Stratton.
*Miss/Ms Isla Stratton if reverted to maiden name

If the prospective bride prefers to be called 'Ms' rather than 'Miss' in the announcement this is perfectly acceptable.

The Parents
Both sets of parents should meet, if they have not already done so. Leaving a first meeting until the engagement party may cause unnecessary nerves and tension for all involved, and it is highly inadvisable to leave it until the wedding day.

The bridegroom's mother traditionally writes to the bride's parents, expressing delight at the forthcoming marriage and suggesting that a date and venue be found for both sides to get together.

If the parents do not already know each other, meeting in a neutral environment, such as a restaurant, may be a good idea so that no one carries the burden of playing host. The bride and bridegroom should make every effort to put both sets of parents at ease. Remember that, first and foremost, this is a celebration – any initial awkwardness is usually forgotten once the discussion of wedding plans is underway.

Engagement Photographs
Sometimes referred to as a 'pre-wedding shoot', many engaged couples have photographs taken by a professional to mark their engagement. It is an opportunity to try out a photographer they may use on the wedding day, and engagement photographs may range from traditional studio portraits to more contemporary styles in meaningful locations. Copies may be sent to family and close friends, as well as being a keepsake for the couple.

Looking Back…

Breach of promise was a tort (civil) law dating back to medieval times which meant that an engagement was considered to be a legal contract to marry. If an engagement was broken off, then the party breaking the contract and not fulfilling the promise of marriage could be liable for damages. It was seen as a safeguard for women who, because they had been engaged, may have been regarded as 'ruined' and would, therefore, have struggled to find another fiancé.

ENGAGEMENTS

CELEBRATIONS

No matter how long a couple have been together, the engagement should still be viewed as a special event.

ENGAGEMENT PARTIES

An engagement party should be held within a month or two of becoming engaged to ensure that it feels relevant to the announcement, but should not be too close to the wedding. The invitations make it clear that the party is being held to mark the engagement. All guests invited to an engagement party should be invited to the wedding; presents should not be expected.

Engagement parties vary according to the wishes and circumstances of the couple and their families. Traditionally, the bride's parents hosted a gathering of family and friends – for example a small dinner party or larger drinks party – and this is still a popular convention. If both sets of parents are well known to each other then they may organise a joint celebration.

The couple may also host a party for their friends. This may be at their home, in a hired venue, or informal drinks in a local pub.

Introductions made at the engagement party will be invaluable on the wedding day, not only for guests to see familiar faces, but also to relieve the hosts of making introductions.

ENGAGEMENT CARDS AND LETTERS

It is customary for friends and family of a newly engaged couple to send a letter or card. Traditionally this was sent to either the bride or bridegroom, never jointly to the couple. The man was offered congratulations, but the woman was not, as it implied she had 'caught' her man. Instead, letters or cards to the bride-to-be focused on the happy news rather than congratulations. This rule is seldom adhered to now, as so many couples live together before marriage and well-wishers simply send a card to them both at their shared address. Friends may wish to send an email or text message, or comment on social media posts, but this is still an occasion where it is appropriate also to put pen to paper.

ENGAGEMENT PRESENTS

Family and close friends may choose to give the bride and bridegroom a present. Friends may send flowers or give a small token but family (parents or grandparents) are often more generous. Heirlooms such as jewellery, furniture or paintings are traditional; a financial contribution towards the cost of the wedding or the honeymoon is a more modern trend. Handwritten thank-you letters for any engagement presents received should be sent as promptly as possible.

226 - 271

Getting Started
Wedding Invitations
The Wedding Party
The Wedding Day
After The Wedding

Weddings

A wedding is the union of two people, witnessed by and celebrated with the community. It is usually the biggest party that the couple and their family will ever organise and it is important that they are as hospitable as possible. Every couple strives to make their day memorable, though this may mean negotiating a minefield of complex family situations, and balancing ambitious plans with a pragmatic acceptance of limitations.

WEDDINGS

Getting Started

The Guest List
Save-the-date Cards
Wedding Presents
Second Marriages

Rites of Passage | Weddings

Setting the Wedding Date

The choice of wedding date is dependent on many factors. There are general considerations, for example the season, as well as more specific details such as the availability of the church or civil venue, reception venue and key guests. It is sensible to avoid clashing with any significant social, sporting or national events, or important guests' personal commitments. In Britain, Saturdays between May and September are the most popular choice of day. Fridays are also an option, but are less popular as they will require guests to take a day off from the working week.

Once the date and guest list is finalised, it may be a good idea to send out save-the-date cards to key people, as invitations may take a long time to organise (*see p 231*).

Who Pays?

Traditionally, the bride's parents were responsible for paying for specific elements of a wedding: the flowers at the church; the order-of-service sheets; the wedding breakfast or reception; the bride's trousseau. The bridegroom was expected to pay for the bride and bridesmaids' bouquets and presents, the church fees and the transport from the church to the reception. Moreover, he was responsible for providing his new bride with a suitable, fully-equipped, home.

Increasingly the responsibilities and division of costs depend on the financial circumstances of the parents and the couple and the age of the couple. It should therefore not necessarily be expected that the bride's family bears the majority of the cost. The bridegroom's parents may offer to pay for a certain element of the day – for example the wine, the wedding cars – or make a contribution towards the total cost of the wedding. It has also become more usual for the bride and bridegroom to fund their own wedding, especially as couples are marrying later in life. In certain circumstances, the wording on the invitation may reflect who has contributed.

See pp 235–243 for invitations

The Guest List

Compiling the guest list is one of the major challenges when planning a wedding. The number of guests is usually determined by the wedding budget, and size of ceremony and reception venue. Inevitably, not everybody can be invited, and wherever the line is drawn there is always someone on the wrong side. Preliminary discussions are recommended before an allowance of guests is allocated – usually to the couple and their parents.

Prioritising the Guest List

Those who are bearing the majority of the wedding costs may feel deserving of a greater allocation of invitations, but this should not be at the expense of other key parties.

As a general rule, family should be prioritised and, if either the bride or the bridegroom has a considerably larger family than the other, an equal split of guests may not be possible between the two sides.

Children

See p 241 for information sheets

In order to compile an accurate guest list, a decision must be made about whether children and babies will be invited. Details of any arrangements about children may be included in the extra information sheet enclosed with the invitation.

Careful consideration should be given to the logistical impact a no-children policy may have on guests. Younger couples, however, may choose more freely not to invite children as many of the guests may not have a young family yet.

If a no-children policy is decided, it is important not to make special allowances for certain guests as it may look inconsiderate to those who have organised special childcare, especially on a weekend.

See pp 248–249 for bridesmaids and pages

An exception is sometimes made for immediate family – for example nieces and nephews of the bride or bridegroom – who may be allowed to attend for a part of the day, or may be participating as a page or bridesmaid.

Sometimes children are invited for part of the day – for example the ceremony and afternoon reception – but are not expected to attend an evening party. If this is the case, it should be made clear on the information sheet. Alternatively, if childcare will be on offer (a crèche, nanny etc), this must also be clarified.

Additional Guests

Some guests may have partners who the bride and bridegroom have not met or do not know very well. If numbers are tight, it is quite acceptable not to invite them.

Both halves of engaged couples should be invited, and those who are in a long-term, established relationship. If an elderly guest is travelling, it is considerate to invite a carer or companion who can assist them.

Size Limits   If the ceremony venue is small, some guests may be invited to the reception only, or just the latter part of the reception (for example the evening, after the food). Each will require a separate invitation or covering note (*see p 239*). Under no circumstances should a guest be invited to the wedding but not to the reception.

Family Tensions   Ensure that everyone invited will attend with the best sentiments. Familial repercussions must be borne in mind where family members are concerned and it is sensible to ensure that none of the key players are upset, or at least surprised, by an individual's attendance.

Reserves   Maintain a record of names of those who did not make the final guest list; it may be possible to extend late invitations after the first round of acceptances/refusals is received. Treat this process with extreme care; it is tactful to ensure that a second round of invitations are not sent out too close to the wedding day.

Save-the-Date Cards

See p 319 for save-the-date cards

Once the date is set and the guest list finalised, save-the-date cards may be sent out, asking guests to keep a particular date free. While an email or simple message in a Christmas card is a possible alternative, it is likely that people will take more note of a dedicated save-the-date card arriving by post. Replies are not sent and hosts should not assume guests will attend: a save-the-date card signals a host's desire and is not a command. The wording should be kept brief; it is usual to include only the geographical location, rather than the venue. For example:

Save the Date

Saturday 15th July 2023

for the marriage of

John Debrett and Charlotte Berkeley

London

Invitation to follow

Wedding Presents

The circumstances and age of the bride and bridegroom will influence the choice of wedding list and presents. Now that many couples are no longer setting up their first home, wedding lists can vary hugely.

Wedding Lists — The wedding list must be in place, and an 'opening' date decided, before the invitations are sent out so that details can be included. Lists are readily available, for example, through department stores, wedding list companies, specialist shops or charities.

Off the List — Although the wedding list is for guidance, it is permissible for a guest to choose a different present and guests are free to do something different if they would prefer to give a unique or individual present, or something with particular meaning.

Money — Asking for money can often be awkward, but it is becoming more accepted. It is important for the bride and bridegroom to communicate clearly that the money is going towards something specific, such as the honeymoon.

Buying a Wedding Present — All guests who attend a wedding will usually buy the bride and bridegroom a wedding present. Brides and bridegrooms should, however, accept gracefully that some guests might not give them one. There should be no correlation between the grandeur of the wedding and the value of the present. It is good form for guests who are invited, but unable to attend, to buy the couple a wedding present.

Presents on the Wedding Day — Some guests may choose to bring a wedding present along on the day, although this is not traditional. Alternatively, they may choose to give the couple a wedding card. On the whole, however, it is inconvenient for the bride and bridegroom when guests bring presents to the wedding.

Looking Back...

Wedding presents were put out on display in a separate room for the guests to admire. They were arranged on tables covered with velvet or dark-coloured cloths, and were grouped by type (for example, china, linen, silver etc). Each present was labelled with the name of the giver. Labelled, empty jewellery boxes were put on display; cheques (without disclosing the amount) or very large items were listed on individual cards. If there were many valuable items, private detectives were hired for security.

Second Marriages

The scale and tone of a second marriage depends on the parties involved. The key is to be sensitive towards everybody involved and to manage their expectations. While it is impossible to please everybody, consideration and good communication can help avoid difficult or upsetting situations.

Style

If both the bride and bridegroom have been married previously, then it is usual to hold a smaller, low key wedding with close friends and family. This may be a simple register office ceremony, followed by a meal in a restaurant or a drinks reception. Much of the pomp and circumstance of traditional weddings is dispensed with. Some churches allow a ceremony for a second marriage; if this is not possible, a service of blessing may be held for those who wish to include a religious aspect.

If, however, the bride is marrying for the first time, then it is likely that the wedding will take more of a grand and traditional route. It may be advisable, especially if children from the first marriage are involved, to acknowledge openly and graciously that this is a second marriage.

Widows and Widowers

If the bride or bridegroom has been widowed, then sensitivity should be shown to the family of the deceased, and their status should be openly acknowledged.

Children

If there are children from the first marriage, then it is usual for them to play a prominent part in the wedding day. A son may take the role of best man, while daughters may be bridesmaids.

Every situation will be different and the logistics of the guest list, style and size of the wedding will depend on the particular details of the situation.

Ex-wives and Ex-husbands

Traditionally, ex-wives and ex-husbands were not invited to the wedding, but if relations are good, then this rule may be relaxed. Ex-wives and ex-husbands who are invited to a former spouse's remarriage should only accept if they are confident that they will be able to meet social expectations and behave well. If there are feelings of residual resentment or bitterness it might be wise to avoid attending.

See p 276 for divorce

WEDDINGS

WEDDING INVITATIONS

TRADITIONAL INVITATIONS
USEFUL FORMS OF ADDRESS
POSTPONEMENT OR CANCELLATION
REPLIES TO INVITATIONS

Traditional Invitations

Traditionally, as the hostess, the bride's mother takes responsibility for sending out the invitations. In practice, the couple may choose to do it themselves.

Recipients

Invitations should be sent to all guests, including the parents – except where any parent is doing the inviting – and the best man, bridesmaids and pages. It is polite to send an invitation to the person conducting the wedding ceremony if he/she is to attend or be invited to the reception.

Courtesy invitations should be sent out to guests who will be unable to attend, for example due to illness or living overseas.

Style of Invitation

The style and formality of the invitation should reflect that of the wedding. The smartest and most traditional (and expensive) invitations are engraved. Flat printing and thermography are alternatives; if opting for thermography a matt ink surface is a better replica of engraving. Letterpress or handmade, artistic invitations are also popular for wedding invitations.

See p 309 for printing techniques

Calligraphy

A calligrapher may be hired to address the invitations and envelopes.

Practicalities

Stationery orders should include plenty of spares to allow for mistakes when writing on them, and enough to send out a second batch once refusals have come in.

A record should be kept of invitations sent so that replies can be methodically logged. Dispatching a second wave of invitations is quite acceptable once refusals are received, so long as they are sent neither too long after the original invitations nor too near to the wedding date.

Dress Codes
See pp 185–195 for dress codes

Traditionally, no dress code is stated on the invitation as it is universally accepted that morning attire or suits are worn at British weddings. If it is felt necessary, the dress code can be noted on the enclosures.

If, however, there is to be a non-traditional dress code – for example black tie – then it should be specified on the invitation in the bottom right-hand corner.

TRADITIONAL WORDING AND STYLE

A traditional wedding invitation is made of white matt card. It should be W6 x H8 inches (W15.2 x H20.3 cm) when folded in half with the text on the first (outer) page, usually in black copperplate script.

The wording on the invitation is dictated by traditional wedding etiquette. The inclusion of the bride and bridegroom's middle name(s) is optional, but should be consistent for both names.

The traditional wording where the parents are married:

The Earl and Countess of Aldford

Mr and Mrs Hugh Berkeley
request the pleasure of
your company at the marriage
of their daughter
Charlotte Jane
to
Mr John Edward Debrett
at St George's Church, Mayfair
on Saturday 15th July 2023
at 3 o'clock
and afterwards at
16 Charles Street, London W1

R.S.V.P.
The Ridings
Chalford
Gloucestershire GL6 1AB

ALTERNATIVE WORDING

Where the bride and bridegroom are the host and hostess:
Mr John Debrett and Miss/Ms Charlotte Berkeley
request the pleasure of
your company at their marriage

If the bride's mother is the hostess:
Mrs Hugh Berkeley or, if preferred, *Mrs Jane Berkeley*
requests the pleasure of
your company at the marriage
of her daughter
Charlotte

If the bride's father is the host:
Mr Hugh Berkeley
requests the pleasure of
your company at the marriage
of his daughter
Charlotte

If the bride's mother and stepfather are the hosts:
Mr and Mrs Timothy Mount-Jones
request the pleasure of
your company at the marriage
of her daughter
Charlotte Berkeley

If the bride's father and her stepmother are the hosts:
Mr and Mrs Hugh [or, if preferred, Catherine] Berkeley
request the pleasure of
your company at the marriage
of his daughter
Charlotte

If the bride's stepmother is the hostess:
Mrs Hugh Berkeley
requests the pleasure of
your company at the marriage
of her stepdaughter
Charlotte

If the bride's father and stepmother, and mother are co-hosting:
Mr and Mrs Hugh Berkeley and Mrs Catherine Berkeley
request the pleasure of
your company at the marriage of
Charlotte

If the bride's divorced parents co-hosting:
Mr Hugh Berkeley and Mrs Catherine Forsythe*
request the pleasure of
your company at the marriage
of their daughter
Charlotte

* 'Mrs Catherine Berkeley' or maiden name if not remarried

If the bridegroom's parents are hosting:
Mr and Mrs George Debrett
request the pleasure of
your company at the marriage of
Charlotte Berkeley to their son John

If the hosts are the bride's relations, guardians or godparents:
Mr and Mrs Gregory Hill
request the pleasure of
your company at the marriage
of [their ward] Charlotte Berkeley*

* The bride's surname may be included if it is different to the host's/hostess's. The phrase 'their ward' is considered formal.

Invitations to the marriage of a same-sex couple can be altered depending on which, of either, set of parents is hosting.

Where a same-sex couple is hosting:
Miss/Ms Sophie McMillan and Miss/Ms Lucy Brightman
request the pleasure of
your company at their marriage

Reception-only Invitations

If the church or ceremony venue is small, then it is acceptable to invite some guests to the reception only. Separate invitations are printed; the same rules relating to the naming of the hosts apply. For example:

Mr and Mrs Hugh Berkeley
request the pleasure of
your company at the reception following the marriage
of their daughter
Charlotte Jane
to
Mr John Edward Debrett
at 16 Charles Street, London W1
on Saturday 15th July 2023 at 4.30 o'clock

A note should also be placed inside the envelope with the reception invitation, for example:

Owing to the small size of St George's Church, it is possible to ask only very few guests to the service. We hope you will forgive this invitation being to the reception only.

Evening Reception Invitations

Sometimes, a further tier of guests may be invited to just the later portion of the reception, after the food and speeches. Separate invitations should be printed.

This section of the day is usually referred to as the 'evening reception' on the invitation. If there is no further food being served, the words 'drinks and dancing' should be included on the invitation to make this clear.

Second and Subsequent Marriages

See p 279 for divorcees
See p 286 for widows

A divorced bride embarking on a second marriage should use whichever example above is applicable to her situation. Traditionally, she is described on the invitation as 'Mrs Charlotte Debrett'; some divorcees revert to their maiden name and would, therefore, be 'Miss/Ms Charlotte Berkeley'. If she is a widow, traditionally she is described as 'Mrs John Debrett'.

Many couples, where one or both of them are marrying for a second time, will choose to host their own wedding and, therefore, the invitation would be prepared in their names. For example: 'Charlotte Debrett and Timothy Curzon request the pleasure' etc.

Guests' Names on Invitations

See pp 229–231 for guest lists

Traditionally, the name of the guest(s) is handwritten in ink in the top left-hand corner. The use of the words 'and guest' should be avoided; it is polite to try to find out their name in advance.

On formal wedding invitations, guests should be addressed by their full title, for example: 'Mr and Mrs Hugh Berkeley', 'Miss Isla Curzon', 'Lady Hermione Cork', 'The Earl and Countess of Tolworth'.

Traditionally, wedding invitations to couples were addressed on the envelope to the wife only. This is now a matter of choice, and a more contemporary style is to address both husband and wife on the envelope.

Useful Forms of Address on Wedding Invitations

	Name on the Invitation	Name on the Envelope
Married couple (traditional)	Mr and Mrs John Debrett	[Mr and] Mrs John Debrett
Married couple (contemporary)	Mr John and Mrs Julia Debrett	Mr John and Mrs Julia Debrett
Married couple with invited children	Mr John and Mrs Julia Debrett, Caroline and James	[Mr and] Mrs John Debrett Mr John and Mrs Julia Debrett
A medical doctor (male)	Dr John and Mrs Julia Debrett	[Dr John and] Mrs Julia Debrett
A medical doctor (female)	Mr John and Dr Julia Debrett	[Mr John and] Dr Julia Debrett
Single man	Mr John Debrett	Mr John Debrett
Single woman	Miss/Ms Charlotte Berkeley	Miss/Ms Charlotte Berkeley
Widow	Mrs John Debrett	Mrs John Debrett
Divorcée (traditional)	Mrs Charlotte Debrett	Mrs Charlotte Debrett
Divorcée (maiden name)	Miss/Ms Charlotte Berkeley	Miss/Ms Charlotte Berkeley
Unmarried couple	Mr John Debrett and Miss/Ms Charlotte Berkeley	Mr John Debrett and Miss/Ms Charlotte Berkeley
Single man where his guest is not well-known to the couple	Mr John Debrett and Miss/Ms Charlotte Berkeley	Mr John Debrett
Single woman where her guest is not well-known to the couple	Miss/Ms Charlotte Berkeley and Mr John Debrett	Miss/Ms Charlotte Berkeley
Same-sex couple, unmarried or married, who use their own names	Mr Richard Maddox and Mr Timothy Curzon	Mr Richard Maddox and Mr Timothy Curzon
Church of England vicar and his wife	The Reverend Anthony and Mrs Susan Lambert	[The Reverend Anthony and] Mrs Susan Lambert
Church of England vicar and her husband	Mr Anthony and The Reverend Susan Lambert	[Mr Anthony and] The Reverend Susan Lambert
Roman Catholic priest	Father Connor	The Reverend Michael Connor
Married peers	The Earl and Countess of Tolworth	[The Earl and] Countess of Tolworth
A married couple where the husband is in the armed forces	Lieutenant-Colonel Hugh and Mrs Anna Chesterfield	[Lieutenant-Colonel and] Mrs Anna Chesterfield
A married couple where the wife is in the armed forces	Mr Hugh and Lieutenant-Colonel Anna Chesterfield	[Mr Hugh and] Lieutenant-Colonel Anna Chesterfield
A couple where the wife is a dame	Dame Gloria and Mr James Hill	Dame Gloria [and Mr James] Hill
A knight and his wife	Sir Reginald and Lady Mount	[Sir Reginald and] Lady Mount
A couple where the husband has the courtesy title of 'Hon'	Mr and Mrs Roger Maddox OR	[The Hon Roger and] Mrs Jane Maddox
A couple where the wife has the courtesy title of 'Hon'	Mr Roger and Mrs Jane Maddox	[Mr Roger and] The Hon Mrs Maddox

Square brackets indicate that, according to traditional etiquette, invitations are addressed to the wife only. This is entirely optional.

Reply Cards	Printed reply cards may be enclosed to assist the hosts in monitoring and updating the guest list. They are usually postcard-sized, with a simple tick box or wording options to indicate whether a guest will be attending. There may be space for guests to specify any dietary requirements or allergies. The reply address is printed on the other side and, preferably, a stamp affixed.
Extra Information	A separate sheet giving practical information may be enclosed with the invitation to inform guests of further details about the day. The style and quality of this sheet should be in keeping with the invitation.
	Directions to the church or wedding venue (especially if it is rural), car parking information, and a range of accommodation – plus any booking codes that have been organised – may be included, as well as a list of local taxi companies.
	It is useful to state the approximate time at which the bride and bridegroom will go away, and the time at which the reception will draw to a close, to help guests book taxis or arrange childcare. Similarly, if transport is being arranged for guests, for example a coach to drop them off at nearby hotels at the end of the night, then details should be included.
See p 230 for children	If there is a no-children policy, then it is sensible to clarify this here, rather than just omitting the names of the children from the invitation. Where possible, it is helpful to provide a reason and make a specific age cut-off point, for example: 'Unfortunately due to the limited size of Charles Street, we have decided not to invite children under the age of eight'.
	If reply cards are not being used, then guests can be requested to inform the hosts of any dietary requirements or allergies.
	Traditionally, wedding guests contacted the bride's mother to find out where the wedding list was held, but it is now usual to enclose details of the wedding list with the invitation.
Websites	Some couples choose to consolidate all the information about the wedding on a personalised website. This may include interactive maps, links to the wedding list, or even a forum for guests to arrange sharing lifts or accommodation. Details of the web address should be included in the extra information sheet.

Postponement or Cancellation

If a wedding is postponed or cancelled due to unforeseen circumstances and the invitations have already been sent out, then a card is sent out. If there is no time for cards to be sent, then every guest must be contacted by telephone or email.

INDEFINITE POSTPONEMENT

If the wedding plans are indefinitely postponed, then the following wording is used:
Owing to the recent death of Lady Hermione Cork, Mr and Mrs Hugh Berkeley deeply regret that they are obliged to cancel the invitations to the marriage of their daughter Charlotte to Mr John Debrett on Saturday 15th July 2023.
Invitations are sent out again when a new date is fixed.

POSTPONEMENT TO A LATER DATE

If the wedding date is postponed to a later date, the following wording is used:
Owing to the illness of Lady Hermione Cork, Mr and Mrs Hugh Berkeley deeply regret that they are obliged to postpone the invitations to the marriage of their daughter Charlotte to Mr John Debrett at St George's Church, Mayfair, from Saturday 15th July 2023 to Saturday 16th September 2023.

CHANGE OF PLAN

If the wedding is to take place quietly, the following wording is used:
Owing to the recent death of her husband, Mrs Hugh Berkeley much regrets that she is obliged to cancel the invitations to the marriage of her daughter Charlotte to Mr John Debrett at St George's Church, Mayfair, on Saturday 15th July 2023, which will now take place very quietly on Thursday, 17th August 2023.

CANCELLATION

If the wedding is cancelled, there is no need to include an explanation of why the wedding will not take place. The following wording is used:
Mr and Mrs Hugh Berkeley regret to announce that the marriage of their daughter Charlotte to Mr John Debrett, which was arranged for Saturday 15th July 2023, will not now take place.

Some families may issue a public statement in the Court Circular pages of, for example, *The Times* or *Telegraph*. For example:
The marriage between Mr John Debrett and Miss Charlotte Berkeley will not now take place.

Any early wedding presents received should be returned by the bride and bridegroom with a letter of thanks.

Replies to Invitations

Guests should take the time to reply to a wedding invitation promptly and correctly.

Traditional Wording

See p 158 for replies to formal invitations

Replies to traditional invitations are addressed to the hosts (as stated on the invitation) and should be handwritten on headed writing paper, with the date handwritten at the bottom-right of the page, in the third person. It is expected that the reply will reiterate all the details outlined in the invitation. The ending expresses whether the guest(s) can attend.

For example:
Mr and Mrs Henry Bruton thank Mr and Mrs Hugh Berkeley for the kind invitation to the marriage of their daughter, Charlotte Jane, to Mr John Edward Debrett at St George's Church, Mayfair, on Saturday 15th July 2023 at 3 o'clock and afterwards at 16 Charles Street, and are delighted to accept or *regret that they are unable to accept.*

Reply Cards

If a reply card is enclosed with the invitation, guests should fill it in and return it even if they also reply formally.

Extra Guests

If an invitation includes 'and guest', then the name of the guest who will be attending should be included in the reply.

If the invitation has arrived and it does not specify 'and guest', it is the height of rudeness to ask to bring one or assume that a partner is invited.

Important Information

Guests should inform their hosts of any dietary requirements or allergies in advance; they will usually be asked to do so, or have the option to mention it on a reply card.

Looking Back...

The bride's father would present his daughter with a sum of money, called a trousseau, with which she would equip herself with the things she would need for married life, for example clothes, undergarments, boots, shoes and gloves. Depending on her situation, she may also have assembled some household items, such as linen.

WEDDINGS

THE WEDDING PARTY

ROLES & RESPONSIBILITIES
DRESS: THE WEDDING PARTY
WEDDING RINGS
DRESS: WEDDING GUESTS

Roles & Responsibilities

The following advice applies to traditional wedding ceremonies; as ways of celebrating marriages and partnerships become more diverse, both opposite sex and same-sex couples who are opting for less conventional ceremonies may choose to incorporate elements of these long-established practices into their own celebrations.

Those who are hosting or contributing to the finances should feel as though they are involved. It is essential that the couple are prepared to handle any fragile family situations that may arise and that they respect the source of the contributions.

The Bride and Bridegroom In most cases, the bride will plan many elements of the wedding (usually with the help of her mother and chief bridesmaid). The bridegroom is usually involved as much as he wishes to be and should be consulted, where appropriate, as decisions are made. Key choices – for example the choice of reception venue, drink, menu, entertainment etc – should be made together.

The Parents of the Bride Traditionally, the mother of the bride plays a hugely influential and prominent role in organising a wedding, particularly if she is hosting the wedding at her home. She may research local suppliers, attend meetings, make appointments and assist the bride in choosing her wedding dress; she may also be responsible for sending out the invitations and managing the responses and guest list.

The bride's father may not have much involvement in the planning, however he usually plays a major role on the wedding day, particularly by giving his daughter away and making a speech.

The Parents of the Bridegroom Traditionally, the bridegroom's parent's role is limited but they may, in practice, have more or less influence depending on their familiarity with the bride's family and their level of financial contribution.

If the bride has strained parental relations or no parents still living, or if the bridegroom's parents are hosting the wedding (for example if the reception is at their house), then the dynamic may change and the bridegroom's parents will often match or assume the roles traditionally fulfilled by the bride's parents. The mother of the bridegroom may also help out with organising the wedding, or be given a specific task.

Divorced Parents

This is a sensitive area that has to be addressed by the family and every case will be different. If there are tensions between children, parents and step-parents, it is important that the bride and bridegroom outline their roles at an early stage so that everyone is aware of the part they will play on the wedding day.

Unless relations are so strained that the only solution is not to invite one of the parties involved, duties should be split. For example, the natural father could walk the bride down the aisle and the stepfather could give a speech. Prominence is often accorded to the party that brought up the bride.

Forward planning is vital when it comes to seating arrangements for the ceremony and lunch/dinner (*see p 265*), and the line-ups in the official photographs.

The Best Man

One of the greatest compliments a man can pay a friend, relation or brother is to ask him to be best man at his wedding. It is a major role and he must be willing to commit fully to the task; high levels of organisation, communication and confidence are required. There is much more to being a best man than organising an unforgettable stag night and making a funny, but not inappropriate, best man speech: with the privilege of the position comes a huge amount of responsibility and many duties. Careful thought should therefore be given to the selection.

It is helpful if the best man is familiar with, or at least able to recognise, key people on the day (parents, grandparents, very close friends of the family and godparents) and that he is aware of any sensitive family situations, such as divorce, estrangement or recent bereavement.

He must also familiarise himself with the ceremony and reception venues, and be briefed fully on the timetable for the day and who is involved (for example caterers, photographers, wedding cars etc).

See pp 256–261 for ceremonies
See pp 267–268 for speeches

On the day, the best man must work discreetly and efficiently to ensure that everything is running smoothly. He must lead the team of ushers, ensuring that they are fulfilling their duties, and he is the first point of contact if there is a problem or query. He plays an important role before, during and after the wedding ceremony. At the reception, he is expected to deliver a speech and is responsible for ensuring that things run to plan from beginning to end.

Best Women

Best women are a non-traditional, but increasingly popular, choice. They should, of course, embody all the qualities of a best man.

The Ushers

The ushers are expected to help things run smoothly and efficiently on the wedding day. Good friends or relations of the bridegroom are usually chosen to be ushers, often along with a relation of the bride, such as her brother.

A chief usher may be nominated to assist the best man and help manage the ushers; sometimes a confident usher with a suitably loud voice may also fill the role of master of ceremonies. The number of ushers depends on the number of wedding guests; a larger wedding will obviously require more ushers than a smaller one.

The role of the ushers is often underestimated but they play an important part in the mechanics of the day. They should be briefed properly and each assigned specific tasks, for example assisting with car parking, seating guests for the ceremony, organising group photographs etc.

They are the first faces that the guests see when they arrive for the ceremony (*see p 259*) and, as a result, play a major part in setting the tone for the wedding day. It is important that they are ready to help out throughout the reception (*see pp 262–266*).

The Choice of Bridesmaids

Some brides choose to have children as their bridesmaids while others like to enlist the help of their close adult girlfriends. Younger brides often opt for adults, while older brides may have friends with young children. If a combination of adults and children is chosen, the numbers, composition and practicalities must be considered carefully. It is sensible to seek a balance between youth and age and experience and, if there are children, ensure that there is a suitable adult to small child ratio.

The chief bridesmaid – traditionally called the maid of honour (unmarried) or matron of honour (married) – is usually a very close friend, relation or sister of the bride. She must be a calm and collected presence who will help and support the bride before and during the wedding.

On the wedding day, the bridesmaids usually play less of an organisational role than the bridegroom's party, but they will have often supported the bride with the planning of the wedding.

The Chief Bridesmaid

The chief bridesmaid is the bride's main helper, from planning the wedding to being her key aide on the actual day. Along with the best man, she should be briefed on the proceedings and the timetable of the day, as well as being aware of the key guests and any relevant family politics.

She will assist her in getting ready on the day and, along with the other bridesmaids, ensure that the bride's party arrives at the ceremony on time. She may help the bride out of the wedding car and arrange her veil; she may also hold her bouquet and assist with the wedding dress train during the ceremony. She should join in the processional with the other bridesmaids, and may sometimes take the arm of the best man in the recessional.

See pp 256–261 for ceremonies

See pp 262–266 for receptions

At the reception, she should communicate with the best man to ensure that everything is running smoothly. It is important that she also keeps a constant eye on the bride to make sure she has everything she needs, or help with her dress as required. She should assist the bride when she is preparing to 'go away'.

Adult Bridesmaids

The adult bridesmaids should assist the bride and chief bridesmaid; their level of involvement will vary depending on the size of the wedding and the wishes of the bride. There are, however, some duties that come with the role.

On the day, the bridesmaids help out with preparations and assist the bride in getting ready. If there are child bridesmaids and pages, the bridesmaids should look after them before and during the service when their parents may not be able to.

At the ceremony, they participate in the processional and recessional, walking up the aisle behind the bride as she enters the ceremony, and then walking down the aisle behind the bride and bridegroom and their parents as they leave. At the reception, the bridesmaids should keep an eye on proceedings and report any problems or difficulties to the chief bridesmaid and best man.

Child Bridesmaids and Pages

Child bridesmaids or pages are often nieces, nephews, cousins, godchildren, children of good friends or children from a previous marriage. Parents of potential bridesmaids and pages should resist the temptation to hint about their own child's suitability. No one can predict how a child will behave on the wedding day, but those who are boisterous or badly behaved never make an ideal choice. Their purpose is, fundamentally, aesthetic and they have very little to do other than look sweet and follow the bride down the aisle. It should be explained to the child that their part in the wedding day is important and they must understand what they will be expected to do and if possible attend a rehearsal beforehand.

Parents should keep an eye on their child and take responsibility for them whenever possible. Very tiny children may need to be retrieved during, or immediately after, the ceremony.

Flower girls and ring bearers are not traditional at British weddings.

Stag and Hen Parties

In days gone by, a stag or hen party would have been an evening with close friends, whereas now anything goes and there really is no set etiquette. Celebrations may last for an evening, weekend or even involve a short holiday; they are usually held a few weeks before the wedding day.

The planning is usually the responsibility of the best man or chief bridesmaid. The bride and bridegroom should provide a guest list and they may hint at what they'd like to do. It doesn't have to be a surprise but some unexpected elements should be included.

Different ideas should be considered to ensure that what is planned is suited to everyone's budget and wishes. Good communication is essential; all costs should be clearly outlined and shared equally or proportionally among the attendees. If possible, the stags and hens should try to cover some of the bride or bridegroom's share.

The stag or hen party should be seen as a both a celebration for the bride or bridegroom, and as an opportunity to get to know the other stags or hens before the wedding day. This is particularly important if they do not already know each other.

Full participation and a sense of fun are essential. If you do not feel able to participate fully or with good grace, consider not going and make an excuse.

Dress: The Wedding Party

Wedding Dress — A wedding dress is likely to be the most significant item of clothing that the bride has ever worn. It is advisable to allow plenty of time to choose, as a wedding dress will need to be altered to fit. Alternatively, a bespoke dress takes around six months to make and the bride is asked to attend several fittings.

The bride must choose a dress that is comfortable and well-fitting. She should remember that, for much of the ceremony, the eyes of the congregation will be focused on her back. Consideration must be given to the style of wedding; a contemporary, city wedding with a civil ceremony would suit a different style of dress from a country church wedding.

Bridal Cover-Ups — Brides who wear a strapless dress in church must consider that it is respectful to cover their shoulders regardless of the season. Winter brides may need a cover-up to stay warm, as may summer brides at the end of the evening.

Veils — The decision on whether to wear a veil is purely a matter of personal choice. They can be worn long or short but the colour should match or coordinate with the dress; family heirlooms or vintage veils often yellow or fade so must be taken along to a dress fitting to check that the colour works.

Bridal Hair and Make-Up — Make-up should enhance, not overpower, the bride's face. Rehearse walking with hair, veil and headpiece in place.

Bridal Jewellery — Jewellery must be chosen carefully; if in doubt, err on the classic side. The style, neckline and details of the dress, veils, headpieces and hairstyles must be considered. Wrists often look better when left plain.

The bride should wear her engagement ring on her right hand so that her finger is empty for the wedding ring. The engagement ring is put back on her left hand after the ceremony.

A headpiece – such as a tiara or ornamental piece – may be worn. Some are chosen as an alternative to a veil, or others worn in addition. It is advisable to take it along to a dress fitting, and essential to have it for a hairstyle rehearsal.

Bridal Bouquet — The bride's bouquet usually reflects the style of the wedding; the shape complements the line of the dress and the size should be in proportion to the height of the bride. The most elegant bouquets are the simplest, with just one or two types of seasonal bloom. The bridal bouquet should be held at hip-height to avoid spoiling the line of the dress.

Adult Bridesmaids

The style of bridesmaids' dresses varies greatly from wedding to wedding but, in general, they should coordinate and look all of a piece. A single colour, modest, full-length dress is the most traditional choice. It is imperative to choose an outfit that will flatter all figures: if bridesmaids vary greatly in size or shape, then subtle variations in styling in dresses of the same colour may be the best option. It is sensible to choose something that may be worn again.

The bridesmaids' bouquets usually reflect the style of wedding, complement the bride's bouquet and coordinate with the buttonholes of the bridegroom's party. They are simpler and more modest in size than the bride's bouquet.

If possible, brides should pay for the bridesmaids' dresses. If the budget does not stretch, then the bridesmaids must be told from the outset that they need to pay. The bride must then be flexible and allow them to have their say.

A compromise may be for the bride to pay for the dresses and then ask the bridesmaids to pay for their shoes and any accessories (cover-ups, wraps, jackets etc). The key is to let them know what is expected from the start.

The chief bridesmaid may have a small bag to hand with some essentials – a phone, key items of make-up for the bride, safety pins, a watch etc. This should be left in a convenient place during the ceremony and reception (rather than carried).

Child Attendants

A well-tried formula is to dress girls in pale dresses, with a sash that coordinates with the adult bridesmaids' dresses, while the main colour of the boys' outfits matches the girls' sashes.

Hair should be neat and tidy; flowers may be worn on a slide or light headpiece. A small posey of flowers, pomander or a basket of flower petals may be carried. The most important thing is that children are neat and tidy and, above all, warm and comfortable.

If parents are being asked to pay for bridesmaids' dresses or pages' outfits this must be made absolutely clear at the outset.

Morning Dress and Suits Morning dress is the accepted dress code for traditional British weddings (*see p 190*) and is traditionally worn by the bridegroom, best man and ushers. For less formal weddings, smart suits may be worn.

Non-traditional Dress Codes Some contemporary weddings may opt for a non-traditional dress code, for example black tie (*see pp 187–189*); this should be stated on the wedding invitation.

Highland Dress Scots may wear Highland dress (*see p 191*), or tartan trews with a morning coat.

Military Uniform Active members of the armed forces may wear military uniform; each armed service, unit and regiment has its own traditions and protocol for weddings.

Top Hats Top hats are not generally worn, but many bridegrooms like their best man and ushers to have them to add a sense of occasion, particularly for the photographs. They are never worn inside a building or church, or in formal photographs – they are carried under the arm instead.

Buttonholes Flowers worn in the buttonhole of the coat/jacket are referred to simply as 'buttonholes' or *boutonnières*. The bridegroom, best man, ushers and usually the fathers of both the bride and bridegroom wear one; sometimes the grandfathers wear one too.

Simple, classic buttonholes – which are not too large or decorative, or have too much greenery such as fern – often look the smartest. Traditionally the bridegroom's buttonhole matches the bride's flowers. The best man's, ushers' and fathers' buttonholes reflect the bridesmaids' flowers. They are worn on the lefthand side. There will be a buttonhole fixing under the lapel of a morning coat – this holds the flower stalk in place and keeps the buttonhole upright.

The Mothers The mother of the bride should wear a hat, avoid white and black, and should confer with the bridegroom's mother to avoid embarrassing clashes or similarities. Head-to-toe colour coordination is not required. Be aware that over-sized broad-brimmed hats may obscure the face in photographs.

The Fathers The fathers of the bride and bridegroom usually follow the same dress code as the bridegroom's party and traditionally wear morning dress.

Wedding Rings

The Bride's Wedding Ring

See p 218 for engagement rings

The bride's wedding ring should complement her engagement ring; they need not necessarily match but if they are not made of the same metal, over time the stronger metal (for example platinum) may wear away the weaker one (for example gold).

The Bridegroom's Wedding Ring

Wedding rings were once the preserve of women alone, but during the Second World War soldiers began to wear them as a reminder of home and their wives. It is now common for married men to wear one, though it is not compulsory.

The ring should be in proportion to the size of the hand and neither too chunky nor too feminine. If a signet ring is worn, the wedding ring may be worn underneath it on the little finger of the left hand.

Practicalities

The wedding rings should be ordered well in advance to allow for alterations; they should both, along with the engagement ring, be insured as soon as possible.

Dress: Wedding Guests

Wedding guests should be appropriately dressed. It is important to remember that weddings are usually a formal affair and people take the time to dress up and look their best.

See p 190 for morning dress
See p 191 for Highland dress
See p 193 for lounge suits

Traditionally men wear morning dress, suits, highland dress or military uniform. Non-traditional dress codes will be stated on the wedding invitation.

Women should be dressed smartly and hats are generally worn. Head-to-toe outfits in white or cream should never be worn and all black, unless cleverly accessorised, may look too sombre. Dress should accord with the season and the time of day; appropriate shoes should be chosen if the wedding is outside or on grass.

Some weddings with a separate dance in the evening require guests to change; the dress code should be communicated to the guests when the invitations are sent out.

WEDDINGS

THE
WEDDING DAY

BEFORE THE CEREMONY
TRANSPORT
THE CEREMONY
TRADITIONAL CHURCH CEREMONIES
CIVIL CEREMONIES
THE RECEPTION
THE SPEECHES
AFTER THE RECEPTION

Before the Ceremony

Photography

See p 223 for engagement photographs

It is worth investing in a good photographer, as photographs are one of the few things the couple will refer back to over years to come. Personal recommendations are often best; an engagement shoot can be a good trial – many photographers will offer this as a complimentary service.

The photographer should be briefed fully on the structure of the day and what is expected of them, including special requests. Contemporary wedding photography usually comprises a mix of both formal portraits and reportage-style shots. A list of formal photographs should be prepared; if there are divorced parents, the positioning must be worked out in advance. Rules about photography inside the church must be checked with the clergy beforehand. The best man and ushers should assist the photographer.

Filming

A wedding video captures the essence of the day, along with moments the bride and bridegroom may otherwise miss. The important thing is to ensure that filming is not intrusive, and to guard against the filming dominating the entire proceeding.

Transport

Wedding Cars

The number of cars required and the logistics of how they are used depend upon the structure of the wedding day and the various locations. Most couples hire a wedding car and, style aside, practicalities are paramount: a large-skirted wedding dress is not easy to fold into a low-slung sports car and open-topped vehicles required to travel at any speed can play havoc with hair, veils and tiaras. All drivers should be briefed properly and given clear directions as to when and where to go.

One car, used just to take the bride and her father to the ceremony and then the bride and bridegroom back to the reception, may be enough. Sometimes, two cars are hired: one for the mother of the bride and the bridesmaids to travel to the ceremony, and a second for the father of the bride and the bride. They are both then used to transport the bride and bridegroom and wedding party to the reception. If the ceremony venue is nearby, one car can be hired to do both of these trips. Plan each journey time carefully; a vintage car may travel much more slowly than expected, especially along narrow country roads.

ACCOMMODATION AND TRANSPORT FOR GUESTS

Local hotels may have been block-booked, or a list of recommended places to stay may be enclosed with the invitation.

If the location of the wedding is short of parking or is very rural with limited taxis, then transport for the wedding guests may need to be provided, for example a coach, vintage bus or minibus.

Guests should ensure, if applicable, that they have somewhere to stay and transport organised in advance.

The Ceremony

There are religious buildings that are registered for the solemnisation of marriage (churches, chapels, cathedrals, synagogues, temples) and register offices or buildings that are approved for civil marriages and partnerships (eg a stately home or hotel). They all have requirements and restrictions that must be addressed before a ceremony can take place.

RELIGIOUS CEREMONIES

There is often a great deal of variation within individual faiths in the United Kingdom. All religious marriage ceremonies are informed by conventions, and the bride and bridegroom will be guided through the regulations and restrictions by the vicar, priest or religious celebrant. There is a framework around which the ceremony can be structured; personal style may be added through music and readings.

Religious organisations can 'opt-in' to offer same-sex weddings, however the law prevents the Church of England and Church in Wales from doing so. The Church of Wales now allows blessings for same-sex couples.

CIVIL CEREMONIES

Since 2019 both opposite and same-sex couples in the United Kingdom can choose between a civil marriage ceremony or civil partnership, which gives a relationship legal recognition as well as legal rights and responsibilities. A civil marriage ceremony has no religious aspects.

Civil ceremonies provide geographical flexibility and more freedom to personalise the ceremony. Many couples choose a venue that has the facility to host both the ceremony and the reception, for example a stately home or hotel. Alternatively, they may choose a register office or other approved venue for the ceremony, and then hold the reception elsewhere.

CIVIL PARTNERSHIPS A ceremony is not legally required for registering a civil partnership, although most couples choose to have one. Couples are required to sign a civil partnership document in front of a registrar and two witnesses. Instead of making traditional vows before the registrar, a requirement in a civil marriage ceremony, the couple may choose to make pledges of commitment.

READINGS Usually close friends, relatives or godparents are asked to read at the ceremony. They should be confident public speakers who will not feel overwhelmed by the prospect. It is sensible to have a balance of both men and women. Readers should be supplied with a copy of the text well in advance so that they have time to practise. Spares should also be to hand on the day.

It is not permitted to use religious words in a civil ceremony, but it may include readings that contain reference to a god as long as they are in an "essentially non-religious context".

MUSIC For a church ceremony, it is a good idea to meet with the organist and ask for advice on the choices of music. They will have a wealth of experience and know what they are able to play well. The church choir may be asked to join in the ceremony; this will add gusto and volume to the hymns. Professional musicians, choirs and soloists can also be hired to perform before and after the ceremony, and during the signing of the register.

A civil ceremony must not contain religious references, so hymns are not permitted. Popular music, folk songs, ballet, classical music or opera are usually acceptable, but all choices should be checked carefully for religious connotations.

THE ORDER OF SERVICE The order of service sheet lists the various stages of the ceremony and includes details of the music and readings. A simple cream or white folded card is the conventional choice, with the names of the bride and bridegroom, the church and the date and time of the service on the front cover. Attention should be paid to the layout and printer proofs should be checked very carefully, especially the dates and people's names.

It is customary to include the full text of the hymns as this dispenses with the need for hymnbooks; ensure that the desired numbers of verses are included. The minister/registrar is acknowledged by name, and the organist, choir or musicians credited. Composers and authors may also be included; readers' names should accompany the title of their reading.

FLOWERS   For a church wedding, the couple should talk to the person who is responsible for the flowers in the church – usually a member of the parish who, along with other volunteers, makes up regular displays. Some may be talented florists who, with a little extra budget from the bride and bridegroom, will increase their usual output for the wedding. Others may not be able to create what the bride has in mind; in this case a florist is used.

Even if they have been provided by the bride and bridegroom, some of the displays should be left behind after the ceremony as a gesture of goodwill. A few may be taken on to the reception, for example the pew ends (and put on the backs of chairs) or entrance garland.

A civil ceremony venue or register office will not usually provide any flowers so they should be included as part of the general wedding floristry.

It is not compulsory to have lots of flowers. While they should look effective, care should be taken to ensure that they are positioned carefully, neither overwhelming the church or room, nor obstructing anyone's vision.

REHEARSALS   The officiant usually organises a rehearsal before the wedding. For small weddings, this may be with just the bride and groom, whereas for larger ceremonies the key members of the wedding party – best man, bridesmaids and the person giving the bride away – may be also asked attend. Everyone should arrive promptly and fully cooperate, even with the pressures of last minute stress or excitement.

Traditional Church Ceremonies

SEATING   Traditionally, the bride's family and friends sit on the left-hand side of the aisle and the bridegroom's on the right. The bride's parents sit in the front-left pew and the bridegroom's parents and best man in the front-right pew. If there are complex family situations – for example divorced and remarried parents – then pews should be allocated to avoid any awkward situations.

The bridesmaids may sit with the bride's parents, if there is room, or alternatively be seated at the altar rails or on stools. Pages and child bridesmaids may sit with them or very young ones may prefer to be with their parents.

Grandparents and siblings sit in the pew behind the bride or bridegroom's parents, followed by immediate family and godparents. Ushers may be provided with lists of family, godparents and other important guests to help them seat guests efficiently and appropriately; ensure that plenty of space is reserved in advance.

The ushers ask guests whether they are a friend or relation of the bride or bridegroom and asks them to sit on the appropriate side. If either side's family is considerably larger than the other, then friends should be seated on the other side to balance it out.

Ushers may sit near the front but it is often more practical for them to be elsewhere. Readers should be near the front or at the end of the row nearest the aisle. It is considerate to allocate seats next to the aisle to parents with babies or young children.

Church Bells
Bells may be booked in advance at an extra cost. Aside from giving the wedding an increased sense of occasion, the bell-ringers are usually keen to participate.

The Arrival of the Bridegroom's Party
It is traditional for the bridegroom, best man and ushers to meet for brunch or lunch before the ceremony. The ushers are then the first to arrive at the church, usually around 45 minutes before the start time. The ushers must be organised and in position when the first guests arrive. They have several key tasks to fulfil: distributing the order of service sheets, checking reserved seating and allocating the buttonholes. If it's a hot day, there should be bottles of water on standby; if it's raining, umbrellas should be to hand and an area organised for guests' umbrellas.

The bridegroom and best man should arrive in good time, shortly after the ushers if they have not travelled together. The best man should check that he has everything he needs for the day: the rings; cheques or cash for suppliers; messages that are to be read out at the reception; a copy of the guest list; a mobile (and important numbers). The best man and bridegroom usually take a seat in the front right-hand pew and wait for the arrival of the bride. They then stand up and wait at the top of the aisle.

The Arrival of the Bride's Party
The mother of the bride, bridesmaids and pages should arrive at least ten minutes before the start. The bridesmaids wait for the bride outside the church. The mother of the bride is traditionally accompanied down the aisle to her seat on the right arm of an usher. She should be the last person to be seated.

The bride and her father (or whoever is giving her away) are the last to arrive. Traditionally, it was the bride's prerogative to arrive 'fashionably late' but, in practice, this puts the bridegroom under unnecessary pressure and just keeps everyone waiting. Extra time should be allowed for the bride, bridesmaids and pages to compose themselves, and arrange veils, trains, and so on.

The Entrance of the Bride and the Processional

The bride takes the right arm of her father (or the person giving her away), the opening music begins and the bride and her father start walking. The pace should have been agreed upon and practised by the whole procession; remember that nerves will naturally speed people up. The bride should remember to hold herself upright with her shoulders back and her bouquet held at hip height.

It is usual for the chief bridesmaid to walk directly behind the bride, followed by the other bridesmaids. If there are baby bridesmaids or pages, they may hold the hand of an adult bridesmaid or walk behind the bride with the adult bridesmaids bringing up the rear.

The Ceremony

During the first hymn, the bride gives her bouquet to the chief bridesmaid and, if she is wearing a veil over her face, it is usually lifted back by her mother or the chief bridesmaid.

Traditionally, the officiant asks, 'who is giving this woman to this man?', the bride's father (or person who is giving her away, standing to her left) takes the bride's right hand, places it in the hand of the officiant, who places it in the bridegroom's right hand. This part of the ceremony is entirely optional.

The vows are usually spoken quietly by the officiant and recited loudly by the bride and bridegroom.

The best man is responsible for providing the rings at the requested moment during the ceremony.

The first kiss should strike a balance between emotion and restraint. A round of applause may follow.

Signing of the Register

The register is signed by the bride and bridegroom, the officiant and two to four witnesses (often the chief bridesmaid, the best man and the parents). The bride signs the register using her maiden name.

The Recessional The bride and bridegroom leave the ceremony by walking back down the aisle; traditionally the bride takes the bridegroom's left arm. They are followed by the bridesmaids, child bridesmaids and pages, who are followed by the mother of the bride and father of the bridegroom and, behind them, the father of the bride and mother of the bridegroom. Sometimes the chief bridesmaid follows behind the newlyweds on the best man's arm.

Confetti Real flower petals should be used where possible. Some of the most appealing are fresh rose petals or dried delphinium petals. Many ceremony venues ban metal confetti and paper confetti may also be restricted.

After The Ceremony Any photography should happen as quickly and efficiently as possible; this is not the time for the full formal photography session as guests will be kept waiting. Similarly, guests should not be kept in the church for too long while the bride and bridegroom pose for photographs as they leave the church.

The best man should see the bride and bridegroom to the bridal car; they leave first to ensure that they are at the reception to receive their guests. The rest of the wedding party should follow as soon as possible, along with some of the ushers and the photographer. The remaining ushers should organise guests and any transport that has been provided. They should clear up order of service sheets, check for belongings left behind and organise for any flower arrangements to be taken on to the reception.

Civil Ceremonies

Practical and non-religious elements from a Church of England ceremony may be applied to a civil or register office wedding.

The style and extent to which non-religious traditions are included depends upon the practicalities of the venue and the preferences of the couple. For example, the bridegroom and best man may choose to await the arrival of the bride at the front; alternatively, the couple may proceed to the front together. Any special vows should have been practised and learnt by heart by the couple. If the reception is being held at a separate venue, it is helpful to have a designated 'best man' (or woman), who should see the couple to the wedding car. If the reception is being held at the same venue, then ushers should be on hand to point guests in the right direction.

The Reception

Style of Reception From a drinks reception to a dinner-dance, the reception should offer as much hospitality as possible. A seated lunch or dinner is the most usual format, however buffets are also popular and, for a short reception, a drinks party-style format with canapés is a practical idea. No format is more correct than another – the key thing is that guests are well cared for and given plenty to eat and drink.

Venues If the reception venue is different from the ceremony venue it should, ideally, be located close by. Guests should not be expected to travel for long distances between locations.

Choosing a suitable reception venue usually boils down to a decision between a marquee at a private house (traditionally the bride's parents' home) or a hired venue, for example a hotel.

A hired wedding venue should have good facilities; it is important that style is not favoured over practicality. If a hotel is chosen, it should not be assumed that guests would want to stay there overnight.

A wedding marquee provides the bride and bridegroom with a blank canvas on which they can impose their own style. A fine balance must be struck between having enough room for comfort and so much space that the marquee lacks atmosphere.

For a marquee or hired venue, there are some key considerations to ensure the best experience for guests: sufficient parking, good signposting, plenty of lavatories, ample seating and suitably sized areas for drinks, dining and, if applicable, dancing. There should be proper heating in cold weather and effective ventilation on warm days, as well as cover from rain, shade from sun and protection from mud. For a marquee wedding, neighbours should be warned about the possibility of noise.

Reception Food Food must be considered carefully and well planned. The menu should suit a range of tastes and the time of year should be considered: shepherd's pie on a hot summer's day is not to everyone's taste, and messy, intricate canapés are impractical for guests who are standing and holding a drink. Anything with a very overpowering smell (fish, curry etc) may also spoil the ambience.

The caterer should be warned in advance of any dietary requirements. Guests should have been asked to let the host know in the extra information sheet sent out with the invitation. The staff – for example the photographer, the band or DJ, the car park attendant – may also need to be catered for.

For a seated meal, it is considerate to provide menu cards on the table; they can also indicate when the cake will be cut and the speeches made.

Reception Drink Champagne or Pimm's are traditionally served at a drinks reception or before the meal; there should also be non-alcoholic choices, as well as tea and coffee, on offer. Wine should be served at the table during the meal, as well as plenty of water and a non-alcoholic option. Glasses should be charged before the speeches begin, ready for the toasts; champagne is the traditional choice.

A bar or table offering drinks should be in place after the meal if the reception carries on into the evening. It is usual to provide drink for the guests during the day; at a hired venue, guests may be required to pay for drinks later on during the evening or when an allocation runs out.

Ambience and Lighting Table centres should not be an inconvenience for guests; sight lines must be kept clear and guests should be able to see everyone at the table without having to peer around large arrangements. Lighting should be intimate yet not so dark that guests struggle to see their food.

Toastmaster A toastmaster, or master of ceremonies, may be used to announce the key moments of the reception to the guests. It is an important role that requires excellent organisation, as well as a loud voice. There are many professional toastmasters that can be hired; choose someone who is a member of an official association. Alternatively, a loud-voiced and confident usher or friend may be asked to be master of ceremonies.

Music and Entertainment Music should enhance rather than intrude on the ambience of the reception. It is not essential at a drinks reception and may be intrusive while guests are eating. If there is background music, it should be at a suitable volume. If there is dancing in the evening, the choice of music should appeal to guests of all ages, at least at the beginning.

WEDDING CAKE A wedding cake is said to symbolise fertility and the couple's shared life together. A traditional wedding cake is a tiered fruitcake, decorated and iced in white royal icing, sometimes sparsely decorated with flowers. Traditionally, the top tier of the fruitcake was kept back for the christening of the first child.

Many couples choose to break with convention and opt for something different, for example a flavoured cake (such as chocolate or lemon).

It has also become increasingly popular to have a wedding cake for pudding and, in this instance, a non-conventional option would be chosen, for example a *croquembouche* or a stack of individual puddings.

Traditionally, the cake is cut after the meal and the speeches, and is announced by the master of ceremonies or toastmaster. If the cake is being served as pudding, then it should obviously be cut after the main course. When cutting the cake, the bridegroom should place his right hand over the bride's right hand. They make the cut together, and the bride takes the first bite, then hands the piece to the bridegroom.

It was customary to send a slice of fruitcake to those unable to attend the wedding, but this habit has died out. Leftover slices of cake may be individually boxed and given to guests as they leave.

WEDDING FAVOURS Wedding favours come in all shapes and sizes but are not essential. They will be well received by children – sweets or something to play with are good choices – while those for adults may include a small box of chocolates or a packet of flower seeds.

LOOKING BACK...

Wedding favours were distributed in the church. The bridesmaids would give them out to family and guests during the signing of the register. Ladies received a sprig of orange blossom with silver leaves and a white ribbon, and men silver oak leaves and acorns. The favours were fixed to the left-hand side of the bodice or coat. Wedding favours were distributed at Queen Victoria's wedding in 1840; it was reported in *The Times* that every lady received a white favour made of 'white satin riband, tied up into bows and mixed with layers of rich silver lace' or simply 'riband intermixed with sprigs of orange flower blossom.'

SEATING PLAN   The seating plan is a critical organisational task of planning the reception and must be done well in advance. However, it becomes an increasingly difficult juggling act as complications arise, people drop out and new guests are added, so last minute changes should be expected.

It should be decided if there will be a traditional top table and whether young and old will be mixed. People's personalities, history and interests should be considered when placing individuals. If possible, each guest should be flanked by people of the opposite sex and be able to recognise at least one other person on their table. Family and close friends should be seated with a good view of the bride, bridegroom and speech-makers.

Tables should be large enough to ensure that guests are not cramped but small enough to feel intimate. Be cautious of seating guests too close to speakers, uplighters, drafts or the entrance to the kitchen. Round tables are usually the most social; if long tables are used, seat someone at each end to ensure that everyone has someone sitting next to them on both sides.

TOP TABLE   A top table should be positioned so guests can see the wedding party – sometimes they are raised – as well as the wedding party having a good view of the room. At a traditional rectangular 'top table', the wedding party sits along one side in a conventional order, facing the table from left to right: the chief bridesmaid, the father of the bridegroom, the mother of the bride, the bridegroom, the bride, the father of the bride, the mother of the bridegroom, the best man. Circular and oval tables are also popular.

If there are difficult family situations then a practical solution must be found. If the parents of the bride or bridegroom are divorced, then a simple solution is to give each parent (and their partner or spouse if applicable) a 'top' table for their friends and family. The bride and bridegroom then host their own table of the best man, bridesmaids and ushers.

TABLE PLANS AND PLACE CARDS   A table plan should be clearly displayed; for large weddings, more than one may be required. Alternatively, small cards with the guest's name one side and a table number on the other can be laid out. This can create interest and conversation as guests establish who is sitting at their table; it is also an easy way to make last minute changes. Place cards should be handwritten and the inclusion of surnames is helpful for other guests.

CHILDREN — Every effort should be made to accommodate children and babies; parents should keep an eye on their children throughout the day. Children of a certain age may sit together; smaller ones should sit with their parents or nannies. It can be sensible to serve a children's menu and provide party bags. Special provisions are sometimes provided: a play-area; an entertainer; face painting; dressing-up; a television showing films suitable for all ages; a room to sleep in with a nanny or child-minder.

RECEIVING LINES — A receiving line allows for the hosts and key members of the wedding party to greet or be introduced to the guests. It does not have to be held at the entrance of the reception; it is best to choose a practical place that will allow for a good flow of people.

Traditionally, the bride and bridegroom and both sets of parents (and sometimes the best man and chief bridesmaid), make up the receiving line. To ensure it does not take too long, it is sensible for those who are receiving the guests to stand opposite each other, rather than side-by-side. This keeps the line moving and makes it easier to make group introductions, rather than meeting or greeting each guest one by one. The ushers should point guests towards the receiving line on arrival at the reception. Guests should be given a drink while they are waiting and provided with a top-up if the line is slow.

Receiving lines are recommended for large weddings or short drinks receptions, but they are not compulsory and can be time-consuming.

SOCIALISING AND HOSTING — Although traditionally the bride's parents are the hosts, the bride and bridegroom must ensure that they mix with all of the guests. They should not allow themselves to be monopolised by close friends and family. It is practical for the couple to visit each of the tables between courses; they should also accept all offers to dance, if applicable.

GUEST ETIQUETTE — Weddings are a time for celebration and the reception will usually take on a party atmosphere. In general, a wedding day lasts for a long time with food served at unconventional times. Care should be taken to pace oneself and last the course. Guests should not monopolise the bride and bridegroom, or upstage them. It is good form to be polite to older guests, and to socialise with everyone and not just mix with existing friends.

The Speeches

The speeches are both a formality, dictated by convention, and a highlight of the wedding day. Traditionally, they begin with the father of the bride; a close friend or godfather, or whoever gave her away, may also give the speech. He is followed by the bridegroom and finally the best man.

Timings   The speeches typically take place towards the end of a drinks reception or, at a sit-down reception, after pudding; sometimes it is preferred that they happen earlier, especially if the speakers are nervous, but guests' needs must be considered and people should not be required to stand for a long time nor should the meal be delayed excessively if guests are hungry and drinking.

Practicalities must also be taken into account: the ushers should discreetly inform the guests that the speeches will be taking place, particularly if people are outside or in the loos; everybody must be able to hear what is being said (a microphone may be required); a glass of champagne for the toasts should be distributed before the speeches start.

Preparation   The speechmakers should spend time preparing and practising their speeches. It is perfectly acceptable to refer to brief notes, so long as the entire speech is not read directly off the page.

Speeches should be appropriate both in content and in length. Indiscreet stories may be embarrassing, and inappropriate and rambling reminiscences – over-extended with in-jokes and witticisms – will challenge the audience's attention span. Speechmakers should be aware of their upcoming responsibilities and ensure that they don't drink too much beforehand.

Thank Yous   The father of the bride and the bridegroom will usually thank those who have helped with the wedding. It should be agreed in advance who is being thanked by whom; it is important not to forget anybody, or mispronounce any names.

The Father of the Bride   Traditionally the father of the bride (or person chosen to give this speech) begins by thanking the guests for coming and those involved with organising the wedding. He may then indulge in some affectionate anecdotes about the bride and her achievements, before welcoming the bridegroom into the family. The father of the bride's speech finishes with a toast to 'the bride and bridegroom'.

The Bridegroom

The bridegroom's speech should consist of some heartfelt words about his new wife, family and the wedding day. First he thanks the father of the bride (or equivalent) on behalf of himself and his new wife – the reference to his 'wife' usually raises a cheer from the audience. He then thanks the guests for coming, the bride's parents (if they are hosting the wedding), his parents for raising him and the best man for supporting him. He then says a few words about his new wife. Traditionally, the bridegroom's speech finishes with a toast to 'the bridesmaids'; in practice, many bridegrooms break with this tradition and also toast their bride.

Some bridegrooms choose to present the mothers (if applicable) with bouquets and give the bridesmaids a present during their speech. While this is not incorrect, it is not traditional nor expected and a quieter, less public time may be chosen to give thank-you presents.

See p 271 for thank-you presents

The Best Man

The best man's speech is expected to be the highlight of the proceedings; a witty, entertaining account of the bridegroom and a sincere reflection on their friendship. He (or, in some cases, she) should begin by responding on behalf of the bridesmaids and thanking the groom, if they were toasted. He may then quickly read out messages – originally telegrams and letters, nowadays usually emails, letters or messages – from friends and relations who couldn't attend. He then tells a selection of anecdotes about the bridegroom, and includes some stories about the couple, how they met, their relationship and a few compliments for the bride.

The aim is to be witty and amusing; stories and jokes should be funny and light-hearted, never rude, uncomfortable or smutty. He finishes with a toast to 'Mr and Mrs [newly-weds' surname]'. He will then announce the cutting of the cake, if applicable.

Other Speakers

Some brides like to make a speech themselves; this would normally happen after the bridegroom's speech. It is not uncommon for the chief bridesmaid also to say something. In unusual or unconventional circumstances, alternative key individuals can make a wedding speech, such as the mother of the bride or the father of the bridegroom, however the number of speechmakers should be limited to make sure that the speeches don't go on for too long.

Impromptu speeches can be unnerving for the speakers and disruptive. All speechmakers should confer beforehand about the order of speaking.

After the Reception

First Dance It is by no means compulsory to have a first dance. For some couples, it is a daunting prospect, whereas others opt for a fully choreographed spectacle. The bride and bridegroom should consider the pace and the length of the song, and check that the sentiment is appropriate. As the song ends and the next one starts, the wedding party joins the couple on the dance floor. Alternativeley, some couples will start by dancing on their own, and then beckon others to join them as the song progresses.

Dancing Traditions Traditionally, the bridegroom should dance with each of the mothers, the bride with both fathers, the mother of the bride with the father of the bridegroom, the father of the bride with the mother of the bridegroom and the best man with the chief bridesmaid. It is customary and good manners for the male guests to ask each of the ladies from their table to dance.

Going Away Traditional manners indicated that guests stayed until after the bride and bridegroom had left, but as modern weddings often end later, it is acceptable for guests to leave before the newlyweds. The couple do not want to be the last ones standing but they should not miss out on the party; an early departure may also upset those who have gone to great trouble to attend.

The couple should agree on a departure time in advance and strictly adhere to it. Timings may have been communicated to guests and a late departure may be inconvenient, for example taxis may have been booked or babysitters organised.

Traditionally, the best man and ushers decorate the going away vehicle, but this can be impractical if it is a taxi or not personally owned. If the bride and bridegroom are staying in the reception venue then there may be less of a formal 'going away' moment.

It should be announced that the couple are about to leave, allowing time for guests to assemble. The chief bridesmaid or mother of the bride will usually attend to the bride. The decision on whether to change out of the wedding dress is totally personal.

Throwing the Bouquet Traditionally, the bride tosses her bouquet backwards over her head into the crowd; the single woman who catches it is believed to have received some of the bride's good fortune and will be the next to marry.

WEDDINGS

AFTER THE WEDDING

Presents and Thank Yous

The bride and bridegroom can show their appreciation of the wedding team's hard work and efforts by buying them a present. Traditionally, the bridegroom buys something for the mothers, bridesmaids, best man and ushers. These presents are usually given out on the morning of the wedding.

The mothers often receive a bouquet of flowers and the bridesmaids a piece of jewellery to wear on the day. These may not always be suitable choices so other more appropriate presents may be given. Occasionally the bridegroom may give out these presents during his speech.

See pp 267–268 for speeches

The bridegroom should give the best man a memorable present he can keep; cufflinks or hip flasks are traditional choices. The ushers' presents need not be as generous as the best man's; a bottle of good-quality whisky or something similar is usual.

Anyone who made a significant contribution to the wedding should also receive a present from the bride and bridegroom.

A thank-you card or letter from the bride and bridegroom should acknowledge every wedding present. Traditionally, these were sent as soon as the present was received. Most couples, however, choose to send out all the thank-you letters promptly on their return from honeymoon; some may even start to write them while they are away.

Guest Thank Yous

While traditionally wedding guests do not write and thank the mother of the bride, a letter of thanks to the hosts – for example, the parents of the bride, or the bride and bridegroom if they have hosted the day – will always be a welcome gesture.

New Names

Both opposite and same-sex couples are now entitled to change their names on marriage. They can opt to retain their original surnames, or the couple can create their own double-barrelled surname by using both of their original surnames. Men have the same rights as women to take their partner's surname.

The British marriage certificate states the surnames of the parties prior to their marriage and is the only supporting evidence required for either party, or both, to change their surname. The same applies to civil partnership certificates.

If the couple adopts a double-barrelled name that does not derive from their surnames, a change of name by deed poll is required.

272 - 279

Social Conventions

Forms of Address

Divorce

Although divorce has become increasingly common and carries no social stigma, it can still lead to a number of social dilemmas, especially on big occasions such as weddings and funerals when juggling the different rights and preferences of divorced couples and their families can be extremely challenging.

Divorce

Social Conventions

Divorce & Weddings
Divorce & Funerals

Even in the most difficult of personal situations, courteous and considerate behavior can help to reduce unnecessary animosity and distress.

Spreading the News — When announcing a divorce to friends and family, ensure that you are the one to spread the news – don't let it permeate your social circle through gossip and innuendo.

Immediate family and close friends should be informed, wherever possible, in person. Other family and friends can then be contacted; an email or brief note can suffice. To counter any possible incredulity, it is always wise to state clearly that the divorce is a difficult decision and a last resort, and to stress that every possible effort has been made to save the marriage.

If children are involved, they will be the focus of many people's concern, and it helps to demonstrate that they are also the number one priority, and that you are working hard to agree amicable arrangements.

Divorced people should be aware of the potential difficulties and embarrassment that their friends and relations may experience and should ensure that they are always flexible and accommodating.

Reactions to Divorce — The friends and family of a divorcing couple may need to employ extreme discretion and to master the art of being non-committal – especially if children are involved – even though their loyalties may naturally incline to one partner.

In socially compromising situations when, for example, you may be invited to an event by one of the ex-partners and feel that attending would be an act of disloyalty to the other partner, confront the problem directly. Talk to the people involved, explain your dilemma, and ask them what they would prefer you to do.

Present Etiquette — The engagement ring is an outright present given to the woman on the condition of marriage, and having met that condition, she is entitled to keep it even after the marriage's dissolution. If the ring is a precious heirloom, handed down to the bridegroom, its return is entirely at the woman's discretion.

Wedding presents are, of course, gifts to both parties. The best guide for distributing these goods after a divorce is to pay attention to their original provenance. If they emanate from the husband's side of the family, then he may have first refusal, and vice versa.

SENDING INVITATIONS TO DIVORCED COUPLES

If you are issuing invitations to a big occasion and want both ex-partners to attend, it is wise to enclose a note with the invitation explaining that the other partner has also been invited – especially if the divorce is recent and social relations have not normalised. When drawing up seating plans for a formal occasion you should respect the estrangement, and ensure that divorced couples are not seated together or in close proximity.

DIVORCE & WEDDINGS

ATTENDING AN EX-PARTNER'S WEDDING

Traditionally, ex-partners weren't invited to remarriages, but social conventions have become more fluid and invitations may be extended. Ex-partners should feel no obligation to attend, even if children are involved, and are quite within their rights to decline gracefully (no apologies or explanations are needed).

SECOND MARRIAGES AND INTEGRATING CHILDREN

It is understandable that the bride and groom will want children from previous relationships to be involved in the celebration of their new marriage. Children are often happy to play a special role, such a being a bridesmaid, pageboy, or even best man, but they should always be consulted in case they wish to stay in the background. The couple must discuss these issues at an early stage, both with the children and with ex-partners.

See p 230 for children at weddings

When embarking on a second marriage, it is advisable to acknowledge previous marriages if this prevents children, friends, and even ex-in-laws from feeling confused or rejected.

When children are in attendance it is quite appropriate to make reference to them and therefore to a previous marriage in the speeches – keep any allusions wry, affectionate and light-hearted.

CHILDREN'S WEDDINGS

Divorced parents who are planning the wedding of a daughter or son will need to bear in mind that they may want both their parents (and their new partners/spouses, if necessary) to attend the wedding. If this is what they want, parents should do their utmost to accommodate their wishes.

See p 246 for divorced parents

Even if divorced parents are not hosting the wedding (eg if their son is marrying, or if their son or daughter is organising the wedding for themselves), the same rules apply. Unless they are completely estranged, they must assume that they are both expected to attend and, whatever the circumstances, should accede to their children's wishes with the minimum of fuss.

Divorce & Funerals

Ex-In-Laws' Funerals

Divorce doesn't necessarily terminate relationships with the ex-partner's family. Many people find that their quarrel is with their ex-partner only, and may feel nothing but affection for his/her parents, siblings and so on. If this is the case, they may well continue to see them regularly, and expect to attend significant family funerals.

In cases like this, it is only natural for divorced partners to want to attend the funerals of former in-laws, and it is quite socially acceptable to do so. They should be careful not to make assumptions about their inclusion within the ranks of the bereaved family and should not head for the family pews at the front, or walk behind the coffin at the end of the service.

The possible exception to this rule is when an ex-partner is accompanying a small child – for example to an ex-father-in-law's funeral. In this case, the relationship with the deceased's grandchild may entitle the divorced parent to 'family status'. If in doubt, they should discreetly ask a member of the family where to sit.

It is wise to maintain a tactful and dignified distance and never upstage the blood family when it comes to displays of grief.

Ex-Partner's Funeral

In some instances, when a divorced partner has remarried and repudiated their first marriage, ex-partners may find themselves airbrushed out of the new family. This exclusion may well extend to the aftermath of a death. In cases like this, it might be wise to avoid the funeral service altogether, or seek guidance from a family friend to check whether your presence might cause distress. If there is a memorial service, attending that may be an easier alternative.

DIVORCE

FORMS OF ADDRESS

Forms of Address

See p 62 for untitled persons

Traditionally, a man's style of address post-divorce did not change, whereas his wife was expected to revert to the style of, for example, Mrs Caroline Debrett (ie retaining her title of 'Mrs' and her married surname 'Debrett', but using her own forename).

This rule may still be followed by some members of the older generation, but it is by no means the rule for younger women. Many women, especially those who combine a working life with a married life, choose not to use their husband's surname at all, retaining their maiden name throughout the marriage. In this circumstance, the dissolution of a marriage will have no effect on the style of address for the female partner; the only question is whether she prefers to be Mrs, Miss or Ms Caroline Davies, for example, or just Caroline Davies with no title.

Some divorced women, who previously assumed their husband's surname, may prefer to revert to their maiden name. Often this happens where there are no children from the marriage. If there are children, however, women may choose to retain their married surnames and continue to use 'Mrs', to avoid a situation where the mother is using a different surname from that of her children.

Writing to an Untitled Divorcee

When writing to a divorcee, therefore, it is advisable to follow the conventional option, and call her 'Mrs Charlotte Debrett' (ie use her forename and her married surname). If in doubt, ask the woman in question or a reliable friend or business colleague.

Peerage and Courtesy Titles

When a peeress obtains a divorce the general rule is that she places her forename before her title, for example Mary, Duchess of Mayfair. This is a practical measure to avoid confusion should the peer in question marry again. If a divorced peer remains unmarried his former wife may continue to use her title without the qualification of her forename.

If Miss Jane Debrett marries the Hon Michael Hill she becomes the Hon Mrs Michael Hill. On divorce she should be Mrs Jane Hill (since the courtesy title belongs to her husband).

When the Hon Alice Hart (daughter of a peer) marries Mr Debrett she becomes the Hon Mrs Debrett rather than the Hon Mrs James Debrett. Unless the woman he remarries is also a peer's daughter, she can continue being named the Hon Mrs (no first name) Debrett, which differentiates her from her successor. However, it is more common now to use the Hon Mrs Alice Debrett, with the first name reinserted.

280 - 303

Communicating the News
Organising a Funeral
Attending a Funeral
Memorial Services

Death

At a time of great sadness and disorientation, falling back on customs and traditions can be very consoling. Within this framework, however, there are many ways of personalising funeral and memorial services, and many choices must be made. The important thing is that the wishes of the bereaved are always respected and honoured.

Death

Communicating the News

Spreading the Word
Death Notices
Condolence Letters

Certain specific customs and codes of behaviour are important and must be respected at a difficult and sensitive time. An established order of conventions may help the bereaved and should be understood, even by those who may choose to dispense with some aspects of it. Funerals are traditionally discreet and understated but, as it is a very personal process, styles will vary.

News of a Death

The initial news of a death is normally broken to family members and close friends over the telephone or indeed in person. More distant relations and old friends living far away would traditionally have been written to and this is still often the case, especially among the older generation, who may take comfort in more formal rituals.

It is practical for relations and close family friends to help chief mourners relay the news by telephoning other friends and acquaintances.

Email is now used for convenience, especially internationally. The email in such a case should be written in the style of a traditional letter. Brief text messages are best avoided.

Social Media

While the more conventional methods of spreading news are usually still adhered to, some people are choosing social media in addition, especially when the person has died young, as it is often considered to be the best way of communicating with the deceased's peer group. Great care and sensitivity needs to be used if this route is chosen, but the bereaved need to use what tools are available at such a hard time and should never be criticised.

Bereaved friends and acquaintances may also wish to post messages on a dedicated page on a social media site, so it is important to monitor online activity to ensure that all the content is respectful and appropriate.

Membership of Groups or Organisations

News of the death of a member of a group, organisation, club or society, who may not have been known personally to others, may be passed on through email, often from the secretary of the organisation, with details of a funeral if the family wish this, in the hope that members may be able to attend. Such emails should be thoughtfully worded and the subject matter should contain a warning, such as the words: 'With regret' or 'Sad news'. The body copy should contain a sentence or two explaining who the person was, such as 'for many years our honorary treasurer'.

However, a full obituary tribute is not called for in this communication. The email should not contain other news.

Deaths may also be listed in regular newsletters or in parish notices, where there is usually a section devoted to this subject. Normally the name alone is listed in this case, but in the case of newsletters there may be separate brief tributes.

Spreading the Word

As the type of funeral may now vary, being of all faiths or none, held in a church, a crematorium or even a garden, a newspaper announcement is often the major indicator of what is expected. The wording will let people know whether or not the funeral is private, whether flowers or a donation to a charity are appropriate and whether or not there may be a memorial service held later.

Style of Funeral — Traditional funerals, encompassing a service followed immediately by a crematorium committal or burial (either for all the mourners or just the immediate family) and then a reception, are still considered the norm.

Some families may choose to have a private committal or burial at a separate time from the funeral service. This may take place before the funeral service or even the following day. Such choices may be dictated by practical considerations, a wish for privacy or by the desire not to inflict the more harrowing aspects of the funeral arrangements on to a larger number of people.

Memorial Service — Memorial services, which used to be the preserve of those who were particularly influential in society or their career, are now more widespread. Funerals may be smaller family affairs, held as soon as practical after the death and usually close to the place of death. Memorial services, traditionally held some time after the funeral, give those from farther afield time to organise attendance and may be held somewhere more central or convenient, such as London. This reflects the fact that many of us lead far less localised lives than may once have been the case.

Death Notices

The public announcement of a death and details of the funeral and/or memorial service are traditionally published in a death notice placed by the family in local or national newspapers, usually *The Times* or *Daily Telegraph*, or both. They vary in length, but should be kept simple and to the point. Essential details include the name of the deceased, sometimes with the addition of names of bereaved family members, where the person lived, date of death and details of the funeral.

Additional wording is an important indicator as to the family's wishes. Where and when services will be held, whether to send flowers and where the charity donations are being sent to, as well as the undertaker's details, are often included. Those intending to go to a funeral may want to get details from the undertaker or funeral director about flowers or location, rather than bothering the family. Notices may also state 'no letters', or may include the phrase 'funeral service private' or 'family flowers only'.

A typical death notice would read:

> *DEBRETT On 19 July at home. John, eldest son of the late Mr and Mrs George Debrett of East Sussex, much loved husband of Charlotte and father of Caroline and Thomas. Funeral at The Church, Lewes, East Sussex on 4 August at 11.30. Family flowers only and donations, if desired, to Marie Curie or the Injured Jockey's Fund c/o William & Co Funeral Services, High Street, Lewes, East Sussex BN7 2DD. Tel: 01273 475111*

Looking Back...

A Victorian widow would follow a very strict code of dress for at least a year following her husband's death while she was in 'deep mourning'. Dresses were made from black, lusterless fabrics with black crape [sic] trim. A simple black bonnet with a long crape veil was worn instead of a hat. Black-bordered handkerchiefs were used; the width of the border decreased as the period of mourning passed. Some women wore mourning dress – known as 'widow's weeds' – for the rest of their lives; others went into half or second mourning after a year when the rules relaxed a little, but subdued dress was still expected. A widow would not enter into society during the period of deep mourning.

Condolence Letters

See p 427 for a sample condolence letter

A letter of condolence should be sent promptly after the death announcement, but it is better to write weeks later than not at all, as letters are known to help the bereaved. A letter need not be very long but should be well thought out and appropriate to the relationship with the deceased or their family.

Letters are written to the individual closest to the deceased, who may be a spouse, partner, parent or sibling. Some people may write to the family member of their own generation they know best, or indeed to more than one person. The letter should always be handwritten in ink on writing paper, not a correspondence card and preferably not an off-the-shelf sympathy card. Email should only be used in exceptional circumstances.

Style

Use your natural voice; the tone need not be too solemn. The letter should be personal, mentioning something relating to the deceased, for example personal recollections, distinguishing characteristics or great achievements. If you only knew the deceased slightly and are writing to support the bereaved person, more general expressions of sympathy are appropriate.

The condolence letter is a formal acknowledgment of what has happened and is in itself a support; it need not be regarded as the vehicle for deeply felt emotions or offers of support, which are best conveyed in person. Conventional phrases such as 'I was so sorry to hear/read about your father...' are perfectly acceptable. It is traditional to end the letter by saying no reply is necessary, although the recipient may well do so.

Titles and Styles

Tradition dictated that widows were addressed as 'Mrs John Debrett' as 'Mrs Jane Debrett' indicated a divorcee. However, while it would be perfectly correct to default to this form in a condolence letter, many widows now choose to use their own first names, especially if they have done so throughout their marriage. It is a matter of personal choice.

Widows of peers were traditionally known as the 'Dowager Countess of Aldford' but many now prefer the style 'Hermione, Countess of Aldford' as this may be more widely understood and more practical. Hereditary peers do not use their new titles until after the funeral of their predecessor, so any condolence letter should be addressed to, for example, 'Viscount Tilncy' rather than 'the Earl of Aldford'.

Replies
: A response to letters of sympathy and condolence is not obligatory but many people will choose to reply. If the person is old or infirm and has received a great many letters then a printed card, with the sender's name and address on the top in the style of a correspondence card, may be sent. The card is signed and, if desired, a short personal message is added by hand.

The printed wording is usually quite simple, for example: *Mrs Jane/Mrs John Debrett would like to thank you very much for your kind letter on the death of her husband.*

She has been unable to reply personally to the many hundreds of letters she received but hopes that all those who took the trouble to write will understand and be assured that their letters were much appreciated at this difficult time and will be treasured in the months to come.

See p 321 for bereavement cards

The bereaved person may also want to thank any individuals who have been especially supportive or helpful, have taken part in the service, or perhaps travelled a very long way to come to the funeral.

Those closely involved in the funeral arrangements, such as the speakers or those who have sent flowers, should be thanked. This can be done in a short handwritten letter thanking them for their time and contribution to the day or over the telephone. Bereaved families have a great deal to get through and such letters may take time to be written.

Looking Back...

A Victorian widow used mourning stationery for a year after her husband's death while she was in 'deep mourning'. Writing paper and envelopes had a black border; replies to letters of condolence were sent on this black-edged paper. Visiting cards also had black edging. Black-edged writing paper was still used on the death of Queen Elizabeth The Queen Mother.

Death

Organising a Funeral

Before the Funeral
The Funeral Service
After the Funeral

Before the Funeral

Opinion from relations and family friends can be sought but it is the prerogative of the chief mourner to make the decisions.

If the family are regular churchgoers, and are involved with their parish, then organising a funeral is relatively straightforward. The undertaker and clergyman will know one another and will liaise and endeavour to make things as simple as possible. The majority of people, however, will have to decide on a venue and a style of funeral, the initial choice being between cremation or burial. Once these decisions have been made and a date has been set, the death notice can then be published, with some indication of the form of the funeral that has been chosen.

Setting the Date — The date of a funeral may be governed by red tape or other issues, including the availability of a chosen church or specific priest or vicar, and of key family members, but most are held within a couple of weeks of a death. It is sensible to allow enough time for scattered relations to plan and travel but it can be too stressful for, say, an elderly widow to delay too long.

Sometimes a second service, which is not a full scale memorial service and is held fairly soon after the funeral, is the solution. People whose lives have been split between two or more places may have more than one service, say in London and Wales or Cornwall, but only one will be the funeral as such. Memorial services are usually several months later.

Types of Funeral — Funerals of all kinds have become less traditional, even when held in church, and there is a range of choices that can reflect the personality and taste of the deceased. Some people take comfort in being individualistic while others find solace in the words of the Book of Common Prayer or the requiem mass. Other faiths have their own rituals and traditions. Services that take place at crematoria, with or without a religious element, can vary considerably. It is also possible to hold services outdoors, in a much-loved garden or wood, and to have a green burial. In all cases, the death is being marked and those who knew the deceased have a structure to help the mourning process.

Personal Choice — There are various ways in which a funeral service can be made more personal. These can all be incorporated within the framework of a traditional religious service if required, or form the basic structure of a secular or non-denominational ceremony.

Some families may choose a traditional church and liturgy. On the other hand if the family prefers something more personal or contemporary they should be able to find a sympathetic venue or celebrant. In a rural area, compromise may be necessary, but the parish priest or vicar will do their best to accommodate the wishes of the family.

In the case of a humanist celebrant there is less tradition involved. Other faiths may be stricter than Christianity and have specific rules and traditions. Mourners may simply have to follow the rules of the relevant clergy, with less room for choice.

Most funerals will last between 45 minutes and an hour. Much longer may be a cause of stress.

The Funeral Service

ORDER OF MOURNERS At very traditional church funerals there is an established order of mourners. Although this strict order is not always followed it is usual for the close family to enter the church or crematorium last and leave first, led by the surviving spouse or chief mourner.

The chief mourner enters the church behind the coffin (unless it is already in situ), accompanied by the eldest child (where applicable), with the other children immediately behind. They are followed by the deceased's parents and siblings. If there is no surviving spouse the children follow in order of age, side by side.

A childless individual, a widow or a widower may be accompanied by a sibling or other near relation and, behind them, other siblings and their spouses and children. The family leaves the church in the same order.

MUSIC Music is customarily played before a funeral service, during the committal (at a cremation) and after the service, but there may also be other hymns or songs. The choice of music may reflect the tastes of the deceased, or act as an evocative memory.

Many places of worship are liberal about the music chosen for funerals, so there is no necessity to adhere to sacred music if this does not feel appropriate. However, if opting for a religious service, talk to the clergy involved to ensure that the choice is acceptable. Certain churches will adhere to strict criteria.

Occasionally a musician or singer who was close to the deceased may be willing to perform, or recorded music can be used. If the church has a choir it is usually necessary for them to be remunerated. Hymns may be chosen to reflect the personal taste of the deceased but it is best to choose one or two that may be known to most people and are not too hard to sing, especially if there is no choir. Many older people leave instructions including their choice of music and readings, and these should be followed.

Readings
It is customary at a church funeral service to incorporate readings that may be delivered by children and family members. At a traditional Christian ceremony these are from the Bible, but other readings such as poetry may be used in addition – the funeral director, vicar or celebrant may provide an anthology of such extracts to which you can refer.

In religious services children or grandchildren of the deceased are increasingly encouraged to read a favourite poem, and – as long as they do not feel coerced – this can be very moving. In non-religious services appropriate readings of all kinds may be chosen and are also often read by different family members, children or friends.

The Eulogy
Most clergy will want to preach as an integral part of the service. It is important to discuss this in advance. If the deceased was well known to the vicar or priest then they can speak of them quite naturally. Otherwise it is best if they are given some indication of the person (preferably on paper), including the name by which they were known, although the sermon will tend to focus on the religious rather than the personal.

There can also be one or more address or eulogy, depending on the desired length of the service. These are usually, but not invariably, delivered by close relations, old friends or a distinguished colleague, and may form part of either a religious or secular service. Addresses were not a part of a requiem mass in the Roman Catholic tradition and will usually come at the end, after the mass itself is finished.

An address may follow a chronological, biographical framework, if appropriate, or it can rely instead on episodic recollections and stories. It may follow the more traditional pattern of a eulogy, in which appropriate respect is paid to the achievements of the deceased, or it may be a personal recollection of a close friend.

Some humour can be injected but memorial services are a more appropriate time for hilarious anecdotes than funerals.

SERVICE SHEETS Order-of-service sheets are very important, especially at a funeral with a larger congregation, and can be time-consuming to prepare. They not only guide people through the proceedings but also act as something of an anchor for those attending, giving them something to look at, and are often kept as a memento.

If you do not have a trusted printer the funeral director will recommend one, but take care they do as the family wishes. Make certain there is time for proofs to be checked, ideally by more than one person, and get the clergy to check the verses and versions of the hymns and ensure they are what you have in mind. Opt for good quality card and printing. The usual choice is white card folded into an A5 format. Do not allow the printer to add what they think are suitable flourishes and touches, or to use ornate fonts, unless you specifically want them.

FRONT COVER On the front cover, the names and dates of the deceased are displayed, as well as the name of the church or crematorium and the time of the service. Some people like a symbol, such as a simple black cross, or a photograph or both, and there may be words such as RIP. The celebrant's name may also appear.

CONTENTS Inside, apart from the hymns and readings, other elements of the service may be included for people to follow. For example, in the case of Roman Catholics, the Order of the Mass helps those less familiar with the service and obviates the need for prayer books and hymnals. Some indication as to whether to stand or sit is also helpful. Some hymns and songs are still in copyright and it is courteous to credit the composer, even with older works.

NAMED PARTICIPANTS If time allows, all participants should be named, for example the priest or vicar, the readers, those who have delivered the address or eulogy, the choir, organist and any musicians. Some further instructions may be included, such as details of a charity collection (if one is to be taken) or arrangements for the interment. A verse, passage of prose or a prayer can be included, as something for the congregation to read to themselves.

An invitation to a reception afterwards may also be included, for example: 'Everyone is invited to join Jane and the family for tea at Park House' or 'Jane and the family hope that everyone will join them for lunch at the Red Lion after the service'.

Pallbearers — Family pallbearers are less common than at one time but there are occasions – for example when there is a large number of sons or grandsons – when they may take this on.

Transport — The funeral director will normally bring the coffin to the church or crematorium. For very grand persons there may be some form of lying in state in the church or elsewhere.

Chief mourners may travel in special cars, organised by the undertaker, or simply use their own. Some care needs to be taken if parking is very limited near a church. Directions to the burial ground or crematorium, if applicable, should be handed out at the end of the service and someone should be delegated to make sure that those who have travelled by public transport are not left stranded without a car at any of the locations.

After the Funeral

It is usual to organise an event after the service, either at home, in a hotel or pub, or at another venue such as a club or hall. Details may be given in the order of service sheet. If the family is going to a private burial a helper can be delegated to welcome the rest of the congregation to the venue. The clergy are normally invited, but if they are busy then they must be excused and no offence taken.

It can be difficult to guess the numbers as people are not obliged to reply and there will not have been an invitation as such. It can be useful for one family member to make tactful enquiries.

Lunch — Older people may prefer an early start and like to get home in daylight. Lunch after a late morning service may comprise a small sit-down affair for family, or perhaps a buffet for a larger number. It may well be just sandwiches, but it should be substantial and generous. It is advisable to get help in the form of caterers or friends and relations if planning to provide refreshments at home.

Tea — If the funeral service takes place in the afternoon then tea afterwards can be easier. It is usual to serve alcoholic drinks as well as tea. A display of mementoes or photographs makes a good talking point or distraction for mourners who do not know any other attendees.

DEATH

Attending a Funeral

Who should Attend?
At the Service
Flowers & Donations
After the Service

Who Should Attend?

People attend funerals to mark the death of the person and to comfort the bereaved. The informal expression 'a good send off' may sound slightly disrespectful but in attending a funeral that is the aim.

In rural areas many funerals are still held in large parish churches and parishioners will attend, not just family and close friends. In the country, memorial services are still relatively uncommon, other than for dignitaries or office holders such as lord-lieutenants. Funerals in cities or where the person has less connection with the area where they died are often far smaller.

Letting the Family Know All funerals are considered public events and there is no question of invitations. It is up to an individual to decide whether or not to attend but it can be helpful to let the family know. Close friends and family who are in touch with the bereaved should let them know if they are able to come. If telephoning seems awkward, a quick letter or email saying how sorry you are and that of course you will be coming is appropriate. It may be followed by a full handwritten condolence letter after the funeral, which can include an element of thanks and praise for a lovely service and very kind hospitality afterwards.

'Private' and 'Public' Funerals The family's wishes are paramount and the words 'private funeral' or 'family funeral' in a death notice mean that the funeral will be small and it would not be correct to go. If the time and place are published, then it is a signal that the family does wish people to come and it is correct to make every effort to do so, as a good turn-out is a great comfort. Lives are often quite compartmentalised and people move around and lose track of one another, so the fact that you knew the person but not the family or vice versa should not inhibit you. If in doubt, go, as your presence will undoubtedly be a great support. It is unacceptable to question someone's reasons for attending.

Service Only Those who feel awkward about attending may choose to go to the service but perhaps not to any lunch or tea afterwards. It is polite, however, to shake the hands of family members on leaving the church and to add a brief word or two of sympathy. The words chosen are less important than your manner and the very fact you are present. Those attending a funeral may also be asked to fill in a card left in the pew or sign a book.

ATTENDING ALONE For practical reasons a husband or wife may well attend the funeral alone. An individual may wish to write either on the card or in the book that he is representing another person, who is unable to be there, or possibly an organisation, but should not embellish this with additional phrases or sentiments. These can be expressed separately in a letter if desired.

CHILDREN Allowing children to come to funerals of close relations is now considered advisable for them, as opposed to shrouding the event in mystery. It may not always be practical to attend with babies or small children but, if they are in the congregation, common sense should apply. If you have a small baby, then sit at the end of an aisle or near the back. Children other than family or godchildren usually only come if there was a special connection or request. In the case of the death of, say, a school child, then the whole school or whole class may come, as may an organisation such as Scouts or the Pony Club. They may also come to support a school friend who has lost a parent or sibling, but less often a grandparent or uncle or aunt, unless that person was involved in their own lives.

Children are expected to behave well and be quiet. It is a good thing to explain to smaller children what will happen and if the funeral is taking place in a church and children are not used to attending, take them to a service the previous Sunday.

AT THE SERVICE

PUNCTUALITY It is vital to arrive early for funerals and inexcusable to be late. If it involves a long journey then make sure you know the way and allow time. It is better not to go at all if it is obvious time is too tight. If a person does arrive late they should wait quietly outside or in the church porch. The congregation should be seated before the arrival of the family and before the funeral party brings in the coffin (in some cases the coffin may already be present). It is best not to greet the chief mourners as they arrive.

SEATING The front pews on the right-hand side are usually reserved for family and close friends. The front pews on the left-hand side can be reserved for prominent individuals from an institution or representatives of the deceased's profession, or for family. This can vary according to the layout of the church or venue, but there should be plenty of space reserved for family. Readers need aisle seats near the front.

At a large funeral there are usually ushers, with a list of people requiring specific seating, who will show people to their pews. Those not on a list should take their places quietly further back or to the side. While it is acceptable to try to sit near friends, who may have already been placed, it is incorrect to make a disturbance by clambering over people or making a fuss. It is best not to talk or look round but acknowledge greetings quietly.

After the service allow the family members to leave first, as at a wedding. Save the social chat until you are outside. Walk slowly and show respect. If there is a plate for offerings for the church or a chosen cause then attend to this as you go out. Have your donation ready so that the people behind you are not held up.

Mobiles and Gadgets

Mobiles should be switched off and all silent activities avoided, for example checking email or sending text messages.

Dress Codes

Black is still the usual colour of mourning but it is not essential to wear unbroken black. A dark colour, such as grey or navy blue, is acceptable.

Men should wear a dark suit with a black tie. Women should dress fairly formally and skirts are still considered more correct than trousers. Showing respect by dressing modestly and smartly is more important than unbroken black. Hats are often worn, but are not essential. They should be relatively simple and appropriate to the season. Remember that very high heels will be difficult to manage in the soft grass of a graveyard.

In cold weather, both men and women should wear a smart tailored coat or jacket rather than a fleece or anorak.

Children should be neat and tidy, with young boys in jackets and girls in dresses and coats if possible.

Occasionally a family will make it known that they want something particular in the way of dress, for instance if the dead person hated black or any kind of formality.

See p 190 for morning dress

At some very formal and grand funerals men may wear morning dress, traditionally worn with not only a black tie, but a black waistcoat. At state occasions military uniforms may also be worn. In such cases, unlike normal funerals, people receive an invitation, which would include instructions.

ROYAL FAMILY — Traditionally the Royal Family does not attend private funerals other than on very exceptional occasions. However, they do send representatives to both funerals and memorial services. The royal representative arrives after the congregation but before the family and will usually be placed at the front on the left. The congregation will rise as the representative makes their way down the aisle.

THE GRAVESIDE — Sometimes the congregation goes to the lunch or tea, while the family attends the burial itself, which may be held away from the church where the service was held. In other cases, especially in the country, everyone goes to the graveside. Different rules apply in different traditions but the celebrant will almost certainly point out any rules or they may be printed on the service sheet. In any case, less close friends should hang back, while allowing the family to stand closer to the grave itself. Usually only family members throw soil, or occasionally flowers, into the grave.

FLOWERS & DONATIONS

Death notices (*see p 285*) often mention flowers. They are becoming less usual than they once were for practical reasons, as they are no longer particularly welcome in hospitals and fewer people are buried in large rural graveyards. Flowers, therefore, are considered by many to be wasteful and less practical than a donation.

CHOOSING THE FLOWERS — Family flowers may be in the form of a wreath or perhaps a cross, and the flowers of close family members are often placed on the coffin. If a non-family member does send flowers a simple bouquet, or flat spray, is more usual than a wreath. A large organisation may send a wreath. Colours are usually white or cream but if it was known that the person whose funeral it is loved, for example, pink, then choose accordingly.

CARDS — It is important to make sure any flowers are clearly and securely marked, as the family will wish to know who they are from and will wish to thank the donor verbally or in writing. If the flowers are being sent because someone is unable to attend, due to absence abroad for example, an explanation may be added to the card; however any message should be primarily addressed to the deceased, rather than the family. For practical reasons the card may have been written by the florist so it is important to check they have the name and wording correct. Ideally the card should be handwritten by the sender but clearly this is not always possible. Simplicity and discretion are crucial.

After the Service

During the funeral service, mourners may be notified about details of the wake; alternatively an invitation may be printed on the order of service. Those not wishing to attend may make a brief excuse on leaving the service. It is not obligatory to attend, nor is the wake intended just for close friends.

Those not at the burial can go directly to the lunch or tea and it is quite in order to be served with drinks or food before the family returns. Be aware that it is not a party, so do not overstay your welcome. However, in certain cultures you will be expected to make a night of it. It is a time for sensitivity and awareness, which, as always, are the essence of etiquette.

Looking Back...

A grand Victorian funeral procession was an ostentatious affair made up of many carriages. The first carriage, the hearse that carried the coffin, was filled with flowers and covered with a canopy of black ostrich feathers. It was pulled by six black horses with black ostrich plumes on their heads, sometimes wearing black velvet cloths to the ground. Further carriages, with drawn blinds, followed this carrying the mourners. The procession was surrounded either side by a line of hired mourners, known as mutes.

Death

Memorial Services

PLANNING THE SERVICE
INSCRIPTIONS & MEMORIALS

Planning the Service

Once the preserve of the very grand, or famous, memorial services have become an increasingly popular way of celebrating the life of an individual.

It is quite customary for a funeral or cremation to be a small and private affair. Then, usually several months after the death, a much wider circle of acquaintances attends a memorial service to celebrate, as well as commemorate, a person's life.

Announcements
If a very large number of people is expected to attend, in the case of a public figure or even a private person who had a large circle of friends, it is customary to place an announcement in a national or local newspaper. Traditional wording for a memorial service announcement might read:

DEBRETT – A memorial service for Mr John Debrett will be held at St Margaret's Church, Westminster, on Tuesday 17th October, at 11am.

In the case of major public figures, a notice may be placed in the Court Circular or Registry pages of one of the newspapers asking people planning to attend to apply for admission tickets. These will rarely be refused but are both a security measure and a way of assessing numbers.

Even for a smaller service an announcement is a good way of spreading the news. Otherwise the telephone, word of mouth or social media can be used, or cards and letters may be sent.

If you do receive a card then reply. However, people can, and do, attend memorial services without having been invited and without letting anyone know. This is particularly the case in larger London churches.

Locations
Conventionally, memorial services were held under the auspices of the Church, although increasingly they can be entirely secular affairs, and may be held within a variety of venues, from halls to theatres, hotels and pubs to beauty spots. Families may choose a place that was particularly meaningful to the deceased or one that works well from a practical point of view.

Schedule
Services usually last between 45 minutes to an hour. Memorial services are almost always held in the late morning. Generally,

people are expected to disperse after a memorial service and make their own arrangements. Occasionally there is some kind of reception or more often a family lunch, to which people are specifically invited. In some cases, especially with a younger person's memorial service, a group of friends will organise an informal gathering.

Format of the Service

There is no established rite for a memorial service in the Book of Common Prayer and families are free to create a service, incorporating prayers, readings, hymns, music and addresses. Old orders of service are often kept as mementoes so referring to them can be a useful source of ideas for structure and readings.

The family or, in some cases, friends of the deceased, can all contribute to the format of a memorial service. They can make their own suggestions for readings, music, speakers and so on, and liaise with the priest, vicar or celebrant to reach an agreed format. Roman Catholics will opt for a memorial mass for the repose of the person's soul, rather than a celebration of their life. However it will be a less solemn occasion than a funeral.
For informal and non-religious services the family may simply devise a programme.

Seating

The seating at a memorial service is as for a funeral. So, in a traditional church setting, the front pews on the right-hand side are usually reserved for family and close friends. The front pews on the left-hand side may be reserved for prominent individuals from an institution or representatives of the deceased's profession, or for family. The immediate family are the last to enter and the first to leave, and the congregation stands for both their entry and departure. A royal representative will enter just before the family and, again, the congregation should rise.

Dress Codes
See p 190 for morning dress

Conventionally, dress is sombre – dark suits and black ties for men, dark clothes for women – but unbroken black is not necessary. At a very grand service, traditional morning dress may be worn, in which case most women would wear formal day dress with hats. However, if the person being commemorated and their family are informal characters, it is not necessary to adhere to a strict dress code.

Service Sheets

As with a funeral, a full order of service is printed. More light-hearted elements, such as photographs and passages from favourite authors, may be included and it is very much seen as a memorialising of the individual's life and tastes.

TONE
With the initial shock and despair of bereavement behind them, mourners are generally more able to contribute to, participate in – and even enjoy – the service. Frequently, recollections and speeches are affectionate and amusing, and laughter is not considered inappropriate or embarrassing.

NEWSPAPER REPORTS AND OBITUARIES
Cards to fill in are often provided in pews or on seats so that the family will know who has come.

In the case of a person of note the broadsheets sometimes send reporters to take names. Lately, however, they are inclined to ask the family to organise this for themselves, which may mean hiring someone who is familiar with titles and precedence to take names and be responsible for getting them to the paper for a deadline as the report will be run the following day.

It is the newspaper's editor's decision as to whether a memorial service will be recorded on the Court Circular page, and family should liaise with them, though editors may already be aware if the service has been announced in their paper's pages. It is also up to the paper whether the person gets an obituary. These may appear many weeks or even months after a death. Some families may want to designate a member to assemble the salient facts, but families need to accept that modern obituaries are not always eulogies.

INSCRIPTIONS & MEMORIALS

Inscriptions, for example on plaques and memorials such as gravestones, usually include all forenames and the surname. Postnominal letters denoting orders, decorations and degrees may also be included. For a peer, all of the forenames are included, with or without the appropriate prefix. If the prefix is used, it is generally given in full, such as 'The Right Honourable' as oppose to 'Rt Hon'. A peer's surname and the territorial designation can also be used. A peer or baronet is sometimes numbered, for example: John Andrew Robert Buxton Cavendish, 11th Duke of Devonshire, KG, MC, PC.

It is a matter of choice as to whether coats of arms are to be displayed. If there is any doubt about their accuracy, reference should be made to the College of Arms or, for Scottish families, to the Lord Lyon King of Arms.

MODERN MANNERS
COMMUNICATION
SOCIAL GRACES
TABLE MANNERS
AT HOME
PUBLIC MANNERS

Modern Manners

306 - 329

STATIONERY

INVITATIONS

CARDS, LETTERS, EMAILS & TEXTS

BUSINESS CORRESPONDENCE

Communication

Whether writing a thank-you letter, a business letter, an invitation email or text, the medium should match the message. Wording, stationery, typographic design and layout should all be used to add clarity and elegance to your communications.

Communication

Stationery

Writing Paper
Visiting Cards

Writing Paper

Good personal stationery shows an attention to detail and appreciation of the finer things in life. It gives correspondence gravitas and helps ensure that it receives the recipient's full attention. If bespoke stationery is not possible, well-chosen writing paper, envelopes and correspondence cards will show that you have taken some trouble.

PRINTING TECHNIQUES — The smartest and most traditional letterheads are engraved, where letters are engraved or etched on to metal dies or plates which are then inked and stamped, creating a raised texture. Raised type may also be produced by thermographic printing. Designed to create the same effect as engraving, thermography is cheaper but is rarely as delicate and is often too shiny. More people will choose flat printing, or lithography, which is a more affordable and versatile alternative. The craft of letterpress printing, which is enjoying a revival, can be a creative choice.

WRITING PAPER — Personal letters are traditionally handwritten on writing paper, with a minimum weight of 100 gsm to avoid show-through. The standard size is either W6¼ x H8 inches (16 x 20 cm) or W5½ x H7 inches (14 x 18 cm). The traditional colours are white or muted shades; more contemporary styles may be in more adventurous colours. Use a lined undersheet to keep text straight. Black or blue ink is recommended. Watermarked paper is usually a sign of good quality.

LETTERHEADS — A personal letterhead should include a postal address and telephone number, traditionally in a dark type. Do not include your name or email address in a letterhead used for purely social, personal correspondence.

Consideration should be given to the layout, style, balance and size of the typeface and the spacing of each line of the address – not all printers will advise you on this or have the expertise.

ENVELOPES — Envelopes for private correspondence should be of a suitable size, allowing for the writing paper to be folded only once or twice. Traditionally, they should have gummed diamond flaps and the colour should match the writing paper. Originally introduced as a means of preventing show-through and therefore increasing security, more expensive envelopes may be tissue-lined, either in a matching or contrasting colour.

STAMPS — Stamps, not franking machines, should be used for personal correspondence.

CORRESPONDENCE CARDS — Correspondence cards should be W6 x H4½ inches (15 x 11 cm), printed or engraved on card of a minimum of 300 gsm. They include the name, address, telephone number and, more frequently now, email address. When a postal address is not permanent, a name, mobile number and email address will suffice. Correspondence cards are always sent in an envelope.

INFORMALS — A rarer, yet useful, variation is a folded card, known as an 'informal', sized W4 x H3 inches (10 x 7.5 cm) with the name printed on the front without any prefixes, for example, 'Charlotte Debrett'. An informal can be used like a personal compliments slip, for example it may be sent along with a present, with a message written, as in a card, on the blank space inside.

A more utilitarian option is a flat-printed postcard, usually on white card, with the name, address and telephone number printed in black above a keyline, laid out in a landscape format.

VISITING CARDS

TRADITIONAL VISITING CARDS — Visiting cards played an important role in the social world when 'calling' was part of everyday life and there was a strict etiquette surrounding their use. Although rare, the use of traditional visiting cards persists in some areas and is a pleasing convention.

Made from the finest quality card, traditional visiting cards are engraved. Names are positioned in the middle with the address in the bottom left-hand corner.

A gentleman's card, usually W3 x H1½ inches (7.6 x 3.8 cm), traditionally gives a title, rank, private or service address (in the bottom left-hand corner or one in each lower corner if two are desired) and club (in the bottom right-hand corner).

A lady's card is traditionally W3¼ x H2¼ inches (8.3 x 5.7 cm), though W3½ x H2½ inches (8.9 x 6.4 cm) is sometimes used.

Joint cards, or those for families, are the same size as a lady's card.

TITLES ON CARDS The name of a peer or peeress is shown by his or her grade, but with no prefix, not even 'The'. For example, 'Duke of Mayfair', 'Earl of Aldford'. Courtesy styles derived from a peerage are shown as 'Lord John Jones', 'Lady Emily Jones' etc, but 'Hon' is not used: those so styled are shown as 'Mr', 'Mrs', 'Ms' or 'Miss' as applicable. A baronet or knight is shown as 'Sir John Jones' – without the suffix 'Bt' or 'Bart' – and his wife as 'Lady Jones'.

OTHER STYLES The only other prefixes used on cards are ecclesiastical titles, ranks in the armed forces, and 'Dr' or 'Professor'. Untitled men precede their surname with 'Mr', followed by their forename and/or initials.

See p 62 for formal address

A married woman may use her husband's forename or initials, although this is increasingly rare. A widow traditionally uses the same style as during her husband's lifetime. A divorced woman uses her own forename or initials and may have chosen to revert to her maiden name.

Suffixes are never used on visiting cards, except those that indicate membership of the armed forces. An archbishop, bishop, dean or archdeacon shows his territorial appointment: for example, 'The Archbishop of Canterbury', 'The Bishop of London', 'The Dean of Norwich' or 'The Archdeacon of Exeter'.

Honours degrees are omitted.

SOCIAL CARDS Social cards are a modern interpretation of traditional visiting cards. Similar to business cards, these are generally printed on thick card of around 350 gsm, and measure W3½ x H2½ inches (8.9 x 6.4 cm) – the same dimensions as a traditional lady's visiting card. They are used in a social environment as a quick and convenient way of exchanging contact details.

Social cards should feature the individual's name, mobile number and email address; the positioning of the text varies but the name is usually positioned centrally. The inclusion of a residential address is optional but rare.

Family social cards, including the names of all the members of the nuclear family – ie those of parents and children – are also an option.

Communication

INVITATIONS

Private Invitations
Formal Invitations
'At Home' Invitations
Contemporary & Informal Invitations
General Considerations
Save-the-Date Cards

Private Invitations

Invitations are minutely calibrated social telegrams, which indicate to guests what they should expect. Their design, layout, printing and quality should always reflect the comparative formality or informality of the occasion; getting it wrong may look pretentious or cause confusion.

Purpose of Invitations

Good invitations give a clear message about all that is needed to be known about the event, including an end time and, where possible, details of food and dress. This information is important to avoid confusion and, potentially, disappointment, which may arise if the host and guest have different expectations.

Invitations to Private Parties

There are three kinds of invitations to private parties:
- formal
- at Home
- contemporary and informal

Traditionally, there were only two types of private invitation: 'Request the pleasure…' and 'at Home', and each would clearly delineate where the event would be held.

Today, 'Request the pleasure…' invitations tend to be reserved for very formal events. At homes are applicable for a number of events, including those that are held in another venue. (On the invitation the 'a' for 'at' is lower case and the 'H' for 'home' is upper case.) Contemporary and informal invitations can provide even more flexibility.

Alternative wording and layouts are acceptable but should be obviously distinct from traditional styles. This will ensure that any deviation is seen as intentional, rather than an error.

Looking Back…

Invitations to private dances were issued in the name of the hostess only. No matter how grand the event, the word 'Ball' would never have appeared on a private invitation card. 'At Home' cards were used with 'Dancing' printed in the corner. The date and timings were filled in by hand in the allotted space, and the guests' names written in the top corner. Some hostesses chose to handwrite the invitations, in which case the word 'Dance' would be included in a friendly note written on small-sized writing paper. Whatever the form of the invitation, a reply would have been expected within three days.

Formal Invitations

> The Earl and Countess of Aldford
> request the pleasure of the company of
> Mr and Mrs John Debrett
> at The Turf Club
> on Friday 9th November
>
> R.S.V.P.
> Park House
> Melton Mowbray
> Leicestershire LE12 6OR
>
> Dinner 8pm
> Black tie
> Carriages at midnight

These are engraved on card of good texture, usually about W6 x H4½ inches (15 x 11 cm) in size, or slightly larger. They are prepared in the name of both the host and hostess. If time is short they may be printed, rather than engraved.

Style — The most traditional and formal style is 'Request(s) the pleasure of the company of…'. Depending on the style of the invitation, the guests' names may be handwritten on the next line. Alternatively, guests' names are handwritten in the top left-hand corner. In this instance, the invitation would read 'Request the pleasure of your company'.

Venue — If the event is to take place at an address other than that to which the replies are to be sent – at a hotel, for example – this is stated on a separate line, before or after the date.

Timings — The time may be placed either after the date or at the bottom right-hand corner before, or in place of, the dress code.

'At Home' Invitations

> Charles and Emma
>
> *Mrs John Debrett*
> *at Home*
> *Sunday 28th September*
>
> R.S.V.P.
> The Lodge
> Little Bealings
> Suffolk IP13 5BT
>
> Lunch
> 1.00 o'clock

An 'at Home' signifies a personal invitation, even if the event will not be held at home.

There are two types of at homes:
- 'closed' at homes for a specific event
- 'open' at homes, with the name of the hostess, 'at Home', RSVP and the address. The date is left open so that the invitations may be used for more than one event.

'Closed' At Home Cards 'Closed' at home invitations for a specific and usually formal event are traditionally engraved on a card of good texture about W6 x H4½ inches (15 x 11 cm) in size, or slightly smaller. In the case of married couples, these are traditionally prepared in the name of the hostess only.

If the time of the event is not a sufficient indication as to its nature, the latter may be stated on the bottom-right: for example, 'Dancing 10 o'clock'. If the invitation extends from 6 to 8.30 pm the description 'cocktails', 'drinks' etc is unnecessary, though it is often included. Guests' names are handwritten in the top left.

'Closed' at home invitations may be sent out by the hostess on behalf of someone else; for example: *at Home for Theo's 21st*.

'Open' At Home Cards With the exception of dances, 'open' at home cards may be used for parties. These are smaller in size than 'closed' at homes, usually W5½ x H3½ inches (14 x 9 cm). The card is printed with the name of the hostess, 'at Home', RSVP and her address. Other details are completed by hand, with the guests' names written top left. A stock of these cards can be ordered for various events.

For small informal parties, simplified 'open' at home cards of the same size – W5½ x H3½ inches (14 x 9 cm) – may be used, which have just 'at Home' and 'RSVP' printed on them.

Contemporary & Informal Invitations

Contemporary Invitations Traditional invitations do not always fit comfortably with contemporary parties, especially those with a theme. With careful consideration and clarity of detail, contemporary invitations may convey to guests the unique look and feel of a party, as well as having the flexibility to include plenty of information. The level of formality of the invitation should accord with that of the occasion.

Informal Invitations It is up to the hosts to choose an invitation style that is appropriate for informal events. Whatever option is chosen, be it a printed invitation, letter, telephone call or email, all the relevant details and arrangements – including the nature of the occasion, timings and dress – must be clearly and successfully conveyed.

James and Helen

Charlotte Debrett

invites you to a party

to celebrate

John's 50th Birthday

on Saturday 25th October

at the Curzon Hotel, W1

R.S.V.P
15 LOTS ROAD
LONDON SW10 8QJ
LOTTIE@GMAIL.COM

NO PRESENTS PLEASE
PLEASE BRING THIS INVITATION WITH YOU

DINNER & DANCING
8.00pm FOR 8.30pm
DRESS: JAZZ AGE

General Considerations

Hosts' Names Where applicable, the exact rank in the peerage of the host and/or hostess is given on all types of invitation.

Joint Parties If there is more than one host or hostess, their names are placed one after the other. The first name corresponds to the address to which the replies are to be sent.

If the host or hostesses are to deal with replies separately, their addresses are placed from left to right at the foot of the card, in the same order as their names.

Dress Codes

See pp 185–195 for dress codes

If the host or hostess considers it necessary to indicate the dress expected to be worn, it should be printed bottom right, eg 'White Tie' for evening dress, 'Black Tie' for dinner jacket.

When necessary, many hosts or hostesses will try to indicate more specifically the level of dress expected, either verbally, in an email, or in a letter or information sheet if one is being sent with the invitation.

Royal Guests

See pp 17–18 for invitations to royal guests

The word 'Decorations' positioned underneath the dress code on a private invitation implies that a member of the Royal Family is expected to be present.

Location If no alternative location is given, it is understood that the event is to be held at the address to which a reply is requested. If the event is taking place in the country, it is useful for a map to be placed on the back of the card or on a separate sheet.

Admission 'Please bring this invitation with you' may be added at the foot of the card. Traditionally this indicated that a member of the Royal Family would be present, but is now used for general security reasons when required.

Sending Out Invitations It is wise to send invitations as early as possible. While a quiet, intimate dinner among close friends may be arranged over the telephone at short notice, it is advisable to give advance warning for a more formal gathering with a larger number of guests.

Names of Guests on Invitations

Guests' names are written in the top left corner, except for formal invitations designed for them to be written on a line in the middle of the card.

The following should be noted:

No prefixes, such as 'The Rt Hon' or 'The Hon', are employed and no letters after the name are included.

The word 'The' is usually omitted for the ranks of marquess and earl, and is always omitted for viscount and baron, as well as for their wives. All peers and peeresses, apart from dukes and duchesses who are referred to by these titles, are given the form 'Lord and Lady Hill'. This is the established custom for all but the most important private events, when the exact rank in the peerage may be given.

Grown-up sons and daughters are usually sent separate invitations even when they live at home. However, when their exact names, or addresses, are not known, it is permissible to add 'and Family', or their forenames, after their parents' names.

The words 'and Guest' or 'and Partner' may be added.

During Ascot week and other occasions for which house parties are given, invitations may show the words 'and House Party' after the names of the guests.

Traditionally, invitations to a married couple, when sent to their home address, are addressed to the wife alone, with both names being inscribed on the invitation card. It has become increasingly common, however, to address the envelope with both names.

Replies

See pp 158–159 for formal replies

Replies are sent on headed writing paper, as for official events, written by hand in the third person. They are traditionally addressed to the hostess even when the invitation is a joint one from both the host and hostess.

When invitations are extended to unnamed guests such as 'and Partner' or 'and Family', the reply should include the names of those attending. A named invitee should be substituted with another guest only if the hostess gives her express permission.

If an invitation is accepted, it is bad form to withdraw that acceptance unless there is a genuine reason (eg illness); another, more appealing, engagement is not an excuse for withdrawing an acceptance. This rule may be further complicated by the public nature of invitations issued via social media. Always bear in mind the importance of the event to others and act accordingly.

Pour Memoire
If an invitation is extended and accepted verbally, for example by telephone, the hostess should send an invitation card on which 'RSVP' has been deleted and 'To remind' or '*Pour mémoire*' substituted. In this case there is no need for acknowledgement.

Save-the-Date Cards

While an email or simple message in a Christmas card may be a practical method of warning guests about an event, a dedicated save-the-date card arriving by post is likely to have more impact.

Timings
Save-the-date cards are practical, as invitations that are sent more than two months in advance – and require a reply – can be restrictive for both sides. Invitations were traditionally sent out a maximum of six weeks before the event, which would ensure that most people were not already booked up, but increasingly, although still correct, this is not sufficient. They may now be sent out up to six months in advance, while key guests can be invited informally as soon as the date is set.

Style
Traditionally, save-the-date cards were slightly smaller than a postcard, and utilitarian in design. Today, they may be more elaborate. The wording should be kept brief and include basic information about the event. Guests' names are not written on the card; it is neither necessary nor correct for guests to reply.

SAVE THE DATE

CHARLES BERKELEY'S 60TH BIRTHDAY PARTY

SATURDAY 9TH DECEMBER 2023

CORNWALL

INVITATION TO FOLLOW

Communication

Social Correspondence

CARDS FOR SPECIAL OCCASIONS
THANK-YOU LETTERS
EMAILS AND TEXT MESSAGES

Cards for Special Occasions

Greetings cards should not be sent when a letter would be more appropriate (for example a letter of thanks or condolence).

Greetings Cards

Cards should always be handwritten in ink. It is traditional for the husband's name to be given before his wife's, but this is a matter of personal choice. The wife's forename is, however, retained. Therefore, a card should be inscribed from 'John and Jane Debrett', rather than from 'Mr and Mrs John Debrett'.

Christmas Cards

Christmas cards are a traditional expression of seasonal goodwill and the sending of cards should be in this spirit, rather than as a means of self-promotion. It is wise to take care when sending cards to those of other faiths: to this end 'Season's Greetings' may be a more appropriate greeting than 'Merry Christmas'.

The card is usually inscribed from 'John and Jane Debrett', rather than from 'Mr and Mrs John Debrett'. A surname will help the recipient to identify the sender quickly.

Christmas cards should preferably be handwritten in ink. If Christmas cards are pre-printed, then the surname should be crossed through or a personal handwritten message included for recipients on first-name terms with the senders.

A short personal letter may be included, but enclosing general round-robin newsletters, or photographs of the family and pets, is not traditionally British and can seem excessive.

Christmas cards are traditionally sent in envelopes with diagonal flaps. Always use stamps on Christmas cards – avoid putting personal cards through the office franking machine.

Change of Address

A card announcing a change of address may be sent out as soon as the essential details have been confirmed. The card should include the names of the sender(s), the new address and telephone number. A moving date is included if the card is being sent out in advance, otherwise the above information is sufficient.

Bereavement Cards
See p 287 for replies to letters of condolence

It is quite acceptable for a bereaved person to convey gratitude for letters of condolence and offers of support in a card. Sometimes a card is specially printed, perhaps with a photograph of the deceased and a simple message of thanks.

Thank-You Letters

On many social occasions, a handwritten letter is preferable to an email, text message or telephone call since it communicates both care and deliberation – for example when thanking a host for hospitality, or when congratulating or wishing someone well. Thank-you letters should always be handwritten and ideally sent within a week to ten days of an event or receipt of a present.

Thank Yous for Presents

Thank-you letters are necessary to acknowledge presents given, for example, for Christmas, christenings, weddings, birthdays and anniversaries. Refer to the present directly and include some details to ensure the tone of the letter is personal.

Children's Thank Yous

Traditionally, children should always write a thank-you letter for presents, but it is becoming more permissible for children to say thank you in person if the giver is there when the present is actually opened. Children should refer to the present in the letter, and make a detailed comment about it ('Thank you for the teddy you gave me for my birthday. I have named him Edward').

See p 426 for a sample children's thank-you letter

Thank Yous After an Event

In our digital age, a handwritten letter is always appreciated so, for maximum impact, make the effort to write promptly after a social event. Traditionally sent to just the hostess, it is now commonplace to address thank-you letters after an event to either the host, hostess or couple as appropriate.

See p 425 for a sample thank-you letter

When thanking someone after an event, the form of the invitation signals the appropriate format of a thank you. Engraved formal invitation cards require a formal handwritten thank-you letter. An 'at Home' card suggests a short letter or note would be acceptable.

A verbal, telephone or email invitation to an informal event needs only a telephone call of thanks afterwards; telephone and email are interchangeable if all parties use both frequently. It is worth remembering, however, that a letter of thanks or a card rarely goes unappreciated.

Other Thank Yous

Thank-you letters should also be sent after being a guest in someone else's house, for example after staying for a weekend or at Christmas. Support during a key event or task – bereavement, wedding, reference for a job – should also be acknowledged with a brief letter of thanks. Email is now generally acceptable for short and informal thank yous.

Emails and Text Messages

Momentous life events should be properly marked. A handwritten note to send condolences on a death, or congratulations on the birth of a child or a new job, will have much more impact and meaning than a short text or email. The effort taken is commensurate with the importance of the occasion.

Emails Emails are extremely convenient; they can be treated as a kind of digital letter, with varying degrees of formality. However, there is a risk of precipitately dispatching missives before reviewing them and assessing their potential to do harm. Be careful about long threads, which may swamp the recipient with irrelevant information, and use the 'cc' and 'bcc' fields discriminately.

Texts The ease of digital communication is particularly dangerous when it comes to texts, as spur-of-the-moment thoughts are immediately transmissible. Try to curb impetuous texting and pause to re-read before sending. Don't rely on emojis to convey nuanced emotion; if you want to do that, choose a more suitable medium. Don't let the convenience of texts lead into bad habits – consistent unpunctuality is always rude, even if you text first.

General Considerations When sending texts and emails be careful to fit the medium to the recipient; older people may find texts awkward and illegible, or may not be comfortable using email.

Don't lapse into abbreviated, text-style language; try to write concisely and clearly, eliminating any potential ambiguity. Although not always used in texts, punctuation adds clarity.

Group Chats Group WhatsApp chats have become an indispensable way of communicating about a myriad of specific topics and situations, but should only be used to talk about subjects that are relevant to the members of the group – don't bombard them with stream-of-consciousness insights or random enquiries.

If you have something particular to say to one individual, message that person directly – the group shouldn't be obliged to eavesdrop on one-to-one conversations. Ask permission of the group before adding a new member, and check with potential new members before adding them.

Always acknowledge messages and try to respond to messages reasonably promptly – it's only polite.

Communication

Business Correspondence

Business Essentials
Digital Communication
Other Business Stationery

Business Essentials

Business letters should be printed on A4 paper that features the sender's company logo, postal address, telephone number and email address, and company number and VAT number where required.

Recipient's Address — This can be ranged left for a clean, modern look, although in some companies the preference is to range the address right. The address will contain the following information: the recipient's title (Mr, Mrs, Ms, Dr, Professor, Lord, Sir etc *see pp 22–61*), the recipient's business title, eg Sales Director, Training Manager etc, the recipient's company name in full, the address and postcode.

Date — The date goes underneath the recipient's name and address. Leave a minimum of one line space before the date. The recommended British style is '15 July 2023', but house styles may vary. Consistency is important.

Salutation — In general, a letter should be addressed 'Dear' followed by the recipient's title (Mr, Ms, Lord, Dr) and surname. To add a personal touch, this may be handwritten. If the sender is familiar with the recipient, then the letter can be addressed using their first name only, eg 'Dear John'. If the sender has already received correspondence from the recipient, then they should mirror the recipient's chosen style of address.

If the sender does not know the name of the recipient, then 'Dear Sir/Madam' can be used. Every effort should be made, however, to find out the recipient's name in order to personalise the letter.

Subject Line — This should be a brief informative line that will help with filing and clarity. It might mention a reference number in response to an earlier letter. Leave one line space after the subject line, before the body of the letter.

The Body of the Letter — Letters are typed with two spaces after a full stop, one space after a comma. This style does not apply to longer text documents, such as company reports. It is advisable to keep business letters concise, to the point and preferably on one side of a sheet of A4 paper.

Sign-off — The sign-off depends on the salutation. Conventionally, 'Yours faithfully' is only used for letters beginning 'Dear Sir' or 'Dear Madam', while 'Yours sincerely' is used for all letters beginning with a salutation by name. The sender's name, in full, is added, with the job title on the line below, underneath the space allocated for the signature.

The inclusion of the sender's title in brackets after the sender's name – for example 'Eliza Curzon (Miss)' – is becoming a less-used tradition. It is, however, helpful as it provides the recipient with the correct form of address for the reply letter.

FINAL NOTATIONS These are traditional notations, which are disappearing from contemporary correspondence. For example, the initials of the person who typed the letter may be added, or the abbreviation 'encl.' to indicate that an enclosure is included with the letter. If the letter is being circulated, the initials 'cc' can be added, with an alphabetical list of all the recipients. Notations are separated with a forward slash.

ENVELOPES Since envelopes are now no longer individually typed, it is acceptable to use adhesive labels for substantial mail-outs.

It is preferable to handwrite addresses on envelopes when sending out important correspondence. Window envelopes are only really appropriate for mass mail-outs or invoices.

DIGITAL COMMUNICATION

EMAIL Email has replaced many traditional forms of communication, including formal written business correspondence, telephone calls and informal verbal communications. It must be remembered that email is digital, and messages may be stored permanently and propagated exponentially. There is no such thing as a secure or confidential email. It should not be used for delicate communications or anything that the sender would not want to be attributed to themselves.

Nothing replaces real paper and ink; email should not be used for formal correspondence, such as replying to postal invitations or sending thank-you letters. These rules also apply to social emails.

ADDRESS AND SUBJECT LINE The subject line is a summary of the content of the email, and should alert the recipient. A well-written subject line will ensure that the message gets the appropriate attention. It is also used for filing and retrieval purposes so it is important that it accurately reflects the topic of the email.

IMPORTANCE LABEL	The 'importance' label should be used discriminately. Otherwise it will be ignored because of its frequent misuse.
CC AND BCC	Copies (cc) can be sent to individuals who only need to view the information for reference. They should be ordered alphabetically, or – in a business environment – by importance.

Blind copying (bcc) should be used with discernment; it is deceptive to the primary recipient. Instead, the email should be forwarded on to the third party, with a short note explaining any confidentiality, after its distribution.

If blind copying is essential – ie for a confidential document where all recipients must remain anonymous – then senders should address the email to themselves, and everyone else as 'bcc' recipients. |
| PUNCTUATION | Ensure that correct punctuation is used. Do not use lower case letters throughout as this can appear lazy. Capital letters, on the other hand, may look over-insistent. If you want to emphasise something, try underlining or using italics. |
| LANGUAGE | Avoid abbreviations and text language. Many recipients will find this irritating or incomprehensible.

Email is a conversational medium, but this should not be reinforced by over-punctuating. As a general rule, emojis and kisses should be avoided in a business context. |
| ATTACHMENTS | Be discriminating about overloading emails with system-slowing extras. Always send a covering note with attachments. |
| SALUTATION AND SIGN-OFF | Retain the same level of formality that you would use in all correspondence (eg 'Dear Sir', 'Dear Mr Brown', 'Dear Bob'). If you're approached with informality, then reciprocate in kind.

In formal emails you might use 'Yours faithfully/sincerely'; in most cases you'll use something more casual (eg 'Best wishes'). In a business context, it's always useful to add your full name, job title and telephone number under your sign-off. |
| THREADS | Maintain threads (all the previous emails on a subject) where appropriate. If it's a long thread a pithy 'I agree' isn't very helpful, so briefly reiterate what you agree with. An itemised, numbered list will add clarity. Always read back through the |

previous threads to check that nothing has been said that the recipient(s) should not read.

TEXT MESSAGES Widely used in both a professional and social context, text messages are for conveying short, instant messages. Important information may need a more lengthy explanation; if in doubt, send an email where you have more flexibility and space.

Do not send a text message if tact or subtlety is required, and bear in mind that there are certain occasions when texting is not really appropriate: never respond to bad news by text message, a handwritten letter or a telephone call is always preferable; if you have to cancel an appointment, make a telephone call; if you're sending a thank you for hospitality, a letter is preferable.

TEXTING LANGUAGE Use as much conventional grammar, punctuation and spelling as necessary for clarity. Whole words or phrases in capital letters may look intemperate. Do not use texts to express strong emotions; angry words may look intimidating on screen. Remember that subtlety and nuance may be lost in a text.

Most texts, unless they are sent in a business context to someone you do not know, do not require a salutation and if the recipient will recognise the sender then no sign-off is required. If they are less well-acquainted, or if the sender is in any doubt that their number will be recognised, a sign-off – eg 'Thanks, Jessica' – should be included at the end of the text message.

OTHER BUSINESS STATIONERY

COMPLIMENTS SLIPS A compliments slip contains the same information that would appear on the standard company letterhead, and is pre-printed with the words 'With compliments'. Usually, these are designed to fit, unfolded, into a standard DL/business envelope. A short handwritten note and signature can be added.

Compliments slips are a convenient shorthand enclosure to attach to, for example, a catalogue or price list that has been requested by a customer. They can be a pleasing addition to a routine mail-out and a way of maintaining good public relations.

They should never be used as a substitute for a handwritten note, and there are many occasions on which a compliments slip is not adequate – for example when you are sending thanks for help or hospitality, or posting a personal package. On these occasions a handwritten note on headed writing paper is always preferable.

Some companies choose to use A5 headed writing paper, or an A5 card, which serves the same function as a compliments slip or can be used for sending out brief, handwritten notes.

FAXES

Faxes are much less prevalent in the era of email communication, but many companies still have fax machines. It should be noted that a fax is legally seen as a method of serving a notice, so faxes should never be dismissed as unimportant.

The cover sheet should include the following essential information: recipient's name, company name and fax number; sender's name, company name, telephone number and fax number. A brief explanation and indication of the number of pages can also be helpful.

BUSINESS CARDS
See p 311 for social cards

These are used primarily for professional or business purposes, but with the decline of the visiting card they have taken on some of its social functions. Social usage should, however, be infrequent. Cards are usually printed, but may be engraved if a smarter impression is thought appropriate.

Business cards are usually about the same size as a credit card and landscape in format (vertical layouts can look striking, but may be inconvenient for recipients' filing systems or cardholders). They should fit into a card holder or the card section of a wallet. They should contain the following: the employee's name, without any prefixes (unless they have professional relevance, eg 'Professor'); the company's full postal address and website address; the company's landline number. The employee's direct line or mobile telephone number may also be included as well as the employee's email address.

On a standard business card, the name and professional title should be centred, in large characters, above the name of the firm, or below the company logo. The address, telephone, fax and email information should appear in smaller characters in the bottom left- and right-hand corners, or spread across the bottom.

See pp 145–153 for letters after the name

On a business card that is intended to show the bearer's qualifications, the appropriate professional letters may be suffixed to the name, for example, FRIBA. First degrees, for example BA (Hons), should not be included.

330 - 345

INTRODUCTIONS

CONVERSATION

Social Graces

Making introductions, enjoying small talk and paying compliments are all enviable social graces. Such social skills will enhance every encounter and occasion, and help any social event run seamlessly.

Social Graces

Introductions

How Do You Do?
Shaking Hands
Social Kissing

How Do You Do?

Performing introductions is an essential social skill and should be an almost automatic action. There are some basic rules to bear in mind to make it simpler.

Hierarchy of Introductions

Precedence and respect is signalled by the name said first. Courtesy gives honour to those who are female, older or more distinguished.

Men should be introduced to women. 'Charlotte, may I introduce John Debrett? John, this is Charlotte Berkeley'. Aim to introduce younger people to their elders or junior employees, say, to more senior people, such as directors. A new arrival should be introduced to a group. Husbands and wives should be introduced separately by name ('John and Emma Debrett'), not as 'the Debretts'.

Procedure

As the person making the introduction you should make sure you have the attention of both parties, but avoid steering them physically, for example with a hand on the shoulder. Wait for an appropriate moment and do not force the person you wish to introduce on to the person you would like them to meet.

Then address the more senior person by name and say: 'John, may I introduce Charles Berkeley? Charles, this is John Debrett.' You may wish then to add a short explanation, or provide some information: 'John is a wine expert', or 'Charles has just moved back to London', or 'I know you are both tennis fans'. It is helpful to give both first name and last name, even in an informal setting, as it provides more information, which is the object of the exercise.

Bear in mind that introductions should help people to decide what mode of address to use. If you know someone very well, and use a nickname, it is more helpful to introduce your friend by the name the other person may be expected to use.

If you suspect that people are likely to have met before, you may want to say: 'Charlotte, I am sure you know John Debrett?'

'Society is like a large piece of frozen water; and skating well is the great art of social life.'
                 Charles Lamb

USE OF TITLES

In a more formal context you may also use titles such as 'Lord' or 'Professor' – older people will expect to be introduced by their title. It is then up to them to say 'Please call me Jane.'

The person you are introducing should not have to guess that the other is, for example, a doctor or a lord, or even someone who would rather be called 'Mrs'. It is considerate for the person making the introduction to provide information that may avert future embarrassment.

It is less common in everyday practice to introduce someone as 'Mr John Debrett', although Mr, Mrs and Miss are titles too. An exception may be when introducing a child to an adult. Some adults wish children to address them as, for example, 'Mrs Debrett'. However, to introduce people using the titles 'Mr', 'Mrs' or 'Miss' for one party and not the other may imply that you are insinuating one party is less important, so you must be sensitive and not appear rude. Remember that certain people are nearly always known professionally as Mr, Mrs or Miss, for example schoolmasters and mistresses and (medical) consultants.

BUSINESS CARDS

See p 329 for business cards
See p 311 for social cards

In a purely social situation in Britain you would not give someone a card on meeting, but you might want to do so on parting, if you have established a rapport and plan to be in contact. As very few people carry cards other than business cards you may wish to apologise for offering a business card in a social setting. An alternative for social situations is to consider using social cards.

FORGETTING NAMES

If you dry up and suddenly cannot remember someone's name and are with two people who are clearly expecting you to make the introduction, the best thing is to act swiftly and blame yourself – perhaps make a charmingly self-deprecating remark about your failing memory.

You may want to remind yourself of the name of someone to whom you have just been introduced by using his or her name once or twice, but try not to overdo it. If someone gets your name wrong, correct them as soon as possible, enunciating clearly and firmly but politely, so there is no mistake. It can be very embarrassing for both parties if such errors persist.

'If you wish to forget anything on the spot, make a note that this thing is to be remembered.'
EDGAR ALLAN POE

IF ALL ELSE FAILS	If you cannot remember someone's name the best thing is to admit it and blame yourself. Alternatively, you can try to stimulate your memory by asking them how long ago you last saw them or where it was. Do not be offended when people cannot get your name into their head, just repeat it patiently. However, if a person blanks you several times at successive gatherings then it is rude of them, unless they have a genuine problem. Try your hardest not to do the same to others. Unfortunately the British cannot use an equivalent of 'Monsieur' or 'Madame' without a last name. You cannot really call someone 'Mrs' or 'Miss' (other than schoolteachers, as above) and should only use 'Sir' for a schoolmaster, or if you are in the forces or a very young man. Men may use 'Sir' appropriately in more circumstances than women, who would usually only do so if serving a client or customer or if addressing a male member of the Royal Family.
WHEN TO MAKE INTRODUCTIONS	In days gone by, when people moved in smaller social circles, it was considered almost rude to make introductions (although at formal occasions names would be announced), as it could imply a person was an outsider if they did not already know the other guests. This is no longer the case and it is now more polite to over-introduce than to assume people know one another.
INTRODUCING YOURSELF	Introducing yourself when you do not know anyone is perfectly acceptable. In a business or professional setting it is an essential skill and it is often the most practical solution in a purely social setting. If you do need to introduce yourself step forward with a smile and say: 'May I introduce myself? I am John Debrett.' The response should be the person's name. 'Charlotte Berkeley.' Or 'Hello' followed by the name. Speaking clearly is polite, as it is maddening for people to have to ask you to repeat yourself.
RESPONSES	Introductions are usually followed by a handshake and the words: 'How do you do?' to which the response is: 'How do you do?' With younger people and in more informal settings you may prefer: 'Hello' or even 'Hi' but resist adding: 'Pleased to meet you.' Never assume that 'How do you do?' means: 'How are you?' If genuinely asked how you are the answer is: 'Very well thank you, how are you?' Do not give a true account of your state of health.

SHAKING HANDS

Shaking hands is a standard form of greeting and may be used socially and professionally, to greet strangers and people you know, and has no age or gender barriers. It is appropriate for both meeting and parting.

WHEN TO SHAKE HANDS Offering to shake hands is never rude, whereas not offering your hand may be seen as standoffish. It may occasionally be somewhat impractical, so if in doubt use your common sense and observe other people. As with all matters of etiquette the best manners do not draw attention to yourself, so to be the only one offering to shake hands on a very informal occasion or one where, for example, the people you meet are occupied or there is some kind of physical barrier, is disruptive and may be seen as attention-seeking.

TIMING It is no longer necessary to wait and see if the woman or more senior person holds their hand out to you. Make and maintain eye contact, step forward with your hand out and shake theirs, firmly but not too hard.

HANDSHAKING TIPS Keep it simple and brief. Do not indulge in double clasps, exaggerated up and down movements, or reeling the person in and patting their back. Some men do a 'war dance' of back and arm patting and bear hugging, but this is just for friends, not on first meeting.

While a very limp handshake can seem unattractive, avoid too much pressure, as this can hurt women wearing rings or anyone with arthritis. Grip the palm not the fingers. Remove your gloves, if applicable, and make sure your palms are not sweaty. Always use your right hand even if you are left-handed. If you have an injury and do not want to shake hands, make it clear quickly so as not to appear rude.

> **LOOKING BACK…**
>
> Handshakes took over from bows and curtseys, which have now almost vanished other than when encountering royalty. The handshake was a sign of friendship, indicating that you were unarmed and so came in peace. A handshake is still a sign of peacemaking and also indicates sportsmanship, for instance between contestants in a boxing match. It is also the sign of an agreement or bargain and that a quarrel has been made up. Exchanging the sign of peace in church usually takes the form of a handshake.

Social Kissing

Kissing is taking over from handshaking, almost as the handshake took over from the bow, although men kissing one another is still unusual (see below). However, kissing is not appropriate in many professional situations. On the whole it should only be used among friends, not at first meeting.

Kissing Guidelines

Social kissing varies according to the age of the people involved. Older people may not want to be kissed at all and even if they do not mind they often only expect one kiss. The double kiss is the norm among younger people.

An air kiss, with no contact at all, may seem rude or impersonal, but at least it is not intrusive – it is simply a social kiss, not a sign of affection to a loved one. A very slight contact is best, and no sound effects are needed.

Who to Kiss

Women routinely kiss other women and men without it denoting anything more than a friendly social interaction. Some men now kiss socially, but kissing is still rare amongst the older generation (older men may find it embarrassing), within more traditional professions or in very rural areas. However, fathers often kiss their sons, even their adult sons and the days of a manly handshake when seeing the 8-year-old off to prep school are over.

Many children hate being kissed by adults they hardly know. By the same token it is inadvisable for parents to force their children to kiss people. Instead they should encourage small children to learn to shake hands, which is seen as charming and a sign that they are well brought-up.

Avoiding a Kiss

If you really object to being kissed by people you hardly know then you may extend a straight arm and offer to shake hands, which should give a clear message. Do not force kisses on people who do extend a hand as a sign.

Hand-Kissing

Hand-kissing, or rather a man bowing over the hand of a married woman, never a young girl, and not quite touching it with his lips, has never really caught on in Britain. It looks affected unless you come from a culture where men are brought up to hand-kiss.

Social Graces

Conversation

Use of First Names
Small Talk
Social Tact

Use of First Names

When introduced you should have learned the person's first and last name and possibly their title. Members of the older generation should be called by their formal title until you are told that this is not necessary. This may mean saying, for example, 'Mrs Debrett', even when she was introduced as 'Emma Debrett'. In practice most people will say 'Emma, please!' though some very senior people may never suggest it.

Anything other than first names would be unusual amongst younger people in an ordinary social or professional situation. However, you should probably not use nicknames unless you know the person, or are invited to do so.

Nicknames and Shortened Names

If you have a childhood or family nickname, and are introduced as such to someone new, you may give a brief explanation of why you have the nickname; by telling the other person your real name you may indicate that you would prefer it to be used, rather than your nickname.

Men often have names based on their last name, such as 'Smithy', but avoid using them when you first meet, even if everyone else is doing so.

With standard abbreviations, such as 'Jo' for Joanna, try to notice how they refer to themselves. It may be that they dislike the contraction.

If in doubt, ask the person if they are always called by their nickname or shortened name, but the safest option is not to use any name at all at first.

Looking Back…

Nicknames have a long and distinguished history in Britain. For example, the Prince Regent was called 'Prinny' and the Duke of Wellington 'Nosey'. They are still popular among the aristocracy. The present Duke of Devonshire is known as 'Stoker' and the future Duke of Devonshire is 'Bunter' to his friends while his (very beautiful and distinguished) sister is called 'Monster'. Public schools and the forces are still bastions of the nickname.

Small Talk

Polite conversation or small talk smooths the way when you first meet someone, making it a valuable tool for social interaction.

Opening Gambits

If you have just been introduced and exchanged 'How do you dos?' you will need to think of something to follow it up. It is polite to make your next remark fairly promptly and not leave a silence. If your hostess or the person who has introduced you has given you a helpful clue then follow that up. Otherwise you may want to ask how they know the host or hostess or try an old royal standby, 'Have you come far?' You can mention the weather or, if you are at a party or an event, make a general comment about the scene. Sport, or a recent sporting event, is also a good ice-breaker.

'Where are you from?', which is standard in America, or 'What do you do?' were traditionally seen as too direct in Britain, so it is best to be more circumspect.

Making Conversation

Do not be afraid of sounding dull. Good eye contact and a ready smile will enliven any conversation. The key thing is to give the other person an easy opportunity to respond. Once the conversation has got going remember to take turns and to listen. When the conversation is one to one, make sure you pay attention and do not look over the person's shoulder for more amusing company, however tempting it may be. If you are trapped by a real bore then it is more polite to escape quickly than to look over their shoulder.

Groups

When you are participating in a group conversation the rule is to share and make sure everyone is included. If a known raconteur has the floor and you know someone else is shy or a natural listener you might want to include the latter as part of your response: 'Charlotte, don't you know southern Spain very well?'

Breaking Off

If someone joins you when you are deep in conversation with one other person you must give it up, however annoying and inconvenient it may be. Include the newcomer and make them welcome by changing the subject or making a link. 'You won't want to hear about our local dramas. How are things with you?' It is possible that you should have been keeping your private or serious conversation for a less public or social occasion.

TOPICS TO AVOID Steer clear of religion and politics and don't talk shop to people other than colleagues. It is unwise to make assumptions, for example that everyone may have the same background or views as yourself.

Ask questions but try not to interrogate or make it seem as if you are trying to get a fix on the person or pigeonhole them by discovering where they live or what they earn. At the same time it is not unreasonable to try to find common ground by asking rather indirect questions. People will usually indicate whether or not they have children, or are married, so don't ask directly.

Small talk can seem like insincerity or a complicated dance but it is tried and tested. Wait until you know someone better before being braver with topics. Trying to be controversial on purpose is really just showing off. One-upmanship is unattractive and can just make you seem insecure rather than impressive. Social interaction is not meant to be a competition.

Avoid catching people out. If someone is talking about a subject you know better than them it is mean, although tempting, to wait until they have finished before saying that you have written ten books about it.

GOSSIP Some gossip can be delightful. Skilled practitioners can make you feel you have heard a wonderful bit of insider scandal, even if it is old news. However, talking about people the others do not know is rude and boring. Name dropping or telling inaccurate stories about celebrities is unattractive and unconvincing. Giving away real secrets is wrong. Discretion is paramount and revelling in bad news is bad manners.

Revealing too much about yourself to a comparative stranger, which is now increasingly common, is not good manners. Do not be in a rush. There may come a time when exchanging confidences is entirely appropriate, but it will not be the first time you meet or sit next to someone at dinner.

'Small talk, you see, is the bridge which links up two or more alien personalities, brought together for a moment by the tide of life... Over this frail bridge of talk your object is to cross in order to discover, if possible, some common denominator of human interest to one or the other which will make the short contact a real thing and leave a pleasant little memory...'
ETIQUETTE AND ENTERTAINING (1938), LADY TROUBRIDGE

Social Tact

Faux Pas

If you stick to the above guidelines you should not make too many *faux pas* but the odd indiscretion cannot be helped. The best way to avoid them is to do twice as much listening as talking (rule of two ears, one mouth) when you first meet someone, so as to get a handle on the situation. You may not realise, for example, that two people are a couple. They may be of the same gender or may have different last names. You may be someone who disdains political correctness, but racist, sexist or homophobic remarks are unacceptable in any circumstances. You may think you are being funny but it is best to keep humour under control.

If you do make a social blunder, apologise as quickly and sincerely as possible, but do not overdo it. A harmless error should be accepted and not regarded as an insult, so do not take offence too easily if you are on the receiving end. Just let the offender know you don't mind as quickly as possible, then move on, either conversationally or even physically if you are feeling very upset.

Compliments

It was considered rude in pre-war society to make remarks about food, drink, houses, pictures or furniture. There are very few places where this still applies. On the whole you are now expected to say the food is delicious and the room lovely.

It is fine to pay people compliments but very personal remarks, which could refer to weight or health issues, are best avoided. Try to keep compliments appropriate to the context and remember that specific beats general. A compliment on a haircut or dress will be much more appreciated that a generic and unimaginative 'You are looking well'.

'It is a great mistake for men to give up paying compliments, for when they give up saying what is charming, they give up thinking what is charming.'
                              OSCAR WILDE

If someone pays you a compliment on what you're wearing, smile and thank them graciously, and do not demur. Try to avoid the British tendency to say 'Oh this old thing', a form of self-deprecation that can make the person paying you the compliment feel they have done the wrong thing and dent their confidence.

Moving On The key to social tact is to do as you would be done by. Put yourself in the other person's shoes and do not press them too hard for information or ignore them and never ask them a single question about themselves. Try to draw people out, but do not patronise them. Do not interrupt. Try not to get on to your hobby horse, for example the latest health fad, and if they get on theirs, try to move the conversation on.

You may have to learn to let it go if people are being provocative or extreme as it is rude to correct people and unattractive to lecture. If you think what the other person is saying is actually harmful or slanderous then you may need to nip it in the bud by obviously changing the subject.

Learn how to move on without giving offence so that you do not get stuck with people or vice versa. You may be able to say you have not seen your host yet to say hello or that you have just seen someone you have been hoping to catch up with. If you're at a seated dinner then you may turn to talk to your other neighbour at the end of each course (*see p 374*).

Above all, stay alert to people's signals and what is going on around you. Successful social life can involve concentrating as well as relaxing.

Looking Back...

It was considered vulgar for a gentleman to talk very loudly, use slang, whisper to others, discuss taboo subjects (religion, politics), gossip or involve himself in long debates. Personal achievement, status, profession or wealth was never discussed. Humour and wit was used carefully and sparingly, the excessive use of puns or anecdote deemed inappropriate and, as a general rule, a gentleman would not ask a lady a direct question.

Social Graces

Polite Actions

Reliabilty, punctuality and acknowledging others with respect are the foundation stones of good manners. Consideration for others is shown through language, for instance in greetings and introductions but also physically, for instance by standing up when someone enters the room.

STANDING UP   It is always polite to stand when someone enters the room for the first time. Traditionally men got to their feet when women came in and younger people for their elders. It is, however, considerate to stand regardless of age and gender, and a host should always stand to greet guests. All introductions should take place standing and it is discourteous to offer your hand to someone while seated. An exception would be an elderly or infirm person. It is correct to stand when someone is leaving a room.

ACKNOWLEDGING   Children and teenagers may be absorbed in playing or watching television when adults, for example guests of their parents, enter the room. They should know to get to their feet, briefly break off what they are doing, and greet the adults. However, it is not necessary for them to get to their feet if the same adults pass through the room again, though they should stand and say goodbye if the guests are leaving. If the adults stay in the room, it is polite for children to stop what they are doing and offer their seats to the adults, or at least to wait until told to carry on.

IN RESTAURANTS   Those already seated at a table should get to their feet when someone arrives or leaves but need not necessarily leave their place. Traditionally it was considered polite to rise when someone left and returned to the table. These days, it is best to use some judgement, for instance to half rise as an acknowledgment rather than disrupt things and draw attention to the person's movements by getting right up.

HELPING WITH COATS   It is polite to take people's coats or bags when they arrive and to help them into coats when they leave, but with judgement, as not everyone likes being fussed over. Hold the coat by the shoulders and position it so that the arms can slip in easily. Lift the coat on to the shoulders, then lift it slightly again.

ENTRANCES AND EXITS   Avoid turning your back on a room. When entering, close the door behind you while remaining face-on and moving forwards into the room.

On exiting, try to reverse, or half-turn, through the door so that the last impression you give isn't of your back.

346 - 365

Table Rules

Challenging Foods

Drinks

Table Manners

Table manners are an everyday example of the old adage 'do as you would be done by'. The essence of consideration for others may be summed up by our behaviour at the table. Thinking of others before gratifying our own desires is important, as is ensuring that dining companions are not offended by inelegant eating habits. All table manners are based on achieving these twin objectives.

TABLE MANNERS

TABLE RULES

ON THE TABLE
PRACTICALITIES
AT THE TABLE

Most people have been taught table manners as children, but surprisingly often such tenets have been forgotten, or are conveniently overlooked, in adulthood. While children may be told not to speak with their mouths full, it is easy for adults to forget to practise what they preach. Modern family life is so frantic that eating together at the table is less usual than it once was, so standards may slip or simply be unfamiliar. In short, the opportunity to monitor and be exposed to good table manners is being lost.

See p 413 for mobiles in social situations

It is not advisable to keep certain manners for 'best' and, even when eating informally or alone, good table manners should still apply. Constant practice will make manners easier to remember so that they come naturally when it really matters. It is worth remembering that it used to be said that the mark of a true gentleman was a man who used a butter knife when dining alone.

As with all manners, it is also important to be accommodating; if someone does something wrong, then never criticise, comment or draw attention to it. The story of the late Queen Elizabeth politely drinking from her fingerbowl as one of her guests had done so in error is probably an urban legend. It does, however, demonstrate that excellent table manners are always flexible and pragmatic, designed to ensure that everyone around the table is comfortable and relaxed.

On the Table

Laying the Table
See p 371 for place settings

Whether it is a formal dinner or a much more casual occasion, the basic rules do not vary when laying the table. Give each person as much elbow room as the table permits. Leave an even amount of space between places. Knives and spoons go on the right, forks on the left. The idea is always to work from the outside in. Formally, it is correct always to lay side plates – even if they are not going to be used – with the napkins simply folded on them.

Knives, Forks and Spoons

The basics are large and small knives, large and small forks, teaspoons, dessert (pudding) spoons and forks, and tablespoons. There may be small blunt knives for butter, fish knives, soup spoons and extra small spoons for coffee, or for salt and mustard. Some people have different shaped spoons for soup and pudding, but cutlery design is not standard. If the dessert spoons are very small, then traditionally tablespoons are used for the soup.

Jam spoons or dessert spoons, not teaspoons, should be used for jam or honey (and the jars and spoons placed on small plates). Teaspoons are also for tea and coffee, or for eating grapefruit or boiled eggs, for which you may sometimes find a type with a more pointed shape.

PLATES AND BOWLS   Soup should be served in shallow bowls. Pudding, unless there is a lot of sauce, is served on small plates. A special dessert service with a decorative pattern may be used, or the same plates as the first course.

The traditional diameters of plates are ten inches or a little more for dinner plates (main course), eight inches for pudding plates and six inches for side plates. With so many contemporary designs and shapes available this is just a guide, not a rule.

PRACTICALITIES

USING CUTLERY   The fork and spoon are the only things that should go into the mouth. Never lick the knife or eat off it. If using a knife and fork together, always keep the tines of the fork pointing downwards and push the food on to the fork. It may be necessary to use mashed potato to make peas stick to the fork but it is incorrect to turn the fork over and scoop.

There are foods that are eaten with just a fork, including some pasta and some fish. In this case use the fork in the right hand and have the tines up, more like a spoon. It is not traditional in England, but quite usual in America, to see someone cut all their food up and then discard the knife and eat with the fork alone.

It is not correct to hold your knife like a pen. The handle lies in the palm of the hand and is secured by the thumb on the side and the index finger on top of the handle. It is permissible in a restaurant to ask for a steak knife, if the meat is tough, but rude to ask for anything extra in a private house.

When finished, the knife and fork (with tines facing upwards) or spoon etc are placed on the plate in a six-thirty position.

SPOON AND FORK   Always eat puddings with a spoon and fork (both should always be laid); the spoon should be a dessert spoon. Ice cream may be eaten with a teaspoon, or a long teaspoon if served in a tall glass. Sorbet, served between courses, is eaten with a teaspoon.

POISE — When eating, bring the fork or spoon to the mouth, rather than lowering the head towards the food. Bring the food promptly to the mouth and do not gesticulate with the knife and fork.

'The world was my oyster but I used the wrong fork.'
OSCAR WILDE

CHOPSTICKS — Hold the chopsticks parallel in one hand. The thumb and forefinger hold and manipulate the top stick. The middle finger rests between the sticks, keeping the bottom stick held still. The top stick is manoeuvred by the thumb and forefinger to grip food and bring it to the mouth. Place the chopsticks by the right-hand side of the plate when they are not in use; there may be special rests for them.

Never use personal chopsticks to pass food to people, and never use them to point at other people. It is best to use a serving spoon to take food from a communal dish if provided, or communal chopsticks (which would be a different colour).

LOCAL FOOD TRADITIONS — Certain foods from different parts of the world have their own traditions, some of which have become commonplace in modern Britain, while others are only going to be encountered rarely. Of these the most obvious is pasta, which 50 years ago was little known. It would be odd today to attack it with a knife and fork or even with a fork and spoon. Learn how to eat it as they do in Italy, with the fork only, but tidily. It is acceptable to bend more closely over the plate than with traditional English food.

If eating Indian food with the hands, it is permissible to lower the head towards the food and preferable to dropping it and making a mess. Chinese food is eaten by bringing the bowl to your mouth, rather that your mouth to the bowl. If in any doubt, say, about whether to eat pizza with a knife and fork or the fingers, remember the golden rule of table manners: think of the person sitting opposite.

LOOKING BACK...

It was usual to provide menu cards at the table, written in French. They were plainly styled, with a title of 'Menu' and the date underneath and to the right-hand side. The food was described in simple terms, without any mention of sauces, vegetables, wines or coffee. For very elaborate dinners, they would have been printed by a stationer but, for less formal dinners, they were handwritten by the lady of the house.

At the Table

Sitting When taking a seat at the table, sit a comfortable distance away, so that with the elbows bent the hands are level with the knives and forks. Do not tilt the chair or hunch forward over the plate. Sit up straight, sit square with hands in the lap and do not fidget. Do not put elbows on the table.

Napkins Napkins should be placed on the lap as soon as you are seated. When you get down from the table, leave the napkin, unfolded on the table, to the left of the place setting (napkins are never left folded as it implies that they may be reused).

Serving and Passing
See p 372 for serving food

Make sure others have been offered anything they might want from the table, such as butter, water, salt or pepper. Help yourself last and never stretch across people. When things are out of reach or have not been passed along, ask a neighbour if they are going to have whatever it is, as a hint, or simply ask them to pass it (traditionally, it was bad manners to ask to be passed the salt).

Serving Spoons and Forks Use the serving spoons and forks to take food from a communal dish. If a spoon and fork or two spoons are provided, hold one in each hand, not in just one hand like a waiter. Use any spoons or ladles for sauces, rather than tipping from the gravy boat or jug.

Salt Traditionally, salt is put on the side of the plate and each forkful of food is lightly dipped into the salt.

Starting Generally do not start before everyone has been served, so look around and take a lead from others. An exception may be if it is a large party and the host asks people to start, as the food may get cold. Those who cannot tolerate very hot food should still pick up the spoon or knife and fork and look as if they are starting at the same time; this will ensure that their neighbours do not feel obliged to wait as well.

Eating and Talking Never eat with your mouth open or talk with your mouth full. It is fine, however, to carry on eating during a conversation. This can be awkward if one person does not pick up their knife and fork out of mistaken courtesy, while the other person is talking. It is not rude just to nod, for example, or to wait a few moments for someone to finish a mouthful. Working out how to eat and talk is part of good table manners and an essential social skill. It is, however, impolite to continue eating during speeches or if there is a performance, such as singing.

Spitting Things Out When encountering an unexpected piece of gristle, or something that may be chewed to no avail, it is polite to be brave and to try to swallow it. If it is something which would be unsafe to eat rather than just unappetising, then cover the mouth with the hand, and quickly and discreetly put the offending item on the side of the plate.

Washing Food Down Avoid washing mouthfuls of food down with gulps of water. It is best to leave a gap between eating and drinking. By the same token take small mouthfuls or sips of water or wine.

Chewing Chewing food thoroughly, keeping the mouth closed as you do so, slows things down to a more civilised pace when eating with others. However, while bolting food is ill-mannered, so is making a production out of endless mastication or chewing in an exaggerated manner. The best table manners are always those that no one notices.

Noises Off Try to avoid making noises of any kind while eating, either with implements against the plate or teeth, or with the actual ingestion of the food, such as slurping soup.

In Britain it is not traditional to say the equivalent of the French *'bon appetit'* or American 'enjoy'. Express appreciation but do so politely. Gestures such as rubbing the tummy or smacking the lips are inappropriate. Similarly, when refusing a second portion, avoid big gestures and decline politely: a simple 'no thank you' covers most situations.

Dipping and Sauces There are foods where dipping is part of the way of eating the food, such as satay or crudités. For most food, however, dipping into any communal bowl – say of mayonnaise – is not recommended. In the case of crudités with a communal dip, never bite the vegetable and then re-dip.

It is very tempting to mop up sauce, or the last few mouthfuls of soup, with bread, but it should be resisted. Eat only what can be eaten easily with a fork or spoon.

Finger Bowls Finger bowls should be put out if serving food such as whole prawns. The water should be tepid and may, especially in restaurants, have a slice of lemon added. Dip the fingers, rub them together gently until any debris is removed, then dry them on the napkin. When clearing the table after a course, remove the finger bowls promptly, as they look unattractive once used.

Table Manners

Challenging Foods

Fruit & Vegetables
Fish & Shellfish
Other Foods

Certain foods can seem daunting, especially if they are unfamiliar. If in doubt, follow other diners' lead and remember that good manners are all about ensuring that fellow diners are never made to feel embarrassed or awkward.

Fruit & Vegetables

Asparagus — Hot asparagus is usually served with melted butter or hollandaise, cold asparagus with vinaigrette. Unless asparagus is a vegetable accompaniment to a dish, or covered in sauce, it should be eaten with the fingers. The asparagus spear should be picked up towards the blunt end of the stem, the budded tip dipped in any accompanying sauce and eaten bite by bite. There's no need to chew through any tough, woody ends of the stems; they should be left neatly on the side of the plate.

Globe Artichokes — The leaves of an artichoke should be peeled off one by one, starting with the outer leaves. Hold each leaf by its pointy tip and dip the rounded base in the butter or sauce. Eat just the tender, swollen base of each leaf, and leave the rest. Place discarded leaves on the side of the plate. When you reach the centre, the smaller leaves and hairy choke are cut away and discarded to reveal the heart, which is cut into pieces and eaten with a knife and fork.

Grapes — Do not pick individual grapes from a bunch. Use either the fingers, or grape scissors, to remove a small bunch.

Lemons — A wedge of lemon usually accompanies fish or seafood. Squeeze the lemon against the tines of a fork, which channel the juice. Keep the lemon wedge low over the plate, cupping a hand around it while squeezing to avoid spraying neighbours. If serving segments of lemon make sure to remove all visible pips. Wedges are best but, if used, half-lemons may be served wrapped in muslin and squeezed with the fingers (without using the fork). Lemons to be used in tea or drinks should be pre-cut into small rounds and possibly then in half again and served on a side plate.

Kumquats — Usually consumed raw, but occasionally cooked, kumquats are eaten whole, including the skin. The top end may be cut off first.

Apples — At the dinner table, apples should be cut into quarters and the core removed from each piece. Then use fingers to eat the quarters. Elsewhere, just hold and crunch.

ORANGES — Either peel the orange by scoring the skin in four quarters with a knife, removing the skin, and then eating the segments. Or, if it is difficult to peel, treat a large orange like a grapefruit and cut it in half and eat with a teaspoon. Tangerines may be peeled and eaten with the fingers.

STRAWBERRIES — Serve strawberries hulled. Do not be tempted to think they look more attractive with the green left on as they are awkward for a diner to eat with a spoon and fork. If they are served as finger food, use a knife and cut the whole leafy end off.

PIPS AND STONES — Pips and stones should be discreetly spat into a cupped left hand and deposited on the side of the plate or discarded. Do not fiddle or play with plum or cherry stones.

FISH & SHELLFISH

LOBSTER — A whole lobster in its shell will typically arrive at the table already cut into two halves, allowing easy access to the flesh. Use a knife and fork, or just a fork, while holding the shell steady with the hand. The big claws usually come cracked but if not, use special lobster crackers and then pull out the meat with a fork. If you want to get meat out of the smaller parts, use a lobster pick. Too much digging can look greedy and messy but too little may seem unappreciative, so aim for a balance.

MUSSELS — Use an empty mussel shell as a pincer to extract the other mussels from their shells. Using a fork is also perfectly acceptable. The sauce around the mussels can be eaten with a spoon, like soup. Put all empty shells on the spare plate or bowl provided and use the fingerbowl as required.

EATING A WHOLE FISH ON THE BONE — Work down one side of the spine at a time, from head-end to tail-end. Ease mouthful-sized pieces from the fish. Never flip the fish over to reach the flesh on the underside – lift the entire skeleton up and gently ease the flesh out from beneath. Small bones should be removed from the mouth with fingers and placed on the side of the plate.

PRAWNS — If the prawn arrives intact, begin by removing the head and tail; do this by giving each end a sharp tug. Peel off the shell, starting from the underside, where the legs meet the body. If the prawn is uncooperative, discreetly bend it against its natural curve to loosen the shell. Finally, remove the black thread from along the back before eating the flesh. To eat a prawn served headless but with its tail attached, use the latter as a handle and discard after eating the flesh. Langoustines may be treated in a similar way. Use the finger bowl as before.

OYSTERS | Raw oysters are served on a bed of ice, accompanied by fresh lemon wedges and sometimes mignonette (shallot and red wine vinegar dressing). They will be already shucked (ie detached), but use your fork to prise the flesh from the shell if any sticks. Squeeze the lemon over the oyster in the shell.

Pick up the shell and bring the widest end to the lips. Tilt, and slide the entire contents of the shell – the oyster and all the juices – directly into the mouth from the shell.

Alternatively, hold the oyster in the left hand and spear the contents with a fork (sometimes special oyster forks are provided), then drink the remaining juice from the shell. Either chew and savour the unique briny, metallic taste of the oyster, or swallow it down in one – opinions vary about which method is best.

LOOKING BACK...

When eating fish, the fork was held in the right hand and a crust of bread in the left. The bread was used instead of a knife to divide and separate the fish. This method was used because the steel of the knife would taint the flavour of the fish and, in turn, the acidic accompaniments to the fish (sauces, lemon or vinegar) would corrode the steel. This habit died out once silver knives and forks became widespread.

CAVIAR | The precious roe of the sturgeon is best eaten as simply as possible, served at room temperature. Accompaniments such as sour cream, onions, chopped egg and lemon are popular, but they disguise the true taste of the caviar.

Caviar should be enjoyed in small quantities and not eaten in bulk. It may be served with blinis, small savoury pancakes. Good caviar should not taste salty. Test it by placing a small amount on the fleshy part of the hand between thumb and index finger; it should not smell. Once opened, caviar should be stored in a glass container, often a champagne flute, in the fridge, never in the tin.

Traditionally, vodka was drunk as an accompaniment, as the oil in the caviar lined the stomach, so large quantities of alcohol could be consumed.

Sushi   Some basic principles should be observed when eating sushi. Soy sauce is poured into the saucer – it is polite to pour for other dining companions too – and then a small amount of wasabi paste mixed in. Sashimi (sliced raw fish on its own) is picked up with the chopsticks, dipped into the sauce and then eaten, if possible, in one mouthful. Sushi rolls and nigiri (blocks of rice with fish on top) should also be picked up with the chopsticks and eaten whole; attempting to bite in two can lead to a scattering of rice across the table.

Other Foods

Soup   Before soup spoons became widespread, soup was eaten with a tablespoon, never a dessert spoon. When eating soup, fill the spoon by pushing it away from you, towards the far side of the bowl. Bring this to the mouth and tip the soup in from the side of the spoon; don't try eating with the spoon at 90 degrees to the mouth. Don't suck or slurp. Tilt the bowl away from you in order to get the last few spoonfuls. Leave your spoon in the bowl when you have finished.

Bread   Bread rolls used to be served inside the napkin. When a guest sat down at the table and placed the napkin on their lap, they removed the bread roll and placed it to the left of their plate.

Bread rolls are eaten from a side plate to the left of a place setting. Break the roll, by hand, into bite-sized pieces that are eaten individually. Break off a new piece for each mouthful, rather than dividing the roll into chunks in advance. Butter, if desired, is taken from the butter dish, using the butter knife and placed on the edge of your side plate. Each piece, or mouthful, is individually buttered. The same applies to the artisan sliced bread often found in restaurants and to melba toast. Hot toast may be buttered all in one go but if it is to be spread with something such as pâté for a first course, follow the bread roll method as above. Brown bread and butter, served with smoked salmon, is ready buttered on the table on a plate, usually cut into halves diagonally.

Cheese   Always use the cheese knife provided to cut cheese from a communal board, not your own knife. Round cheese, such as Camembert, must be treated like a cake: cut triangular portions. It is correct to slice a whole large cheddar or Stilton horizontally but, if already cut like a cake, follow suit. With a wedge such as

Brie, cut slivers lengthways. Never cut the nose off a triangular wedge. Stilton is usually sliced, but if a spoon is provided, scoop a portion of cheese from the middle.

Rind may be eaten or left. Bite-sized morsels of cheese on individual pieces of biscuit should be brought to the mouth, rather than biting off mouthfuls from a large piece of cheese on an entire cracker. It is fine to use fingers to eat hard, non-messy cheese with no biscuits or bread, perhaps with celery or grapes. Cut it into small pieces first.

Quails' Eggs and Gulls' Eggs Tiny speckled quails' eggs are usually served hard-boiled in their shells, with celery salt on the side. Peel off the shell (loosen by crushing the surface lightly), dip into the salt and eat whole. The larger gulls' eggs, that have a short season (April-May), are eaten the same way.

Snails Usually served with their shells intact, snails require a little manual dexterity to consume and the use of special implements. Grip the shell with the snail tongs, and remove the meat with the small two-pronged fork. Whether mopping up the juices with bread is acceptable is debatable but in very formal company (or if in doubt), abstention is safer. The golden rule of being aware of the view presented to the person sitting opposite should never be forgotten.

Whole Birds Whole small game birds such as grouse are usually served one per person. Tackle by slicing the breast off from the bone. With a bigger bird, like a partridge, tackle the leg meat with a knife and fork. With very small birds it may be simpler to leave the legs. It is usually not appropriate to pick up bones and gnaw on them but sometimes a host will suggest everyone should do so. (At an informal gathering, such as a barbecue or picnic, it is fine to eat a chicken wing or spare rib with the fingers.)

Looking Back...

In Tudor times, food was eaten with the fingers, or a knife and spoon (forks were not used in England until the 17th century), from a communal bowl known as a mess. Generally, four people shared each mess, however those of high social standing shared between two and those with the highest precedence did not share at all. Good manners required diners to keep the tablecloth and their hands as clean as possible, so napkins were tied around the wrist or placed over the left shoulder for convenience. Bowls of water – often scented with rose leaves, herbs or orange peel – and towels were offered in order of precedence, for guests to wash their hands before and after a meal.

Table Manners

Drinks

Wines & Spirits
Coffee
Traditional Tea

Wines & Spirits

Drinking manners are an integral part of table manners. How to hold the cup or glass, when and how much to drink, and how to do so in an appropriate and civilised fashion, is as important as eating food the right way.

Glasses — The two most basic kinds of glasses are tumblers for water or soft drinks, and wine glasses. These should be on the right-hand side of a place setting and slightly above it, either grouped or lined up. It is usual, when serving both white and red wine, to provide a smaller glass for white and a larger for red.

Special Glasses — Champagne is usually served in flutes or narrow glasses. Shallow saucer-shaped glasses were traditional but have fallen out of favour.

Other glasses that may be useful include narrow sherry glasses, brandy balloons and triangular, stemmed glasses for martinis and other cocktails, but it is not incorrect to manage without these. It is more important that glasses should be immaculately clean, plentiful and of as good quality as possible.

What to Serve — If hosting, it is good manners to serve the best wine possible and quality should be as important as quantity. It is important as a host to keep the supplies flowing and not leave empty glasses, but at the same time never force people to drink more than they want. Always provide plenty of water and soft drinks.

How to Serve Wine — A wine glass should be only one third full. It is better to underfill, rather than overfill, a glass. Red wine should be served at the 'old-fashioned' pre-central heating room temperature of 17–18°C (63°F) in a larger glass with a bigger bowl, to release the bouquet.

Whites are served in a smaller, narrower glass that should be held by the stem to avoid warming the wine. Fine white wine only needs around 20 minutes in the fridge (including Sauternes); too much chilling will hide the complexity of good wines. It is best, however, to chill cheaper bottles right down. Ice buckets are most effective when filled with a mix of ice and water.

'Let us have wine and women, mirth and laughter, sermons and soda water the day after.'
                                    Lord Byron

Wait to be served by the host or, if the host has put bottles out and asked people to serve themselves, offer others before helping yourself. Wine is usually served from the right-hand side. Avoid touching the top of the glass with the bottle when you pour.

How to Drink Wine

Take small sips and avoid making noises or 'wine tasting' gestures such as ostentatious sniffs or swirls. It is best to confine any remarks to general appreciation unless specifically asked. Opinions are best left to acknowledged experts and, even then, err on the side of politeness over honesty.

Decanters

Some wines are served in a decanter. The process of decanting a red wine allows it to breathe, separating mature wine from the sediment. It mellows and 'brings out' younger reds. Contact with the air livens it and, in a sense, 'accelerates' the ageing process.

Decanting should take place a couple of hours before drinking but less, perhaps, for older wines that can fall away through the shock of air contact.

Before decanting, ensure that the glass decanter is clean and soap-free. Pour the bottle at a reasonably rapid rate, being careful towards the end to ensure that any sediment remains in the bottle. Simply removing the cork from the bottle will not have the same (if any) effect; white wines are not usually decanted.

Champagne

Champagne should be served chilled (optimum temperature is about 7°C), in tulip-shaped flutes that are held by the stem (to avoid the heat of one's hands warming the champagne through the glass). The sign of a good champagne is a consistent stream of small bubbles that create a light froth on top, which is called the 'mousse'.

Vintage champagne comes from the crop of a single year so always has a date on its label; non-vintage (nv) champagne is blended from the crop of different years and therefore there will be no date on the label.

Aperitifs

An aperitif is a pre-meal drink that stimulates the appetite and palate. Traditional choices include chilled dry sherry, vermouth and Campari. Spirit-based drinks are also suitable; a cocktail, gin and tonic or vodka and a mixer. A simpler, and popular, option is a glass of chilled dry white wine or champagne.

Port

Port is usually served in a decanter and comes at the end of the dinner after pudding. In the days when women withdrew it was served to men only but today it is usually circulated to everyone, while they are still seated, often at about the same time as coffee. Unlike other after-dinner drinks or digestifs such as brandy, it is not normally served away from the table, for instance in a drawing room. If, however, you have been given wonderful port and have not had time to finish, it is fine to carry the glass through with you.

See p 373 for serving port

A port decanter will be placed on the table so that people can help themselves and then pass it on. Always pass the port to the left. If the port passes you by without your glass being filled don't ask for the port and make it change direction. Either send the empty glass after the port decanter and ask for it to be filled or better still wait for it to come round again.

Digestif

A digestif is drunk to aid digestion after a large meal. They are usually strong and dark coloured spirits, such as brandy, cognac and whisky. Fortified wines, such as port or Madeira, are also traditional options, as well as sweet liqueurs.

Brandy and Whisky

Brandy is served in a bulbous brandy balloon that is cradled in the palm to warm the spirit, intensifying the bouquet and enhancing the flavour.

Whisky is served in a short, heavy-based tumbler. Adding water to a single malt is generally no longer frowned upon, but adding ice is still thought to interfere with the aromas.

Looking Back...

The tradition of passing the port originates from naval dinners where the port was always passed 'port to port' around the table – ie to the left. Remembering to pass the port, which had arrived silently to a person's right, was something which could get forgotten, especially by those who did not drink it themselves. If this happened a trick was to remind the right-hand neighbour by saying: 'Did you know the Bishop of Norwich? No? He was a charming man but never remembered to pass the port.' In certain circles this tradition still stands.

Coffee

When to Serve

Coffee is most often served at breakfast, mid-morning or after lunch or dinner. In Britain it is not usually served during a formal main meal. Traditionally tea took the place of coffee in the afternoon, with coffee being served again after dinner. An exception is iced coffee, which is very much a part of the summer social season and is served as an afternoon alternative to hot tea in such enclaves as the President's Tent at the Chelsea Flower Show, White's Club Marquee during Royal Ascot, and at tea on the Royal Yacht Squadron Lawn during Cowes Week.

See pp 429–431 for a guide to the Season

What to Serve

Freshly ground coffee is preferable to instant coffee, other than very informally in the kitchen. However there is no need for private individuals to offer complicated espressos or a huge range of blends to guests in their own home. It is considerate to offer decaffeinated coffee.

How to Serve

Morning coffee should be served on a tray in cups with saucers and teaspoons on each. Mugs are only for informal use. It is best to serve coffee with cold milk and sugar, which people may add themselves. It is not necessary to provide sweeteners. At breakfast it is best practice to provide a pot of hot milk as well.

The coffee may be in a coffee pot or a cafetière. If it has been made by using a filter or coffee machine, then decant it into a plain coffee pot. It is best not to serve coffee still showing any of the equipment used in its making, such as bags, individual filters etc, other than a cafetière. The cups should be breakfast-sized for morning coffee and deep enough to ensure that the coffee does not get cold too quickly. Servings should be generous.

See p 375 for serving coffee

After-dinner coffee is traditionally served in small cups also called *demi-tasses*. Traditionally only cream would have been on the tray but it is thoughtful to offer milk as well. Special coffee sugar and small coffee spoons should be used.

Coffee in Restaurants

Coffee may be ordered at the same time as others are having pudding or cheese. It is not considered bad manners to drink coffee while others are still eating. Small cups are more elegant and espresso or filter coffee, with milk on the side, are a more sophisticated and appropriate choice than large milky drinks after dinner.

Traditional Tea

When having formal tea in the afternoon, it is usual to serve two kinds of tea: Indian such as Assam, and China such as Lapsang Souchong. Lapsang Souchong and Earl Grey are taken weak, with either a slice of lemon or milk. Separate hot water is usually served to dilute the tea. Black teas, such as Assam, are generally served with milk which is added after the tea has been poured.

Serving Tea — The tea is poured by the hostess or a nominated pourer. If leaf tea is served, a tea strainer is used. The tea is handed out one cup at a time after being poured, rather than pouring a few and handing them out in one go. The milk jug and sugar is passed around and each person adds their own. Use the teaspoon to stir the tea (without clinking) and then place it back on the saucer. Cups are held by the handle – being careful not to raise the little finger – and placed back on the saucer between sips. Saucers remain on the table and are never raised when the cup is lifted up. Away from the table, for example in an armchair, the cup and saucer are raised together and then put down between sips.

Traditional accompaniments include cucumber sandwiches, scones and cakes that are passed around. Cakes should be either very small – for example mini éclairs – or cleanly sliced. Cake that needs to be eaten with a fork should not be served.

Scones — Scones are broken by hand, not cut with a knife. As with bread rolls, the jam and cream is spooned on to the plate first, not directly on to the scone (unless the cream is runny, in which case it can be put straight on to the scone). It is traditional in Cornwall to spread jam on a scone before cream, whereas in Devon cream is traditionally put on first. County differences aside, it is generally considered that the most practical and neatest method is to spread the cream first, before the jam.

Looking Back...

The tradition of tea, served at 4pm with cakes, savouries and sweets, was started by Anna, Seventh Duchess of Bedford, in 1840. The evening meal in her household was served fashionably late at eight o'clock, thus leaving a long period of time between lunch and dinner. The Duchess would feel hungry around four o'clock in the afternoon and asked that a tray of tea, bread and butter, and cake be brought to her room during the late afternoon. This became a habit of hers and she began inviting friends to join her. This pause for tea became a fashionable social event, and was established as a regular and lasting fixture of British life.

366 - 395

Dinner Parties

Drinks Parties

Overnight Stays

AT HOME

Whatever the occasion, whether a formal dinner party or an overnight stay, the same principle of hospitality applies: the guests' enjoyment is always paramount. Hosts must do their utmost to shape their guests' expectations and to ensure that they have a pleasurable and convivial time. Guests owe it to their hosts to make an effort, arrive on time, talk to as many people as possible and not outstay their welcome. Thank you letters sent after enjoying hospitality are *de rigueur*.

At Home

Dinner Parties

Formal Dinners
Informal Suppers
Buffets

Formal Dinners

Dinner parties are usually for at least eight people and consist of three courses, at a formally laid table, in a dining room if one is available. Both host and guest should make an effort with dress.

Planning See pp 313–319 for invitations	The invitation should indicate the level of formality of the occasion. A printed card sent several weeks in advance with the dress code 'black tie' would indicate a formal event; a phone call a few days ahead would obviously signal informality. In either case the host should prepare the guests as to what to wear and what to expect, and be specific about times. If there is a special occasion, such as a birthday, hosts should mention it beforehand so that guests aren't taken by surprise.
Dress See pp 185–195 for dress codes	Black tie is usually confined to grand houses, or formal or special occasions. For less formal occasions, a helpful host will mention the dress code. As a general rule, the choice of outfit should show that an effort has been made. Change into something that is different from normal day clothes and, if coming straight from work, consider changing shoes or jewellery. What people actually choose to wear varies considerably according to age and location (for example, events in the country may be less formal than those in the city), but to make no effort would seem disrespectful to the host.
Arrivals	Guests should arrive a little after the stated time. At this point hosts should be organised enough to welcome guests and serve drinks, ideally in a different room from where dinner will be served. Couples can divide the roles of 'cook' and 'butler'. If the host is also the cook, then a simple menu should be planned so that they are free to welcome guests and make introductions; otherwise consider enlisting some help. Drinks may last for anything from 15 minutes to an hour, but resist anything longer. If people are running really late then dinner can be started without them. If drinks are protracted, provide substantial canapés or serve an informal first course with the drinks. This can work well, particularly if it is known in advance that guests will be arriving at different times.
Table Plans	The traditional plan is for the host and hostess to sit at either end of the table, with the most important female guest on the host's right and the most important man on the hostess's right. Some hosts prefer to sit opposite each other in the middle. Hosts who

need to go in and out to the kitchen should sit near the door. Any peculiarities of the room – for example, drafts, proximity to fires or radiators, low ceilings – should be noted and guests can be seated accordingly.

Men and women are alternated where possible and couples should not be seated next to one another (traditionally this rule was relaxed for engaged couples who would always be seated together). Try to avoid seating together workmates or those who see one another all the time.

Even numbers are traditional but not essential. Inviting someone just to make up numbers can be awkward or even offensive, but it is still considered bad luck to host a dinner party for 13.

Seating Plan

Often but incorrectly called *placement*, the formal term for a seating plan or list is *place à table*.

During the pre-dinner drinks, guests should aim to talk to those whom they will not be sitting next to during dinner. A table planner may be out on display allowing guests to identify who their neighbours at the table will be. Alternatively, a good trick is to speak to members of the same sex before dinner as guests will probably be seated next to members of the opposite sex.

When it is time to move to the table, the hostess (in the case of a couple) should lead her guests while the host brings up the rear. Male guests should also hold back and let the ladies through first. The hostess will tell people where to sit as they come through. It is fine to carry a list and read from it as people are seated but it is smarter to write place cards and put them out in advance.

See p 159 for place cards

Place cards may be displayed in special holders or just rested flat on the table above the place setting. Cards should be handwritten in ink, and may either show first names or full names with titles. If titles are used they should be social not formal, for example 'Lord Gainsborough' rather than 'The Earl of Gainsborough'.

Seating

Seating people correctly is important but so is ensuring guests' comfort. There should be plenty of leg-room and elbow-room. Chairs should be at the same height and be comfortable.

Traditional rectangular dining tables should be wide enough to look generous but narrow enough to talk across easily. With long, narrow, refectory-type tables or trestle tables for a big party, beware of stranding anyone at the end with only one neighbour.

PLACE SETTINGS   Place settings should be an even distance apart and no less than 20 inches wide to allow plenty of space. Formal place settings always have side plates (even if they will not be used) as they automatically provide sufficient elbow room.

It is helpful to have a table mat, correctly positioned about an inch from the table's edge. Fashionable chargers may be used in preference to table mats, but avoid piling up too many plates at each place setting.

Knives and spoons should be on the right of the setting and forks on the left. Guests should work from the outside in for each new course. While most first courses are eaten with just a fork, the small starter knife should still be laid (except when soup will be served and only a soup spoon is required). For formal dinners, pudding spoons and forks should be laid innermost and not above the place setting. If short of space, bring them to the table when pudding is served.

Glasses should be grouped or lined up on the right above the knives. A tumbler for water and two wine glasses, with the larger one for red wine, is usually enough. Napkins should be linen or cotton, folded simply or rolled, and can be put on the table mat or the side plate. Avoid elaborate arrangements in glasses.

DECORATIONS   Decorating tables is a very personal matter and there are really no rules, other than taste. Flowers are traditional and can look beautiful but arrangements should be low enough for guests to see over. Silver or ornamental objects may decorate a table. A theme, driven by colour or occasion, is fun, but a simple, immaculate, white double damask cloth is always attractive.

Candles alone provide a flattering ambience, but plenty should be used to ensure that everyone can see their food – the old rule was six candles, in pairs, for eight people and so on. Soft, additional indirect lighting such as picture lights, or down or uplighters, can help to get the right balance.

If silver is being used, clean it ahead of time to avoid the room smelling of polish. Both silver and glasses will usually benefit from a final polish once the table is laid.

Menus

A standard dinner party usually consists of three courses or three courses plus cheese. The traditional array of soup, fish, meat, pudding, savoury and dessert (fruit) is rarely encountered in a private house outside the world of PG Wodehouse or period television dramas.

Menus should be kept well within one's skill set when assuming the roles of both cook and host. The simplest dishes, perfectly executed and using the best ingredients, are often the most successful. Avoid anything that needs last-minute attention or precision timing such as a soufflé.

Steer clear of very hot and spicy dishes, and food guests may object to, such as *foie gras*. Try to have separate dishes, such as distinct meat and vegetables, rather than composite dishes, so that guests can choose and avoid dishes they won't enjoy.

Think of all the courses and try to keep your menu balanced. If you're serving a hearty main course keep the starters and puddings light.

Special Diets

If guests require a special diet then they must let the host know in advance. A considerate host may choose to serve a flexible menu to accommodate vegetarian or vegan guests, or those who are avoiding carbohydrates.

As a guest, if arrangements have not been made in advance, it is more polite just to refuse certain dishes as unobtrusively as possible, so that no one will notice. Avoid boring others with fads; if a very strict but temporary regime is being adhered to, consider staying at home.

Serving Food
See p 352 for table manners

Apart from the first course, which may be plated up individually and set out, do not serve food already on the plate as in a restaurant. Aim to present the food in big dishes from which people may help themselves or be served.

Carve meat away from the table for a dinner party, as opposed to a Sunday lunch, and serve on a platter. Make sure there is plenty of everything; aim to be able to offer second helpings.

It is not necessary to serve bread rolls as in a restaurant. If bread is required for a specific dish – for example bread and butter with smoked salmon – put butter out on small plates, with a butter knife, at intervals along the table.

STAFF/SERVICE When serving seated guests, the staff or host should offer food from the left (fork side). The dish should be held low and steady, with the serving implements placed so that people can help themselves easily. In a private house, plates are also cleared from the fork side, contrary to the way waiting staff are often trained.

Wine should be poured from the right and either be offered by staff, if there are any, or the host. Alternatively, bottles may be placed on the table at convenient intervals and the host can suggest that guests help themselves. Men should help the women first, then neighbours, then themselves. Do not overfill glasses. Put water on the table so guests may pass it to one another.

Staff should serve the principal woman guest first, then go round the table, finishing with the host. Meat or fish, with sauce if there is one, is offered first, then vegetables and finally potatoes.

Salt and pepper and mustard, if applicable, should be on the table, placed at intervals if it is large. Sauces or gravy should be served but cream, to go with pudding, may be served or passed round the table.

DRINKS
See pp 336–363 for drinks

Pre-dinner drinks – usually wine, champagne or cocktails, and soft drinks – are ideally served in a reception room. Generally it is fine for guests to carry unfinished wine or champagne through to the table. In a very grand setting, or if there are serving staff, it is best to finish your drink or leave it behind.

At dinner there should be both white and red wine, with separate glasses for each, plenty of water and perhaps a soft drink. Always keep the wine flowing but never force it on guests, who may have many reasons for not drinking.

If a pudding wine or champagne is served, a third, smaller wine glass is needed, though it does not necessarily have to be a champagne glass or flute.

PORT
See p 363 for port

If port is served then separate glasses are needed. Port is circulated in a decanter, starting with the host, in a clockwise direction around the table. It is correct to pass it on promptly, without putting it down, even if not drinking any.

Brandy and other after-dinner drinks may be served at the dining table with coffee, or in the sitting room. It is considerate to have more soft drinks available after dinner.

PACING   The host will usually say 'Do start' when people are being served hot food, but it is polite to wait for everyone else if food such as a cold first course is already on the plate.

The host needs to keep things moving and ensure the courses progress smoothly, without hurrying people. There is almost always someone very slow but nothing should be cleared before everyone has finished. Twenty minutes per course is about right. If there is an unanticipated delay in the kitchen, it is often best to inform guests.

Guests should try to pace their eating and keep an eye on others. They should also speak to one neighbour during the first course then turn the other way so that no one gets left out. A woman will usually turn first to her left. If there is a gap, perhaps because the host or hostess is doing something in the kitchen, then talk across it till they sit down.

'So long as you chatter, Fanny, it's of no consequence what you say, better recite out of the ABC than sit like a deaf mute. Think of your poor hostess, it simply isn't fair on her.'
                           NANCY MITFORD, LOVE IN A COLD CLIMATE

CLEARING   Clear away plates two at a time and avoid stacking or scraping as this can look unattractive and be noisy. Accept offers to help clear but if everyone starts getting up from the table then appoint one, or at the most two, helpers to avoid too much disruption. Avoid excessively clearing up in the kitchen or being absent from the table for a long time between courses.

Everything from the first and main course, including salt and pepper, should be removed before pudding. Side plates are left if there is going to be cheese.

AFTER DINNER   The days when men stayed in the dining room over the port and cigars and the ladies withdrew are over, other than in the most formal settings. A more informal version may naturally take place and it is often the case that everyone ends up staying at the table. There are, however, many practical and considerate reasons to get down. Those who have not had a chance to talk to each other at the table may wish to do so, or guests may want to wash their hands, move to a more comfortable chair, stretch their legs, or even smoke. Taking people through into another room allows for all this to happen fairly naturally.

Coffee
See p 364 for coffee

Coffee may be served at the table or in a reception room. Small cups, sometimes called *demi-tasses*, are often used. Avoid serving coffee in large mugs. A considerate host will offer decaffeinated coffee and herb teas. Cream is traditional with after-dinner coffee, as is special coffee sugar, but many people prefer milk. After-dinner drinks may be served. It is also the time to open and offer round any chocolates that have been received.

Parting

Guests should be alert to signals from the host. They may be verbal, such as mentioning an early start, or non-verbal, such as not offering more drinks. If the host gets to their feet or starts tidying, it is definitely time to go. It is usual to leave reasonably promptly after dinner on a weekday night.

As a host, if someone is outstaying their welcome, a balance must be struck between being polite yet fairly clear. Very occasionally it is necessary to be absolutely direct, but always take the blame: 'I am so sorry, I am exhausted. I have not really recovered from our long journey the other day.'

If you are hosting overnight guests, you can go to bed and leave them downstairs on their own. Often one of the hosts will do so, leaving the other on duty. Talk of putting dogs out and locking doors may help late night carousers get the message.

Afterwards
See p 425 for sample thank-you letter

It is very important for guests to thank their hosts properly and promptly for having them to dinner. A letter is best but a postcard is also acceptable, unless it was a very formal affair. If the host is a close friend then a telephone call may be sufficient. An email, while not ideal, may be suitable under some circumstances. If the event was sensational, then send flowers.

Above all, guests must reciprocate and invite their hosts back; not to do so is very bad manners. If they really can't manage a dinner party then something else should be proposed instead. Be aware, however, that asking someone who hosted a dinner back for just a drink is not good enough.

Looking Back...

When pudding was over, the hostess would signal to the lady of the highest rank that it was time for the ladies to leave the dining room. The gentlemen would stand and then the host would move into the hostess's seat so he was near the principal male guests. The gentlemen would enjoy more wine, and cigarettes or cigars. The ladies would go through to the drawing room for coffee and, after a little while, be re-joined by the men.

Informal Suppers

Informal dinners or suppers, sometimes called kitchen suppers, are different from dinner parties. Supper parties typically start at an hour that is convenient for everyone and will last for a shorter amount of time than a formal dinner party. When inviting, hosts should make it clear if they are hosting a supper party, rather than a dinner party.

Menu There may or may not be a first course but the main dish will be something simple like fish pie or pasta, served with a salad, followed by pudding and cheese, or just cheese. Guests will help themselves, either from the table or from the side, or the food may already be on their plates.

Practicalities It is fine to use paper napkins and everyday plates, knives and forks but apply some basic rules. Ensure that the table looks attractive and pay attention to seating people where they will mix best. Formalities, such as seating the most important senior guest on the host's right or splitting couples, need not be observed; the emphasis should be on ease and conviviality.

Contributions from friends such as wine, cheese, chocolates or homemade preserves may be very welcome. Wine can be put on the table and guests asked to help themselves.

Children or teenagers may well be included and it is fine to let them leave after eating when permission is asked, but while they are there they should eat properly, offer to help and be included in the conversation.

Looking Back...

Full evening dress was customary for dinner parties. Referred to as 'dressing for dinner', this meant tailcoats for gentlemen and full evening dresses for ladies. An exception was made for less formal supper parties when, if the hostess specified that it was to be a more casual evening, gentlemen could dress down and wear black tie.

BUFFETS

PLANNING A buffet table should be positioned to allow plenty of space for guests to move along and serve themselves. Dishes should be arranged so that people are not forced to wait for too long or stretch over each other. Plates should be in a prominent position and always provide more than may be needed – no one wants to feel that they are bringing up the rear. If there are no formal tables, there should be provision for guests to sit casually and eat.

FORMAL BUFFETS At formal buffets when there is a proper seated meal, guests are usually asked, by table, to go and get food. This request should be responded to promptly and it is polite to check that everyone on the table, particularly older guests, is able to go and get themselves something or is being looked after.

INFORMAL BUFFETS Timing is less crucial at informal buffet parties and generally guests will help themselves at a convenient moment. It is, however, a help to the hosts (and caterers) to keep an eye on the rest of the room and eat with the majority rather than holding up the clearing of the main courses and the serving of pudding.

PRACTICALITIES Move along the buffet at a reasonable speed to maintain the flow, and be polite and accommodating to waiting staff who may be on hand to serve. Be aware of people behind you and offer to help where necessary, either by handing them a plate, knife and fork or napkin, or by serving them where practical. Take plenty, but avoid overloading your plate or finishing dishes that look like they may not get replenished. Usually there will be the opportunity for second helpings, but multiple visits to the buffet table may look greedy.

Pudding is generally served at a more relaxed pace, with guests helping themselves when it suits them. It is polite to offer to fetch pudding for other guests, particularly for gentlemen to offer to help the ladies sitting next to them. The same considerations apply for coffee or tea.

CHILDREN Parents should keep an eye on their children and make sure that they do not keep helping themselves to the buffet or touch the food in the serving dishes.

At Home

Drinks Parties

Party Planning
At The Party

Party Planning

Drinks parties or cocktail parties can be a practical, flexible and comparatively economical way of entertaining larger numbers. Traditionally they are held before dinner, often from 6.30–8.30pm but, especially in the country, may be before lunch. Increasingly, drinks parties last for a whole evening from 7pm until around 9–10pm. Slightly more substantial food is served and then guests may take themselves on to dinner or go home. Occasionally, people may be asked for after-dinner drinks.

Venues — Unlike most dinner parties, drinks parties may be held at a venue other than the host's house, for example gardens, clubs, other people's large houses or hired rooms in museums, even on boats.

Staff and Service — Drinks parties are where waiting staff, or at least help of some sort, is most worthwhile. Having a bar person and one or two waiters makes a real difference, as does having someone to greet guests and take coats. A club or venue's own staff, or possibly those from an agency or the caterer, may be used. At home, if professionals are not wanted, then the host's (or their friends') teenage children, plus a friend or two, may be a good option, but always ensure they are well-briefed beforehand. If there is no help, a host needs to be very organised, with drinks set out ready poured and a few friends enlisted to circulate with refills.

Practicalities — If hosting a party at home then a single room that is big enough is preferable – while parties that overflow into more than one room can allow for different ambiences, they can be tricky. If multiple rooms must be used, then set up a bar in one and provide some, but not too much, seating in another. Most people will stand and circulate, but some seats are considerate for older guests. In summer, allow the party to spill outside if possible.

Flowers are a bonus but music is not essential. Signs for the lavatories and where to leave coats (if not tended to on arrival) may be helpful.

Drinks — Drinks can range from champagne or sparkling wine to cocktails. Always serve a good selection of soft drinks and perhaps a non-alcoholic cocktail. Have a bottle of whisky to hand for the guest who only drinks Scotch. Get too much of everything, including extra glasses, as demand can never be anticipated and drinks often get mislaid or spilt.

FOOD   Some food needs to be served at a drinks party, even though it is not central to the event. Canapés are customary and may be provided by a caterer, shop-bought or homemade. It is smartest to serve just one type of canapé per tray and, most importantly, they should be easy to eat in one bite, without cutlery.

Serve canapés in stages, introducing new kinds progressively throughout the evening. For a party of a hundred people then six different canapés, three hot and three cold, would be about right, but this may be impractical or require too much cooking if professional caterers are not being used. It is not always necessary to provide little napkins. If food is served on sticks or skewers then thought should be given as to their disposal. Receptacles should be provided on the canapé tray, or be offered separately.

DRESS   Dress can range from glamorous cocktail dresses for women and suits for men to more casual clothes for a summer drinks party in a garden. The invitation should give a clue, although dress codes as such do not always appear on invitations to drinks.

A large, formal party is indicated by a card arriving weeks or even months ahead of time – if it is taking place at a smart venue you may assume that it is best to dress up. A telephone call asking if you are free the following night and want to come round for a drink with one or two friends is obviously different. Whatever the case, make an effort to change from work or day clothes into something more appropriate. At the very least, women can use accessories (jewellery, handbag etc) to adapt the overall look of their outfit so that it suits a social event.

AT THE PARTY

HOSTS   Hosts must be ready to greet their guests on arrival and make sure they have drinks. Ideally, someone else should open the door and take coats. Guests should be introduced as much as possible, especially in the early stages of the party. Once most people have arrived, the host can move to the middle of the room to check that people are meeting one another and that no one is stuck or isolated. If there is no help, it is sensible for the host to take a bottle with them as they circulate. This will keep glasses topped up and signal to guests that the host cannot linger for a long chat. Towards the end of the party the host may stand fairly near the exit, so that guests can thank them and say goodbye.

GUESTS   It is not important to be absolutely punctual for drinks parties; some people like to arrive and leave promptly, while others come later on and stay to the end. Unless helping out, it may seem a little excessive to be the first to arrive and the last to leave.

Guests should greet their host on arrival, have a brief chat and then try to talk to anyone they are introduced to. Aim to meet at least two sets of new people and do not just talk to friends or cling to a partner or spouse. Introduce people to one another. If guests hardly know anyone, they may need to approach strangers and introduce themselves.

Do not look over people's shoulders to see who else is at the party but it is reasonable after a short time to make an excuse and move on. Keep it simple and honest: 'There are so many old friends I need to catch up with so I am going to circulate' or 'It has been so lovely talking to you but I suppose we should circulate'. Alternatively, go in search of a drink or the host. Do not plead an imminent departure and then spend hours talking to someone feet away from the person who has just been left.

Find the host to say goodbye and thank you but do not monopolise them so that a queue forms. Drinks parties are suitable for quick catch-ups and possibly meeting new people and not for long, private chats.

AFTERWARDS   It is perfectly in order to stop serving drinks to signal the end of a party. Hosts may find it problematic if they are expecting certain people to stay on for dinner and others will not leave, especially if the party is being held at home.

If the party is in a venue and the host is aiming to go on to a restaurant, then it is easiest to apologise to any stragglers and let them know that everyone has to vacate the premises by a certain time.

When booking a restaurant for after the party, it is wise to choose somewhere that is very flexible or likely to have space, as a few extra people are bound to join in. The host is neither expected to pay for a post-party dinner they have arranged, nor have any responsibility for what happens later. If, however, the host is extending their hospitality to include dinner then they should make it clear in advance to any guests who will be joining them.

AT HOME

OVERNIGHT STAYS

HOSPITALITY
GUEST ETIQUETTE
CHILDREN

Hospitality

Whether you're having an old friend to stay or hosting a weekend gathering, the same fundamental principles of hospitality apply, as the aim is to make sure that guests feel at home and are as comfortable as possible.

Hosts need to make an effort and stay attentive to guests' needs without exhausting themselves. A programme should be planned, without scheduling every moment. While plenty of good food and drink must be served, the host should not allow their own responsibilities to become a burden so that they do not enjoy themselves. Guests must remember that they are going to someone's house, not a hotel.

Preparation It is best to invite people well ahead of time – weeks rather than days – and to let them know if there is anything in particular involved, such as a day at the races. It is much more usual to speak to guests in person or on the telephone, but this may be followed up with a letter, or an email, with directions, times and full contact details.

As much as possible should be done in advance, as it is more important to spend time with guests than rush around doing last-minute jobs. It is more relaxing and welcoming if guests are greeted by a calm, relaxed and well-presented host, than someone in an apron, looking fraught and as if everything is hard work, or that they wish they had asked their guests to arrive later.

Priorities While meals are important, they should not completely dominate the proceedings. Take short cuts, such as having a simple cold first course ready prepared and a main course that does not need last-minute attention. Stews and soups prepared earlier in the week are useful. If you are having a large influx of people, consider hiring some help. Plan meals so that some are very simple, accompanied by salad, cheese and fruit, and make one – usually Saturday dinner – a main event.

Accommodation Make sure the spare room, however simple or small, works perfectly. The best way to test this is for hosts to sleep there from time to time. The beds and mattresses should be of as good quality as possible. Twin beds may provide more flexibility and the type that can be pushed together when required are ideal. Remember that beds with a fixed foot board can be uncomfortable for very tall people.

Windows should be easy to open and shut and the curtains easy to draw and heavy enough to keep out the light. If the heating is not good, provide an electric heater that is easy to switch on and off. Electric blankets may be useful in cold country houses, while cosy hot water bottles are still a tradition in some houses.

Avoid using a spare room for too much storage (especially drawers and hanging cupboards) and try to keep surfaces uncluttered.

FURNITURE
The room should have bedside tables with good reading lights (check the bulbs regularly) either side and plenty of accessible sockets for hairdryers and for charging telephones and gadgets. Ideally there should be a chest of drawers and a hanging cupboard with plenty of hangers of every kind.

A dressing table, ideally with a well-lit mirror and a chair, an armchair and somewhere to put a suitcase when unpacking – either a folding rack or a chaise longue or ottoman at the foot of the bed – will all enhance the room. Traditionally hosts would provide a desk with writing paper and envelopes.

GETTING THE ROOM READY
Bedclothes, preferably either cotton or linen, should be freshly aired and ironed if possible. Be aware that guests may have allergies so launder duvets and pillows regularly and consider man-made fibre rather than down fillings in spare rooms. Give each guest two good-quality large pillows. A radio may be appreciated but a television is not needed.

Providing tea and coffee in the room may make it look like a bed and breakfast but in some circumstances it is practical and thoughtful. Avoid sachets and provide proper milk in a jug and sugar lumps in a bowl. Put out water and glasses, either a carafe or a bottled mineral water. Before guests arrive, put fresh flowers in the room and some suitable books on the bedside table.

Some hosts like to put cotton wool in a china bowl, paper tissues on the dressing table and provide a hairdryer. It is considerate to provide the WiFi password, perhaps on a printed card.

'A host is like a general: calamities often reveal his genius.'
HORACE

BATHROOMS   If guests have their own bathroom put towels there. A bath towel, a medium-sized towel for hair, a hand towel and a bathmat will be needed. There is no need to provide face flannels. If they are sharing a bathroom with other guests, leave the clean towels in the bedroom, either folded on the bed or on a towel rail.

It is not necessary to provide body lotion, as in a hotel, but there should be some untouched soap and possibly bath essence, shower gel and shampoo in the bathroom. Keeping a stock of toothbrushes and other essentials for the forgetful in a drawer or cupboard is thoughtful.

ON ARRIVAL   When guests arrive they should be shown to the room and bathroom, if separate. Show them how things work, such as the heater or light switches, and warn them of any quirks such as complicated blinds, uneven floors or temperamental hot water.

Give them some idea of the programme: they may, for example, be invited down for a cup of tea, or invited to relax, have a bath and join everyone for drinks at 7.30. It helps people relax if they know in advance about timings but do not bombard them with information. Wait until bedtime to discuss breakfast arrangements and on no account start asking about when they are going to leave as soon as they arrive. Once guests are in their rooms it is their territory, so never barge in unannounced.

BREAKFAST   Make sure that everyone understands what breakfast will involve. Some hosts choose to leave things out so people can help themselves, especially if they are known to get up very early. It is, however, easier for everyone if the host is clear about timings, giving guests a start and a cut-off time.

Generally, the host should be dressed and on breakfast duty before anyone appears, ideally with a tidy kitchen and the table laid. If breakfast is at a specific time, such as 8.30, guests should be down before 8.45, bathed and dressed. This may be flexible in certain circumstances, for example at a country cottage with close friends where dressing gowns would not seem out of place (save skimpy night clothes for the privacy of the bedroom).

If laying breakfast, lay the small plate as a side plate and place the cereal bowl in the centre; do not put one under the other. It is more traditional to lay only the side plate and to leave the bowls near the cereal for people to help themselves.

As a minimum, try to offer tea, coffee, juice, cereal, toast and marmalade, honey or jam. A considerate host may also ensure that newspapers are available for their guests.

Cooked breakfast may be served on a sideboard from which everybody helps themselves. In smart country houses, where cooked breakfast is served in dining rooms to large parties, hotplates and hostess trolleys are often used to keep food and plates warm, especially if the kitchens are a long way away and guests are likely to come down for breakfast at different times.

It is not necessary to make a cooked breakfast every morning, especially on a Sunday when a large lunch may be served. One quick and simple cooked element, for example bacon sandwiches, warm muffins, scrambled eggs, mushrooms on toast or pre-prepared kedgeree, can be provided to ensure that the host spends plenty of time with their guests, rather than cooking in the kitchen.

If anyone is very late it is reasonable to serve just coffee or tea in another room so that hosts can get on with preparing lunch.

STAFF   In a very grand house, guests may have their suitcases unpacked and their beds turned down, and perhaps a hot-water bottle placed in their beds during dinner. Staff will also make the beds in the morning while the guests are at breakfast.

If you have no help then it is not necessary to go into the room at all to do any tidying until guests leave. Guests should feel that they can retire to their rooms to relax, rest or read and be undisturbed.

LOOKING BACK...

At large country house parties, for example during the shooting season, the women would breakfast in their bedroom, while the men were expected to go downstairs. Breakfast was a more informal meal and, unlike dinner, no order of precedence was observed. The gentlemen would take their seats as they came in, exchange a brief morning greeting and begin to eat without waiting for others. It was expected that breakfast would be taken in a comfortable silence.

Guest Etiquette

Arrivals and Departures

Weekend guests should try to find out what the programme is likely to be so that the right clothes and shoes are packed. If waterproofs and gumboots will be needed, guests should bring their own rather than expecting to be kitted out.

For a traditional weekend in the country, guests are expected to arrive on the Friday night in time for dinner. If it is not going to be possible for a guest to arrive in time for dinner on Friday, they can suggest that they will either arrive late in the evening (and will have already eaten *en route*) or come on Saturday in time for lunch. Either way, it is important to be definite about times.

'Few things tend more to alienate friendship than a want of punctuality in our engagements. I have known the breach of a promise to dine or sup to break up more than one intimacy.'
WILLIAM HAZLITT

Guests should find out about distances and directions in advance. In the sat nav/smartphone era it is inconsiderate to get lost, but if the place is very inaccessible, be sure to have left plenty of time and that the phone number is to hand. Be wary of hosts' estimates of journey times as they may be familiar with the local area and short cuts.

If running late, call ahead in good time rather than leaving it until it is very close to the expected time of arrival. If travelling by train, guests can expect to be met at the station but should make sure times are convenient and distances not too great. Check what other guests may be doing in case shared lifts are possible, or offer to get a taxi.

The usual time to leave would be after lunch on Sunday, or possibly after tea, but it is inconsiderate to expect Sunday night supper. If it is not possible to stay for Sunday lunch then hosts should be told in advance, rather than on arrival, as food may have been bought and prepared in advance.

Bearing Gifts
See p 425 for sample thank-you letter

While they are not essential and may vary according to the situation, house presents are increasingly common. Popular choices include wine, chocolates, candles or small items for children. It is, however, more important to write a proper and prompt thank-you letter afterwards – a present does not replace the need for this.

Wine is usually very welcome, but do not be offended if the wine is put away or opened last, as it may not go with the menu or other wines. The safest bet may be to bring a bottle of chilled champagne, or sparkling wine, which may be opened straightaway or kept.

Bringing food and drink is not suitable for a very formal or grand house party, but may well be appreciated on other occasions. If the hosts are good friends then ask what would be a helpful contribution.

In certain circumstances it may be more considerate for guests to suggest that they buy their hosts lunch in a local pub or restaurant, perhaps on the Saturday, if it fits with everyone's plans, than to spend money on a big present. If the stay is any longer than a weekend then guests should certainly take their hosts out at least once.

GUEST BEHAVIOUR Guests must remember that they are staying in someone's house, not a hotel, and should therefore not expect hotel standards such as endless hot water. They will be expected to fit in, which means being punctual for meals and outings and not staying in bed all morning or being anti-social when, for example, the neighbours come for drinks.

GUESTS' ROOMS A guest's room is theirs for their stay. It is their space to relax in and spread their things around, but wet towels should not be left on furniture or too much mess made. If there is a bed cover, do not lie on it; take it off and fold it on a chair.

A polite and considerate guest will adopt a positive demeanour during their stay. They will always tell their host, in a genuine manner, that they have slept well and that the food is delicious, even if the opposite is true.

It is important that guests are sensitive to the routines and rituals of the house and its occupants. For example, avoid parking in the space where the family car is always parked, or sitting in the host's favourite armchair, unless invited to do so.

MAKING YOURSELF AT HOME Even though hosts will want guests to feel at home, food should not be taken from the kitchen or drinks from the fridge, or even tea made without asking. Don't leave your possessions lying around in communal spaces. Avoid using or borrowing things like hats or wellingtons, or playing with games or toys, unless they are offered. Do not turn on the radio or CD player without asking or being asked to do so. Put things back where they were found and stow them away properly. Be open to the host's suggestions and if asked to play a game such as croquet, always abide by 'house rules' however unfamiliar or unfair they seem.

TECHNOLOGY Guests may find that their hosts have provided them with the WiFi password. Guests must not make a fuss or complain if WiFi is not available or there is only a weak signal. If there is a genuine need to stay in touch, or there is a business matter or urgent private or family matter pending, then this should be explained. There is usually the opportunity to use a landline or to drive somewhere and get reception if needs be.

As a general rule, guests should use their own room for making calls or checking emails, unless there is some relaxing television or reading time when it would seem appropriate and unintrusive to check messages. Everyone is there to socialise, however, not to work or keep up with social media. Do not obviously carry a phone round and keep checking it.

TELEVISION If a guest particularly wishes to watch something on television, they should not make demands or turn on the host's television without prior consent. With modern technology, it is simple enough to record or watch something later. If the host suggests watching something, then guests should agree; avoid talking during those programmes unless they are suited to communal viewing, for example sports programmes.

STAFF At grand house parties guests may find that there are staff. Treat them in a friendly manner: for instance say good morning, but do not get over-familiar or try to gossip. If in doubt of the 'house style', refer formally to the host: 'Is Mr Debrett back yet?' rather than 'John'. The same goes for spouses: 'Mrs Berkeley will be down in a minute.'

If staff are known by their last name, such as 'Beech', then call them 'Beech' but children should be taught to say 'Mr Beech'. If their first name is used then only use that. Remembering names of staff and using them is polite and shows respect.

Guests should not give an instruction to private staff, as they might to restaurant or hotel staff, but should let them do their job – for example if they offer to take a case up or even unpack – without being embarrassed. Remember to thank them.

HELPING If the host is undertaking all the cooking, then offer to help without hovering or asking endless questions: 'Where are the forks? Which knives?' On the other hand, do not appear when all the work is clearly finished and ask if there is anything to do. Helping with a specific task, such as peeling the potatoes, may be the best option. Be aware that some hosts may want the kitchen to themselves – this is not the time to take charge or pass on any unwanted culinary tips.

Try to be sensitive and ask what would be the best way to be of help: for example, to entertain other guests, look after the children, walk the dog or just keep out of the way.

Always help clear away plates during dinner and hand things round. Offer to wash up if the host has no help but do not insist and dive in. Some hosts may prefer leaving things until the morning or have a special routine.

At the end of the stay, offer to strip the bed and tidy the bathroom, but the host should not expect guests to do real housework.

DRINKING Overnight stays may be seen as a good opportunity to overdo it as there is no requirement to drive anywhere after dinner or get up for work, and hosts are usually very generous.

If guests want to be asked back then they should take it easy. It is rude to drink a host out of house and home or demand that more bottles are opened. A guest who keeps the hosts or fellow guests up into the small hours against their wishes will generally be regarded as a social bore – they are almost certainly not being as entertaining, witty and amusing as they imagine.

If the evening does get very late and people overindulge, it should be assumed that the usual house rules will apply the next morning. Guests must be up for breakfast at the arranged time, unless the host tells them otherwise, and should keep their hangover to themselves.

SMOKING Take the lead from the hosts and never ask to smoke or assume it is acceptable. Guests should never smoke in bedrooms, but may smoke with permission in reception rooms if there are ashtrays already out and if one of the hosts smokes. Some hosts may offer after-dinner cigars, in which case smoking is permitted at the table.

If a host really hates smoking then it should be made clear before guests arrive. If a guest of smokers really hates smoking they will probably have to suffer in silence, but can speak up if they have a medical condition such as asthma.

In practice most people are used to having to smoke outside or not smoking. When smoking in the garden, dispose of cigarette ends tidily.

The same general rules apply to vaping; ask permission from your host, abstain or go outside.

Tipping — If there are household staff they should be tipped. On departure a tip is left on the dressing table, either in an envelope or just on its own, or the host is asked for advice. Traditionally men also tipped the butler, but in grand households there may be a pooling system so anything from the dressing table will be shared.

Traditionally, guests ask the host if something should be left as a tip for a cleaner or daily who comes during the week. This is increasingly rare; many hosts will not observe this practice and see it as an outdated custom.

Pets — Only take a dog that is happy sleeping in the car, as it may not be welcome in the house. Even then it is essential to ask first as the host's dogs may not like other dogs on their patch. The exception would be a shooting dog, but always check first. Guests should bring along their own dog's food, basket etc.

Looking Back...

Country house parties lasting three to five days were usual between August and the end of January, during the hunting and shooting seasons. They also were held to coincide with local social or sporting events, for example Glorious Goodwood or the Royal Highland Show. They loom large in the golden age of British crime fiction, especially Agatha Christie, who found house parties (which she often located in Devon where she lived) fertile ground for murder. In real life, murder was rare, but adultery was another matter. Edwardian memoirs show that 'corridor creeping' was rife – most likely aided by the old-fashioned practice of a guest's name being on the door of their room.

Children

Many people have 'help' with their children, either looking after them during the daytime while parents work, or on a more permanent basis living in their houses.

The strict hierarchical rules of days gone by have disappeared and, as a result, modern relationships between parents and children, parents and nannies (or au pairs) and, in particular, nannies and others are less clear-cut.

Bringing Children

Some people with very small babies may refuse overnight invitations until their child is older. Conversely, others choose to socialise with a very small baby and then refuse invitations during the challenging toddler years. It depends on the situation, the nature of the weekend away and, ultimately, on the child.

It is important for hosts to be sensitive to parents' needs and wishes. Some parents may be delighted to have a weekend away without their baby or small children taking centre stage, whereas others would be appalled at the idea of leaving them behind. Working parents in particular may treasure their weekends and want to spend time with their children.

When accepting an invitation, a guest should clarify to the host the number and ages of children who are attending, if it isn't already obvious.

Communications

It is essential that the expectations of both the host and guest are managed well in advance, as every situation varies. If either the host or guest has very strong views about children then discuss these so that a plan, or compromise, can be made.

As a general rule, the host's views should take precedence, but a good host will also be flexible. Routines and sleeping and eating arrangements must be discussed as openly as possible. If a nanny is coming too, or will be on duty, then this must be made clear.

Nannies or au pairs – whether the guests' or the hosts' – must be properly briefed so that they have a clear understanding of what is expected of them both by the host, and by the guest family.

Children who are well-behaved when they are away from home will be welcome everywhere. Moreover, they will be confident with a range of age groups, which is an essential life skill.

Good Behaviour	As a guest in someone else's house, parents must take full responsibility for their babies and children at all times. This also means bringing everything a baby will need from home, including food, bedding and equipment.
Responsibility	Parents cannot abdicate responsibility for their children, even if it means missing out on some of the weekend activities or forgoing late night excesses. Most importantly, guests should not use their hosts as nannies or expect the host's nanny to take over childcare, especially early in the morning, unless offered. A guest's baby must never spoil or impede on other people's fun – for example parents asking everyone to keep quiet during the evening – but other guests should, of course, be considerate.
Safety	While hosts should not be expected to baby-proof their house, it is sensible to be practical about any potential hazards for crawling babies, toddlers or small children. For example, keep certain doors shut, move anything very fragile out of reach, warn parents about the pond in the garden or request that a certain area or room in the house is out of bounds.
Routines	Routines vary from the super-strict to the ultra-liberal. A baby will understandably require some sort of routine, but parents should aim to be flexible and not impose their rules. If it seems too hard to adapt or fit in with the weekend's plans, do not go. Ideally the baby should have its tea or evening feed, be bathed and then put to bed to allow parents to go down to dinner at the normal time with all the other adults. If you are not happy to be separated, for example from a very small baby, then hosts should be warned beforehand.
Food and Drink	Night-feeds and breakfast should also be organised so as not to disturb others.
Adult Time	A baby or small child who has a set bedtime will be more popular than one who expects to stay up for dinner with the grown-ups. Guests must remember that house rules will apply so, even if they are used to eating with their own children at 6.30pm, if a host is planning an adults' dinner then this must be respected and the children should be put to bed at an appropriate hour. Similarly, if the hosts have arranged a babysitter or other help to facilitate an adult evening, it would be rude for guests' children to be allowed to stay up unless invited to do so.

Older children may be allowed to stay up and commune with their laptops or watch television rather than joining in at dinner – they should be urged not to interrupt the adults unnecessarily.

Parents should remember to keep conversation relevant to all guests, especially those who do not have children (for example avoid long discussions about schools).

CHILDREN'S MEALS

Usually children will be expected to join in at breakfast and lunch. Guests should bring food and snacks for babies and very small children who do not yet eat adult food. At any age, children should try to eat as tidily as possible and parents should take responsibility for clearing up after messy babies and toddlers. Generally, it is up to the host to say that younger children may 'get down' and play or watch TV if lunch goes on for a long time.

As a rule of thumb, a guest's nanny or other helper would join in at breakfast and lunch, but not dinner. To avoid embarrassment, a guest should confirm with the host in advance where and when the nanny will take meals.

FUSSINESS

Ideally children should eat what is put in front of them and have good table manners. If the parents know that they really will not eat certain foods then tell the children quietly to leave them on the side of the plate. At someone else's table, parents should neither make special requests on behalf of their child, nor battle with them to eat. Young children can be discreetly helped with their food.

Guests should confer with the host to confirm whether older children will be joining the family for dinner. It is important for children to learn to speak to people of all ages, including those they do not know. On the other hand they should not 'perform' or show off. Some hosts intersperse children and adults but, if there are a number of young, then having a junior end to the table works well.

ENTERTAINMENT

Guests should bring toys and books for small children and babies, but they must be kept as tidy as possible and be out of sight once the children are in bed. A laptop or tablet may be useful for occupying small children in their bedrooms either at bedtime or early in the morning.

SEEKING PERMISSION   Children should not be allowed to put on the host's television by themselves unless the host has suggested it. If there are children of different ages, programmes or entertainment should be vetted to ensure they are suitable for the youngest. They should also be told not to help themselves to food or drink from the host's fridge.

OLDER CHILDREN AND TEENAGERS   Older children will usually be given their own rooms or share with a child of the host. They should have suitable clothes in their own case and be taught to unpack. Guests should check that their children are not making too much mess in their room.

REQUIREMENTS   Parents should check in advance what their children may need, for example outdoor clothes, boots or something smart.

PRESENTS   Be aware when giving presents to a host's children what kind of parents they are. Avoid anything that may be controversial or too extravagant.

A nanny or au pair who provides substantial assistance with another family's children – be it the hosts' or the guests' – should be thanked and given a present or gift voucher.

LOOKING BACK...

In large, fully-staffed country houses two or three generations ago there was an upstairs/downstairs division, with the family in the dining room and the servants eating in the servants' hall below. The top floor was a third realm: the nursery. There, Nanny presided over yet another table with the help of a nursery maid. In the very biggest houses, a nursery footman brought the food up from the kitchen for her and her charges. Visiting children would bring their own nanny and they too would eat and sleep in the nursery wing. The children were brought down after tea to play with their parents until it was time for the latter to think about changing for dinner and the children went to bed. Nannies, who were neither servants nor family, often found themselves isolated in a strange netherworld, dependent on other families' nannies for social contact.

396 - 421

On the Street

Transport

Daily Life

Culture & Sport

In the Country

Public Manners

Good manners are paramount in the public arena: thrust together in close proximity with our fellow human beings, it is important that we treat each other with consideration and respect. Good manners make the world a more civilised place, ensuring everyday encounters and contacts are a positive, rather than a debilitating, experience.

Public Manners

On the Street

General Awareness

General Awareness

If the watchword for manners at home is consideration, the equivalent when out and about is courtesy. Both are about awareness of others but they are expressed somewhat differently, as the latter involves engaging with strangers and projecting a public persona.

Many signals of courtesy and co-operation when out and about are more physical than verbal, for instance acknowledging other motorists. It is important to be aware of the wider world, and to be alert and look where you are going. In public, heedlessness and selfish behaviour inconveniences others and at worst may actually endanger people or cause accidents. The great British tradition of forming an orderly queue is essentially a civilised and courteous display of awareness of other people.

Pedestrians — Pedestrians should be aware of their surroundings and act accordingly. Avoid slowing down or stopping suddenly in a busy place. If there is a need to slow down or stop, move aside. Walking more than two abreast is anti-social.

Pace — Ideally people on a crowded pavement should move at roughly the same pace and know where they are going, but in practice this is not always so. It is courteous to allow time and space for the elderly, less able people or indeed confused tourists, without showing anger or impatience.

Mobiles on the Move — The key to good public manners is to engage with the world. Negotiating a crowded pavement without bumping or jostling fellow-pedestrians requires care and attention. Multi-tasking and thinking all communication too important to ignore for even a few seconds is tempting but self-aggrandising. Realistically almost everything can wait for a few moments. Scrutinising a screen while walking along, especially when wearing headphones, may cause accidents or impede other pedestrians.

Meeting Friends in the Street — When meeting an acquaintance in the street, move to one side to avoid blocking the way for others. If hailed by a friend when there is no time to talk properly, smile and wave and perhaps follow up with a text or short explanation about being in a hurry. Try not to be distracted, for example by your mobile, and cut friends dead in the street. On the other hand, be aware that some people may be lost in thought, so do not take it personally if it happens to you.

ENCUMBRANCES   If carrying lots of bulky bags then make sure they do not impede others, for example at bus stops or on escalators. Those with trailing suitcases also need to be spatially aware. Similarly, those wearing backpacks need to be aware that if they stop or turn they may hit someone behind them.

UMBRELLAS   Look around before putting up an umbrella and have some regard for height differences. When wielding an umbrella, be spatially aware and avoid poking passing pedestrians in the eye. On meeting a fellow umbrella-user head-on, adopt the following strategy: the person on the inside edge should move closer to the wall/buildings, while raising their umbrella to avoid collision; the person on the outside lane should lower their umbrella and edge towards the road.

DOGS   Do not assume that everyone loves dogs (even in the country) and be aware that some people may fear them. Big dogs can often frighten small children, and dogs who rush up to strangers can be alarming, even if their owner says that they are only being friendly.

Dogs should always be under control and never jump up, growl or bark at strangers. In towns all dogs should be on short leads that do not stretch over the width of the pavement. Do not insist on bringing a dog into other people's houses or restaurants, though some may be dog-friendly. It goes without saying that any mess must be dealt with.

PUSHCHAIRS   When using a pushchair, be considerate and ensure that everyone in the vicinity is inconvenienced as little as possible. Two pushers abreast, deep in conversation and oblivious to the world, shows a lack of courtesy to other pedestrians. Always offer to help those struggling with a pushchair – lifting the front to assist with steps or stairs, or holding open doors.

CHILDREN   Small children on scooters must be kept close and under control, and older children should not cycle on the pavement. Once toddlers are able to walk, they should be encouraged to look where they are going and to respect others.

SMOKING AND VAPING   With smoking banned in public places indoors, smoking and vaping on the street has become a common practice. It goes without saying that littering the street with cigarette ends is anti-social. Always use the designated area, if there is one, or congregate in places where smokers won't form an impediment.

EATING IN THE STREET Eating away from the table was once confined to picnics but is now a part of daily life. Eating while walking down the street would have been frowned on in the past and is still to be approached with caution. 'Street food' is now very fashionable but, if possible, try to eat it sitting down or standing still rather than walking along, when food might be a distraction that impedes awareness of fellow pedestrians.

LITTER Many town centres are defiled by litter dropped by inconsiderate pedestrians, so whether eating, drinking, or smoking outside, it is absolutely imperative that all rubbish is disposed of properly. That means holding on to it until a rubbish bin is available, and if necessary taking it home and disposing of it there.

PEDESTRIAN PRIORITY Pavements are for pedestrians, pushchairs, wheelchairs and mobility scooters. People on bikes should be using the roads or designated bike lanes. However, pedestrians should aways be vigilant and aware of other pavement-users and should look before stepping out or changing direction.

IN AND OUT It is courteous to hold doors open for people, especially those who are elderly or less able. Do so with a smile.

See p 345 for polite actions It was traditionally considered polite for men to hold doors open for women and allow them through first, but it now works both ways. Everyone should check behind them and not let the door slam in someone's face. Young people should give way to adults.

STAIRS Younger, more able people or those coming down should pause on narrow stairways to let others up. If someone clearly needs the banister, allow them to stay on that side. If someone is courteous the other person must acknowledge and thank them, with a word, smile or even a brief gesture. When following someone up stairs, avoid getting too close by keeping a gap of a few stairs between you.

LOOKING BACK...

The tradition of men walking on the roadside of the pavement was referred to as 'giving the wall'. The roads had filthy gutters, called kennels, so the man would walk on the outside to protect the lady from the dirt, therefore 'giving her the wall'. It is still gentlemanly and seen as chivalrous.

Public Manners

Transport

Driving
Public Transport
Aeroplanes

Driving

Driving is governed by law, as well as manners, but there are many areas where manners and courtesy beyond the legal also apply. Allowing people out or to change lanes, or acknowledging being allowed out into a stream of traffic would be the most common examples. Being patient when having to wait for others to park or turn is courteous and best practice, as is consideration for learner drivers and the elderly.

Threatening or aggressive gestures are never correct, even when on the receiving end of discourtesy. Road rage is not only rude but may be dangerous and self-defeating.

Getting In It is chivalrous for men to let women into a car before getting in themselves. Younger people should open doors for older people or the elderly. Everyone should be ready to help someone in need, regardless of age or gender.

Where to Sit If parents and children are passengers in someone else's car, then every effort should be made to keep the children entertained and prevent them from distracting the driver.

Etiquette used to dictate that women used the front passenger seat, but when men are very tall it is no longer considered incorrect for women to sit in the back. Sensible arrangements based on leg length are best; if seats are moved backwards and forwards, it is polite to return the seat to where it was at the end of the journey.

Elderly or less able people should be offered a choice. Younger people should know to sit in the back and allow their elders to take the front seat.

In the Car Passengers are effectively guests in the car, so drivers should be considerate, keep the car clean and avoid driving aggressively. There should, however, also be some give and take between the driver and passenger.

It is the driver's right to choose the in-car entertainment but drivers should be considerate of their passengers – for example, asking if they would like to stop and take a break if the journey is a long one. The driver may choose the temperature in the car and, unless it is unbearable, the passenger should tolerate this and not fiddle with the controls or ask for it to be changed.

Smoking or vaping in cars may be considered anti-social by many. Passengers should always clear up their litter and thank the driver at the end of the journey.

Directions Passengers should not be backseat drivers. They may map read if asked but should not argue about routes. Sat navs have helped in this area but they can make mistakes and may need to be overruled if, for example, a passenger has good local knowledge.

Distractions Talking too much and distracting the driver should be avoided but uncommunicativeness may be seen as rude. A balance can be struck, but passengers should be sensitive to when the driver may need quiet to concentrate, for example when joining a motorway, changing lane or parking.

Lifts If someone gives you a lift on a regular basis or over a long distance, such as back to London from a weekend in the country, it is correct to offer them some petrol money if it is not possible to take turns.

Getting Out When dropping someone off, the driver should get out and open the door, especially for anyone elderly or less able, and help with children or luggage. It is rude to stay seated, unless this is essential for practical reasons.

Cyclists Drivers should be sympathetic and considerate to cyclists. Be particularly careful of opening a car door without checking. Cyclists should stay off pavements and obey the rules of the road. They must be aware of pedestrians at all times and remember that pedestrians have priority – ring two tings of the bell, if there is one, when approaching. Pass people carefully and slowly, and never cycle too quickly. Pedestrians should allow cyclists to pass wherever possible.

Both cyclists and pedestrians should be considerate to each other, exchange greetings when on country lanes or paths, and generally acknowledge any courtesy.

Looking Back...

When out driving in a carriage, the men would sit with their backs to the horses; the ladies sat facing forward. The right-hand side was considered the best, and precedence for this seat was given to women who were older, married or guests. The gentlemen would always dismount from the carriage first so that they could assist the ladies and ensure that their dresses did not get dirtied by the carriage wheels.

Public Transport

On the Bus

Bus queues were once an iconic part of the British street scene but an actual line is no longer always practical. However, there is still an order of boarding, even if it is not always explicit, and it is rude to barge in, rather than allowing those who were there first on to the bus.

Be alert, make some eye contact with other passengers and smile. Have your card or fare ready and not spend ages fumbling in a huge bag. After boarding, move swiftly down the bus.

Do not take up a priority seat and offer a seat to those who may need one. If worried about offending someone (eg if you are unsure whether they are pregnant) just get up discreetly and the other person may sit if they wish. Children should be seated and not allowed to wander around. Bags should be kept on laps or the floor, rather than taking up a spare seat. If forced to stand, avoid blocking the exit doors and move out of people's way as they move to disembark.

Trains

See p 413 for mobiles on public transport

The key thing to bear in mind on trains is that passengers are in a public space, in close proximity to others, and not in a private bubble. Applying full make-up or conducting loud conversations with companions or on a mobile are all best avoided. Take newspapers away with you and throw away any litter.

Luggage and feet should be kept off seats. Do not wait to be asked to move a bag and don't hog the aisle seat, forcing other passengers to climb over or ask you to move. It is courteous to help anyone struggling to put luggage on the high rack and to help them with big cases when getting on and off trains. Any help should of course be recognised with a smile and thanks.

Ask people if it's acceptable to open windows. Open doors for people if they require assistance. If seated, do not impinge on the aisle space. In other words, be aware of limited space and others' needs at all times. Always offer seats to people who need them more than you and if you are offered a seat, accept it with good grace and don't embarrass the good Samaritan.

On the Tube

Do not dawdle and ensure that you have your ticket to hand when going through the barriers. Stand to the right when on the escalator, allowing other passengers to walk up or down on the left. Before boarding the tube, always stand to one side to allow passengers off the train first. Board promptly and try to move down the carriage to allow everyone else behind you to get on easily and efficiently.

Even on crowded tubes, try to respect personal space and keep bags under control; avoid placing them on seats or where they may trip people up. Do not sit with your knees wide apart taking up as much room as possible, as if to show who is king of the jungle. Be considerate with large newspapers. It is fine to be plugged in and to text or email. Very loud conversation is anti-social but quiet talking is acceptable. On the other hand, avid eavesdropping is not.

Giving up seats also applies on the tube and is effectively gender neutral and more a matter of age and health. If offered a seat, it is polite to accept it and say thank you.

Speaking to people and acknowledging things such as diversions or helping with directions is normal practice on buses, but people tend to keep more to themselves on the underground.

Eating on Public Transport Eating on public transport can be particularly offensive to others, so be considerate about both choice of food and how to eat it. Very best practice is not to do so but if it is unavoidable then stick to neat, non-pungent food. Take rubbish with you, tidy up any mess from cups of tea or coffee and do not leave wet marks on the tray-table.

Headphones When listening to music on headphones, or watching movies on a laptop, ensure that the headphones are adequate to the task, and that neighbours are not being bombarded with a maddening barrage of percussive sound. Always use headphones – it is the worst sort of noise pollution to inflict private listening choices on other people.

Taxis In cities certain taxis may be hailed from the street by raising an arm. It is traditional to give the destination and to pay the driver through the window on the passenger side; a tip of approximately 10 per cent is usual.

If you use a taxi app, it is polite to tip the driver and leave a positive review if you have had a good experience.

Aeroplanes

The days of flying being in any way glamorous are long gone for most air-travellers, but common courtesy should still apply, whether in first class or on a no-frills carrier.

Airports

It is polite to others to be organised: queue patiently, have your documentation ready and be prepared for security checks.

In airport lounges, respect the ambience and atmosphere. If fellow-passengers are attempting to work, then loud conversations (with friends and colleagues, or on mobiles) should be avoided. Similarly, avoid conducting confidential or sensitive business calls in earshot of fellow passengers.

On the Plane

Be polite to the crew and queue calmly and patiently to board; do not push and shove or attempt to queue-barge. Once on board, try to sit down as quickly as possible. Avoid blocking the aisle when stowing bags in the overhead lockers and be aware of those of a smaller build who may need help lifting up bags and cases.

Stay within your own designated space and do not hog the armrest. In addition it is selfish to put the seat right back during short flights, especially during mealtimes when tray-tables are in use. If you are preparing to recline your seat, check the person behind to ensure you won't be tipping drink or a computer into his or her lap. Avoid kicking the back of the seat in front.

Be courteous to a neighbour by getting up to let them out into the aisle, not making them scramble over you. The back of the seat in front of you should not be used to help you get up on to your feet.

It is fine to avoid all but the most essential conversation and best to make it clear that you do not wish to talk by shutting your eyes, reading or putting on your headphones, even if nothing is playing.

Children on Planes

Children should not kick, jolt, or otherwise interfere with, the seat in front. They should not run up and down the aisle, especially when the lights are off. If a baby or child is upset during the flight, parents can try getting up and walking around – cabin space is limited, but a child may respond well to a change of scene. Nobody wants a child to cry on the plane, so other passengers should avoid showing irritation.

PUBLIC MANNERS

Daily Life

Restaurants & Pubs
Hotels
Shops
Mobiles and Laptops in Public Places
Managing Children in Public
In Church

Restaurants & Pubs

If a table has been booked, be punctual and greet staff politely. If the table offered is unsuitable then ask firmly and politely for another one if possible. The host or organiser should take charge and be the person who deals with the restaurant staff. It is best when booking a table to mention any special requirements in advance.

Treat waiting staff well and with respect for them as professionals, but not as new best friends. In their turn they should try to offer good professional service.

Hosting   It is the responsibility of the host or organiser to tell people where to sit at the table and to respond when the waiter comes to ask about drinks or goes through the specials. Guests may order separately or through the host (the host should make it clear which they would prefer). It is also the host's job to set the tone, for example by ordering a bottle of champagne.

Ordering   A host should make it clear that guests should order whatever they wish but the guests should show some restraint. Guests should choose reasonably promptly and say simply, for example, the beef or the salmon. It is reasonable to ask the waiter for an explanation of a dish but it may be boring to others to embark on a long dialogue. Be decisive; it is rude to keep an entire table waiting while prevaricating over choices.

Power Ordering   Asking for food that is not on the menu, or for food that is listed to be cooked or served a special way is increasingly common as so many people follow diets or have allergies or intolerances. It can, however, be rude to the host to make too much of a fuss or to hold everyone up, so keep it brief and include the host, explaining and apologising, rather than monopolising the waiter with complex demands. If you are the one paying it is less rude but may appear arrogant or neurotic, so keep it in proportion.

Wine   The waiter will normally bring the wine list to the person they perceive as the host or organiser. If you are the host and it is given to someone else then you may ask them to pass it over and take charge, but do consult others.

Guests may respond if asked about particular likes or dislikes but should not try to take charge unless they are invited to do so – if, for example, they are respected wine connoisseurs.

PAYING   It is usual for the person who has invited the guests or suggested the dinner to pay. If this is not the case then this should be made clear when the evening is being planned. If a guest wishes to contribute then they may offer or perhaps suggest a return match another time if the host insists on paying.

LARGE GROUPS   If a large group of friends is sharing the bill then it is best to have an outline agreement, such as sticking to the set menu or only having one course. The normal thing is to divide the bill equally at the end and not to argue about what any one person has ordered. However, those who order very expensive dishes with supplements, or additional wine or after-dinner drinks such as brandy, should offer to pay extra.

COMPLAINING   If things go wrong then complaining is not rude; it should be undertaken firmly but discreetly. If food needs to be sent back or wine is corked, mention it immediately. If a bill is wrong then point this out but do not spoil the occasion and embarrass others.

As a guest, do not criticise the food and wine, or take on a senior position that may undermine the host. It is not the moment to show off but to accept gracefully the host's generosity.

TIPS   Many restaurants include service, in which case a tip is not necessary other than for exceptional service. It is traditional to leave 10 per cent, but up to 15 per cent is now commonplace for good service. Try to have a coin for cloakroom attendants.

PUBS   The most fundamental requirement in pubs is to respect the rules of buying rounds. Be sensitive to the occasion and go with the flow, not ordering complicated cocktails when others are drinking lager. There is no need to be persuaded to drink alcohol and non-drinkers must never be put under pressure to do so.

Respect the atmosphere of the individual pub and be aware that regulars may have places they regard as their territory. Some pubs encourage joining in and others are more like restaurants where it would be unusual to talk to strangers. On the whole, be friendly but do not intrude. Large, dominant groups should not be allowed to dictate the ambience.

Tips are not necessary when just drinking in pubs, but bar staff who have been particularly helpful may be bought a drink. If, however, you have eaten in a pub and received table service, it is appropriate to leave a tip.

Restaurants and Pubs with Children

The suitability of a restaurant or pub – food, ambience, space – should be considered carefully when children are involved. Young children who accompany adults to restaurants or pubs in the evening should be especially quiet and well-behaved.

Children should be able to sit up at the table for the duration of the meal or drink, without being disruptive. If they are very fidgety, then a parent or adult can take them for a walk or quiet look around. Children should be discouraged from getting down and running around as they may disturb others. Parents may give smaller children some quiet toys or activities and ensure that they order promptly to avoid a hungry wait for food.

Pub gardens offer a little more freedom for children but, even in a spacious area in the open air, loud noise or boisterous play must be controlled.

Teenagers and Young Adults

Groups of teenagers or young people should avoid intruding on other people's space, especially if they are standing and others are seated. The ambience of the pub should be respected and, if necessary, noise levels moderated.

Hotels

Correct behaviour in a hotel will vary greatly depending on the location, style and standard of the hotel.

Noise

Be considerate to people in other rooms – especially late at night or early in the morning – by avoiding loud conversations, moderating the volume levels of televisions, radios and alarms, not slamming doors and being quiet in the corridors.

Complaints

If the room is not adequate then say so immediately and deal with the front desk or reception staff in the first instance. If there is no response then ask for the manager.

Tipping

In the past, tips would be expected by doormen and porters on every interaction. Increasingly this is a judgement call, dependent on the quality and speed of service, and the level of expectation of the hotel and its staff.

Seasoned travellers often choose to give something at the beginning and end of their stay; they will also be well-prepared with small notes and change for quick tips.

ROOM SERVICE — When using room service be prepared to answer the door looking presentable and make sure that the room is in a reasonable state. Room service that is signed for may have service included. If you are not leaving a single, large tip at the end of the stay, then it is usual to tip when the order arrives.

SPECIAL REQUIREMENTS — In luxury hotels it is expected that clients may have particular requirements and satisfaction may be taken in meeting these, so do not suffer in silence if expectations are not met. However, guests should be always be courteous, allowing time for services to be delivered, and treat staff as professionals.

SHOPS

SHOP STAFF — Customers should treat staff with civility and respect. It is not necessary to say good morning as you go into a shop and transactions may take place in silence without giving offence, but a few words and a smile or some eye contact are good form.

It is considerate to be sensitive to queues in shops – avoid spending ages searching bags for money or cards.

It is totally unacceptable to talk on a mobile while being served. Treating staff with courtesy and as human beings is not only polite, but can result in better service. Similarly, it is ill-mannered for someone working in a shop to ignore the customer in front of them to take a call, speak to a colleague, or attend to their own administrative tasks.

CHILDREN IN SHOPS — Children should be supervised in shops and not be allowed to touch or pick up items or be left to play in a different area of the shop. In supermarkets, children who are shouting, screaming, running up and down the aisles or 'riding' the trolleys will be an irritation or even a danger to other customers. It is sensible to sit smaller toddlers in the designated trolley-seat.

MOBILES AND LAPTOPS IN PUBLIC PLACES

IN PUBLIC — Be aware that there are many situations in which using mobiles is inappropriate: they should be switched off in theatres, cinemas, art galleries, or any public space where silence is desired. Respect quiet zones on trains and remember that audible mobile conversations can be distracting for other people.

Modern Manners | Public Manners

On Public Transport
See p 405 for trains

It is imperative, on buses and trains, only to use mobiles when they will not disturb other passengers (for example when neighbours are also talking). Loud ringtones can be intrusive, so it is wise to switch mobiles to vibrate or silent in public situations. Use headphones to minimise leaking noise pollution.

In Social Situations

It is always rude to pay more attention to a mobile than a person in the flesh, so mobiles should always be put away when transacting other business – for example in shops, when buying tickets, at the bank or post office, and so on. If there is an emergency or crisis, always apologise for using a mobile.

Answering phonecalls, texting, or repeatedly glancing at the screen in a social situation is never acceptable. Mobiles should be put away at the dining table (whether at home or eating out) and calls should only be taken, away from the table, in exceptional circumstances. Parents should encourage their children and teenagers to use their mobiles appropriately and unintrusively.

Working on a Laptop

Increasingly, with new hybrid working practices becoming ever more popular, people are choosing to work away from the office, either in a home office, or in a public space such as a café.

When planning to work in a café, choose one where there is plenty of room and table space is not at a premium. If other people are already working on their laptops, this is a good sign. If not, ask the manager politely if it's alright to work and use the café's power outlets and WiFi.

When settling in for the long haul, order food and drink at regular intervals. Be observant and sensitive to what is happening around you. If queues build up at the counter and people are waiting for tables, pack up and leave – a crowded café is not a suitable working environment.

Never look askance at near neighbours because their animated conversation or crying baby is playing havoc with your work-related concentration.

Using Laptops with Consideration

When working on a laptop that emits sound (playing a video for example) in a public place, always wear headphones or ear buds. Avoid video calls or conferences when in public, if possible, as it may look unprofessional. If there is no choice, explain and apologise for background distractions. When not speaking, always remember to mute the sound.

Managing Children in Public

Parents must be aware of the impact their child is having on other adults around them, especially in places where people can reasonably go with the expectation of some peace and quiet – train carriages, restaurants, pubs and so on. Children's tantrums and parents' overly-loud praise or 'baby talk' can be equally intrusive and distracting for others.

Parents' Reactons Parents' reactions to their child should be well moderated. If they are angry because of his/her behaviour in a public place (a shop, for example), shouting or dramatic behaviour should be avoided. While tantrums may be par for the course with toddlers, uncontrollable public displays of anger require careful management. If the situation is getting out of control, a quiet corner away from others is the best place to resolve the situation.

Ps and Qs Remind children frequently about their ps and qs; an automatic 'please' and 'thank you' response is a basic requirement. Parents should also be consistent about what they will not tolerate, for example, loud shouting or screeching, pushing and shoving, interrupting, pointing or making remarks about other people.

Parents must lead by example. Their good manners will inevitably rub off on their children, so it is important for parents to be polite at all times and show consideration for people in public places. It is realistic, however, to accept that there are always going to be times when children misbehave. In this situation, damage limitation and the attempt to regain control is preferable to dramatic exasperation or capitulation.

Other People's Reactions If a child is behaving inappropriately or intrusively in a public place, other people should refrain from offering advice or passing immediate judgement. Sometimes it is hard to soothe a crying baby or calm down a toddler who is in the middle of a tantrum. If the situation is too much to bear, then try to move away, for example change seat on the train or move table in the pub.

School Gate Etiquette For many parents, the school gate is an important daily social interaction. While for some it can be a pleasure, others may, for example, feel excluded by cliques and boastful parents. Look out for lone parents and try to include them.

Keep conversation light and non-competitive; the playground is not the place to display your own social status or professional credentials. Similarly, boasting about your child's achievements can cause offence. Resist the temptation to question other parents about how well their child is doing – talking directly with the teacher is more sensible. Never gossip about other children – their behaviour or failings – with fellow parents. Similarly, resist the urge to gossip about other parents: this sort of poison leaks out (possibly with the children as the unwitting conduit) and can cause real distress.

THE PARENT-SCHOOL RELATIONSHIP

Take your concerns about the school directly to your child's teacher or to the head. Even if there is a serious grievance, it is wise to keep tempers in check and language moderate – anger will only make people defensive.

Drive safely and park considerately outside the school. Express willingness, if possible, to help with pick-ups, after-school visits, school-runs etc, especially if you are hoping that other people will reciprocate. If other parents are looking after your child after school, be punctilious about arrangements and timings.

Always do your best to turn up punctually for regular meetings with the teacher. If this isn't possible, find an alternative option – being 'too busy' to discuss a child's progress will be frowned upon. Always fill out all the material that comes from the school, and do it promptly.

Never embarrass a child in front of his/her fellow pupils or teacher. Parents accompanying their children on a school trip, for example, should always take their cue from their children. Behaviour that is acceptable in the privacy of the family home may be absolutely mortifying in a school context.

IN CHURCH

DRESS

It is correct to dress respectfully in a church, and indeed in a mosque, synagogue or temple, and to adhere to the appropriate dress codes, for example covering heads or removing hats.

BEHAVIOUR

Be punctual and ensure mobiles are turned off. Conversations should be minimal and whispered, and children should be supplied with quiet toys and books. Do not take aisle seats, forcing others to climb over you. Try to follow customs such as standing, sitting and other gestures, even if you are not of the same denomination, and be tolerant of differences.

Public Manners

Culture & Sport

Performances
Sporting Events

Performances

At the Theatre

Although dressing up for the theatre is no longer *de rigueur*, dressing well shows respect. Very casual clothes are not appropriate in formal theatres. Plan ahead, pre-order drinks and, if need be, supper and transport. Punctuality is vital and latecomers must expect to wait until the end of an act or even the interval before taking their seats. When squeezing along a row, face the seated people so as not to present your back to people's faces; if space is very tight, people should stand. It's convenient for others if people with seats at the end of a row wait before sitting down; try to be extra punctual if seated in the middle.

Noisy consumption of food and drink is anti-social and mobiles should be off, if possible, never just on vibrate. Avoid writing text messages, as the illuminated screen is distracting for others. Do not make a mess round the seat and keep coats and bags nearby. Fidgeting is annoying so try to keep still. While members of the audience should join in at pantomimes, loud criticism, singing along, or excessive laughter or applause would be inappropriate at most theatre performances. The same rules of good behaviour also apply to the cinema.

At the Opera, Classical Concerts and Ballet

At the opera certain codes of behaviour are expected. Do not applaud till the end of an act but if in doubt follow others' lead. Exceptional individual arias may be applauded with the words 'Bravo' (or 'Brava' for a woman). It is correct to clap when the conductor takes to the podium, both at the very beginning and after the interval, at the end of an act and at the final bows. It is not traditional British behaviour to whoop or stamp.

Country House Opera
See pp 429–431 for a guide to the Season

Country house opera is a highlight of the Season. Performances begin in the late afternoon and are punctuated by a lengthy 90-minute interval during which it is customary to have a picnic in the grounds or dine in one of the restaurants. Reasonably grand picnics with tables, chairs, china and glass are common. Gentlemen wear black tie (*see pp 187–189*) and ladies should wear the equivalent, for example long evening dresses.

Events in Large Venues

When attending a large venue, cooperate with security checks and be polite to the ushers. If seated, sit in the seats allocated on the ticket. Don't stand up and block people's view; keen dancers should opt for standing tickets. If standing in a crowd, accept that you may get jostled. Tall people should move to allow those shorter than them to stand further forward or have a decent view.

Sporting Events

Dress Codes
See pp 185–195 for dress codes

Dress codes may be enforced and should always be checked in advance and keenly observed; failure to do so may result in entry being refused. Where there is no dress code, it is sensible for spectators to dress appropriately for the formality of the event and for the weather.

At some sporting events, there may be specific dress codes for an enclosure or ticketed area. For example, in the Royal Enclosure at Royal Ascot, morning dress must be worn or, in the Stewards' Enclosure at Henley Royal Regatta, ladies' hemlines must come below the knee. Other dress codes may be more casual, for example, traditional linen suits or blazers, ties and Panama hats in the Richmond Enclosure at Goodwood.

Seated Events

Spectators at seated events should be sitting down before play begins, and can only enter and exit the stands at specific points, for example between overs in cricket or during a change of ends in tennis. Even at sporting events where coming and going is the norm, try not to disturb whole rows of people by frequently going to get food or drinks. Never impede the view of others, either by standing up to watch or by wearing a huge hat.

Spectators are expected to keep quiet at times when competitors may be distracted. Keep conversation to a minimum during play. Mobiles should be switched to silent and not used to make or answer calls. Applause should be at appropriate moments and the customs of the sport should be followed.

Boxes

Guests in corporate or private boxes – for example at football, rugby, tennis or cricket – should socialise with other guests in the party as well as spectate, and remember that it is polite to display an interest in the sporting action. Enjoy the hospitality but do not overindulge. Hosts should inform guests of dress codes (for example jackets for the men) in advance; guests should dress appropriately. Guests should send hosts written thanks.

Competitive Spirit

Ardent fans attending team sports are advised to make sure they are in the appropriate area of any stadium or the correct enclosure. Bad language or insulting behaviour is not acceptable.

School Sports

Parents should not be overly competitive or cheer unsportingly. Criticism of other team players is unacceptable, as is boasting about their own child's sporting prowess.

FOOD AND DRINK   Different sports have different traditions, from picnics in car parks to hot dogs in the stands. Whatever the tradition, eat tidily, do not leave litter, and be aware of others.

RACING   Spectators should take care not to frighten the horses with sudden movements, such as opening an umbrella, or by making a loud noise. This is particularly important at smaller race meetings, such as point-to-points, where spectators are close to the horses.

It is anti-social to block the view of others and to push into busy grandstand crowds just before a race starts. Shout your horse home, but do not use bad language or show distress if it loses. Lucky winners usually buy drinks for their party. Only genuine connections of horse owners and trainers are allowed into the paddock or winners' enclosure. It is bad form to push into the private celebrations of a win; it is acceptable to offer a brief word of congratulation to a winning owner you may encounter on the course, or to cheer a horse being led in.

BETTING   Betting is an integral part of a day at the races and a racecard (never called a programme) provides information on the horses running in each race. Restraint and self-control should be employed, however, and losses accepted with equanimity. Winners can enjoy a quiet sense of satisfaction, but never gloat or get too over-excited.

GOLF   Be silent and still when players are about to play the ball. If a ball comes towards the crowd, move away and never touch or move it. Never ask for autographs or attempt to engage a player during a round. Spectators should not move towards the next hole before everyone in a playing group has putted. Be aware of restrictions on photography and use of mobiles.

Some clubs have strict dress codes but, as a general rule, soft shoes such as trainers should be worn when walking on the course. Golf is taken very seriously so laughter, shouting, jokey advice, knowing remarks or even gasps should be moderated.

POLO PRACTICALITIES   Polo dress varies and ordinary country clothes are acceptable at many matches and tournaments. However, at the finals of major tournaments or at fashionable sponsored events, spectators should dress for a summer garden party. Flat shoes or wedges should be worn as high heels sink in the grass and make holes in the ground; wellingtons are worn when it's very wet.

PUBLIC MANNERS

IN THE COUNTRY

Country Code

There is still a distinction between acceptable behaviour in town and the country, and much of it is to do with pace. While it is quite normal to carry out a transaction in a city shop in silence and inconsiderate to hold up the person behind you, in the country it is customary and correct to pass the time of day, even if quite briefly, during any transaction. It is ill-mannered to lose patience if the person in front of you is discussing local matters.

Common Courtesies

Please and thank you, good morning, goodbye and goodnight should be used habitually by well-mannered people, but these courtesies are essential out of town. There is more formality and the use of titles, such as 'Mrs' or 'Colonel', especially for older people, is still expected.

Highways and Byways

Drivers should be aware of mud and puddles and avoid splashing pedestrians or forcing them into a ditch. On narrow roads, give way to vehicles coming uphill where possible, and be prepared to back up, especially if you are closer to a passing space. If neither party is prepared to reverse, get out and talk to the other person rather than enduring a battle of wills. Never park in gateways or passing places.

Be tolerant of cattle, tractors or mud on lanes from farm vehicles. Always give horses and riders a wide berth and drive slowly past them as they can be skittish. Acknowledge riders with a wave.

It is also correct to wave in acknowledgement of other motorists who have pulled over; pedestrians, dog walkers and riders should also thank and acknowledge motorists. Wave at any car you recognise, and its occupants, including local tradespeople, postmen etc.

If out walking, then greet others, even if you do not know them. Keep dogs on leads on lanes and under control on agricultural land and in forestry. Ask permission before crossing any private land that is not a right of way and be aware of sporting seasons, such as shooting, and the farming calendar, especially lambing and harvest. The country is a workplace not a leisure park.

> **Looking Back...**
>
> Landowners were fiercely protective of their private property in the past and legend has it that gamekeepers even used mantraps in the 19th and early 20th century to catch poachers and trespassers. It is worth knowing that the polite enquiry: "May I help you?" is contemporary code for: "Get off my land!"

Appendices

Sample Letters

The Season

Orders, Medals & Decorations

APPENDICES

Sample Letters

Thanks For Hospitality
Thanks For a Present
Condolences

Thanks For Hospitality

See pp 369–395 for entertaining at home

Thank-you letters should be sent promptly after the event. As well as a general statement of thanks, more specific reference should be made to the hospitality (delicious food, convivial company, interesting outings etc.).

Dear Charlotte,

GENERAL THANKS

Thank you so much for having us to stay last weekend. It was so kind of you and we had a wonderful time and very much enjoyed it all. It was lovely to catch up quietly on Friday night but great fun to meet so many interesting new people at dinner on Saturday, as well as some old friends. I hope you are not too exhausted!

SPECIFIC THANKS

We both very much enjoyed looking round the gardens at Rosings, Jane as our guide was fascinating. I fear my fingers will never be green enough to create such perfection but it was certainly an inspiration.

NEWS

OFFER OF RECIPROCAL HOSPITALITY

We got home in good time in spite of all the roadworks. The next couple of weeks are going to be rather frantic, as there is such a lot to do before we go away. Once we are back we must make a plan and get you over here. The autumn show is a great local occasion but other than half term we are going to be here so even if that does not appeal I am sure we can work out a date.

REPEAT THANKS

Many thanks again for having us.

Love from

Jane and Edward

Thanks For a Present

A simple thank-you for a present is not adequate; the writer should go on to explain specifically why it is appreciated, why it is a good choice, and give – if possible – some indication of how it will be used/enjoyed.

Dear Godmother Charlotte,

GENERAL THANKS

Thank you so much for the very generous Christmas present. It was just what I wanted. I really needed some new headphones as I broke my old ones which were not nearly as good as these anyway. We are going skiing next week and I am really looking forward to taking them. My brother Tom is really jealous as he only has the basic ones that came with his phone.

SPECIFIC THANKS/
WHY GOOD CHOICE

NEWS/GENERAL CHAT

We had a very good Christmas with all the uncles and aunts at my grandparents' house but they insist on making us all get up for a mega-walk on Boxing Day, so I was very pleased to get home and be able to relax and enjoy my presents, especially the incredible bike my parents got me.

FURTHER NEWS

I am hoping to be in the Under-15 football team next term, fingers crossed. I really hope you will be able to come to my confirmation this summer but anyway see you soon.

REPEAT THANKS

Thanks again for the brilliant headphones.

Love

Luke

Condolences

If possible, refer to the writer's relationship with the deceased, including personal recollections and an appreciation of their qualities. When writing about someone who is not personally known (eg a friend's grandmother), general sympathy and fellow-feeling for the bereaved is sufficient.

Dear Charlotte,

GENERAL CONDOLENCE

I was so very sorry to hear that your father had died. He was a wonderful man and will be very much missed by all who knew him. I have so many happy memories of our childhood holidays together and his amazing sandcastles and our adventurous if not always very fruitful mackerel fishing expeditions. Of course I had no idea when we were children how incredible his life had been, both during the war and afterwards. That generation were extraordinary and we will never see their like again.

REFER TO YOUR OWN RELATIONSHIP WITH THE PERSON

ABOUT THE PERSON

Your father was always so encouraging to young people and I can remember him being so kind and helpful when I was worried about leaving my first job and going off to Australia.

WISHES TO THE FAMILY

Please do give my love to your mother and tell her how sorry I am. Even though he had been so ill it must be a terrible shock, as I know it was for my mother.

WISHES FROM THE WRITER'S FAMILY

Tom and the children send their very best wishes to you all. Of course he only knew your father as an older man but he admired him very much and I think they also shared a sense of humour, not to mention a love of real ale.

CONVENTIONAL PHRASE

Please do not reply.

With much love

Jane

APPENDICES

THE SEASON

A BRIEF HISTORY
CALENDAR OF EVENTS

The Season: A Brief History

The origins of the Season can be traced to the 18th century when the court, and therefore the aristocracy, followed the movements of the Royal Family, who spent April to July in or near London. Upper-class girls of 17 or 18 were presented to the monarch at court and introduced into society, a tradition known as 'coming out' (as a debutante) that continued to the mid-20th century. The debutante's parents gave her a dance or party and she took part in a whirlwind season of sporting, cultural and social events designed to help her meet her peers and ideally a future husband.

Society has become increasingly egalitarian and young people more independent, so the Season is no longer focused on debutantes but experienced through a series of traditional events, still regarded as highlights of the social calendar, including Royal Ascot, Wimbledon, Henley Royal Regatta and Cowes Week. The historical roots of the Season are evident in the social conventions that continue to be respected at many of the events, especially those associated with certain formalities and dress codes.

The Season: Calendar of Events

MARCH **The Cheltenham Festival** Four days of top-class National Hunt racing at the Cheltenham racecourse featuring the Cheltenham Gold Cup steeplechase and the Champion Hurdle.

APRIL **The Boat Race** The Oxford and Cambridge Boat Race, first held in 1829, sees amateur coxed eights, known respectively as the Dark Blues and the Light Blues, race on the tidal River Thames over four miles 374 yards, from Putney to Mortlake.

The Grand National The three-day meeting at Aintree, outside Liverpool, features the world's most famous steeplechase, run over four miles, which includes legendary fences such as The Chair and Becher's Brook.

MAY **Polo** The British outdoor summer polo season gets underway at clubs throughout the country.

Glyndebourne The Glyndebourne Festival Opera season opens at the East Sussex country house of the Christie family, who founded the festival in 1934. Black tie is worn.

The Guineas Festival The 1000 Guineas for three-year-old fillies and the 2000 Guineas for three-year-old colts are run on successive days over Newmarket's Rowley Mile. They are the first leg of the Classic Flat races of the Season.

Badminton Horse Trials Britain's premier three-day event is held on the Duke of Beaufort's estate in Gloucestershire, offering both top international competition and a huge shopping village.

The Royal Windsor Horse Show Held over five days in the private Home Park and including international carriage driving, top-level show jumping and showing classes. Members of the Royal Family both compete and spectate.

Lords Test Match The opening international Test cricket match of the season between England and a touring team is held on the hallowed turf in St John's Wood, north London.

The Chelsea Flower Show Held over five days in the grounds of the Royal Hospital, this is the premier event of the Royal Horticultural Society, famous for its show gardens by the world's best designers. Its Gala Charity Preview event is a social highlight.

JUNE **The Epsom Derby** The second and most important leg of the five Classic Flat races. The Derby and the Oaks are run over one-and-a-half miles on successive days. Morning dress is worn in The Queen Elizabeth II Stand on Derby Day.

The Royal Academy Summer Exhibition Held for three months at Burlington House in Piccadilly this is a unique exhibition, for which any artist may submit their work for selection by an expert panel. The preview party is a social highlight.

Trooping the Colour The annual parade takes place on Horse Guards Parade, near Buckingham Palace, in the presence of The King and other members of the Royal Family and is the premier military ceremonial event of the Season.

Royal Ascot With five days of first class racing, this is the central event of the Social Season, and it includes the daily royal carriage procession down the course. The Thursday is Gold Cup Day, also known as Ladies' Day. Dress codes are clearly specified, and in the Royal Enclosure morning dress is required for men and formal day dress, with hats, for women.

The Queen's Cup This high-goal tournament is held at Guards Polo Club at Smith's lawn in Windsor Great Park from early June. The final is a major social and royal event; the late Queen used to regularly present the prizes.

Wimbledon A fortnight's tennis in south-west London, from late June into early July, Wimbledon is a major world tournament and the only grand slam played on grass.

Henley Royal Regatta The five-day rowing regatta has many unique traditions for participants and spectators. Dress code in the Stewards' Enclosure is strictly enforced; women must wear below-the-knee dresses or skirts or tailored trousers.

JULY

The July Meeting at Newmarket Held on the pretty July course at racing's headquarters, the three-day meeting features the July Cup and has a relaxed atmosphere, attracting both racing fans and summer revellers.

The Gold Cup Regarded as the British high-goal championship, this polo tournament takes place at Cowdray Park in Sussex for the first three weeks of July. The final is a fashionable high-summer social highlight.

Glorious Goodwood Five days of outstanding racing on the Duke of Richmond's estate, where the racecourse is located high on the Sussex Downs. It famously has a garden party atmosphere, with Panama hats and linen suits, and is regarded as the end-of-term event of the Season.

AUGUST

Cowes Week The international sailing regatta takes place over the first five days of August in the waters off the Isle of Wight. Craft from sailing dinghies to ocean-going yachts compete and social life ranges from discos along the seafront to private balls in the yacht clubs, notably the exclusive Royal Yacht Squadron Ball. There is a spectacular firework finale on the Friday evening.

A NOTE ON DRESS

The majority of Season events are held outside and go on into the evening when it can be quite chilly, so it is sensible to bring something warm – a jacket, wrap or pashmina – to keep warm.

As a general rule, velvet, long boots or felt hats are not worn between early May and the end of September. Similarly, linen, open-toed sandals or straw hats are not worn between the end of September and the beginning of May.

Appendices

Orders, Medals & Decorations

How to Wear Orders, Medals & Decorations
Foreign & Commonwealth Orders

How To Wear Orders, Medals & Decorations

Full Evening Dress

The occasions when decorations may be worn can be divided into two categories:
- When The King, or a member of the Royal Family who is a royal highness, is present. The host should ascertain from the member of the appropriate household whether it is desired that decorations should be worn.
- On occasions when the host has decided that the nature or importance of the occasion makes it appropriate for decorations to be worn. Instructions would then be issued on the invitations, which should state 'Evening Dress—Decorations'.

The method of wearing orders, decorations and miniatures when 'Decorations' are prescribed is as follows:

(i) Knights of the Garter and Knights of the Thistle; Knights and Dames Grand Cross, Knights Grand Commander: broad riband and badge of the senior British order, unless it is more appropriate on certain occasions to wear the riband and badge of a junior British or foreign order.

Up to four stars may be worn on the left side of the coat or dress. When wearing more than one star the precedence of the position of each star is (looking at the wearer):

Four Stars	Three Stars	Two Stars
1	1	1
2 3	2 3	2
4		

One neck badge suspended on a ribbon (miniature width) of the order may be worn under the collar and hanging close up below the tie. Miniature badges of all orders and medals are worn on a medal bar. (The Garter, Thistle, Order of Merit, Companion of Honour and baronet's badge are not worn in miniature.) Collars are not worn.

(ii) Knights and Dames Commander: up to four stars may be worn on the left side of the coat or dress, as above. One neck badge suspended on a ribbon (miniature width) of the order is worn under the collar and hanging close up below the tie. Miniature badges of all orders, decorations and medals are worn on a medal bar. (The Order of Merit, Companion of Honour and baronet's badge are not worn in miniature.) The ladies' badge is worn on a bow, below the miniatures, on the left side.

(iii) Companions and Commanders: one neck badge suspended on a ribbon (miniature width) of the order is worn under the collar and hanging close up below the tie. Miniature badges of all orders, decorations and medals are worn on a medal bar. (The Order of Merit and Companion of Honour Badge are not worn in miniature.) The badges of a Companion of the Distinguished Service Order or Imperial Service Order are worn in miniature on a medal bar and not as a neck badge. The ladies' badge is worn on a bow, below the miniatures, on the left side.

(iv) Officers, Lieutenants and Members: miniature badges are worn on a medal bar.

(v) Order of Merit, Companion of Honour: these are neck badges suspended on a ribbon (miniature width) of the order worn under the collar and hanging close up below the tie. Only one neck badge may be worn. Miniature badges of all other orders, decorations and medals are worn on a medal bar. (The OM and CH badges are not worn in miniature.) The ladies' badge is worn on a bow, below the miniatures, on the left side.

(vi) Baronet: this badge is worn as a neck badge suspended on a ribbon (miniature width), worn under the collar and hanging close up below the tie. Miniature badges of all other orders, decorations and medals are worn on a medal bar. (The baronet's badge is not worn in miniature.)

(vii) Knight Bachelor: this badge is worn as a neck badge suspended on a ribbon (miniature width) under the collar and hanging close up below the tie. It may also, if desired, be worn as an order star. The badge is also worn in miniature on a medal bar in the same manner as miniature badges or orders, decorations and medals.

(viii) The Royal Victorian Chain: this chain is worn round the neck by men in place of a neck badge and is adapted for wear by ladies on a bow of the ribbon of the Royal Victorian Order and worn on the left side above miniatures.

DINNER JACKET

On occasions when it is desired that dinner jackets (and not full evening dress) with decorations are to be worn, invitations should state 'Dinner Jacket—Decorations'.

In addition to miniatures, only one star (or the breast badge of a knight bachelor) and one neck badge may be worn.

The method of wearing orders, decorations, miniatures and medals with a dinner jacket is as follows:

(i) Knights of the Garter, Knights of the Thistle: one star is worn on the left breast. The gold sash badge is transferred from the broad riband to a miniature width ribbon and worn around the neck under the collar and close up below the tie. Miniature badges of all orders, decorations and medals are worn on a medal bar. (The Garter, Thistle, Order of Merit, Companion of Honour and baronet's badge are not worn in miniature.) The collar and broad riband are not worn.

(ii) Knights Grand Cross, Knights Grand Commander: one star is worn on the left breast. Miniature badges of all orders, decorations and medals are worn on a medal bar. (The Order of Merit, Companion of Honour and baronet's badge are not worn in miniature.) Neither collar nor broad riband and badge are worn.

(iii) Knights Commander: one star is worn on the left breast and one neck badge suspended on a ribbon (miniature width) of the order is worn under the collar and hanging close up below the tie. Miniature badges of all orders, decorations and medals are worn on the medal bar. (The Order of Merit, Companion of Honour and baronet's badge are not worn in miniature.)

(iv) Companions and Commanders: one neck badge suspended on a ribbon (miniature width) of the order is worn under the collar and hanging close up below the tie. Miniature badges of all orders, decorations and medals are worn on a medal bar. (The Order of Merit and Companion of Honour Badge are not worn in miniature.) The badges of a Companion of the Distinguished Service Order or Imperial Service Order are worn in miniature on a medal bar and not as a neck badge.

(v) Officers, Lieutenants and Members: miniature badges are worn on a medal bar.

(vi) Order of Merit, Companion of Honour: these are neck badges suspended on a ribbon (miniature width) of the order worn under the collar and hanging close up below the tie. Only one neck badge may be worn. These badges are not worn in miniature.

(vii) Baronet: this badge is worn as a neck badge suspended on a ribbon (miniature width) worn under the collar and hanging close up below the tie. This badge is not worn in miniature.

(viii) Knight Bachelor: this badge is worn as a neck badge suspended on a ribbon (miniature width) under the collar and hanging close up below the tie. It may also, if desired, be worn as an order star. The badge is also worn in miniature on a medal bar in the same manner as miniature badges or orders, decorations and medals.

(ix) The Royal Victorian Chain: the chain may be worn round the neck in place of a neck badge.

Ladies should follow the same rules as those given under 'Full Evening Dress' (but only one star is worn).

MORNING DRESS

The occasions when orders, decorations and medals are worn with morning dress are comparatively rare. Such occasions may include special official public functions, religious services connected with the orders of chivalry or memorial services. If it is indicated that the wearing of decorations would be appropriate, no more than four stars, one neck badge and full size medals should be worn. If a star and neck badge are worn they must be of different orders.

(i) Knights of the Garter, Knights of the Thistle; Knights and Dames Grand Cross, Knights Grand Commander: one star only is worn on the left breast or, for ladies, in a corresponding place on the dress. The broad riband and badge is not worn. Collars are only worn on appointed 'Collar Days'.

(ii) Knights and Dames Commander: one star only is worn on the left breast or, for ladies, in a corresponding place on the dress. The neck badge of a Knight Commander or the corresponding badge of a Dame Commander may only be worn if belonging to a second Order. If worn with full-size medals the ladies' badge, on a bow, is worn below the medal bar.

(iii) Companions and Commanders: one neck badge suspended on a ribbon (miniature width) of the order is worn under the collar. The badge should hang three quarters of an inch below the tie knot in front of the tie. The ladies' badge is worn on a bow on the left side. If worn with full-size medals, the badge is worn below the medal bar.

(iv) Officers, Lieutenants and Members: the full-size badge, whether worn singly or mounted on a medal bar, is worn on the left side in the same manner with civilian dress as with uniform. Companions of the Distinguished Service Order or Imperial Service Order wear their insignia in this manner and not as a neck decoration. The ladies' badge, if worn separately, is worn on a bow on the left side of the dress. If worn with other medals it is normally mounted on a medal bar and worn in the same manner with civilian dress as with uniform.

(v) Order of Merit, Companion of Honour: one neck badge suspended on a ribbon (miniature width) of the order is worn under the collar. The badge should hang three quarters of an inch below the tie knot in front of the tie. The ladies' badge is worn on a bow on the left side. If worn with full-size medals, the badge is worn below the medal bar.

(vi) Baronet: this badge is worn as a neck badge, suspended on a ribbon (miniature width) under the collar. The badge hangs three quarters of an inch below the tie knot in front of the tie.

(vii) Knight Bachelor: this badge is worn as a neck badge suspended on a ribbon (miniature width) under the collar. The badge should hang three quarters of an inch below the tie knot in front of the tie. It may also, if desired, be worn as an order star.

(viii) The Royal Victorian Chain: the chain may be worn round the neck in place of a neck badge.

LOUNGE SUITS

There are some occasions, such as Remembrance Sunday services or regimental gatherings, at which those attending are requested to wear medals with lounge suits. On such occasions it is not customary to wear either broad ribands with badges, stars or the Royal Victorian Chain. One neck badge is suspended on a ribbon (miniature width) of the order, worn under the collar and hanging close up below the tie knot in front of the tie; full-size insignia mounted on a medal bar are worn on the left side as with uniform.

CIVILIAN DRESS

Appropriate strips of ribbon, unattached to any insiginia, of orders, decorations and medals may be worn on all occasions, with all forms of civilian dress, at the discretion of the holder. If worn they should be sewn on the coat or dress or on to a medal bar and worn on the left hand side.

OVERCOATS Full-size medals may be worn on an overcoat, on the left-hand side. No other insignia should be worn.

Foreign & Commonwealth Orders

ORDERS AND DECORATIONS The following regulations concerning the wearing of orders, decorations and medals conferred by heads or governments of foreign states and by members of the Commonwealth overseas of which The King is not the head of state apply:

(i) No person in the service of the Crown may accept and wear the insignia of any order or decoration without His Majesty's permission. Such permission, if granted, will be either:

(a) unrestricted, allowing the insignia to be worn on any occasion.
(b) restricted, allowing the insignia to be worn only on particular occasions associated with the country concerned.

The grant of both unrestricted and restricted permission will be conveyed by letter from His Majesty's Private Secretary.

(ii) Full and unrestricted permission is contemplated in the case of orders conferred:
(a) for distinguished services in saving or attempting to save life.
(b) on any officer in the Royal Navy, Army or Royal Air Force, or any United Kingdom official, in recognition of services either while lent to a Commonwealth government or while lent to a foreign government, provided that he is not in receipt of any emoluments from British public funds during this period.

(iii) Restricted permission is contemplated in the case of orders or decorations conferred in recognition of personal attention to a head of state, or a member of the Royal Family of a foreign or Commonwealth country, on state or official visits.

(iv) Restricted permission will also be given for the wearing of insignia of orders and decorations conferred:
(a) on United Kingdom officials in connection with a state visit by The King;
(b) on members of deputations of British regiments to heads of states;
(c) on members of special missions when The King is represented

at a coronation, wedding, funeral, or similar occasion; or on any diplomatic representative, when specially accredited to represent His Majesty on such occasions (but not on the members of their staff).

Permission will not be given to:
(a) the heads, or other members, of His Majesty's diplomatic or consular establishments abroad, when leaving, whether on transfer or on final retirement;
(b) officers of British naval, military or air squadrons or units visiting foreign countries and member countries of the Commonwealth overseas, except as provided at (ii) above.

(v) Applications for The King's permission, whether full or restricted, will be submitted to His Majesty by His Principal Secretary of State for Foreign and Commonwealth Affairs, who shall be under no obligation to consider them unless, before the bestowal of the order or decoration, the country concerned has ascertained through the British diplomatic representative there or through its diplomatic representative at His Majesty's Court, that the award would not give rise to any objection.

Applications cannot be considered in respect of orders conferred more than five years previously, or offered in connection with events so long prior to the proposal to award them.

(vi) Permission will not be granted for the wearing of the insignia of orders and decorations conferred otherwise than by the heads or governments of states recognised by His Majesty.

(vii) Medals with the exceptions specified below, and state decorations not indicating membership of an order of chivalry, are subject to the regulations in the same manner as orders. If granted, unrestricted permission is given by letter; restricted permission is given by certificate.

(viii) Medals for saving or attempting to save life whether conferred on behalf of the head of government of a foreign or Commonwealth state or by private life-saving societies or institutions, may be accepted and worn, subject only to the restrictions imposed by the regulations for the services concerned.

Applications for permission to wear other medals conferred by private societies or institutions cannot be entertained.

(ix) Applications for permission to wear medals gained in warlike operations will not be entertained if permission would be at variance with considerations of general policy or public interest.

(x) The wives of persons in the service of the Crown are regarded for the purposes of these regulations as sharing the disabilities of their husbands concerning the acceptance of foreign or Commonwealth awards.

Persons employed in the commissioned or salaried service of the Crown on a temporary basis are subject to these regulations.

GENERAL — *Regulations concerning the acceptance and wearing by persons NOT in the service of the Crown of orders, decorations and medals conferred by heads or governments of foreign states and by members of the Commonwealth overseas of which The King is not the head of state.*

PERSONS NOT IN SERVICE OF THE CROWN

(i) It is The King's wish that His Majesty's subjects should not accept and wear the insignia of any order or decoration without His Majesty's permission.

(ii) Permission, if granted, will allow the insignia to be worn on any occasion, and will be conveyed by letter from His Majesty's Private Secretary.

(iii) Permission will not be given:
(a) when considerations of general policy or public interest must be held to preclude it;
(b) in respect of orders relating to services rendered more than five years before the question of eligibility is raised;
(c) unless authoritative evidence of the award is forthcoming, preferably in the form of a notification through one of the channels prescribed in Rule iv.

(iv) Applications for The King's permission will be submitted to His Majesty by His Principal Secretary of State for Foreign and Commonwealth Affairs, who shall be under no obligation to consider them unless, before the bestowal of the order, the government of the foreign or Commonwealth country concerned has ascertained, through the British diplomatic representative there, or through its diplomatic representative at His Majesty's Court, that having regard to these regulations the award would not give rise to any objection.

(v) Permission will not be granted for the wearing of the insignia of orders and decorations conferred otherwise than by the heads of governments or states recognised by His Majesty.

(vi) Medals*, with the exceptions specified below, and state decorations not indicating membership of an order of chivalry, are subject to the regulations in the same manner as orders. No permission is needed for the acceptance of a foreign or Commonwealth medal if it is not designed to be worn.

(vii) Medals for saving or attempting to save life, whether awarded by the head or government of a foreign or Commonwealth state or by private life-saving societies or institutions, may be accepted and worn without permission; but such medals, if given by private organisations, should be worn on the right breast and not on the left with state awards, and not more than two awards in all should be worn in relation to one act of bravery. Applications to wear other medals conferred by private societies or institutions cannot be entertained.

(viii) Applications for permission to wear foreign or Commonwealth medals gained in warlike operations will not be entertained if permission would be at variance with considerations of general policy or public interest.

(ix) The regulations shall be regarded as applying, in the same way as to British subjects, to British-protected persons who are such by virtue of their connection with a protectorate or trust territory administered under the supervision of His Majesty's Principal Secretary of State for Foreign and Commonwealth Affairs. They also apply in the same manner to British-protected persons who are such by virtue of their connection with a protected state administered under the supervision of the said Principal Secretary of State, but orders, decorations and medals conferred upon such British-protected persons by their rulers are not regarded as falling within the scope of these regulations.

These Regulations do not relate to awards of campaign or commemorative war medals.

Appendices

The Tables of Precedence

Gentlemen in England & Wales
Ladies in England & Wales
Gentlemen in Scotland
Ladies in Scotland

The Table of Precedence amongst Gentlemen in England & Wales

THE KING
The Heir Apparent
The Sovereign's Younger Son
The Sovereign's Grandsons
The Sovereign's Brothers
The Sovereign's Nephews
The Sovereign's Cousins
Archbishop of Canterbury
Lord High Chancellor
Archbishop of York
Archbishop of Wales
The Prime Minister*
Lord High Treasurer (when existing)
Lord President of the Council
Speaker of the House of Commons
Speaker of the House of Lords
President of the Supreme Court
Lord Chief Justice of England and Wales
Lord Privy Seal
Ambassadors and High Commissioners
Lord Great Chamberlain (when in performance of official duty)
Lord High Constable (when existing)
Earl Marshal
Lord Steward of the Household
Lord Chamberlain of the Household
Master of the Horse
Dukes of England
Dukes of Scotland
Dukes of Great Britain
Dukes of Ireland
Dukes of UK and Ireland since the Union
Eldest Sons of Dukes of the Blood Royal
Ministers, Envoys, and other very important visitors from foreign countries
Marquesses of England
Marquesses of Scotland
Marquesses of Great Britain
Marquesses of Ireland
Marquesses of UK and Ireland since the Union
Eldest Sons of Dukes
Earls of England

Earls of Scotland
Earls of Great Britain
Earls of Ireland
Earls of UK and Ireland since the Union
Younger Sons of Dukes of the Blood Royal
Marquesses' Eldest Sons
Dukes' Younger Sons
Viscounts of England
Viscounts of Scotland
Viscounts of Great Britain
Viscounts of Ireland
Viscounts of UK and Ireland since the Union
Earls' Eldest Sons
Marquesses' Younger Sons
Bishop of London
Bishop of Durham
Bishop of Winchester
Other English Diocesan Bishops according to seniority of consecration
Retired Church of England Diocesan Bishops according to seniority of consecration
Suffragan Bishops according to seniority of consecration
Secretaries of State if of Baronial rank
Barons of England
Lords of Parliament, Scotland
Barons of Great Britain
Barons of Ireland
Barons of UK and Ireland since the Union, including Life Barons
Master of the Rolls
Deputy President of the Supreme Court
Justices of the Supreme Court
Lords Commissioners of the Great Seal (when existing)
Treasurer of the Household
Comptroller of the Household
Vice-Chamberlain of the Household
Secretaries of State, being under Baronial rank
Viscounts' Eldest Sons
Earls' Younger Sons
Barons' Eldest Sons
Knights of the Garter
Privy Counsellors
Chancellor of the Order of the Garter
Chancellor of the Exchequer
Chancellor of the Duchy of Lancaster

President of the King's Bench Division
President of the Family Division
Chancellor of the High Court
Lord Justices of Appeal according to seniority of appointment
Judges of High Court of Justice according to seniority of appointment
Viscounts' Younger Sons
Barons' Younger Sons
Sons of Life Peers and Lords of Appeal in Ordinary
Baronets, according to date of Patent
Knights of the Thistle
Knights Grand Cross of the Order of the Bath
Knights Grand Commander of the Order of the Star of India
Knights Grand Cross of the Order of St Michael and St George
Knights Grand Cross of the Royal Victorian Order
Knights Grand Cross of the Order of the British Empire
Knights Commander of the Order of the Bath
Knights Commander of the Order of St Michael and St George
Knights Commander of the Royal Victorian Order
Knights Commander of the Order of the British Empire
Knights Bachelor
Circuit Judges in England and Wales
Master of the Court of Protection
Companions of the Order of the Bath
Companions of the Order of St Michael and St George
Commanders of the Royal Victorian Order
Commanders of the Order of the British Empire
Companions of the Distinguished Service Order
Lieutenants of the Royal Victorian Order
Officers of the Order of the British Empire
Companions of the Imperial Service Order
Eldest Sons of the Younger Sons of Peers
Eldest Sons of Baronets
Eldest Sons of Knights of the Orders of Chivalry (according to the precedence of their fathers)
Members of the Royal Victorian Order
Members of the Order of the British Empire
Younger Sons of Baronets
Younger Sons of Knights
Esquires
Gentlemen

*When a senior position is held by a woman, such as Prime Minister etc, her place in the order of precedence is the same as it would be were the incumbent male.

Table of Precedence amongst Ladies in England & Wales

Protocol dictates that when The Princess of Wales and The Duchess of Sussex are not accompanied by their husbands, Princesses of the Royal Blood, such as Princess Anne, Beatrice and Eugenie, rank above them. However, when Wales and Sussex are accompanied by their husbands, the roles are reversed and they outrank the princesses.

THE QUEEN CONSORT
The Princess of Wales
The Princess Royal
The Sovereign's Granddaughters
The Sovereign's Nieces
The Sovereign's Cousins
Wives of the Younger Son of the Sovereign
Wives of Dukes of the Blood Royal
Wives of Princes of the Blood Royal
Duchesses of England
Duchesses of Scotland
Duchesses of Great Britain
Duchesses of Ireland
Duchesses of UK and Ireland since the Union
Wives of Eldest Sons of Dukes of the Blood Royal
Marchionesses of England
Marchionesses of Scotland
Marchionesses of Great Britain
Marchionesses of Ireland
Marchionesses of UK and Ireland since the Union
Wives of Eldest Sons of Dukes
Daughters of Dukes
Countesses of England
Countesses of Scotland
Countesses of Great Britain
Countesses of Ireland
Countesses of UK and Ireland since the Union
Wives of Younger Sons of Dukes of the Blood Royal
Wives of Eldest Sons of Marquesses
Daughters of Marquesses
Wives of Younger Sons of Dukes
Viscountesses of England
Viscountesses of Scotland
Viscountesses of Great Britain
Viscountesses of Ireland

Viscountesses of UK and Ireland since the Union
Wives of Eldest Sons of Earls
Daughters of Earls
Wives of Younger Sons of Marquesses
Baronesses of England
Ladies of Parliament
Baronesses of Great Britain
Baronesses of Ireland
Baronesses of UK and Ireland since the Union, including Life Baronesses and Wives of Life Barons
Wives of the Eldest Sons of Viscounts
Daughters of Viscounts
Wives of Younger Sons of Earls
Wives of the Eldest Sons of Barons
Daughters of Barons
Ladies of the Garter
Wives of Knights of the Garter
Privy Counsellors (Women)
Wives of Younger Sons of Viscounts
Wives of Younger Sons of Barons
Wives of Sons of Life Peers
Wives of Baronets, according to their husbands' Patents
Wives of Knights of the Thistle
Dames Grand Cross of the Order of the Bath
Dames Grand Cross of the Order of St Michael and St George
Dames Grand Cross of the Royal Victorian Order
Dames Grand Cross of the Order of the British Empire
Wives of Knights Grand Cross of the Order of the Bath
Wives of Knights Grand Cross of the Order of St Michael and St George
Wives of Knights Grand Cross of the Royal Victorian Order
Wives of Knights Grand Cross of the Order of the British Empire
Dames Commander of the Order of the Bath
Dames Commander of the Order of St Michael and St George
Dames Commander of the Royal Victorian Order
Dames Commander of the Order of the British Empire
Wives of Knights Commander of the Order of the Bath
Wives of Knights Commander of the Order of St Michael and St George
Wives of Knights Commander of the Royal Victorian Order
Wives of Knights Commander of the Order of the British Empire
Wives of Knights Bachelor
Companions of the Order of the Bath

Companions of the Order of St Michael and St George
Commanders of the Royal Victorian Order
Commanders of the Order of the British Empire
Wives of Companions of the Order of the Bath
Wives of Companions of the Order of St Michael and St George
Wives of Commanders of the Royal Victorian Order
Wives of Commanders of the Order of the British Empire
Wives of Companions of the Distinguished Service Order
Lieutenants of the Royal Victorian Order
Officers of the Order of the British Empire
Wives of Members of the Royal Victorian Order (4th Class)
Wives of Officers of the Order of the British Empire
Companions of the Imperial Service Order
Wives of Companions of the Imperial Service Order
Wives of the Eldest Sons of the Younger Sons of Peers
Daughters of the Younger Sons of Peers
Wives of the Eldest Sons of Baronets
Daughters of Baronets
Wives of the Eldest Sons of Knights of the Garter
Wives of the Eldest Sons of Knights
Daughters of Knights
Members of the Royal Victorian Order
Members of the Order of the British Empire
Wives of Members of the Royal Victorian Order
Wives of Members of the Order of the British Empire
Wives of the Younger Sons of Baronets
Wives of the Younger Sons of Knights
Wives of Esquires
Wives of Gentlemen

In Scotland the Prince and Princess of Wales are known as the Duke and Duchess of Rothesay (see Scottish Tables of Precedence).

SAME SEX PARTNERS AND SPOUSES — If an office holder is in a same-sex partnership/marriage, the same rule of precedence for their partner apply as for wives.

Table of Precedence Amongst Gentlemen in Scotland

THE KING
Lord High Commissioner to the General Assembly of the Church of Scotland (during sitting of the General Assembly)
Duke of Rothesay
The Sovereign's Younger Son
The Sovereign's Grandsons
The Sovereign's Brothers
The Sovereign's Cousins
Lord-Lieutenants of Counties
Lord Provosts of Cities being ex-officio Lord-Lieutenants of those Cities
Sheriffs Principal
Lord Chancellor of Great Britain
Moderator of the General Assembly of the Church of Scotland (during office)
Keeper of the Great Seal of Scotland (the First Minister)
Presiding Officer
Secretary of State for Scotland
Hereditary High Constable of Scotland
Hereditary Master of the Household in Scotland
Dukes (*as in English Table*)
Eldest Sons of Dukes of the Blood Royal
Marquesses (as in English Table)
Eldest Sons of Dukes
Earls (*as in English Table*)
Younger Sons of Dukes of the Blood Royal
Eldest Sons of Marquesses
Younger Sons of Dukes
Lord Justice-General
Lord Clerk Register
Lord Advocate
Advocate General
Lord Justice-Clerk
Viscounts (*as in English Table*)
Eldest Sons of Earls
Younger Sons of Marquesses
Barons or Lords of Parliament (Scotland) (*as in English Table*)
Eldest Sons of Viscounts
Younger Sons of Earls
Eldest Sons of Barons or Lords of Parliament
Knights of the Garter
Knights of the Thistle

Privy Counsellors
Senators of the College of Justice (Lords of Session), including Chair of the Scottish Land Court
Younger Sons of Viscounts
Younger Sons of Barons or Lords of Parliament
Baronets
Knights Grand Cross and Knights Grand Commanders of Orders (*as in English Table*)
Knights Commanders of Orders (*as in English Table*)
Solicitor-General for Scotland
Lord Lyon King of Arms
Sheriffs Principal (when not within own county)
Knights Bachelor
Sheriffs
Companions of the Order of the Bath
Thence as in English Table

Table of Precedence Amongst Ladies in Scotland

THE QUEEN CONSORT
Duchess of Rothesay
The Wife of the Younger Son of the Sovereign
Granddaughters of the Sovereign
Wives of Grandsons of the Sovereign
Nieces of the Sovereign
Wives of nephews of the Sovereign
Duchesses (*as in English Table*)
Wives of Eldest Sons of Dukes of the Blood Royal
Marchionesses (*as in English Table*)
Wives of Eldest Sons of Dukes
Daughters of Dukes
Wives of Younger Sons of Dukes of the Blood Royal
Wives of Eldest Sons of Marquesses
Daughters of Marquesses
Wives of Younger Sons of Dukes
Countesses (*as in English Table*)
Viscountesses (*as in English Table*)
Wives of Eldest Sons of Earls
Daughters of Earls
Wives of Younger Sons of Marquesses
Baronesses, or Ladies of Parliament (Scotland) (*as in English Table*)
Wives of Eldest Sons of Viscounts

Daughters of Viscounts
Wives of Younger Sons of Earls
Wives of Eldest Sons of Barons or Lords of Parliament
Daughters of Barons or Lords of Parliament
Ladies of the Order of the Garter
Wives of Knights of the Garter
Ladies of the Order of the Thistle
Wives of Knights of the Thistle
Privy Counsellors (Women)
Wives of the Younger Sons of Viscounts
Wives of the Younger Sons of Barons
Wives of Baronets
Dames Grand Cross of Orders (*as in English Table*)
Wives of Knights Grand Cross and Knights Grand Commanders of Orders (*as in English Tables*)
Wives of Knights Bachelor, and Wives of Senators of the College of Justice (Lords of Session) including the wife of the Chair of the Scottish Land Court
Companions of the Order of the Bath
Thence as in English Table

APPENDICES

SURNAME PRONUNCIATION

Surname	Pronunciation
Abercrombie	Aber-crum-by
Abergavenny	Aber-*genny* (title - town pronounced as spelt)
Abinger	Abin-jer
Acheson	Atchesson
Adye	Aydi
Aldous	*All*-dus
Alleyne	Alleen (sometimes pronounced as spelt)
Alnwick	Annick
Althorp	*All*-thorp (since 2000, previously *All*-trup)
Altrincham	Altringham
Alvingham	All-ving-am
Alman	Amman
Ampthill	Ampt-hill
Annesley	*Anns*-li
Apethorpe	App-thorp
Arbuthnot, Arbuthnott	A-*buth*-not
Ardee	A-*dee*
Arundel	*Arun*-del
Ashburnham	Ash-*burn*-am
Assheton	Ash-ton
Atholl	*Uh*-thol or *Ah*-thol
Auchinleck	Affleck or *Ock*-inleck
Audley	*Awd*-li
Ava	Ah-va
Ayscough	Askew
Babington	*Babb*-ington
Baden-Powell	Bayden-Poell
Bagot	*Bag*-ot
Balcarres	Bal-*carris*
Balogh	Balog ('Bal' as in 'Hal')
Bampfylde	*Bam*-fielda
Baring	*Bear*-ing
Barnardiston	*Bar*-nar-*dis*-ton
Barttelot	Bartlot
Basing	Bayzing
Bathurst	*Bath*-urst ('a' as in 'cat')
Bazalgette	Bazl-jet
Beauchamp	Beecham
Beauclerk	Bo-clare
Beaudesert	Bodezair
Beaufort	*Bo*-foot

Beaulieu	*Bew*-ley
Beaumont	Bo-mont
Becher	Beacher
Bechervaise	*Besh*-er-vayse
Bedingfeld	Beddingfield
Behrens	Barens
Belfast	Bel-*fast*
Bellew	*Bell*-ew
Bellingham	Bellingjam or Bellingum
Belvoir	Beevor
Bengough	Ben-*goff*
Beresford	*Berris*-fud
Berkeley	Barkli
Bertie	Barti
Betham	*Bee*-tham
Bethune	Beaton
Bicester	Bister
Blakiston	Blackiston
Bledisloe	Bledslow
Blenheim	*Blen*-im
Bligh	Bly
Blithfield	Bliffield
Blois	Bloyss
Blomefield	Bloomfield
Blount	Blunt
Blyth	Bly
Boevey	Boovey or Buvey (short 'u')
Boleyn	*Bull*-in
Bolingbroke	*Bulling*-brook
Boord	Board
Boreel	Borale
Borrowes	Burrows
Borwick	Borrick
Bosham	*Bos*-am
Bosanquet	*Bozen*-ket
Boscawen	Bos-*cowen*
Botetourt	Botti-tort
Boughey	Boey
Boughton	Bought-on (village pronounced 'Bough-ton')
Bourchier	*Bough*-cher
Bourke	Burke
Bourne	Boorn

Bowden	Bowden (as in 'no')
Bowes	Bose (to rhyme with 'rose')
Bowman	Boman
Bowyer	Bo-yer (as in 'no')
Brabazon	*Brab*-azon
Brabourne	*Bray*-burn
Breadalbane	Bread-*au*burn
Breitmeyer	Bright-mire
Brereton	Breer-ton
Brise	Brize
Brocas	Brockas
Broke	Brook (HMS *Broke* as spelt)
Bromhead	Brumhead
Brougham	Broom *or* Brooham
Broughton	Brawton
Broun	Brune
Bruntisfield	Bruntsfield
Brynkir	Brinkeer
Buccleuch	Bu-*cloo*
Bulkeley	Buckley
Burgh	Borough
Burghersh	Burg-ish
Burghley	Ber-li
Bury	Berry (England), Bure-y (Ireland)
Caccia	Catch-a
Cadogan	Ka-*dugan*
Caius	Keys (Cambridge college)
Caldecote	Call-di-cot
Calderon	*Call*-dron
Callaghan	*Calla*-han
Calver	Carver
Calverley	*Car*-verly or *Calf*-ley
Camoys	Cam-oyz
Capell	*Cay*ple
Carew	As spelt (Cary has become archaic)
Calthorpe	*Call*-thorpe (Cal-trop has become archaic)
Carnegie	Car-*neggie*
Carteret	*Carter*-et
Cassilis	Cassels
Castlereagh	*Castle*-ray
Carthcart	Cath-*cart*
Cathie	*Cay*-thie

Cato	*Kate*-o
Cator	*Cay*-tor
Caulfield	*Caw*-field
Cavan	*Cav*-en ('a' as in 'cat')
Cavanagh	*Cava*-na
Cecil	*Ci*cil
Chandos	Shandos
Charlemont	Shar-le-mont
Charteris	As spelt (Charters is archaic)
Chattan	Hattan
Chenevix	*Sheeni*vix or *Shenne*vy
Chernocke	Char-nock
Chetwode	Chetwood
Chetwynd	Chetwind
Cheylesmore	*Chyles*-more
Cheyne	Chain, Chainy or Cheen
Chichele	*Chich*-ley
Chisholm	*Chis*-um
Cholmeley, Cholmondeley	*Chum*-li
Cilcennin	Kil-*kennin*
Claverhouse	Clayvers
Clerk	Clark
Cloete	Clootie
Clough	Cluff
Clowes	Clues
Clwyd	*Cloo*-id
Cochrane	*Coch*-ran
Cockburn	Co-burn
Coghlan	Co-lan
Coke	Cook (sometimes as spelt)
Coleraine	Cole-*rain*
Colquhoun	Ca-hoon
Colville	*Col*-ville or Col-ville
Combe	Coom
Combermere	*Cumber*-mere
Compton	Cumpton
Conesford	*Connis*-ford
Conolly	*Con*-olly
Constable	*Cun*stable
Conyngham, Conynghame	Cunningham
Cosham	As spelt

Cottenham	*Cot*-nam
Cottesloe	*Cots*-low
Couchman	Cowchman
Courthope	Cort-hope
Cowper	Cooper
Cozens	Cuzzens
Cracroft	*Cray*-croft
Craigavon	Craig-*avv*-on
Craster	Crarster
Creagh	Cray
Creighton	Cryton
Crespigny	*Crepp*-ni
Crichton	Cryton
Cromartie	*Crum*-aty
Crombie	Crumbie
Culme	Cullum (Sometimes as spelt)
Cuming	Cumming
Cunynghame	Cunningham
D'Abrell	*Dab*-roo
Dacre	Dayker
Dalbiac	*Dawl*-biac
Dalhousie	Dal-*howsi*
Dalmeny	Dul-*menny*
Dalyell	Dee-el or Dayli-el
Dalzell	Dee-el or Dayli-el
Darcy de Knayth	Darcy de Nayth
Daresbury	Darsbury
Daubeney	*Daub*-ny
Daventry	As spelt ('Daintry' is archaic)
Davies	Davis
De Blacquiere	De *Black*-yer
De Burgh	De *Burg*
Decies	Deeshies
De Courcy	De Koursey
De Crespigny	De *Crepp*-ni
De Freyne	De *Frain*
De Hoghton	De Hawton
De la Warr	Della-ware
Delamere	Della-mare
De la Poer	De la *Poor*
De la Rue	Della-rue

De L'Isle	De Lyle
De Lotbiniere	De Lobin-yare
De Moleyns	*Demo*-lins
Dering	*Deer*-ing
De Ros	De *Roos*
Derwent	Darwent
De Salis	De Saals or De Sal-is
Devereux	Dev-rooks or Dever-oo
De Vesci	De Vessy
De Villiers	De Villers
Diomede	Di-o-meed
Dilhorne	*Dill*'n
Dominguez	Dum-*ing*-ez
Doneraile	Dunnaral
Donoughmore	Duno-more
Doune	Doun
Douro	*Dur*-o
Drogheda	*Droyi*-da
Drumalbyn	Drum-*albin*
Duchesnes	Du *Karn(s)* (sometimes French 'Du-shayn')
Ducie	*Dew*-si
Du Cros	Du *Crow*
Dukinfield	*Duckin*-field
Dumaresq	Du-*merrick*
Dunally	Dun-*alley*
Dundas	Dun-*das*
Dungarvan	Dun-*gar*-van
Dunglass	Dun-*glass*
Dunsany	Dun-*saney*
Duntze	Dunts
Du Plat	Du-Pla
Dupplin	*Dupp*-lin
Durand	*Du*-rand or Dur-*rand*
Dymoke	Dimmock
Dynevor	*Dinny*-yer
Dysart	Dy-z't
Ebury	*Ee*-bri
Echlin	Eck-lin
Edwardes	Edwards
Egan	*Ee*-gan
Egerton	*Edger*-ton

Elcho	Elco
Elgin	El-gin (hard 'g')
Elibank	Elli-bank
Elphinstone	*Elfin*-ston
Elveden	*Elve*-den (Place 'Elden')
Elwes	*El*-wes
Erle	Earl
Ernle	Earnley
Erskine	*Ers*-kin
Eveleigh	*Eve*-ley
Eyre	Air
Every	As spelt
Eyton	*I*-tun
Falconer	Fawkner
Falkiner	Fawkner
Faringdon	Farringdon
Farquhar	Farkwar (Farker in Scotland)
Farquharson	Farkwerson (Farkerson in Scotland)
Fayrer	*Fair*-er
Featherstonhaugh	Fetherston-haugh or Fetherston
Feilding	*Field*-ing
Fenwick	*Fenn*-ick
Fergussen	Ferguson
Fermor	Farmer
Feversham	Fevver-sham (Place 'Favversham')
ffolliott	*Foll*-y-ot
ffolkes	Foaks
Fiennes	Fines
Fingall	Fin-*gawl*
Fitzhardinge	Fitzharding
Foljambe	Full-jum
Forestier	Forest-tier
Fortuin	Fortayne
Foulis	Fowls
Fowke	Foke
Fremantle	*Free*-mantle
Freyburg	*Fry*-burg
Froude	Frood
Furneaux	*Fur*-no
Gairdner	Gardner
Galston	*Gaul*-ston

Galway	Gaulway
Garioch	Gary (to rhyme with 'Mary' or Geary)
Garvagh	*Gar*-va
Gathorne	Gaythorn
Geoghegan	*Gay*-gan
Gerrard	Jerrard
Gervis	Jervis
Giffard	Jiffard
Gill	As spelt (hard 'g')
Gillespie	Gill-*es*-py (hard 'g')
Gilmour	Gillmoor (hard 'g')
Glamis	Glahms
Glasgow	*Glass*-go
Glenavy	Glen-*avy* (as in 'day')
Glerawly	Gler-*awly*
Gorges	Gorjes
Gormanstown	*Gor*-mans-ton
Goschen	*Go*-shen
Gough	Goff
Goulding	Goolding
Gower	Gore (place names as spelt)
Graeme	Grame (to rhyme with 'frame')
Grantham	*Gran*-tham
Greaves	Graves
Greig	Gregg
Grosvenor	*Grove*-nor
Guise	Gyze
Gwynedd	*Gwinn*-eth
Haden-Guest	Hayden-Gest (hard 'g')
Haldane	*Hall*-dane
Halsey	*Hall*-sey
Halsbury	*Halls*-bry
Hamond	Hammond
Harcourt	*Har*-cut
Hardinge	Harding
Harewood	*Har*-wood (village pronounced Hare-wood)
Harington	Harrington
Harwich	Harrich
Hawarden	*Hay*-warden
Haworth	*Hay*-worth (Harden for title is archaic)
Heathcoat	Heth-cut
Heathcote	Heth-cut

Heneage	Hennidge
Hepburn	*Heb*-b'n
Herschell	Her-shell
Hertford	*Har*-ford
Hervey	Harvey
Hever	Heaver
Heytesbury	*Hetts*-b'ry
Heywood	Haywood
Hindlip	*Hynd*-lip
Hippesley	*Hips*-ley
Hobart	Hubbard (city as spelt)
Hogan	*Ho*-gan
Holbech	*Hole*-beech
Home	Hume
Honywood	Honeywood
Hopetoun	Hopetown
Horsbrugh	Horsbro
Hotham	*Huth*-am
Housman	House-man
Howick	Hoyk
Hugessen	*Hu*-ges-son (hard 'g')
Huth	Hooth
Hylton	Hilton
Iddesleigh	*Idd*-sli
Ikerrin	I-kerrin
Iliffe	I-liffe
Inchiquin	Inch-quin
Inchrye	Inch-rye
Inchyra	Inch-*eye-ra*
Inge	Ing
Ingestre	Ingustry (like 'industry')
Inglis	Ingles or as spelt
Inigo	*Inni*-go
Innes	Inniss
Inveraray	Inver-*air*-a
Ionides	Ion-ee-diz
Isham	I-sham
Iveagh	I-va
Jervis	As spelt or Jarvis
Jervoise	Jervis
Jocelyn	Josslin
Jolliffe	*Joll*-iff

Kaberry	*Kay*-berry
Kavenagh	*Kavan*-a
Kekewich	*Keck*-which
Keighley	*Keith*-li
Kemeys	Kemmis
Kennard	Ken-*ard*
Kenyon	*Ken*-yon
Ker, Kerr	Car or Cur
Keynes	Kaynes
Killanin	Kil-*lah*-nin
Kilmorey	Kil-*murray*
Kingsale	King-*sale*
Kinnoull	Kin-*ool*
Kirkcudbright	Cuck-*coo*-bri
Knollys	Nowles
Kylsant	Kill-*sant*
Knyvett	Nivett
Lacon	*Lay*-kon
Laffan	Laf-*fan*
Lamplugh	*Lamp*-loo
Lascelles	*Lass*-ells
Lathom	*Lay*-thom
LaTouche	La *Toosh*
Latymer	Latimer
Laurie	Lorry
Layard	Laird
Leacock	Laycock or Leccock
Lechmere	Letchmere
Le Fanu	*Leff*-new
Lefevre	Le-*fever*
Legard	Le-jard
Legh	Lee
Leighton	Layton
Leinster	Linster
Leitrim	Leetrim
Le Mesurier	Le *Mezz*-erer
Leominster	Lemster
Leven	*Lee*-ven
Leverhulme	*Leaver*-hume
Leveson-Gower	Loosun-Gore
Levinge	As spelt (hard 'g')
Levy	Levvy or Levi

Ley	Lay or Lee
Leycester	Lester
Liardet	Lee-ardet
Liddell	*Lid*-el
Lisle	Lyle
Listowel	Lis-*toe*-ell
Lombe	Loam (sometimes Lumb)
Londesborough	Londs-bro'
Londonderry	*Londond*'ry (city pronounced London-Derry)
Loudon	*Loud*-on
Loughborough	*Luff*-bro
Louth	'th' as in 'mouth' (Ireland 'th' as in 'breathe')
Lovat	Luv-at
Lowson	Lo-son ('lo' as in 'go')
Lowther	*Low*-thr ('low' as in 'now')
Lycett	Lisset
Lygon	Liggon
Lyon	Lion
Lysaght	Ly-set
Lyveden	*Live*-den (as in 'give')
Macara	Mac-*ara*
Macbean	Mac-*bain*
McCorquodale	M'*cork*-o-dale
McCulloch	M'*cull*-och
McDonagh	Mac-*Donna*
McEvoy	*Mac*-evoy
McEwan	Mac-*ewen*
McFadzean	Mac-*fadd*-yen
McGillycuddy	*Mac*-li-*cuddy*
Machell	*May*-chell
McIvor	Mac-*Ivor*
McKay	M'*Kye* (as in 'eye')
McKie	*Mack*-ie (occasionally pronounced M'*Kye*)
Maclean	Mac-*layne*
Macleay	Mac-*lay*
Macleod	Mac-*loud*
McLachlan	Mac-*lochlan*
Macnaghten	Mac-*nawton*
Macmahon	Mac-*mahn*
Maelor	Myla
Magdala	Mag-*dahla*
Magdalen, Magdalene	Maudlin

Magrath	Ma-*grah*
Mahon	Mahn or Ma-*han*
Mahony	*Mah*-ni
Mainwaring	*Manner*-ing
Mais	Mayz
Majendic	Ma-*jendy*
Makgill	Mc-*gill* (hard 'g')
Malpas	*Mawl*-pas
Malet	Mallet
Malmsbury	*Marms*-bri
Mandeville	Mande-ville (first 'e' slightly inflected)
Mander	Mahnder
Mansergh	Manser
Margesson	*Mar*-jesson
Marjoribanks	Marchbanks
Marlborough	*Maul*-bro
Marquand	Mark-wand
Martineau	Martinowe
Masham	*Mass*-ham
Masserene	Mazereen
Mathias	Math-*ias*
Maughan	Mawm
Mauchline	*Mauch* (as in 'loch')-lynn
Maunsell	*Man*-sel
Maxse	Maxie
Meath	Meeth ('th' as in 'breathe')
Meiklejohn	*Mickel*-john
Melhuish	*Mell*-ish
Menteth	Men-*teeth*
Menzies	Ming-iz
Merioneth	Merry-*on*-eth
Mereworth	*Merry*-worth
Metcalfe	Met-calf
Methuen	Meth-wen
Meux	Mews
Meynell	*Men*-el
Meyrick	Merr-ick
Mitchelham	*Mitch*-lam
Michie	Micky
Midleton	*Middle*-ton
Millais	*Mill*-ay
Mocatta	Mow-*catta*

Molyneux	*Mully*-neux or Mully-nu
Monaco	*Mon*-aco
Monck	Munk
Monckton	Munkton
Monro	Mun-*roe*
Monson	*Mun*-sun
Montagu	*Mon*-tagu
Montgomery, Montgomerie	Mun-*gum*-eri
Monzie	M'*nee*
Moran	Moor-*an*
Moray	Murray
Mordaunt	*Mor*-dant
Mosicy	Mozeley
Mostyn	*Moss*-tin
Mottistone	Mottiston
Moulton	*Mole*-ton
Mountmorres	Mount-morris
Mowbray	*Mo*-bray
Mowll	Mole
Moynihan	*Moy*-ni-han
Munro	Mun-*roe*
Myddelton	Middle-ton
Mytton	Mitton
Naas	Nace
Naesmyth	*Nay*-smith
Nall	Nawl
Napier	*Nay*-pier
Nathan	Naythan
Nepean	Ne-*peen*
Newburgh	*New*-bro'
Niven	Nivven
Northcote	*North*-cut
Nunburnholme	Nun-burnham
Ochterlony	Ochter-*lony*
Offaly	*Off*-aly
Ogilvie, Ogilvy	*Ogle*-vi
O'Hagan	O'*Hay*-gan
Olivier	O-livier
O'Loghlen	O'*Loch*-len
Ormonde	*Or*-mund
O'Rourke	O'Rork
Outram	*Oot*-ram

Pakington	Packington
Paget	*Paj*-it
Pakenham	*Pack*-en'um
Pasley	*Pais*-li
Paton	Payton
Paulet	*Paul*-et
Paunceforte, Pauncefote	*Pawns*-fort
Pechell	*Peach*-ell
Pennefather	*Penn*-ifither or Penny-feather
Pennycuick	*Penny*-cook
Pepys	Peppis (Peeps has become archaic, except for the diarist and the Pepys Cockerell family)
Perceval	Percival
Pery	Pairy
Peto	*Peet*-o
Petre	Peter
Petrie	*Peet*-rie
Peyton	Payton
Phayre	Fair
Pierpoint	Pierpont
Pleydell	Pleddel
Plowden	Ploughden
Plumtre	*Plum*-tri
Pole	Pole or Pool (see also Carew)
Poltimore	Pole-ti-more
Polwarth	*Pol*-worth
Pomeroy	*Pom*-roy
Pomfret	*Pum*-fret
Ponsonby	Punsunby
Poulett	*Paul*-et
Powell	Powell or Poell
Powerscourt	*Poers*-caut
Powis	*Po*-iss
Powlett	*Paul*-et
Powys	Po-iss (name) (place pronounced 'Powiss')
Praed	Praid
Prevost	*Prev*-o
Prideaux	Priddo
Puleston	*Pill*-ston
Purefuy	Pure-foy
Pytchley	*Pietch*-li
Quibell	Quy-*bel* (as in 'high')

Raleigh	*Raw*-li
Ranfurly	*Ran*-fully
Rankeillour	Rank-illour
Ratendone	Ratten-dun
Rathdonnell	Rath-*donnell*
Rea	Ree
Rearsby	*Rears*-bi
Reay	Ray
Redesdale	*Reads*-dale
Renwick	*Renn*-ick
Reresby	*Rears*-bi
Reuter	*Roy*-ter
Rhyl	Rill
Rhys	Rees or Rice
Riddell	*Riddle*
Rideau	*Reed*-owe
Roborough	*Roe*-bra'
Roche	Roach or Rosh
Roden	Roe-den
Rolfe	Roaf (as in 'loaf')
Rolleston	*Roll*-ston
Romilly	*Rum*-illy
Romney	Rumney
Ronaldshay	*Ron*-alld-shay
Rotherwick	As spelt
Rothes	*Roth*-is
Rous, Rouse	Rowse (as in 'grouse')
Rowley	*Roe*-li
Roxburghe	Rox-bro
Ruabon	Ru-*a*-bon
Ruthin	Ruth-in
Ruthven	Rivven
Sacheverall	Sash-*ever*-al
Sacheverell	Sash-*ev*-rell
St Aubyn	S'nt *Aw*-bin
St Clair	Sinclair or as spelt
St Cyres	S'nt Sires (to rhyme with 'fires')
St John	Sin-jun
St Leger	*Sill*-inger or St Leger
St Levan	S'nt Leaven (as in 'leaven' for bread)
St Maur	S'nt *More*
Salisbury	*Sawls*-bri

Salkeld	Saul-keld
Saltoun	*Salt*-on
Salisbury	*Sawls*-bri
Sandbach	Sandbatch
Sandeman	*Sandy*-man
Sandys	Sands
Sanquhar	Sanker (Sanwer is historically correct)
Saumarez	Summer-ez or *Saumer-ez*
Sausmarez	Summer-ez or *Saumer-ez*
Savernake	Savver-nack
Savile	Saville
Saye and Sele	Say and Seal
Schilizzi	Skil-it-zy
Schuster	*Shoo*-ster
Sclater	Slater
Scone	Scoon
Scudamore	*Scooda*-more
Scrymgeour	*Scrim*-jer
Sedburgh	Sed-ber
Segal	Seagal
Segrave	Sea-grave
Sele	Seal
Sempill	Semple
Seton	Seaton
Seymour	Seamer or as spelt
Shakerley	Shackerley
Shaughnessy	Shawnessy
Sherborne	Shirb'n
Shrewsbury	*Shrows*-b'ry (town has alternative pronunciation of *Shrewsb*'ry)
Shuckburgh	*Shuck*-bro'
Sieff	Seef
Simey	Symey
Skene	Skeen
Skrine	Screen
Smijth	Smyth
Smyth	Smith or Smythe
Smythe	Smythe
Sneyd	Sneed
Somers	Summers
Somerset	Summerset
Sotheby	*Sutha*-by
Soulbury	*Sool*-bri

Southwark	*Suth*-erk
Southwell	*Suth*-ell
Sowerby	Sour-by
Spottiswoode	Spotswood
Stanhope	Stannup
Staordale	*Stav*-erdale
Stonor	Stone-er
Stourton	Sturton
Strabane	Stra-*bann*
Strabolgi	Stra-*bogie* (hard 'g')
Strachan	Strawn
Straghan	Strawn
Strahan	Strawn
Strachi	*Stray*-chie
Stratheden	Strath-*eden*
Strathspey	Strath-*spay*
Stratfield	Stret-field
Stucley	*Stewk*-li
Suirdale	Sure-dale
Sysonby	*Size*-on-by
Synge	Sing
Talbot	*Tall*-bot
Tangye	Tang-y
Taverne	Tav-*erne*
Taylour	Taylor
Teignmouth	*Tin*-muth
Terregles	Terry-*glaze*
Teynham	*Ten*-'am
Thame	Tame
Thellusson	*Tellus*-son
Theobald	Tibbald or as spelt
Thesiger	*Thesi*-jer
Thorold	Thurrald
Thynne	Thin
Tichbourne	*Titch*-bourne
Tighe	Tie
Tollemache	*Tol*-mash (Tall-mash is archaic)
Torphichen	Tor-*kken*
Touchet	*Touch*-et
Tovey	Tuvvy
Trafalgar	Traffle-*gar* (title only)
Traquair	Tra-*quare*

Tredegar	Tre-*deegar*
Trefusis	Tre-*fusis*
Trevelyan	Tre-*villian*
Trimlestown	*Trimmels*-ton
Trowbridge	Troobridge
Tuchet	*Touch*-et
Tuite	Tute
Tullibardine	Tulli-*bard*-in
Turnour	Turner
Tuvey	Tuvvy
Twohy	*Too*-y
Twysden	Twis-den
Tynte	Tint
Tyrrell	Tirrell
Tyrwhitt	Tirrit
Tyzack	*Tie*-sack
Urquhart	*Urk*-ut
Uvedale	*Youv*-dale
Vachell	*Vay*-chell
Valentia	Val-*en*-shia
Valletort	Valley-tort
Van Straubenzee	Van Straw-*ben*-zie
Vaughan	Vawn
Vaux	Vokes
Vavasour	*Vav*-assur
Verschoyle	Ver-*skoil*
Vesey	Veezy
Vigor	Vygor
Villiers	Villers
Vyvyan	Vivian
Waechter	Vechter (guttural 'ch')
Wagner	As spelt
Waldegrave	Waldgrave or Wargrave
Waleran	*Wall*-ran
Walmer	*Wall*-mer
Walrond	*Wall*-rond
Walsingham	*Wall*-sing'm
Walwyn	Wall-wyn
Wathen	Wothen
Wauchope	*Walk*-up ('ch' as in 'loch')
Waugh	As spelt, to rhyme with 'flaw'
Wavell	*Way*-vell

Weighall	*Wy*-gall
Weighill	*Wey*-hill
Wellesley	*Wells*-li
Wemyss	Weems
Wernher	Werner
Westenra	*Westen*-ra
Westmeath	West-*meath* ('th' as in 'breathe')
Westmorland	*West*-morland
Wharton	*Whor*-ton
Wigoder	*Wigg*-oder
Wigram	*Wigg*-ram
Wilbraham	*Will*-bram
Willoughby de Eresby	*Willow*-bi deersby
Willoughby de Broke	*Willow*-bi de Brook
Winder	*Winn*-der
Woburn	*Woo*-burn
Wodehouse	*Wood*-house
Wollaston	*Wool*-aston
Wolley	Wooly
Wolmer	*Wool*-mer
Wolrige	*Wool*-ridge
Wolseley	*Wool*-sli
Wombwell	*Woom*-well
Wontner	Wantner
Worsley	*Wers*-li or Werz-li
Wortley	*Wert*-li
Wriothesley	Rottisli
Wrottesley	*Rotts*-li
Wykeham	*Wick*-am
Wyllie	*Wy*-lie
Wyndham	*Wind*-'am
Wynford	*Win*-fud
Wynyard	Win-yard
Wythenshaw	*With*-in-shaw
Yeatman	Yaytman
Yerburgh	*Yar*-bra'
Yonge	Young
Zouch	Zooch

APPENDICES

INDEX

A

Abbots	125, 127
Academic forms of address	67-73
Academic qualifications	150
Academicians, Royal	152
Accommodation, for overnight guests	383-384
Address, forms of	
academic	67-73
armed forces	75-85
chaplains	122
baronets and families	45-47
courtesy titles	39-41
dames	55-56
diplomatic Service	137-141
divorced persons	279
government	100-101
joint	62, 157, 158
judiciary	103-109
knights and families	49-54
Ladies of the Garter	52-53
Ladies of the Thistle	52-53
letters after names	143-153
local government	92-97
medical	131-133
on invitations	318
peerage	23-44, 279, 286
memorial inscriptions	303
police	87-89
privy counsellors	61
religion	111-129
Royal Family	15-21
private secretaries	18-19
King, HM The	15
Scottish titles	57-60
untitled persons	62
widows	286
Address cards, change of	321
Admirals	75, 78, 79
Admission cards	159
Adopted children, titles	40
Adoption cards	202
Afternoon tea	365
Agents-general Commonwealth	141
Air commodores	75, 85
Air marshals	75, 84
Air travel	407
Ambassadors	137-139
Announcements	
birth	201-202
death	283-285
engagement	221-222
memorial services	301
Aperitifs	362
Apples	355
Appointments, royal	149
Archbishops	113-114, 119
Roman Catholic	124, 126
Archbishops' Council	112
Archdeacons	117, 119
Armed forces	
forms of address	75-85
chaplains	122
letters after names	153
Army, British	
forms of address	80-83, 153
Artichokes, globe	355
Ascot, Royal	430-431
Asparagus	355
Assemblies	
Wales	100
Northern Ireland	100
At home invitations	315-316
Attorney General	104
Australia, Order of	148

B

Baby showers	203
Badminton Horse Trials	430
Ballet	417
Baptisms	205-209
Bar and bat mitzvahs	212
Baronets	
wearing of badges	434, 436, 437
Baronets and families	
forms of address	45-47
Barons and families	
forms of address	36-38
Scottish feudal	60
Baronesses	
forms of address	37
Barristers	106
Bathrooms, for guests	385
Bedford, Seventh Duchess of, Anna	365
Bereavement cards	321
Best man, duties	246, 259
speech	267-268
Betting	419
Birds, whole, eating	359
Birth, announcements	201-202
visiting after	202-203
Bishops	115-116, 119
Roman Catholic	124-125, 126
Black tie, dress code	187-189
Boat Race	429
Bouquets, bridal	250-251
Bowls, finger	353
Bowls and plates	350
Boxes, at sporting events	418
Brandy	363, 373
Breach of promise	223
Bread	358
Breakfasts, for guests	385, 386
Bridesmaids	247-249
Brigadiers	75, 80, 82
Buffets	377
Buses	405
Business cards	329, 334
Business correspondence	325-329
Business stationery	328

C

Cakes, wedding	264
Canada, Order of	148
Canapés	380
Candles	371
Canons	117-118, 119
Roman Catholic	125, 127
Captains	
Army	75, 81, 82
Navy	75, 79
Cardinals	124, 126
Cards	
admission	159
bereavement	321
business	329, 334
change of address	321
Christmas	321
correspondence	310
engagement	225
greetings	321
menu	351
place	159, 265
save-the-date	231
social	311, 334
visiting	310-311
mourning, Victorian	287

Carriages, traditions	405	
Cars		
driving	403-404, 421	
funeral	293	
wedding	255-256	
Catholic Church		
Roman	123-127	
Cavalry, Household	83	
Caviar	357	
Ceremonies, wedding	256-261	
Chairman of the Land Court,		
Scotland	108	
Chairmen of councils	96-97	
Challenging foods	355-359	
Champagne	362	
glasses	361	
Chancellor, Lord	103, 107	
Chancellor of the Exchequer	101	
Chancellor of the High Court	107	
Chancellors and vice-chancellors,		
forms of address	67, 73	
Change of address cards	321	
Chaplains	122	
Charity events	175	
Cheese	358-359	
Chelsea Flower Show	430	
Cheltenham Festival	429	
Chewing food	353	
Chief rabbi	128-129	
Chiefs and chieftains		
forms of address	58-59	
Children		
as pedestrians	400	
at buffets	377	
at informal suppers	376	
in public	414	
in restaurants and pubs	411	
in shops	412	
on planes	407	
overnight stays	392-395	
Chivalry, orders of		
wearing	433-441	
Chopsticks	351	
Christenings	205-209	
Christmas cards	321	
Church		
behaviour in	415	
of England	111-119	
of Ireland	112, 116	
of Scotland	120-121	

Scottish Episcopal	116, 119	
in Wales	112	
Cinema	417	
Civil ceremonies, weddings	261	
Clergy, forms of address	113-119	
in speeches	171	
Coats, helping with	345	
Cocktail parties	379-381	
Coffee	364, 375	
Colleges		
heads of, titles	68-71	
Royal Medical	132	
Colonels	81, 82	
Coming of age	213	
Commanders		
navy	75, 78, 79	
police	89	
Commissioners		
church	112	
commonwealth high		
commissioners	139	
police	87	
police and crime	88	
Commodores		
air	75, 85	
navy	75, 78, 79	
Commonwealth		
diplomatic titles	140-141	
high commissioners	139	
orders and decorations	148	
Complaints	410, 411	
Compliments	342	
Compliments slips	328-329	
Concerts	417	
Condolence letters	286-287	
sample	427	
Confetti	261	
Confirmations	211	
Consuls	138	
Conversation	340-343	
Correspondence cards	310	
Councillors, local government	97	
Counsel, King's	106, 149	
Countesses, forms of address	30	
Country		
clothing	195	
etiquette	421	
house opera	417	
house parties	386-387, 391	
Court of Appeal		

Lord Justice of	107	
Courtesy	399-419	
Courtesy titles		
forms of address	39-41	
Cowes Week	431	
Cricket, Lords test match	430	
Crown honours	146-147	
Cutlery	349-351, 371, 376	
serving	352	
Cyclists	404	

D

Dames		
forms of address	55-56	
Deaconesses, methodist	121	
Deans		
church	117, 119, 121	
college	70	
Death announcements	283-285	
Decanters	362	
Decorations, table	371	
Decorations, wearing	187, 433-441	
at royal events	178-179, 317	
Degrees, order of letters		
after names	72, 150	
Dental officers, Royal Navy	79	
Dentists, forms of address	131	
Deputy lord-lieutenants	92, 149	
Derby, Epsom	430	
Diets, special, catering for	372	
Digestifs	363	
Digital nomads	41	
Dinner jackets	187-189	
Dinner parties, formal	369-375	
Dinners, informal	376	
Diplomatic service	137-141	
Diplomats, precedence	163	
Dipping sauces	353	
Directors		
colleges and institutes	71	
Disclaimed peerages		
forms of address	43-44	
Divorce, conventions	273-279	
Divorced women		
forms of address	62	
Doctorates	71, 73	
medical	133	
Doctors, medical	131	
Dogs	391, 400	
Donations, funeral	298	

Doors, holding open 401
Dress codes 173, 182-195
    baptisms and christenings 209
    bar and bat mitzvahs 212
    black tie 187-189
    dinner parties 369, 376
    drinks parties 380
    funerals 297
    golf spectators 419
    Highland dress 191
    lounge suits 193
    memorial services 302
    morning dress 190
    mourning, Victorian 285
    on invitations 158, 317
    parties 189
    places of worship 415
    polo matches 419
    royal events 178
    smart casual 194
    sporting events 418
    theatre 417
    weddings 235, 252
    white tie 185-187
Drinks 361-363
    dinner parties 373
    overnight guests 390
    wedding receptions 263
Drinks parties 379-381
Driving 403-404
    in the country 421
Dukes and families
    forms of address 24-26

E

Earls and families
    forms of address 30-32
Eating
    buffets 377
    canapés 380
    dinner parties 369-375
    informal suppers 376
    in the street 401
    public transport 406
    restaurants 409-411
    sporting events 419
    table manners 347-365
Eating and talking 352
Eggs, quails' and gulls' 359
Emails, business 326-328
Emails, social 323
Engagements 215-225
Entrances and exits 345
Envelopes 309, 326
Epsom Derby 430
Eulogies, funeral 291-292
Evening dress 185-189, 376
Exits and entrances 345

F

Family Division, President of 107
Faxes 329
Fellowships and memberships
    medical 134-135
    professional 151-152
Feudal baronies, Scottish
    forms of address 60
Field marshals 75, 80, 82
Finger bowls 353
First names, usage 339
Fish and shellfish 356-357
Flowers
    dinner party 371
    funeral 298-299
    wedding 258
        bridal bouquets 250-251
        buttonholes 252
Flying officers 85
Food, local 351
Forgetting names 334-335
Forms of address
    academic 67-73
    armed forces 75-85
        chaplains 122
    baronets and families 45-47
    courtesy titles 39-41
    dames 55-56
    diplomatic service 137-141
    divorced persons 279
    government 100-101
    joint 62, 157, 158
    judiciary 103-109
    knights and families 49-54
    Ladies of the Garter 52
    Ladies of the Thistle 52
    letters after names 143-153
    local government 92-97
    medical 131-133
    on invitations 318
    peerage 23-44, 279, 286
    police 87-89
    privy counsellors 61
    religion 111-129
    Royal Family 15-21
        private secretaries 18-19
        King, HM The 15
    Scottish titles 57-60
    untitled persons 62
    widows 286
Funerals 289-299
    announcements 284-285
    divorced family members 277

G

Game birds, eating 359
Garden parties, royal 179-180
    invitations to 21
Garter, Ladies of the
    forms of address 52-53
General Synod 111-112
Generals 75, 80, 82
Glasses 361, 371
Globe artichokes 355
Gloves 186
Glyndebourne Festival
    Opera Season 429
Godparents 206-207
Golf 419
Goodwood 431
Gossip 341
Government 99-101
    local, order of precedence 94
    local, structure 91
Governors and governors-general,
    Commonwealth 140
Grace, saying 167
Grand National 429
Grapes 355
Greetings cards 321
Group chats 323
Guards' Division, Household
    Cavalry 83
Guest lists
    baptisms, christenings 208-209
    weddings 229-231
        divorced couples 276
Guests, etiquette
    at buffets 377
    at dinner parties 369-375
    at drinks parties 381

at formal events 173-180
at informal suppers 376
at royal events 177-180
at weddings 266
overnight guests 375, 383-395
Guests of honour 171
The Guineas at Newmarket 430

H

Handshakes 336
Headphones 406
Hen and stag parties 249
Henley Royal Regatta 431
High commissioners
   commonwealth 139
High Court 104-105
   Chancellor of 107
High Sheriffs 94
High tables 174
Highland dress 191
Honours, Crown 146-147
   Commonwealth 148
Horse Show, Royal Windsor 430
Hosts' duties
   at dinner parties 374
   at drinks parties 380-381
   at sporting events 418
   for overnight guests 385-386
   in restaurants 409-410
Hotels 411-412
Household Division
   British Army 83

I

Iced coffee 364
Informal suppers 376
Informals, cards 310
Inscriptions, memorial 303
Introductions 333-335
Invitations 157-158, 313-319
   at home 315
   baptisms, christenings 207-208
   bar and bat mitzvahs 212
   coming of age parties 213
   dinner parties 369
   divorced couples 276
   dress codes 158, 317
   from the Royal Family 21
   informal and contemporary 316
   joint forms of address 62, 157

   private parties 313
   replies 158, 208, 212, 243, 318-319
   to married couples 158
   to the Royal family 17-18, 181
   wedding 235-243
Ireland, Church of 112, 116
Irish hereditary knights 60
Islam 128

J

Joint forms of address 62, 157, 158
Judaism 128-129
Judges 105-106, 107
Judiciary
   forms of address 103-109
   Scotland 108-109
Justice of the Supreme Court 107
Justices of the Peace 106, 149

K

King, HM The
   forms of address 15
   invitations from 21
   presentation to 15
King's Bench Division,
   President of 107
King's Counsel 106, 149
Kissing, social 337
Kitchen suppers 376
Knights, Irish hereditary 60
Knights and families
   forms of address 49-54
   letters after names 50-52
Kumquats 355

L

Lairds and families
   forms of address 58-59
Land Court, Scotland
   Chairman of 108
Langoustines 357
Laptops 413
Laying the table 349-350
Leap years 217
Learned societies 151
Lemons 355
Letterheads 309
   business 325

Letters
   business 325-326
   condolence 286-287
   sample 427
   thank-you 175, 180, 181, 202, 207, 225, 271, 322-323, 375, 387
   samples 425-426
Letters after names 143-153
   armed forces 153
   degrees 72, 150
   knights 50-52
   medical 133-135
   order of
   professional institutions
     and associations 152
Lieutenant colonels 75, 81, 82
Lieutenant generals 75, 80, 82
Lieutenant-governors 140
Lieutenants
   army 81, 82
   lord-lieutenants 92-93
   navy 75, 78, 79
Life peers 43
   forms of address 36-38
Lists, official 164-165
Litter 401
Lobsters 356
Local government
   order of precedence 94
   structure 91
Lord Advocate, Scotland 108
Lord Chancellor 103, 107
Lord Chief Justice 103, 107
Lord High Commissioner
   Church of Scotland 120-121
Lord Justice Clerk
   Scotland 108, 109
Lord Justice General
   Scotland 108, 109
Lord-lieutenants 92-93
Lord mayors 95, 97, 163
Lord President, Scotland 108, 109
Lord Privy Seal 101
Lords justices of appeal 104, 107
Lords spiritual 114
Lords test match 430
Lounge suits, dress code 193
Loving cups 175
Loyal toasts 167-168, 171

M

Magistrates	106
Major generals	75, 80, 82
Majors	75, 81, 82
Manners, table	347-365
Marines, Royal	78, 153
Marquesses and families	
forms of address	27-29
Marriage proposals	217
Married women	
forms of address	62
Marshals, Royal Air Force	84, 85
Master, Scottish	
courtesy title	41-42, 57
Master of the Rolls	104, 107
Masters, college	69-70
Mayoresses	96-97
Mayors and civic heads	95-97, 163
Medals and decorations	
wearing	187, 433-441
Medical fellowships and	
memberships	134-135
Medical Officers, Royal Navy	79
Medical qualifications	132-133, 150
Medical Royal colleges	
and faculties	132
Members of Parliament	100-101, 153
Memberships and fellowships,	
medical	134-135
Memorial inscriptions	303
Memorial services	284, 301-303
Menus	
cards	351
dinner party	372
informal supper	376
Methodist Church	121
Midshipmen	78
Military honours	146-147
Ministers	
Church of Scotland	121
government	101
Judaism	129
Methodist	121
Mobile phones	399, 413
Moderators	
Church of Scotland	120-121
Monsignors	125, 127
Morning dress	
dress code	190
Mourners, order of	290
Mourning, Victorian	285, 287
Music	
funerals	290
headphones	406
wedding ceremonies	257
wedding receptions	263
Mussels	356

N

Names	
change after marriage	271
first, usage	339
forgetting	334-335
introductions	333
Naming ceremonies	209
Nannies	392, 394, 395
Napkins	352, 371, 376
National Assembly for Wales	100
Navy, Royal,	
forms of address	77-79, 153
loyal toast	171
New Zealand, Order of	
and Order of Merit	148
Newmarket	430
The Guineas	430
July meeting	431
Nicknames, usage	339
Non-commissioned officers	81
Northern Ireland Assembly	100
Nurseries, customs	395

O

Obituaries	303
Opera and ballet	417
country house opera	429
Oranges	356
Orders, medals and decorations,	
wearing	433-441
Orders of service	
funerals	292
memorial services	302
weddings	257
Overnight guests	375, 383-395
Oysters	357

P

Paper, writing	309
Parent-school relationships	415
Parties	
coming of age	213
dinner	369-375
dress code	189
drinks	379-381
engagement	225
invitations	313
stag and hen	249
wedding receptions	262-269
Paying in restaurants	410
Pedestrians	399-401
Phones, mobile	399, 413
Photographs	
at baptisms and christenings	209
at royal events	180
engagement	223
wedding	255
Physicians	131
Pilot officers	85
Pips and stones	356
Place à table	370
Place cards	159, 265
Place settings	349-350, 371
Plane travel	407
Plates and bowls	350
Police, forms of address	87-89
Police and crime	
commissioners	88
Polo	419, 429, 431
Pope	124, 126
Port	363, 373
Prawns	356-357
Prebendaries	118, 119
Precedence	
order of	94, 163-165, 169-170
tables of	443-451
Presents	
christening	206
coming of age	213
confirmation	211
engagement	218, 225
etiquette after divorce	275
thank-you letter, sample	426
wedding	232, 271
weekend visits	387-388, 395
President	
of the Family Division	107
of the King's Bench	
Division	107
Presidents, college	69

Priests, Roman Catholic 127
Prime Minister 101
Principals, college 68-69
Printing, stationery 309
Priors 127
Private secretaries (royal) 18-19
Privy Council 99
Privy counsellors
   forms of address 61, 100
   letters after name 149
Processions, Victorian funeral 299
Professional institutions and
   associations 152
Professions and societies, letters
   after names 151-153
Professors, forms of address 71, 73
Pronunciation of surnames 453-471
Proposals, marriage 217
Provincials 125, 127
Provosts
   clergy 119
   college 71
Public transport 405-407
Pubs 410-411
Pushchairs 400

Q
Queen's Cup 431
Quails' eggs 359
Qualifications
   academic 150
   medical 132-133, 150

R
Rabbis 128-129
Racing
   Season events 429-431
   etiquette 419
Ranks
   armed forces 75-83
   police 87
Readers, Judaism 129
Receiving lines
   formal events 173
   wedding receptions 266
Receptions
   christenings, baptisms 208-209
   wedding 262-269
Recorders (judiciary) 106

Rectors
   clergy 118, 119
   college 70
Regard rings 219
Regatta, Royal Henley 431
Regents, college 70
Religious orders and
   communities 118, 150
Restaurants
   coffee in 364
   dining in 409-411
   greeting others 345
Retired army officers
   forms of address 81
Retired clergy
   forms of address 114-115
Retired naval officers
   forms of address 78-79
Retired Royal Air Force officers
   forms of address 85
Rings
   engagement 218
   regard 219
   wedding 253
Roman Catholic Church 123-127
Room service 412
Rose bowls 175
Rowing, Henley Royal Regatta 431
Royal Academicians 152
Royal Academy Summer
   Exhibition 430
Royal Air Force
   forms of address 84-85, 153
Royal appointments 149
Royal Ascot 430-431
Royal events 177-181
Royal Family
   attendance at funerals 298
   entertaining 20, 181
   forms of address 15-21
   invitations from 21
   invitations to 17-18
   presentation to 16
   private secretaries 18-19
Royal Marines 78, 153
Royal Navy
   forms of address 77-79, 153
   loyal toast 171
Royal Windsor Horse Show 430

S
Sailing, Cowes Week 431
Salt 352
Salutations, business
   correspondence 325
Sauces, dipping 353
Same-sex couples 256-7, 271
Save-the-date cards 231, 319
School gate etiquette 414-415
School-parent relationships 415
School sports 418
Scones 365
Scotland
   Church of Scotland 120-121
   judiciary 108-109
   Scottish Episcopal Church 116, 119
Scottish titles
   forms of address 57-60
   Highland dress 191
Season, The 429-431
Seating
   funeral services 296-297
   informal suppers 376
   memorial services 302
   wedding ceremonies 258-259
Seating plans 161-165
   dinner parties 370-371
   divorced couples 276
   royal guests 20
   wedding receptions 265
Senators of College
   of Justice, Scotland 108, 109
Service sheets
   funerals 292
   memorial services 302
   weddings 257
Serving and passing
   at the table 352, 372-373
Shaking hands 336
Shellfish 357
Sheriffs 171
   high sheriffs 94
   Scotland 109
Shops 412
Signet, Writers to the 153
Signing off, business
   correspondence 325-326
   emails 327
Sitting at the table 352

Small talk	340-341	
Smart casual, dress code	194-195	
Smoking	390-391, 401	
Snails	359	
Social cards	311, 334	
Social kissing	337	
Societies, learned	151	
Societies and professions		
letters after names	151-153	
Solicitor General	104	
Soup	358	
Speaker, House of Commons	100	
Speaker, Lord,		
House of Lords	100-101	
Speeches	168-169	
wedding	267-268	
Sporting events	419-420	
Squadron leaders	75	
Staff	373, 379, 389	
shop	412	
Stag and hen parties	249	
Stairs	401	
Standing up	345	
Stationery	309-311	
Stones and pips	356	
Strawberries	356	
Supper parties, informal	376	
Supreme Court	103	
Justice of	107	
Surgeons	138	
Surnames, pronunciation	453-471	
Sushi	359	
Synod, General	111-112	

T

Table decorations	371
Table manners	347-365
Tables of precedence	443-451
Table plans	
dinner parties	369-370
royal guests	20
wedding receptions	265
Table settings	349-350, 371
Tact	343
Talking and eating	352
Tartans	191
Taxis	406
Tea	365
Telephones, mobile	399, 413
Television	389

Tennis, Wimbledon Championships	431
Test match, Lords	430
Text messages, business	328
Text messages, social	323
Thank-you letters	175, 180, 181, 202, 207, 225, 271, 322-323, 375, 387
samples	425-426
Theatre	417
Thistle, Ladies of the	
form of address	52-53
Tipping	391, 395, 406, 410, 411
Titles	23-63
courtesy	39-41
on visiting cards	311
use in introductions	334
Toastmasters	263
Toasts	167-168
Topics of conversation	341
Traditions and history	
conversation	343
dances	313
eating and drinking	351, 357, 359, 363, 365, 375
engagement	223
dress	186, 376
funerals	299
game-keeping	421
handshakes	336
house parties	386, 391, 395
letter-writing	323
mourning	285, 287
nicknames	339
proposals	217
rings	219
toasts	171
travelling	401, 404
wedding	232, 243, 264, 269
Trains, travelling on	405
Travel	
cyclists	404
in cars	403-404
on planes	407
on the train	405
on the tube	405-406
taxis	406
Trooping the Colour	430
Trousseaux	243
Tubes, travelling on	405-406

U

Umbrellas	403
Universities	
degrees, order of letters	
in forms of address	72
hierarchy of posts	67-68
titles, academic forms	
of address	67-73
Ushers, wedding, duties	247, 259

V

Vaping	391, 400
Video calls	413
Vicars	118, 119
Vice-chancellors,	
forms of address	67, 73
Viscounts and families	
forms of address	33-35
Volunteer Reserve	
Royal Air Force	85

W

Wales	
Church in	112, 116
National Assembly	100
Wardens, college	70
Weddings	227-271
WhatsApp	323
Whisky	363
White tie, dress code	185-187
Widows, forms of address	62
WiFi	389
Wimbledon Championships	431
Windsor, Royal Horse Show	430
Wines and spirits	361-363
in restaurants	409
serving	373
Writers to the Signet	153
Writing paper	309

Acknowledgements

Sir Jeremy Stuart-Smith;
Alistair Harrison, Marshal of the Diplomatic Corps;
Jonathan Spencer, Assistant Comptroller Lord Chamberlain's Office;
Patric Dickinson, Secretary of the Order of the Garter;
Mrs Sophie Reilly, Court of the Lord Lyon;
Ross Gillson, Secretary to the House of Bishops